The New Politics of Public Policy

The New Politics of Public Policy

EDITED BY

MARC K. LANDY & MARTIN A. LEVIN

THE JOHNS HOPKINS UNIVERSITY PRESS
BALTIMORE AND LONDON

© 1995 The Johns Hopkins University Press
All rights reserved. Published 1995
Printed in the United States of America on acid-free paper
04 03 02 01 00 99 98 97 96 95   5 4 3 2 1

The Johns Hopkins University Press
2715 North Charles Street
Baltimore, Maryland 21218-4319
The Johns Hopkins Press Ltd., London

Library of Congress Cataloging-in-Publication Data will be found
at the end of this book.

A catalog record for this book is available from the British Library

ISBN 0-8018-4877-6
ISBN 0-8018-4878-4 (pbk.)

For Aaron Wildavsky

Contents

Preface

This book argues that there is a new politics of public policy. During the past two decades, major changes in the structure and dynamics of our political system have led to unexpected policy outcomes that are broad in scope and that carry large price tags. This conclusion was arrived at, not through abstract theorizing, but through the deliberations between scholars and practitioners which are the raison d'être of the Gordon Public Policy Center.

The center seeks to bridge the world of action and the world of ideas. By paying close attention to what those who make policy say about what they are doing, scholars can escape their insularity and become better attuned to what is actually happening, rather than clinging to what their often shopworn theories tell them *ought* to be happening.

This book was born from such an encounter between practitioners and scholars. In 1988, Stanford Ross, former Social Security commissioner and a prominent Washington attorney, led a Gordon Center seminar about the politics of 1986 tax reform and remarked that, at a critical point in the congressional deliberations over tax reform, all of the lobbyists, even the most well placed, were totally excluded from the process. A hush fell over the room. "Everybody knows" that lobbyists dominate the legislative process, especially when it involves such a detailed and arcane question as the revision of the tax code. And yet we were being given this counterintuitive information by a very shrewd person who was actually *there*.

Later, a group of center fellows—Shep Melnick, Sidney Milkis, Morton Keller, and the editors—met to consider the implications of Ross's account. The more we thought about it, the more we began to ponder what else about current policy making might defy conventional wisdom.

The more we looked, the more the prevailing explanations about public policy formulation seemed, at best, inadequate and, at worst, just plain wrong. The sheer number and scope of the innovations in the 1970s and 1980s belied the conventional notion that the legislative process is biased against change, dominated by obstructionary interests, and characterized by incrementalism. Moreover, many of these policy innovations were propelled neither by crisis nor by scandal and were enacted during a period when conservatives won five of the six presidential elections.

In short, the postwar era's paradigms of American politics do not seem to explain the policy making of the past two decades. The model of a slow-moving, incremental political system, biased against change and constrained by organized interests, is no longer accurate. Nor can it be said that most of these policies were the result of a ground swell of public demand. Whether or not one likes these new policies, they are emblematic of a drastic shift in the pattern of public policy making.

To gain a better understanding of these vast changes, we recruited several prominent scholars of the policy process to examine them in light of the policy issues with which the scholars are most familiar. This volume is the result. It contains an in-depth exploration of several of the most important policy reforms of the 1970s and 1980s, including the 1986 and 1990 immigration reform acts, the 1986 Tax Reform Act, Aid to Children with Special Needs, Superfund, and the Clean Air Act. It also looks more broadly at the most important arenas of modern domestic policy reform—health, entitlements, the environment, and tax—as well as at the changes that have taken place in the key policy-making institutions—Congress, the executive, the states, and the courts.

Despite the variety of policy arenas considered, there is a remarkable degree of cohesion and consensus among the authors regarding the fact that a new politics of public policy exists and about the critical elements that constitute it. There is little talk of "gridlock," "iron triangles," or "incrementalism." Rather, the chapters are suffused with such concepts as the role of ideas, adversarial legalism, the rights revolution, the lowering of the legitimacy barrier, the drive for perfect justice, a new constitutional order, the fragmentation of authority, and the weakening of integrative institutions.

In the introduction, Martin Shapiro places these specific arguments and investigations in the context of the major debates that dominate contemporary political science. In explaining the rapidity with which these new policies often developed, he suggests that a shift has taken place from a "politics of interests" (which tend to be fixed and thus to change slowly) to a "politics of values and ideas" (which tend to be more open, fluid, and responsive to change and reason).

The six specific explorations of the new politics of public policy are grouped into three separate categories—Adversarial Legalism and the Rights Revolution, Taxing and Spending, and Regulation and Deregulation. In their concluding chapters Wilson C. McWilliams and James Q. Wilson each provide an interpretation of how best to understand these developments. McWilliams describes a "two-tiered polity" in which the "thick" politics of the Capitol uneasily coexists with the "thin" politics of the country at large. Wilson stresses the dissonance between the elite interests that dominate much of the policy-making apparatus and the mass interests that receive consideration only sporadically. In the final essay, the editors synthesize and develop the volume's most important themes.

"Divided government" is not a central theme of this analysis. Thus, as we move back and forth between divided and undivided government, we are confident that the major arguments made in this volume will continue to hold true. So far, the experience of the Clinton administration has served only to accentuate the relevance and importance of these arguments.

The authors in this volume vary considerably in their ideological and scholarly predispositions, but they do share some important traits. They do not try to reduce politics to the mere interplay of "interests," as if preferences were fixed in advance and participants were never moved by new ideas or never used their reasoning powers to change their minds. The authors are comfortable using purely political categories of analysis like "leadership," "deliberation," and "constituency." They do not make the naive and mistaken assumption that politics is epiphenomenal and that political analysis should be derivative of culture, economics, or social class.

Also, their analyses are informed by deep respect for American political and constitutional history. The authors understand that policies have a past that predates the current presidential administration and that broader constitutional questions will influence narrower policy outcomes. As Martin Shapiro notes in his introduction, this book makes an argument about political science as well as about the politics of public policy. It seeks to uphold the dignity and seriousness of an enterprise that is continually in danger of trivializing itself by donning the intellectual and academic fashions of the day.

We are grateful to our Gordon Center colleagues, including Michael O'Hare, Dennis Hale, James Gomes, Scott Rasmussen, and John Tierney, whose advice and criticism have made this a stronger volume. Martin Shapiro, in addition to contributing a thoughtful and thought-provoking introduction, provided wise intellectual counsel and shrewd practical advice.

Our profound gratitude goes to Stephen Rockwell and Dennis Hale for their superb work on the revision and editing of chapter 6 after the untimely death of our friend and colleague, Aaron Wildavsky. Dennis Hale also expertly contributed his wise editorial pen to chapters 3 and 4.

We also thank the Harvard Program for Constitutional Government; its co-chairs, Harvey Mansfield, Jr., and Shep Melnick; and the Harry and Lynde Bradley Foundation for providing the funds to hold a preparatory conference on this topic and to commission the chapters that make up the volume. We are especially indebted to Sidney Milkis, who provided crucial advice and criticism and whose ideas so strongly inform our own conclusion.

Most of all, we thank the trustees of the Gordon Foundation—John Adelsdorf, Sandford Bank, Burton Feldman, Robert Green, and David Silverberg—whose faith in this project and in the other endeavors of the Gordon Center has been so steadfast, gracious, and enduring.

Introduction

Of Interests and Values:
The New Politics and the
New Political Science

MARTIN SHAPIRO

We are wont to speak these days of the new American politics. And when we are political scientists, there is often some confusion between changes in the real world and changes in the political science learning about it. Sometimes we speak as if a new, correct political science theory or concept were displacing an earlier one proven wrong, when in reality all that is happening is that a fairly accurate description of the politics of 1940 is being replaced by a fairly accurate picture of the changed politics of 1990. Thus, it might be useful to start with the changes in politics before considering the changes in political science.

Certainly, politics has changed. The voters have changed. More voters say they are independent or even conservative, split their ticket, and vote for incumbent legislators. A significant enough number to determine outcomes frequently vote for Republican presidential candidates and Democratic congressional ones. Campaigns and their financing have changed. The use of television and thus the increased costs of campaigning, the institution of limits on campaign contributions and spending, the increased reliance on direct mail solicitation, the constant awareness of hair-trigger polling and hair-trigger candidate response to poll results, the dominance of primaries over convention bargaining—all of these have changed elections. The South has become the sun belt, with two-party competition and black voting. The parties have changed—most particularly the Democratic party, where the massive New Deal coalition has attenuated, the Northern liberal, Southern conservative dynamic has disappeared, and younger, white voters have drifted away. To some degree single-issue politics, abortion, affirmative action, gun control, and the great environmental awakening have become more important and party politics has become less important.

Congress has changed, with a wider distribution of power among more of its members, a Democratic leadership often in command of firm majorities no longer dependent on southern conservative Democrats, and the growth of staffs more able to compete with the resources of the executive branch. The policies coming out of Congress have changed, with major and sweeping civil rights, environmental, and safety legislation. The presidency has changed, becoming less "imperial" as Republican presidents have faced a Democratic Congress. The administrative process has changed as the judicial process has changed. The judicial process has changed from the judicial passivity engendered by the New Deal victory over the nine old men to a judicial activism so intrusive that every act of government is challenged in court and passed on by judges and much of administrative procedure is forced to ape judicial procedure to win judicial approval. The nature of the Washington policy-making process may even have changed or at least moved much further in the direction of an "open" process, in which anyone with a claim to interest and expertise is a welcome participant and policy authority is diffused. Finally, the international environment has changed dramatically: the rise of China, the events in the Soviet Empire, the economic power of Japan and Germany, the trade deficit. And, as the trade deficit reminds us, the new politics exists in the context of a new economics: an unprecedentedly long period of slow but almost uninterrupted economic growth with low unemployment, relatively low inflation, steadily rising or only slightly declining real income among various segments of the population, a rising governmental debt burden (in absolute numbers but not relative to the gross national product), and a federal deficit produced by relatively high spending and low taxation.

The changes in political science in part are merely reflective of real-world changes and in part are due to broader ideological changes in the West as a whole. Some of them may even represent increases in scientific understanding. Party identification, which once promised to be the $E = MC^2$ of political science, has lost its central explanatory role as the electorate and the parties seem to have changed. The "strong presidency," both as an empirical concept and as a normative totem, has also lost centrality, in part because of real-world change and in part because political scientists are mostly main-line Democrats and the presidents mostly have not been of late. Theories of the legislative process built up out of constituency influence, interest group pressure, committee power, internal norms of expertise and seniority, brokerage by the leadership, coattail effects, and presidential initiative have eroded under the force of incumbent security, the "democratization" of the House, and the situation of a Democratic Congress and a Republican president as a normal condition. Most importantly, the rather elegant theory that built to the conclusion that Congress could pass legislation that diffused costs among the taxpayers in general while concentrating benefits on specific interest groups and could not pass legislation that concentrated costs on identifiable groups but created diffuse or "public" benefits has been confounded by much of the major legislative product of the Congress during the past thirty years.

Most central, of course, to the new political science is the whole furor over pluralism. At an empirical level there has been much less revolution than meets the eye. At that level group theories of politics, far from having been demolished, are with us in new and even more professionally rewarding forms, now under the name of *public choice.* Indeed, the very emperor of the social sciences has adopted the oldest, most orthodox political science group theories and parades them forth in gorgeous new colors as the "economic theory of legislation," in which guise they have become one of the latest fascinations of academic lawyers. In the age of single-issue politics, the feminist movement, the Natural Resources Defense Council, political action committees, the National Rifle Association, and group-sponsored litigation in every court house, no one is prepared to argue that interest groups do not in fact play a large role in politics and that most policy processes are not characterized by multiple players and considerable permeability. Indeed, much of the new political science is directed at describing the multiplicity of participants and the diffusion and disruption of the policy-making process. Even at the empirical level, however, there is something amiss in group theory, which could not have readily predicted the wave of public interest in health, safety, and environmental legislation or even much of the "deregulation" legislation. At some point the general swings in overall popular sentiment that are reflected in general swings of the type of legislators who get elected seem to overwhelm the play of groups in the legislative arena. Part of the new political science involves facing up to the fact that policy makers are not the mere playthings of group pressures but are also purposive actors bent on achieving their own visions of public values. Indeed, much of the "new institutionalism" that is now declared to be the leading edge of the new political science is not actually about institutions in the narrower or everyday sense of that word, but about values that dwell in individual political actors, persist over time, and play a major role in shaping political outcomes.

Although the recognition of human values that persist over time as empirical realities shaping and constraining political behavior is a kind of halfway house between the empirical and the normative, the major battle over pluralism lies at the normative level, although the battlers often confuse empirical and normative issues. Everybody agrees that the groups are there, but the short and dirty of it is that the pluralists like groups and the postpluralists do not. Or at least that's what the post-pluralists say. They paint the group theories of Bentley, Truman, and Dahl and company's New Havens everywhere as both empirical descriptions and applause of what is described.[1] Various groups and their representatives and agents will struggle with one another, and out of the struggle democratic results (i.e., the successful accommodation of all preferences) will emerge. The postpluralists, instead of applauding, begin from the Orwellian vision that some groups are more equal than others and that the product of the group struggle is not democratic, fair, or equal, but favors those groups with the greatest political resources. (The pluralists, of course, deny that they were guaranteeing good outcomes.)

Various alternative cures to the evils depicted by the postpluralists have been pursued. Ted Lowi, in the book that has come to be the symbol of postpluralism (most particularly for those who have not actually read it), suggested that Congress should not delegate so much of its law-making authority to the administrative agencies.[2] If Congress retained its authority, the influence of the unequal group struggle or "capture" in the administrative law-making process would be reduced simply by dint of the administrative process doing less and the Congress doing more of the law making. Lowi's solution has been applied to a degree in much of U.S. environmental, health, and safety legislation, which contains substantial amounts of specific legislated standards. The same statutes, however, contain massive delegations.

Another solution has actually created a major reshaping of American politics, the curing of the diseases of pluralism by the injection of still more pluralism. Led by the courts, with assistance from Congress and from the agencies themselves, administrators have made massive attempts to restructure the administrative process so that all groups will have access, will have relatively equal resources with which to present their positions, and will get equal attention from the agencies. (In the jargon of administrative law, this is the "dialogue," "rule-making record," "hard look," "reasoned elaboration," "standing" stuff.) There has even been some funding of the lobbying costs of the poorer groups. There is less talk of "capture" than there used to be. Indeed, there is vast complaint that having to listen to everybody equally and over and over again has slowed administrative decision making to a crawl. Alas, nobody really is prepared to assert that the groups have been or can be sufficiently equalized to guarantee truly democratic or equal or fair outcomes. Moreover, even if the ideal of more pluralism were achieved, we would still be left with the Rousseauian question of whether the outcome would really be the public interest or only the sum of the interests of the groups.

Neither of these solutions deals with what to do about the group struggle in Congress. The newest prescription, and one that does deal with both the legislative and the executive branches, is deliberation; like most political prescriptions, *deliberation* rather deliberately conflates empirical and normative elements. The basic premise is that legislatures and administrative agencies should be more than arenas to which all groups have equal access in which to struggle toward an accommodation of their various interests. In such a vision the outcome is merely passively recorded as law by the government, which has been holding the coats of the interest groups. Instead, legislation and administration should be purposive processes of moral discourse in which the participants, both government officials and interest group spokesmen, will seek to achieve a policy product that is better, more dedicated to the public interest, than the mere pluralist, compromised sum of the preferences of interest groups. Such deliberation is seen not as a utopian prescription but as an emphasis on phenomena already present in the governing process but deemphasized and obscured by pluralist analysis.

The concern for deliberation and discourse is part of a broader aspect of the new political science, its concern not only for the policy-making process but also for the substantive merits of the policy that emerges. Pluralism, at least in its opponent's version, defined a good policy entirely in procedural terms. Any policy that emerged from a democratic process, a process in which all interested groups participated, was by definition a good policy. Or, put slightly differently, the goodness or badness of policy was the degree to which it *satisfied* the preferences of the contending groups. As a matter of the real-world ideology of the new politics, rather than the new political science, there has been increasing interest in moving beyond goodness as mere preference and toward notions of some sort of "real" or objective goodness.

Earlier we noted the new openness of the policy process to all who have ideas and claim expertise rather than simply to those who assert interest and preferences. This openness occurs precisely because of concern for the substantive goodness of policy. Those who can persuasively assert that they have invented the better mousetrap can claim political attention. Ideas, and those who have mastered them, come to play a larger role than they would in pure preference politics. As Peter Schuck convincingly demonstrates in Chapter 3, "Immigration politics in the 1980s exemplifies this independent causal role of ideas. Certain distinctive notions about immigration and its effects propelled the reform impulse in directions that were more expansionist than interests, entrepreneurship, and events alone would have dictated." He shows that ideas perform necessary political functions; they help cement coalitions, change how people think, mobilize potent symbols, reinforce existing arrangements, and reduce cognitive dissonance.

At the most elevated levels, this theme may be seen as the growth of anti-utilitarian or postconsequentialist ethics, which teaches that moral deliberation can arrive at better, if not absolutely true, moral knowledge. Values are not seen as the utilitarians saw them, as mere preferences—I like chocolate; you like vanilla—to be summated by the political process into the greatest satisfaction of preferences for the greatest number. Instead, politics is about shaping policies in the light of true or at least better statements of the good. Political processes are to be philosophy seminars in ethics writ large. Legislatures and administrative agencies are to deliberate the good rather than merely register preferences.

For a great many years, students of politics and policy neglected moral philosophy as both a way of evaluating policy and a motivating force in politics. The dominant moral philosophy of the late nineteenth and early twentieth centuries had been utilitarianism, a philosophic technique that purported to bridge the gap between fact and value in politics. In fact, each individual preferred some things to others and so preferred some public policies to others. In fact, each individual sought pleasure and avoided pain. In fact, each individual was better situated to know his or her own pleasures and pains than was any other individual or institution. So, normatively, the good public policy was that which supplied the greatest pleasure and the least pain for the greatest number of individuals. If political processes could be constructed so as to allow all of these individual preferences to be registered and summated, the only political good that in fact existed would be achieved.

Pluralist theories of both legislation and administration flowed easily from utilitarian moral philosophy. In politics, preference-holding individuals bundled themselves into preference-holding groups, and group preferences were bundled into legislation. If the legislative process was good, in the sense of facilitating this bundling so as to give as many groups as possible what they wanted, then the legislation was also substantively good by the utilitarian measure of substantive goodness, maximizing pleasure and minimizing pain for the greatest number. If each individual knew what was best for him or her, then groups as bundles of individuals also knew best, and so the only good we could really know was good was achieved by legislation that maximized what the groups wanted.

If administration could be seen as the purely rational, instrumental carrying out of these deal bundles, then an administrative process that accurately carried out the deals was both procedurally and substantively good. If, instead, it were revealed that administration involved making deals as well as implementing them, then an administrative process that mirrored the legislative process of preference bargaining and summation would arrive at substantively good deals to supplement the substantively good legislative deals.

The final pinnacle of this moral philosophy of utilitarianism is modern economics, which provides us an unquestioned moral norm for politics: efficiency. Who of us dares to say that inefficient policy is better than efficient policy? The normative persuasiveness of efficiency rests, however, entirely on the utilitarian premises that people do and should seek pleasure and avoid pain and that they know better than anyone else what pleasures and pains them. It follows that efficiency, providing the most of what pleases people (benefits) for the least of what pains them (costs), is the one sure moral norm.

By the 1930s utilitarianism had lost its dominance as a moral philosophy, for it became increasingly clear that the greatest good for the greatest number was not a very satisfying moral norm if you happened to be one of those in the least number. Utilitarianism eroded, but nothing replaced it. Normative moral and political philosophy almost ceased as an intellectual enterprise. Philosophers turned to the task of making language more precise, and political theorists turned to the history of political thought. Not daring to claim that they knew what was good, they resorted to recounting what earlier theorists had said was good. In such an intellectual climate, where no one claimed to be able to know what was substantively good, defining the political good entirely in procedural terms, as whatever came out of a properly pluralistic political process, seemed the only normative move available.

Somehow, for reasons no one quite understands, Western civilization regained its moral self-confidence shortly after midcentury. This moral sea change is reflected in the rise of a postutilitarian or postconsequentialist epistemology and moral theory and in new work in normative political and legal philosophy. For those familiar with the academic world, the most easily observable evidence is that young "political theorists" are now actually doing political theory instead of being historians of other peoples' political thought and that the works of Dworkin and Rawls are now commonplace on undergraduate reading lists. In 1950, who would have believed that Kantian or contractarian moral philosophy could ever be written again.

In moral philosophy itself, the new beginning and, indeed, probably the be-all is a new epistemological self-confidence. It is now again confidently asserted that, although we may not be able to know the good in an absolute sense, we can know the better. No statement of the good may be absolutely true even for one time and place, let alone for all times and places, but some statements of the good are truer than others, and there are ways through which we can know which moral statements are truer than others, at least for a particular set of circumstances. It is this revived faith in moral knowledge, that man *can know* the good, or at least the better, which is the soul of the new politics.

The new ethics has not entirely worked out or unified its prescription for how we are to know. There are various contending schools and a thousand nuances. Basically, however, a methodological faith is proclaimed. If persons of good faith engage in a mutual exchange of tentative claims about the good, fully cognizant of the rich complexity of the social and technological context of the claims and the contingency of human experience, they will arrive at statements of the good (or at public policies) that are different from and more agreed to be true than the initial claims made. These statements or policies will contain an element of moral truth above and beyond the mere summation of the pleasure-pain preferences of those making the initial claims.

It is from this movement in moral philosophy that the intellectual energy of the new theories of political deliberation comes. At the most popular level, this search for the substantive rather than merely procedural good may be seen in the great green wave of environmentalism, which firmly believes that, if the fish in the river die, the policy that caused them to die is bad, no mater how neatly contrived was the process that produced the policy. Indeed, much of the rhetoric of rights that pervades contemporary political discourse, from the right to choose to the rights of trees, is really an assertion that there are substantive goods and evils that trump the assertion that a policy was made by a properly pluralistic process. This confidence about knowing the good and the consequent enthusiasm for doing it right now, no matter what, is to be seen in James Morone's description of the "democratic wish" in health policy (see chapter 7). Even the new popularity of political economy moves us from process to substance, for political economists ask not only how the policy was made but whether it is economically efficient. And, although the concept of economic efficiency rests not on the notion of an objective good but only on the summation of subjective individual preferences, nevertheless, it does serve as a kind of objective, exterior, and substantive measure of the goodness of policy; at least it tells us that whatever deliberation reveals to be good ought to be achieved at the lowest possible cost.

No doubt, it is something of an unfair parody of the new fascination with deliberation to say that it seeks to turn the legislative chamber and the administrative agency into philosophy department seminar rooms. And certainly there is a kind of pseudosophistication and willful suppression of reality in visions of such chambers and agencies as places in which decision makers deliberately eschew any rational pursuit of the good in favor of total immersion in the pork barrel. Nevertheless, lurking behind much of the appeal of the deliberative prescription is a kind of "groves of academe" image of reasonable people calmly talking together.

One hint of this background image is the appeal of the judiciary to many of the deliberative school, or at least the lawyers among them. If legislatures and agencies should fail to truly deliberate, perhaps courts should repair their deficiencies. Our current faith in courts as policy makers stems in part from the closer approximation provided by two lawyers engaging in reasoned argument with one another in front of a third to the ordered exchange of views of the seminar room than is provided by the messy back-stairs struggles of legislatures and executive agencies.

The new politics has not quite faced up to the question of whether and how much you can deliberate in political settings that are rife with high-stakes interests, coercions, and rent seekings that rarely arise in the seminar room. And, surely, retreat to the courtroom is not a very satisfactory answer, at least for those of us who put even less faith in the moral skills of lawyers than in those of philosophy professors. Yet, compared to the half-empty glass of pluralist and public choice analysts, the half-full glass of deliberators holds some attractions. If we are entitled sometimes to simplify our analysis by assuming that all legislators and administrators are motivated solely by the hope of maximizing their particular individual preferences and thus also the preferences of the groups that will give them the best exchange, why not sometimes simplify by assuming that legislators and administrators seek solely to discover and implement the common good?

The emergence of deliberation as central to the new political science and its general concerns with policy as well as process is a reflection of the tendencies among both intellectual elites and common citizens to aspire not only to democratic processes but also to the good life. More and more political science turns to the proof of the pudding and in ways that suggest that there are answers beyond that some like the way it tastes and some don't.

Group approaches to politics generated their own decision theory, the theory of incrementalism which, as both description and prescription, explained how organizations as alliances of groups or interests could arrive at policies that sufficiently satisfied (in Simon's term *satisficed*)[3] each of the participant interests and so allowed the organization to continue. Although incrementalists rarely suggested that incremental decision strategy led to substantively good policies—they hardly concerned themselves with such, to them, nonquestions—there was more than a hint that such strategies at least led to more successful or survivable policies through the process of small change, feedback, and adjustment to feedback that was central to the incremental prescription. Both the new politics and the new political science have come to question incrementalism in part because it seems to council against large-scale attacks on what are seen as large problems but ultimately because it defined the *good* as whatever the groups can compromise on rather than in any substantive way. There is no guarantee that the small steps will be down the path to goodness rather than badness. Increasingly, both the Congress in its legislation and the courts in their review insist that complex, administrative organizations act synoptically, that they have considered everything and arrived at correct or at least the best available solutions. And more and more of the new political science that concentrates on policy tends to attribute deficiencies in the policies it examines to the incremental processes by which they were made and implemented.

A similar story can be told about the "new institutionalism," which rejects the vision of the individual as a mere atomized bearer of preferences, groups as mere agglomerations of preferences, and organizations as mere coalitions of preferences. Instead, individuals are treated as moral entities embedded within institutions with persistent repertoires, structures, and norms. And among the phenomena treated as institutions are not only organizational entities but also long-term cultural values and world views. Rather than the relatively static computer of preference sums, politics then becomes an ongoing purposive endeavor in which institutions are both the products and the constituters of political values. Ultimately, then, both the new politics and the new political science represent a shift of concern from interests to values, from procedure to substance, from the correlation of preferences to the attainment of the good, or at least the better, or perhaps (to put the matter more succinctly) a movement from will to reason.

A significant symptom of this shift is to be seen in the preoccupation of many of the chapters in this book with litigation and particularly with constitutional litigation and judicial review of administrative decision making. In chapter 4 Rober Kagan writes that "government authority is constrained, buffeted and superseded by legal rights and duties, by threats of litigation and judicial deadlock." This condition, which did not exist in the 1940s and 1950s, is largely the result of a peculiar feature of Anglo-American politicolegal culture, a feature that empowers and is nurtured by courts and lawyers. To a marked degree, for English speakers everywhere, the legislative and administrative process and product are thought of as the realm of will and the judicial process and its product as the realm of reason. It is enough for a legislature to give the people, or the majority, what it wants and for the executive faithfully to execute those wants or whatever wants the president sees manifest in the mandate given by the last presidential election. As Peter Schuck points out in chapter 3, whatever reputation for reason, in the shape of "expertise," was once enjoyed by administrative agencies has withered under perceptions of capture and inertia and under the perception distortion that comes from excessive specialization. Rightly or wrongly and for better or worse, Americans have perceived courts as institutions acknowledging an obligation to "principled" argument about and reasoned elaboration of their own decisions and as authorities who could force legislatures, presidents, and agencies into at least some elements of the same allegiance. While everyone else may be in pursuit of naked preferences in institutions that are mere arenas for clashing wills, courts at least are in search of those elements in our collective psyche that are about our common search for the good person in the good state.

In addition to the preoccupation with litigation, another obvious leitmotif of this book is the powerful contemporary surge of egalitarianism. What we encounter again and again, however, is not the clash of egalitarian and other values, but a situation in which egalitarians have seized the high ground of values—and equality is a persuasive value—while nonegalitarians seem only to be defending existing interests. In this clash between value and interests, value has enormous appeal. All of the contributors to this volume reflect in one way or another this interest in moving beyond interests, typically expressed as *rights,* and toward something else that revolves around reason, values, and deliberation, although some use more of the older and some more of the newer language.

Marc Landy most clearly mirrors the new concerns. Indeed, this new work of his has an almost eerie quality of following the predictions about further intellectual developments in regulation and administrative law made in my book, *Who Guards the Guardians?*[4] In his work on the Environmental Protection Agency (chapter 8), he describes the policy problems that arise when "rights" become the common coin of policy talk and action. He shows how environmental policy suffered when "there simply was no readily available repository of intellectual discourse that both displayed sympathy for [environmental] claimants, proposed to help them, and yet rejected their rights claims." His proposed solution is a "reconstituted environmental protection agency . . . to . . . lead . . . a sustained, comprehensive deliberation which . . . must involve all the interested parties as well as the broader public." He emphasizes the duty of the agency to educate the public. Rather than engaging in "policy entrepreneurship," civil servants should be "provokers of deliberation."

Of course, Landy does acknowledge that the participants in environmental policy making would bring strongly felt interests to the deliberation he proposes, many of them interests that do not necessarily push them toward learning new truths. His argument is very much of the half-full variety, but the quest toward filling the glass as full of deliberation as possible is also very much there. His work shows the new focus on and power of substantive values. In attempting to restructure the environmental debate around risk and quality of life, he is actually attempting to integrate the values of "health" and economic efficiency and is calling on the president and the agencies to lead a civic education seminar about them.

Risk is, of course, now the special terrain of Aaron Wildavsky. In his leading 1987 article in the *American Political Science Review*, he dramatically showed the shift from interests to values as the building block of political analysis and explicitly registered this shift, although he carefully did not embrace the new moral epistemology.[5] His "preferences," which are actually overarching values rather than abstractions of mere self-interest, are elements of political culture which he treats positivistically. They remain "I like chocolate, you like vanilla," rather than the "better" moral statements that deliberation is supposed to yield. Nonetheless, political culture, in the sense of values (e.g., the attitude toward risk), become major explanatory variables. Such variables surely better explain than does pluralism alone such phenomena as the one that Landy notes at the beginning of chapter 8: "the ability of the environmental movement and its congressional allies to dominate" the politics of environmental regulation.

Wildavsky's analysis in terms of hierarchs and egalitarians tells us something further about the new concern for substantive values. Often treated as a conflict between elitists and democrats, or Republicans and Democrats, this is also a conflict between process and substance. The egalitarians subscribe to equality not only as a procedural value, that all should have an equal voice in politics or an equal opportunity in economics, but also as a substantive value, that the outcomes of politics and economics should be more equalized. And their ultimate evaluation of a political and economic system rests far more heavily on the equal outcomes and far less heavily on equal process than did that of earlier egalitarians. The egalitarian substantive values of contemporary American political culture stressed by Wildavsky *when combined with the new confidence that moral truth may be known* lead, among other things, to the current vogue in "politically correct" speech. For, if the truth can be known, and the truth is substantive equality, why should anyone be allowed to obstruct the teaching of that truth to the citizenry? More fundamentally, the belief in substantive equality and the confidence in the moral truth of the value leads to unbounded enthusiasm for the claims of anyone successful in claiming underdog designation. Politics becomes the struggle to pursuade others of one's claim to genuine underdog status.

In the conclusion of chapter 4, Robert Kagan sounds the same notes as does Landy. He prescribes the "dialogic community" and "public deliberation . . . in a disbelieving age to restore faith in the competence and public-spiritedness of governmental authority." Here we have government as the maker of good decisions rather than the mere summater of preferences. Kagan is pointing to the role of political talk not only in the formulation of good policy, but also in the constituting of government itself. We came to disbelieve in government, it might be argued, because we came to disbelieve in any mode of value creation at all. If we now again believe that "better," even if not "best," value statements can be made, that is a necessary if not perhaps sufficient condition for believing that government can make them.

In chapter 10 James Q. Wilson is wide ranging and certainly touches often on the movement from interests to values. His most recent book, although it speaks largely in the conventional language of administrative discretion, is an attempt of the sort Kagan prescribes to restore faith in government as the maker of good decisions.[6] Indeed, nearly all of the language of deliberation can readily be translated into the language of discretion. On its negative side, the call for administrative discretion is a call to leave the agencies some breathing space, some refuge from the constant cat-and-dog fights of the interest groups and from the supervision by litigation which is just the same cat-and-dog fights by another name. On the positive side, the discretion called for is the discretion to arrive at a better solution than one that merely satisfies the groups. Wilson's comments in chapter 10 illustrate how far we may be swinging back toward government as constituter of the good life rather than registrar of preferences.

In this work and in much of his earlier work, Wilson has pointed to the central change in contemporary American political culture as a shift from notions of limited government to the almost automatic assumption that, if society encounters a problem, government bears responsibility for fixing it. Here, Wilson reminds us of the rights dimension to this shift. He notes that whether or not, à la Dworkin, rights ought to be trumps, they are certainly treated that way today. This trumpness of rights is, of course, largely a matter of confidence in our ability to know substantive truths, for rights, even rights to equality, are ultimately claims that we are very sure that some social goals and some arrangements of society are substantively better than others. Wilson's chapter provides a focus for and culmination of the leitmotif of environmentalism that appears throughout this volume. As he shows, we have become surer of the dominance of substantive goods in the environmental area than in any other. If the fish in the stream die, the policy is wrong, no matter how good the process that arrived at the policy.

Paul Quirk's chapter adopts the older discourse of general or public interest versus special interests, with the insoluble problem of that form of discourse. Standing on its own, such a discourse can never tell us what the public interest is, except negatively. The public interest is something other than one of or the sum of the special interests. Indeed, Quirk still tends to define the good in terms of "diffuse interests," a rather awkward device of David Truman's to sandwich values into the group theory of politics. From a postconsequentialist point of view, diffuse interests are not necessarily morally superior to concentrated ones. Quirk uses the word *deliberation* in an older, more general sense of being "thorough, accurate, and unbiased in identifying and weighing information relevant to decisions." For him the key public interest criterion is "whether Congress makes the same decision it would make if all of the members were in possession of and fully understood all of the relevant information."

All of this certainly implies a kind of postpluralist move toward synopticism but leaves obscure the questions of values and moral growth. Quirk does say that "there must be dialogue; understanding develops through a process of exchanging claims, criticisms, and counterclaims," which seems to suggest the ethics seminar engaged in John Dewey's or Richard Rorty's endeavor, but then he goes on, "that become more refined and accurate," which tends to suggest mere factual inquiry rather than moral growth.

Quirk wants for Congress what Landy wants for the administrative agency, that it become a place of deliberation. But for Quirk deliberation is rational decision by experts that adequately discounts special interests and adequately serves diffuse or general interests. He sees quite clearly the shift from interests to values in American politics, but he speaks of that shift in terms of the lamentable incapacity of Congress to "discount the biases and misconceptions of mass opinion" because, "in the current era, the pressure to conform to public sentiment is probably greater than the pressure to comply with interest-group demands." We shall see shortly that James Morone identifies a similar shift from interest groups based on expertise to an imagined democratic value consensus. However, Landy and Quirk solve the problem of popular mistake in diametrically opposed ways. Landy calls upon the agencies to engage in civic education, and Quirk calls upon Congress to isolate itself as an expert elite. Yet Quirk speaks of "issue-oriented" legislators and rejects public choice theories of legislative behavior, which are the old pluralism in new guise, in favor of a "perspective [that] acknowledges that members promote policies designed to achieve ideological or broadly based programmatic objectives." In the final analysis Quirk may be searching for a postconsequentialist notion of legislative deliberation as a search for the good rather than a mere reflection of public preferences. From there, it is only one step to Landy's position that the seminar not only must find the good but also has some responsibility for constituting it, that is, persuading the public to subscribe to it.

In chapter 2 Shep Melnick perfectly illustrates the current movement from will to reason and the powerful identification of courts with reason. "American legal reasoning and legal culture are more substantive than formal . . . tak[ing] . . . account [of] . . . moral, policy-oriented, and other substantive considerations." One reason Congress vests a judicially enforceable right to adequate education in the handicapped is so that it can take a position and claim credit without paying the bills or facing the outrage of those who do have to pay them. Another reason, as in all rights-creating legislation, is that it wants these bills to be paid. But another reason yet is that it does not trust local and state education bureaucracies to make good decisions, and it does trust courts to do so. Like Landy and Wilson, Melnick sees the distrust of the ability of agencies, conceived of as interest group arenas, to arrive at substantively right decisions as crucial to the new politics. Like Kagan (and Lowi before him), he also sees that, when Congress has not stated clearly what values are being preserved and what the tradeoffs between various values should be, adversary legalism will take over. The group struggle will simply be transferred from agencies to courts or, more precisely, to the interaction between them. Melnick does not seem to share the faith that litigation is a better medium of deliberation than are the legislative and administrative processes.

In chapter 7 James Morone provides a cautionary tale about the new politics. The old politics of health care were group politics, expert politics, and capture politics, with the American Medical Association (AMA) as the group, the expert and the capturer—the very model of both the flourishing and the diseases of pluralist politics. And to cure these diseases, Congress went to the very model of the new value-oriented and deliberative politics. Morone refers to "the democratic wish, . . . a vague program that promised communal consensus," that is, "direct citizen participation in local community agencies where—with the assistance of scientific technique—the people would form a consensus about the public interest without resorting to narrow power, politics, or politicians."

No clearer vision of the philosophy seminar could be imagined. The experts are on tap, not on top, but there, for proponents of deliberation do not slight facts and technical expertise. The deliberators are not supposed to be know-nothings. They must have the facts at their command but without suffering the narrowing and distortion of perspectives that is the inevitable concomitant of expert specialization. The goal is not merely the summation of the various preferences brought to the seminar room but the working up of an agreed better truth among the seminar participants. In this instance, because politicians are not seen as deliberators but only as interest bearers, they are excluded in favor of concerned but, it is hoped, not interested citizens.

And the results of this magnificent attempt at the new politics of deliberation? In Morone's view they are not encouraging. The wish for deliberation is not necessarily father to the deed. Of course, it could be argued that what Morone's story actually shows is that, if Congress has not truly deliberated and administrative agencies have not truly deliberated, it does no good to shift the burden of deliberation to the public, particularly a public that has not received a civic education in deliberation.

Perhaps at this point we ought to return to Landy, the most enthusiastic about deliberation of our contributors. Although he rejects the older pluralism because of its inattention to values beyond preferences, he treats civic education not as education in substantive values but only as education in facts and in a sense of responsibility. The care of the government should be to sustain the values of education, responsiveness, and respect for merits by promoting liberation, integration, and accountability. There is a faith here that the substantive merits, the better moral and policy truth, will arise from the deliberation if only government will foster the prerequisites for deliberation. Shall we ascribe the failure of deliberation that Morone describes to the failure of civic education in these prerequisites or to the attempt to conduct the deliberation in an unsuitable setting with unqualified participants. Or is deliberation just the next liberal democratic pipe dream—a way of softening the deformities of pluralism in a haze of aspirational ethics.

Whether or not deliberation is possible or probable, the shift from a politics of interests to a politics of values and ideas implies a major change in the tempo and scale of politics. All other things being equal, a politics of interests will as often arrive at a standoff as at a winning coalition, as often at the dreaded cycling as at the blessed equilibrium of public choice theory. All other things, of course, are far from equal in our constitutional and internal congressional, executive, and judicial arrangements. They are full of checks and bottlenecks that reinforce the sluggishness of interest group politics. Not only is the pace likely to be slow, but also the steps are likely to be short. Interest group politics and incremental decision making are but two names for the same game. A politics of values and ideas brings a dynamic force to the political arena that more easily sweeps over and through these other things. A politics of ideas is more open, fluid, and responsive to economic, social, and technological change than is a politics of interests. And, more attracted to the shared processes of reason, it is more confident of generating successful, large policy changes than is a politics of interests, which focuses on individual or group wills seen as largely intractable. The new politics is a faster, bigger politics. Its prototype is the politics of environmentalism, which keeps damning the cost torpedoes while legislating full speed ahead.

One thing that is clear from the chapters in this volume is that the shift from interests to values and the new calls for deliberation leave whatever the new political science is in a tight place. Political scientists are increasingly comfortable treating values as variables, that is, acknowledging that widely shared and persistent value propositions or assertions in fact do play a major role in shaping public policy and political life, a role perhaps as or more important than the array of personal and group preferences. They remain uncomfortable with actually dealing with substantive value questions and with evaluating governmental performance on the basis of substantive value conclusions. Even Landy, with his array of criteria for good government, does not include getting the right answer, arriving at the right policy, among them. If getting the right answer were adopted as the test of good government, then political scientists would have to claim to know what the right answer was before claiming to make accurate assessments of governmental performance. And political scientists remain wary of such claims.

Thus, the call for more deliberation in government or more discretion in the agencies or more real law making by Congress may turn out to be yet another relatively empty procedural slogan, like the call for access of the pluralists. How will we know when true deliberation rather than the mere summating of preferences has occurred? The only ultimate test of deliberation is whether what comes out of it is better, represents a real moral growth over the sum of the preferences brought to it by the individual deliberators. So we can only apply the test if we are prepared to claim that we can tell better from worse.

Perhaps, until we feel comfortable making such a claim, it is possible to deal in imperfect and surrogate measures, such as equal access and respectful attention to all opinions, consensus, careful attention to facts, and a willingness to reach a clear, consistent, integrated policy rather than transferring the responsibility to others and some seat-of-the-pants evaluation of whether outcomes seem to favor particular interests excessively or seem to be meeting to some practical degree more general moral aspirations. Perhaps all we are seeing is an urge to reject cynicism and to reassert the authority and capacity of government or to instill in government the will to use the authority and capacity it has. All of the contributors want to say that government ought to be something more than the coat holder, referee, and score keeper for interest groups, something more than a passive arena in which the group struggle proceeds. All seem to agree that government ought to take responsibility for arriving at the good rather than merely summating preferences. This volume is, then, part of a sea change in American political life and thought, but do the blessed isles lie ahead?

Adversarial Legalism and the Rights Revolution

Separation of Powers and the Strategy of Rights: The Expansion of Special Education

R. SHEP MELNICK

Over the past two decades, special education policy at the federal, state, and local levels has undergone a dramatic change. Despite a decline in the total public school population, the number of children in special education rose from 2.3 million in 1968 to 4.3 million in 1986. The number of special education teachers increased from 179,000 in 1977 to 275,000 in 1986. Although accurate cost estimates are hard to find, the "excess" cost for special education (i.e., the total cost minus the cost of educating an equal number of regular students) is probably between $25 billion and $30 billion per year. The federal government spends $2 billion annually on special education (up from $92 million in 1972), making this the second largest program administered by the Department of Education. Over the past two decades, special education programs have been the fastest growing part of the state and local school budget. Not only does the United States now devote more resources to education of the handicapped than do most European nations, but it also imposes more controls from outside the local school and offers more opportunities for parents to participate in decisions about the education of their handicapped children. None of this was true before 1975.[1]

A major cause of these changes was passage of the Education for All Handicapped Children Act (EAHCA) of 1975. Among the important provisions of the act are the following:

— it mandates school systems to provide a "free appropriate public education" to *all* handicapped children;
— it requires teachers and administrators to hold yearly conferences with parents to establish an "individualized educational program" for each handicapped child;

— it offers parents dissatisfied with this "individualized educational program" the opportunity to receive an "impartial due process hearing" first before a local independent hearing officer, then before a review board at the state level, and ultimately before a federal district court judge;

— it requires schools to "assure that, to the maximum extent appropriate, handicapped children . . . are educated with children who are not handicapped";

— and it requires schools to provide handicapped children with "related services" such as occupational and physical therapy, psychological services, and counseling.

In a reversal of well-established practices, federal regulation of state and local school systems has far outstripped the federal money provided by the 1975 act. Appropriations remain well below the cost imposed by federal mandates. John Pittenger and Peter Kuriloff described the act as "the most prescriptive educational statute ever passed by Congress."[2] The 1980s brought surprisingly little relaxation of federal control. The Reagan administration's efforts to give state and local administrators more discretion were stymied by Congress.

This federal prescription is particularly surprising in light of the notorious decentralization of public education in the United States. Efforts to provide federal aid to elementary and secondary schools and to desegregate southern schools were frustrated for decades and were highly controversial when they finally came to fruition in the 1960s. Both desegregation and federal funding are classic examples of "breakthrough" politics. After years of debate a powerful, determined president overcame the opposition of determined minorities in Congress to enact landmark legislation, the Civil Rights Act of 1964 and the Elementary and Secondary Education Act of 1965.

Passage of the Education of All Handicapped Children Act was much different. Despite its intrusiveness, this federal legislation generated little controversy or concerted opposition. Bipartisanship prevailed. In the Senate Republicans were as vocal as Democrats in their support for the legislation. To say that presidential leadership was not a central factor is an understatement. President Nixon repeatedly opposed the legislation, and President Ford signed it only after seeing that Congress would surely override a veto.

How did advocates for the handicapped manage to pass legislation transforming special education without the advantages of presidential leadership, party support, lobbying by established interest groups, or a significant shift in public opinion? Part of the answer lies in the courts. As with civil rights, unilateral judicial action put the issue on the national agenda. In 1972 two federal district courts ordered school systems to provide an "appropriate education" and "due process hearings" to handicapped children. But these two cases, *Pennsylvania Association for Retarded Children (PARC) v. Commonwealth of Pennsylvania* and *Mills v. Board of Education of the District of Columbia*,[3] were unusually shaky legal precedents. One was a consent decree; the other was based primarily on local law in the District of Columbia. Moreover, soon after these two court rulings, the Supreme Court announced in *San Antonio v. Rodriguez* that the courts should not use the Equal Protection Clause to establish novel educational policies.[4] If Congress had not passed the Education for All Handicapped Children Act, the two lower court decisions would most likely have become exhibits in the museum of Warren-era initiatives abandoned by the Burger Court. Since 1975 the courts have been active in special education policy, but only through statutory interpretation, not constitutional adjudication. The judiciary, in short, has been active but far less than "imperial" in this area. The interesting question is why other institutions were so ready to respond to the decisions of these two courts.

Of central importance to the development of federal policy is the fact that from 1970 onward the issues in special education have been framed in terms of *individual rights*. According to David Neal and David Kirp, "the language of rights and the mechanisms of due process were introduced into an area that had previously relied on the professional discretion of teachers, psychologists, and school administrators."[5] This approach is peculiarly American. When the British revamped their special education system after passage of the EAHCA, they consciously rejected the American model. The British have continued to stress professional judgment and bureaucratic discretion rather than parental involvement and adversarial proceedings. The chair of the Committee of Enquiry that reviewed special education policy for Parliament displayed the prevailing British attitude when she said, "There is something deeply unattractive about the spectacle of someone demanding his own rights."[6] The attitude underlying the new American policies, in contrast, is that there is something deeply unattractive about handicapped students being subject to the whim of school officials. This rights orientation has permeated special education policy making at every level of government.

In this chapter I show how the language of rights combined with American separation of powers in an era of divided government to produce significant program expansion and extension of federal control. In particular, I develop four themes about the political significance of the language of rights.

First, in both the passage and the implementation of the 1975 act, rights were more than mere symbols but less than "trumps" (to use Ronald Dworkin's term). The focus on individual rights, both substantive and procedural, was the central feature of the act. Yet few of the key actors (including the most devoted advocates for the handicapped) believed that the costs of educational programs for the handicapped would be or even should be irrelevant. Questions of resource allocation were never far from anyone's mind. Rather, the focus on rights was the linchpin of a sophisticated political strategy that allowed advocates for the handicapped to unite a highly diverse reform coalition, to use victories in the courtroom as leverage in other political forums, and to place themselves in an advantageous bargaining position during implementation of the act.

Second, although the emphasis on rights was at first perceived by special education professionals as an attack on their expertise and discretion (a perception obviously shared by British officials), these professionals soon realized that this approach could increase their control over special education policy. The interest group most active in shaping the act was the Council for Exceptional Children (CEC), the principal national association of special education professionals. Leaders of the CEC argued that creating such legal rights would not only increase the resources going to special education, but also reduce the extent to which principals, superintendents, and school boards scrutinized the professional activities of the organization's members. The act, as Senator Robert Stafford put it, affirms "the best and most progressive professional practice of all who are involved in the instructional development of exceptional children."[7]

Third, despite its sponsors' claim that federal legislation would reduce the role played by the courts, litigation has increased dramatically since passage of the EAHCA. Congress has encouraged litigation not only by creating legal rights to a "free appropriate public education" and to "impartial due process hearings," but also by giving federal district courts substantial discretion to review the decisions of school administrators. When the Supreme Court ruled that the 1975 act does not authorize judges to award attorneys' fees to parents winning EAHCA cases, Congress amended the act to provide attorneys' fees for both administrative and judicial proceedings.

Finally, what is perhaps most intriguing about education of the handicapped is how policy became more ambitious as it traveled from one institution to another. Federal and state court decisions forced some states to increase substantially their spending on special education. These states then appealed to Congress for financial support. Congressional sponsors of federal legislation agreed that the states needed help but insisted that federal money be coupled with guarantees that the states protect the "constitutional" rights of handicapped children. Since no one knew precisely what these rights were, the federal legislation spelled out the procedures that school systems must follow. Once the legislation was in place, the courts reentered the picture, insisting on a literal interpretation of some phrases (such as the requirement that states educate *all* handicapped children) and giving a liberal interpretation to others (such as "related services"). Each institution made incremental changes that seemed small when viewed individually but that constituted major, rapid change when put together.

The Courts Set the Stage

The influence of the *PARC* and *Mills* decisions was twofold.[8] First, the substance of the act was drawn from the court orders. The duty to provide all handicapped children with a "free appropriate public education," the requirement that schools work with parents in preparing a plan to meet the unique needs of each handicapped student, the elaborate requirements for "impartial due process hearings," and the preference for mainstreaming all came from the courts. In the words of Senator Harrison Williams (D-NJ), the act's chief sponsor, "the courts have helped us define the right to an education in the last few years. That is what we are trying to find, the means to carry out the fundamental law of the land."[9]

Second, the decisions led the states to demand that the federal government help pay for the judicial mandates. Court rulings helped push up state expenditures on special education from $900 million in 1972 to over $2 billion in 1974.[10] The goal of the plaintiffs had always been to use the courts to spur further legislative action. As one advocate put it, the strategy was "to cook the school districts until they came to Congress demanding the funds that we [need] to provide appropriate programs."[11]

PARC and *Mills* were peculiar "landmark" cases. The plaintiffs and the defendants did not disagree on much. In *PARC* the defendant, the Commonwealth of Pennsylvania, settled the case after a single day of testimony by the plaintiff's witnesses. Local school systems later complained that the state had colluded with the plaintiffs to fashion a remedy that the local schools would be forced to implement. In the District of Columbia, the school system was struggling to deal with a large number of problems, including desegregation. The beleaguered school board accepted the court's ruling in principle but did little to put it into practice. The two courts addressed constitutional issues only in the most oblique fashion. In *PARC* the court stated that "the plaintiffs have established a colorable claim" under the Fourteenth Amendment. Both courts relied primarily on their interpretation of state law.

This did not stop the two courts from issuing extensive, detailed orders. The thrust of the two decisions was similar. First, schools were ordered to launch a major effort to locate handicapped students excluded from public school. Second, schools must "provide to each child of school age a free and suitable publicly-supported education regardless of the degree of the child's mental, physical or emotional disability or impairment." They cannot exclude any child "on the basis of a claim of insufficient resources."[12] Third, before placing a child in special education school officials must "notify his parent or guardian of the proposed educational placement, the reasons therefore, and the right to a hearing before a Hearing Officer if there is an objection to the proposed placement." Parents have the right to be represented by legal counsel, to examine school records, and to cross-examine school officials. Fourth, school officials cannot suspend a handicapped child without affording him a hearing and "providing for his education during the period of any such suspension." Finally, both courts expressed a preference for "mainstreaming," that is, educating handicapped students in classrooms with their nonhandicapped peers.

FROM EXCLUSION TO APPROPRIATENESS

With education of the handicapped, as with desegregation, the courts started out with issues of "simple justice" and before long faced complex administrative issues. The most compelling argument the courts heard in *PARC, Mills*, and similar cases around the country was that some children were receiving *no* education, either because they had been excluded as "uneducable" or because they had been suspended for behavior related to their handicap. Such exclusion not only violated state laws mandating public education for all capable of benefiting from it, but also raised equal protection issues in a particularly stark way. According to *Brown v. Board of Education*, the fountainhead of contemporary constitutional jurisprudence, once a state establishes a system of public education, education becomes "a right which must be made available to all on equal terms."[13] In *San Antonio School District v. Rodriguez*, the Supreme Court upheld Texas's school financing law because it did *not* result in "an *absolute deprivation* of a meaningful opportunity to enjoy that benefit."[14]

The *PARC* trial began and ended with expert testimony on the educability of all retarded children. The state of Pennsylvania originally claimed that it excluded only the uneducable. The plaintiff's four experts claimed that "there is no such thing as an uneducable or untrainable child."[15] In the middle of the trial, the state announced its agreement with these experts and offered to settle the case. The state department of education was eager to accept the controversial assertions of academic experts. Other state officials were anxious to get rid of a case that made them appear heartless.

More surprising than the defendants' quick capitulation on the issue of exclusion was how effortlessly the parties and the court moved from nonexclusion to the right to an *appropriate* education. The due process hearings originally designed to prevent exclusion were given the additional task of establishing the appropriateness of instruction within the classroom. This is by no means a necessary progression. Regular students, who presumably have a similar right to an education, seldom receive an individualized hearing on the appropriateness of their education. Nor do they have the opportunity to appeal school decisions. "Appropriateness" is precisely the type of judgment the Supreme Court has told judges to avoid.

Advocates for the handicapped, distrustful of local officials and concerned at least as much about the quality of special education as about exclusion, were adamant on the issue of "appropriateness." What good is merely sitting in a classroom, they argued, if the education provided by the state is not suited to the student? School officials, assuming that they would be the ones to determine appropriateness, decided not to object.

Ironically, it later became clear that exclusion was not nearly as great a problem as advocates had claimed. Although the plaintiffs in *PARC* claimed that the number of children receiving no education in Pennsylvania was 100,000, the extensive court-mandated effort to find these children turned up only 2,500 children who were not in any educational program.[16] Results were similar at the national level. The act announced that "one million of the handicapped children in the U.S. are excluded entirely from the public school system"; the Senate Report put the number at 1.75 million.[17] By 1981 both the General Accounting Office (GAO) and the Office of Civil Rights (OCR) had concluded that these figures were far too high.[18] But by then everyone's attention had shifted away from exclusion to the *quality* of special education.

THE REFORM COALITION

One of the central achievements of the litigation of the early 1970s was to bring together a broad coalition of groups dedicated to reforming special education. The *PARC* and *Mills* cases were well publicized—including front page stories and editorials in the *New York Times*. Subsequent litigation gave state and local organizations concrete tasks and helped the CEC and the National Association for Retarded Children (NARC) to build a national network of supporters. Most importantly, the emphasis on individual rights allowed a highly diverse coalition to come together and stay together. This coalition included parents of children with an array of handicaps, special educational professionals, and civil rights groups.

The variety of handicaps that afflicts children of school age is enormous. They stretch from profound retardation to dyslexia, from autism to blindness, from emotional disturbances to spina bifida. Before 1970 parents tended to organize around particular handicaps—if they organized at all. Consequently, the blind, the deaf, the retarded, the physically disabled, and those with learning disabilities competed with one another for scarce resources. Even within these smaller groups, there were disagreements about proper treatment—for example, home care versus institutionalization for the profoundly retarded and sign language versus lipreading for the deaf.[19] About the only thing everyone could agree upon was that each child should receive an education "appropriate" to that child's "unique capacities."

Robert Katzmann's discussion of the American Coalition for Citizens with Disabilities (ACCD), an umbrella organization concerned primarily with accessible transportation, applies equally well to the coalition put together by the CEC and NARC.

> If government defined federal policy toward the disabled as a matter of claims involving the allocation of finite resources, then presumably each of the many groups within the ACCD would have competed with the others to secure funds for its own constituency. But because the government defined the issue in terms of rights, questions of cost became irrelevant: each group could champion the demands of others without financial sacrifice.[20]

Indeed, the events examined by Katzmann—passage and implementation of section 504 of the Rehabilitation Act of 1973—helped make clear to advocates for handicapped children the advantages of a rights-based approach.

The driving force behind most of the litigation and lobbying at the state and federal levels was the Council for Exceptional Children. An association of more than seventy thousand special education professionals, the CEC provided the expert testimony in *PARC*. It wrote the model statute that was the basis for many state laws and, ultimately, the EAHCA. The CEC explained to local groups how to bring court suits and how to use these suits as leverage for passing legislation. The CEC took pains to explain to its members how in the long run litigation would enhance their position within the school system. Thomas Gilhool, the lead attorney in *PARC*, told a CEC conference, "We have with some ease adopted the agenda that you, the professionals, have set and we have taken it to court."[21] Professionals should not interpret court suits as an attack on their authority. Experience shows that "defendants, if they are good professionals, welcome litigation as an opportunity to advance the agenda which they share." Another CEC official explained that in some instances "named defendants have spent days preparing defenses for the suit, and nights assisting the plaintiffs to prepare their arguments." In short, "litigation (or the threat of litigation) may be used as a lever to bring about the action desired by both the potential defendant and the plaintiff."[22]

Parents, lawyers, and professionals shared not only a common set of enemies, but also a commitment to individualized treatment for each handicapped child. Individual needs, in the end, would be determined by special education experts now insulated from pressure by cost-conscious administrators and politicians. These factors brought parents, lawyers, and professionals together in early litigation and eventually produced a formidable alliance dedicated to protecting the EAHCA.

For all of the brave talk about a constitutional right to a "free appropriate public education," the law on the subject was remarkably thin. Advocates for the handicapped won some state court cases after *PARC* and *Mills*. But at the same time they were losing cases in other federal courts.[23] One year after *PARC* and *Mills*, the Supreme Court announced that it "is not the province of this Court to create substantive constitutional rights in the name of guaranteeing equal protection of the laws."[24] CEC's lobbyists and lawyers were painfully aware of their tenuous legal position. According to Jack Tweedie, they "avoided appellate resolution of the issue," fearing "that an increasingly conservative U.S. Supreme Court would reject a constitutional right to education for the handicapped."[25]

CEC's political genius was to convert a stalled judicial strategy into a successful legislative campaign. Working first at the state level, advocates discovered that legislators and governors were happy to appropriate more money and to impose regulations on local schools so long as they could pass the blame to the federal courts. Before long advocates for the handicapped turned their attention to Congress. They joined with state and local officials to demand that the federal government help pay for the mandates of *PARC* and *Mills*. They also argued that federal legislation would put an end to the unnerving uncertainty created by pending litigation. As it turned out, though, the federal legislation passed in 1975 forced them to deal even more frequently with the courts.

A Bill of Rights Becomes a Law

For a bill that has been described as "the single most important piece of federal education legislation passed during the 1970s" and "the most significant child welfare legislation of the 1970s,"[26] the EAHCA generated remarkably little opposition. Not one interest group opposed the bill. Only the White House and the Secretary of Health, Education and Welfare (HEW) spoke against it. The bill passed both houses by margins so lopsided that President Ford decided not to veto it. Republicans in the House stated that, with a few minor changes, "this bill would truly represent one of the finest Acts ever produced by Congress."[27]

Three factors help explain Congress's support for education of the handicapped. First and most obvious is the entrepreneurial role of the two authorizing committees, the House Education and Labor Committee and the Senate Labor and Public Welfare Committee. These committees have been aggressive in their support for federal aid to education and for assistance for the handicapped. In the early 1970s members of these committees were looking for an opportunity to expand the federal role in special education. *PARC* and *Mills* created a fiscal problem for which these entrepreneurs had a ready policy solution.

Second, education of the handicapped is an issue that cuts across party lines. The best indication of this came in 1981 when the Republicans gained control of the Senate. Senator Lowell Weicker, the new chairman of the Subcommittee on the Handicapped, was at least as vocal in his opposition to the Reagan administration as were Democrats on the panel. Weicker, to be sure, is hardly a typical Republican. But such atypical Republicans gravitate to the two education committees. Senators Robert Stafford, Jacob Javits, and Charles Mathias, as well as Representatives Albert Quie and James Jeffords, were all instrumental in the passage of the EAHCA. Just as importantly, their more conservative Republican colleagues made little effort to oppose them on the floor. Handicaps such as retardation, spina bifida, blindness, autism, and learning disabilities are universally viewed as tragedies that fall upon all ethnic groups, upon rich and poor, and upon residents of inner cities, suburbs, and farm districts—even upon members of Congress and their families.

Third, the benefits of the new federal program are clear and of great importance to parents and professionals, but the costs are hard to trace. Only a small part of the cost of special education is borne by the federal government. Who pays for the services required by the EAHCA? Local taxpayers? State taxpayers? Teachers who are expected to take on extra duties? Regular students who receive fewer resources and experience the disruptive consequences of mainstreaming? No one can say for sure. This ambiguity—an ambiguity created largely by the rights-based structure of the act—has proved highly significant politically.

THE POLITICAL CONTEXT, 1965–1972

In 1965 members of the two education committees swallowed their pride and accepted *in toto* the version of the Elementary and Secondary Education bill negotiated by the Johnson administration and education interest groups.[28] But by 1966 they were rushing to champion causes that they believed the executive branch had ignored. Over the objection of the White House (which opposed funding increases) and the Office of Education (which opposed congressional meddling with administrative structures), Congress established a small authorization for education of the handicapped and created a Bureau of Education for the Handicapped (BEH) within the Office of Education.[29]

This pattern of executive resistance and committee insistence became more pronounced under President Nixon. The Nixon administration sought to reduce both federal spending on education and federal demands on the states. Congress's response was to create more and larger categorical programs. Education became both a Democratic and a congressional issue. The more education bills Nixon threatened to veto, the more Democrats presented theirs as the party of education. The more Democrats took credit for education programs, the more congressional Republicans backed away from Nixon and presented the issue as Congress versus the president rather than Democrats versus Republicans. The time was ripe for new initiatives in education.

THE HANDICAPPED TO THE FORE

In 1970 Senator Harrison Williams rose to the chairmanship of the Senate committee. Williams was looking for an issue to call his own and decided to make the handicapped his top priority. It soon became apparent that "rights of the handicapped" was an issue with a vocal clientele and significant political appeal. Over the next several years, Congress enacted the Developmental Disabilities and Bill of Rights Act, the Civil Rights for Institutionalized Persons Act, and section 504 of the Rehabilitation Act, which outlawed discrimination on the basis of handicap in any program receiving federal assistance.

Senator Williams' proposed legislation on education for the handicapped was different from previous education laws, which had stressed both federal funding and cooperation between professionals at the federal, state, and local levels. His legislation's detailed mandates on "free appropriate public education," "related services," and "due process hearings" were the products not of the older staff members, with their ties to the Office of Education, but of an "alternative policy network" created by Williams.[30] Williams' staffers worked closely with the CEC, whose model statute formed the core of this bill. Strict enforcement of federal rules and confrontation with the educational "establishment" replaced cooperation as the goals of reformers.

S.6 was but one of many programs competing for money and floor time before the "resurgent" Congress of the mid-1970s. Of decisive importance to the bill's success was the fact that state officials lined up to testify that they needed help. State officials, committee members, and advocates for the handicapped created the image of a right-to-education juggernaut that would crush the states unless they received a massive injection of federal funds. The Nixon administration lamely replied that the states had more money in their coffers than did the federal government. The Democratic leadership realized that this created an opportunity to curry favor with state and local officials. Republicans in Congress quickly distanced themselves from the administration.

The political change wrought by the court decisions was evident in the congressional action on the Education Amendments of 1974. Senator Charles Mathias (R-MD) offered a floor amendment increasing the authorization for education of the handicapped. Mathias explained that state court decisions had dramatically increased the cost of special education in Maryland and warned that "the set of conditions found in Maryland are replicated throughout this country."[31] The amendment passed by voice vote and was accepted by the House in conference.

Added to the Mathias amendment was an unprinted floor amendment that, in the words of its sponsor, Senator Robert Stafford, "simply attaches guarantees to Mr. Mathias's amendment, which conform to the court decrees."[32] Stafford's amendment established the goal of a "free appropriate public education" for all handicapped children. It required states to provide "procedural safeguards," including prior notice of placement, an opportunity for parents to obtain "impartial due process hearings" and "independent educational evaluation of the child," as well as "procedures to insure that, to the maximum extent appropriate, handicapped children . . . are educated with children who are not handicapped." This amendment, too, faced no opposition on the floor or in conference.

No one wished to challenge the contention that when states receive federal money they should protect children's constitutional rights. Moreover, these amendments were presented as stopgap measures designed to tide the states over until Congress could put together a more comprehensive response. Just as Stafford claimed in 1974 that he was doing little more than codifying court rulings, in 1975 Senator Williams and his cosponsors claimed that they were doing little more than providing more money and guidance for carrying out the Stafford amendment. Ironically, members of Congress treated the *PARC* and *Mills* decisions as etched in stone, even though other federal courts did not.

THE FINAL HURDLES

Even in an ordinary year the prospects for increased federal funding and a concomitant increase in federal regulation would have been good. Given the popularity of both education and assistance for the handicapped, passage of some variation on S.6 seemed assured. And 1975 was no ordinary year. The 1974 election had produced a "veto-proof" Congress with 291 Democrats in the House and 60 in the Senate. Democrats were already building a legislative record in anticipation of the 1976 presidential election.

The only real challenge to passage of the act came in the conference committee. Conferees faced two issues, money and compliance mechanisms. They quickly reached a compromise on the former but nearly deadlocked on the latter. Advocates for the handicapped insisted on elaborate appeals procedures that were strenuously opposed by the National School Board Association and other education groups. Given the vagueness of the act's substantive mandate, compliance procedures are in effect a mechanism for deciding who sets federal policy. Advocates for the handicapped, many of whom had spent years battling school districts, understood this better than did the lobbyists for school groups.

The architect of the conference committee's solution was first-term congressman George Miller (D-CA), a "Watergate baby" who has made children's issues one of his major issues. Miller worked closely with the Children's Defense Fund and the California Rural Legal Assistance Foundation, both of which had been involved in litigation on behalf of handicapped students and were highly suspicious of the education "establishment."[33] The lengthy and detailed proposal written by these two groups and put forth by Miller were weakened somewhat to make them more palatable to traditional education interest groups.

The final version of the EAHCA contained these provisions:

1. A parent dissatisfied with an individualized educational program (IEP) can demand an "impartial due process hearing" at the local level. The hearing officer may not be "an employee of such agency or unit involved in the education or care of the child." Parties to the hearing have the right to be accompanied by legal counsel, to compel attendance by witnesses, to cross-examine witnesses, and to receive a written explanation of the hearing officer's decision.

2. Either party may appeal the outcome of the first hearing at the state level. The state agency "shall conduct an impartial review . . . and make an independent decision."

3. Aggrieved parties can appeal this decision in federal district court. The court shall review the record of the prior hearings, "hear additional evidence at the request of a party," and "basing its decision on the preponderance of the evidence, shall grant such relief as the court determines is appropriate." The conference report added that the federal court should make an "independent" judgment as to the adequacy of the IEP.

This compliance mechanism not only gives a significant role to the federal court, but also makes each administrative hearing relatively formal and courtlike. Just as importantly, the arrangement shifts control over IEP decisions away from those who bear compliance costs. Hearing officers at each level are to be "independent," which means, above all, not readily subjected to reprisal by school administrators. Most independent of all are the federal judges who have the final say over what constitutes an "appropriate" education.

Why did school systems ultimately accept this intrusion into their traditional area of autonomy? The conference bill was less obnoxious than either the House or the Senate bill. State and local education agencies could choose the hearing officers, and the initial review was at the local rather than the state level. Moreover, the change from the Stafford amendment with its vague "due process" requirement did not seem large. To be sure, the conference bill expanded the role of the courts. But hadn't the courts played a significant role even without federal legislation? Looming over everything else was the carrot of federal money. Why put authorizing legislation in jeopardy over procedural issues, especially since the courts might impose more stringent procedural requirements if the legislation were to fail?

On 29 November 1975, President Ford signed PL 94-142. He warned that the bill "promises more than the federal government can deliver" and that its "vast array of detailed, complex, and costly administrative requirements" would "unnecessarily assert federal control over traditional state and local government functions."[34] In 1975 such arguments fell on deaf ears—which is probably why Ford declined to veto the bill.

SUBSTANCE AND PROCEDURE

The legislation passed by Congress in 1975 was indeed complex and detailed in its procedures, but it was surprisingly vague in its substantive mandates. State applications for federal money, local applications to the states, IEP meetings, due process hearings—all these were spelled out in elaborate statutory provisions. Yet the heart of the act, the right to a "free appropriate public education" and "related services," became the educational equivalent of the Holy Ghost: everyone considers them sacred, but no one really knows what they are. Legislators talked blithely about providing equal educational opportunity and allowing individuals to maximize their potential, without giving serious thought to what this might mean in practice.

Although it is always tempting to criticize Congress for failing to make hard choices, given the huge variety of handicapping conditions and the extent of disagreement over how to treat each one, it is difficult to see how Congress could possibly have come up with specific substantive requirements. Nor did Congress get much help from special education professionals. It had become a matter of faith for them that general rules are always arbitrary; trained professionals must consider the unique needs of each handicapped child. This article of faith conveniently dovetailed with the courts' insistence on individualized treatment of handicapped children—and, of course, with legislators' incentives to avoid unnecessary controversy.

How could one hope to change educational practices in fifteen thousand local school systems—many of which appeared to have provided inadequate services to the handicapped in the past—without providing substantive guidelines? Elaborate procedures seemed to provide the only way out of the dilemma. In designing these procedures groups like CEC, NARC, the Children's Defense Fund, and the California Rural Legal Assistance Foundation had an important advantage. They had spent years fighting and suing school systems. As a result they had a fairly good sense of which procedures provided leverage against recalcitrant school officials. The Washington representatives of traditional education groups, in contrast, were far removed from such local confrontations, were accustomed to seeing financial issues as paramount, and thus were not nearly as sophisticated at estimating the likely consequences of procedural change. With the help of congressional allies such as George Miller and Harrison Williams, advocates for the handicapped won the day.

Although state and local officials supported the EAHCA to get federal money for newly mandated programs, federal appropriations never came close to authorizations and are almost certainly less than the added costs imposed by the new law. Familiar only with federal programs that provided money with easily evaded strings, many state and local officials only later realized that federal mandates could become "millstones."[35] An additional reason for state and local support for the EAHCA was these officials' distaste for litigation, with its uncertainty and adversarial tenor. Sponsors of the federal law repeatedly argued that the legislation would take these matters out of court. As the following discussion will show, just the opposite happened. The number of court cases grew enormously. Ironically, just as the Supreme Court was pulling the federal judiciary away from educational policy making, Congress was pushing it back in.

Coming Full Circle: Court Action under the EAHCA

Implementation of the EAHCA was bound to be contentious. Throughout the legislative process members of Congress had acted under the assumption that what constitutes an "appropriate education" could be determined through a relatively straightforward application of professional judgment. Professional norms, though, proved far weaker than expected. Many of the disagreements ended up in court.

That the courts should be so involved in administration of the act is, in retrospect, not surprising. Parents with severely handicapped children have a great deal at stake; residential placement can cost $50,000 or more per year. Private attorneys soon started to specialize in education of the handicapped. District and circuit court judges who chafed under the Burger Court's restrictive reading of the equal protection clause in education cases welcomed the opportunity to make an "independent" finding on the adequacy of educational plans.

The extensive federal case law on education of the handicapped defies easy description. The typical federal case involves competing professional judgments about the treatment of severely handicapped children. Usually the parent is seeking residential placement, tuition for a private day school, or special services such as psychotherapy, a sign language interpreter, or catheterization. The school district claims either that a less expensive program would be equally appropriate or that the service requested is not mandated by the act. On a few matters—for example, the legality of the 180-day school year and the outer bounds of "related services"—the federal courts have spoken clearly enough to create a "black letter law" of education for the handicapped. But on the central issue of "appropriateness" and the amount of deference due school systems and hearing examiners, there are serious and lasting disagreements among federal judges. Although the Supreme Court came down squarely on the side of judicial deference to local school systems, it has not been successful in convincing the lower courts to comply.

THE EXTENDED SCHOOL YEAR

The case law on the extended school year provides a useful first look at EAHCA litigation. Most states limit the school year to about 180 days. When parents of some handicapped children asked for year-round educational services, most school systems argued that this would be too expensive and was not mandated by the statute. The National School Board Association was particularly aggressive in opposing the extended school year.

The courts have been unanimous in their opposition to any across-the-board limits on the length of the school year. According to the Court of Appeals for the Third Circuit, "The 180 day rule imposes with rigid certainty a program restriction which may be wholly inappropriate to the child's educational objective" and thus "incompatible with the Act's emphasis on the individual."[36] The rule of thumb to be applied in such cases was stated by the Court of Appeals for the Fifth Circuit: "If a child will experience severe or substantial regression during the summer months in the absence of a summer program, the handicapped child may be entitled to year round services."[37]

Since, as many judges recognized, all children experience some regression over the summer, the real issue in these cases is not regression itself but its severity. Most federal courts have held that the school officials, hearing officers, and judges who make these complex determinations must be guided above all by the needs of handicapped students, not by the cost of extended school year programs.[38] On occasion judges have ordered school districts to provide an extended school year program even when experts are divided over its usefulness for the child in question.[39]

RELATED SERVICES

Few issues have been as frequently litigated or have involved as many unusual circumstances as the meaning of "related services." The act defines "related services" as "transportation and such developmental, corrective, and other supportive services . . . as may be required to assist a handicapped child to benefit from special education" (section 1401(1)(17)). It specifies that "related services" does *not* include "medical services" other than those used for "diagnostic and evaluative purposes." This raises two issues of great importance to schools and parents: What services are "required to assist" a particular handicapped child to "benefit from special education"? What services are exempt because they are "medical"? At stake is not just the extent of services received by handicapped children, but also the distribution of costs among state and local agencies. In many states social service agencies have used the EAHCA to transfer to the schools a variety of responsibilities.

The courts have generally taken an "inclusionary" approach to "related services."[40] When residential placement and extensive programming is needed to deal with a child's severe psychological problems, these become "related services" because "the emotional needs of this plaintiff are closely interwoven with his educational needs."[41] "Where what is being taught is how to pay attention, talk, respond to words of warning, and dress and feed oneself," the First Circuit explained, "a suitably staffed and structured residential environment providing continual training and reinforcement in those skills serves an educational purpose."[42] Judges have agreed that when residential placement is "appropriate" the school must pay all nonmedical costs.[43]

Judges and hearing officers have required schools to provide what one law review article called "a bewildering array of services, including music therapy, 'therapeutic recreation,' myofunctional therapy, sign language training for parents, detoxification, and the assistance of a 'visual computer.'"[44] Many (but not all) courts have found extensive psychotherapy and group therapy to be appropriate "related services."[45] In one unusual case a federal court ruled that the insertion of a tracheotomy tube into a child's stomach is a service covered by the act.[46]

In its only decision on the subject, the Supreme Court followed the lead of the lower courts in adopting a broad reading of "related services" and a narrow reading of the "medical services" exception. In *Tatro v. Texas* the Court ruled that periodic reattachment of a catheter (a procedure required by those with spina bifida) is a related, nonmedical service.[47] Services that can be provided by school nurses rather than solely by physicians, Chief Justice Burger found, do not fall within the medical exception. "School nurses have long been a part of the educational system, and the Secretary could thereby reasonably conclude that the school nursing services are not the sort of burden the Congress intended to exclude as a 'medical' service." This was as far as the Court has gone in giving direction to the lower courts on the meaning of "related services."

DEFINING AN APPROPRIATE EDUCATION

What constitutes an "appropriate education" for a child with a particular concatenation of handicaps? This is the question that has plagued almost everyone affected by the EAHCA. The act allows parents to appeal decisions of state and local hearing officers in federal district court. The district court must consult the administrative record, hear additional evidence, and "basing its decision on the preponderance of the evidence, shall grant such relief as the court determines is appropriate." Most judges, following the 1975 conference report, have interpreted this to mean that they must make an "independent" decision on the merits. In the late 1970s judges and commentators voiced confidence in the courts' ability to create a coherent "common law" for education of the handicapped.[48]

Despite years of experience and hundreds of cases, judicially manageable standards of appropriateness remain elusive. Some judges announced that they would overturn decisions of school officials and hearing officers only if they were "clearly erroneous" or failed to provide the handicapped student with "some educational benefit." According to these judges, not only do school officials have more educational expertise than judges, but weighing the cost of alternative placements is an inevitable and legitimate part of a school administrator's job. The act, one judge maintained, does not create a right for parents "to write a prescription for an ideal education for their children and to have the prescription filled at public expense."[49] Many other judges, though, have rejected this circumscribed judicial role. Willingness to listen carefully to parents' experts, to place the burden of proof on school officials, and to come up with an independent evaluation is what characterized this more aggressive approach to judicial review.[50]

In *Hendrick Hudson District Board of Education v. Rowley*, the Supreme Court clearly sided with the deferential judges.[51] The case involved Amy Rowley, a highly motivated deaf girl with an IQ of over 120. Her school had placed her in a regular class and provided her with daily individual tutoring, a weekly session with a speech therapist, and a special FM hearing aid. School administrators also took sign language classes to communicate with Amy's parents, who are themselves deaf. But the school refused to honor her parents' request for a sign language interpreter to accompany Amy in class.

The Rowleys sued the school, and the district court agreed with them. Without the interpreter, the court found, Amy could understand only 59 percent of what was said in class. The lower court concluded that the gap between Amy's potential and her performance in school is "precisely the kind of deficiency which the Act addresses in requiring that every handicapped child be given an appropriate education."[52]

In a 6–3 decision the Supreme Court overturned the lower court's decision. The majority and dissenting opinions present a classic confrontation between judges who rely on legislative history to support judicial activism through statutory interpretation and those who rely on federalism and strict construction of statutes to justify judicial restraint. Justice Rehnquist's majority opinion noted that the statutory definition of *free appropriate public education* "tends toward the cryptic . . . Noticeably absent from the language of the statute is any substantive standard prescribing the level of education to be accorded to handicapped children." The lower court had mistakenly concluded that this silence coupled with the act's liberal judicial review provision indicated a congressional intent for the court to fashion its own substantive standards. The mere use of the words *preponderance of the evidence,* Rehnquist argued, is "by no means an invitation to the courts to substitute their own notions of sound educational policy for those of the school authorities which they review." Not only are the courts ill-suited to engage in educational policy making, but the lower courts' approach also violates a key tenet of federalism. If Congress had meant to impose obligations such as those ordered by the district court, then it would have done so "unambiguously" rather than through definitional silence.[53] According to Rehnquist, "The intent of the Act was more to open the door of public education to handicapped children on appropriate terms than to guarantee any particular level of education once inside." All the act requires is "that the education to which access is provided be sufficient to confer *some* educational benefit upon the handicapped child."[54]

Justice White's dissenting opinion relied heavily on the act's legislative history, which is full of references to "equal educational opportunity" and allowing each handicapped child to "achieve his or her maximum potential." According to White the purpose of the act "is to eliminate the effect of the handicap, at least to the extent that the child will be given an equal opportunity to learn if that is reasonably possible" (at 215). Moreover, the change in judicial review provisions made by the conference committee "demonstrated that Congress intended the court to conduct a far more searching inquiry."

The fact that Justice Rehnquist garnered more votes in the Supreme Court than did Justice White did not put an end to the debate within the judicial branch. Although judges routinely cite *Rowley*, only some follow its command of deference. Judges who chose to take a more activist stance can easily evade Supreme Court review. According to a Legal Services publication, "judges have not been unduly constrained" by *Rowley*. "They still make independent decisions based on all the evidence before them."[55]

Consider, for example, *Doe v. Anrig*. A district court decision issued before *Rowley* had explicitly relied on the standard of review subsequently rejected by the Supreme Court. Shortly after *Rowley* the First Circuit upheld the ruling of the trial judge. It stated that, although "the district court's statement that the 'administrative decision is entitled to no special deference' may seem at odds with the thrust of the *Rowley* requirement that courts give 'due weight' to state proceedings, we find nothing in the record before us to suggest that 'due weight' was not accorded." At issue, the court explained, "was not a choice of educational policy, but resolution of an individualized factual issue." Resolution of such factual issues "falls within the scope of the question which *Rowley* says is for the court."[56] In other cases, too, decisions initially based on the reading of the statute rejected in *Rowley* were upheld by circuit judges claiming fealty to that decision.[57]

Another way that some judges have circumvented *Rowley* is by relying on state laws that seem to set a substantive standard more rigorous than "some educational benefit." Massachusetts law, for example, refers to the "maximum possible development of handicapped children." A New Jersey statute establishes the principle that all students "be assured the fullest possible opportunity to develop their intellectual capacities." The First, Third, and Ninth Circuits have all argued that the EAHCA "incorporates by reference" such state laws. This incorporation of state law into the federal statute is "bottomed on both the statutory language and authoritative legislative history."[58] As a consequence, federal judges hearing cases in these states can revert to their aggressive pre-*Rowley* stance.[59] The history of *Rowley* shows above all how hard it is for the Supreme Court to control the lower courts when determinations of "appropriateness" are tied so closely to particular, often highly unusual factual circumstances.

The Political Appeal of Rights

When the courts announced their decisions on the extended school year, related services, residential placement, and "appropriate education," Congress reacted not at all—no hearings, no appropriations riders, no legislation. Yet when the Supreme Court ruled in *Smith v. Rob-*

inson that plaintiffs who prevail in EAHCA cases cannot collect attorneys' fees, the halls of Congress rang with denunciations of this "misinterpretation of Congress' intent" which "threaten the rights of handicapped children" and will have "a devastating effect on the ability of parents to secure a free appropriate public education for disabled children."[60] Both houses unanimously passed legislation to allow courts to award attorneys' fees. The Handicapped Children Protection Act of 1986 did more than reestablish the *status quo ante*. It allowed these awards to cover attorneys' fees incurred in administrative as well as judicial proceedings. Congress clearly has no aversion to the intervention of courts and lawyers in special education.

Why did Congress react with such vehemence on this particular issue? The argument that the Supreme Court flaunted the clear intent of Congress is weak. The "American rule" has long held that attorney's fees cannot be awarded by federal courts unless explicitly authorized by Congress. In 1975, several months before the conference committee wrote the judicial review provision of the EAHCA, the Supreme Court issued a widely publicized decision reaffirming its commitment to the "American rule."[61] Congress responded to this decision by passing the Civil Rights Attorneys Award Act of 1976, which covered the Voting Rights Act, the Civil Rights Act of 1964, and the Fair Housing Act of 1968. In 1978, it extended attorneys' fees to cases brought under section 504 of the Rehabilitation Act. No mention of attorneys' fees appears in the EAHCA, and no mention of the EAHCA appears in either of these two attorneys' fees statutes.

Congress's reaffirmation of its commitment to adversarial procedures came at a time when school officials, parents, and academics were attacking the act as a leading example of rights gone wrong.[62] School officials decried the increase in paperwork, the amount of time spent at conferences and hearings, the cost of lawyers, and the harm done to the parent-teacher relationship by adversarial proceedings. Parents find the proceedings "emotionally straining, overly formal, and primarily concerned with procedures and rules of law rather than issues of substance." Often the experience was "so intimidating and threatening that parents felt unable to act on their own, feeling strongly the need for an attorney or advocate." As one mother put it, "It's been hell. Absolute hell." Said another, "I've been through seizures and everything else with her, and this has been the worst affair of my life."[63]

Part of the explanation for Congress's delegation of authority to the courts is that this arrangement allows legislators to engage in both credit claiming and blame avoidance. In effect, members of Congress can say, "We have passed legislation to educate the handicapped, help the states, and protect the Constitution. For that we should be praised. And if you don't like any specific result, blame the courts." Yet if members of Congress wanted to insulate themselves from blame, why wasn't it sufficient to follow the traditional route of delegating authority either to state and local governments or to federal administrators? As Morris Fiorina has argued, members of Congress frequently take credit for program benefits while blaming *bureaucrats* for their costs.[64]

The structure created by the Education for All Handicapped Children Act was in large part the product of the way the issue came onto the congressional agenda. The act was sold as a way to vindicate the constitutional rights of handicapped children. Most of the bill's supporters, both inside and outside Congress, saw the issue in terms of individual rights and had more faith in courts than in other governmental institutions. To the extent that the courts serve as "agenda setters," they will frequently be the recipients of delegated authority.

Just as importantly, the principal sponsors of the act were serious about changing the practices of state and local educational systems. To change the locus of decision making to give parents and special education professionals more control over the education of handicapped children became a central purpose of the legislation. Simple delegation to state and local officials was out of the question.

Advocates for the handicapped did not trust the federal Department of Education much more than they trusted state and local school systems. The department had always emphasized the development of cooperative relations with local administrators. Its principal enforcement mechanism, the funding cutoff, was seldom effective. The courts, in contrast, were not tied to the "educational establishment" and had at their disposal an effective enforcement tool—the injunction. To advocates for the handicapped, relying on the courts was the only effective way to overcome the obstacles created by the decentralized American educational system.

If education for the handicapped makes clear the special problems resulting from decentralization, it also demonstrates the fragmented American political system's capacity for rapid and substantial policy change. The Education for All Handicapped Children Act increased both the number of services available to children with disabilities and the extent of federal control over state and local school systems. This transformation took place in an era of divided government. Presidential leadership was conspicuously absent. The impetus for change came from the lower courts, congressional subcommittees, and public interest groups. What galvanized this coalition was its commitment to protecting the *rights* of handicapped children.

The conventional wisdom on federalism and the separation of powers is that these features of our political system create multiple veto points and lead almost inevitably to either the frustration or the watering down of reform initiatives. Here the opposite was true: federalism and separation of powers created "opportunity points" rather than "veto points." Reformers skillfully used victories in one forum to press for further action in another. Decisions by federal district courts and state courts forced some states to spend more for special education. Congressional committees offered financial assistance in exchange for more specific federal requirements. Subsequent action by the lower courts turned ambiguous statutory phrases into costly federal mandates. A series of seemingly small steps produced a major change in American education.

Education for the handicapped thus illustrates an important feature of American politics over the last twenty-five years: American politics has been nationalized, but authority at the national level has become more fragmented than ever before. The central government is now more powerful but less capable of speaking with a single voice. The lower courts and congressional subcommittees proved highly responsive to impassioned pleas for government assistance, and the courts showed that they could force state and local governments to comply with federal demands. Yet these institutions had great difficulty establishing uniform policies and establishing spending priorities. Special education policy is the sum of thousands of decisions made on an ad hoc basis by school officials, hearing officers, and federal and state judges. The Supreme Court's inability to control the lower courts provides a graphic illustration of the dispersion of power within the national government. Despite the Supreme Court's insistence on greater deference to state and local officials, many federal district and circuit courts continue to impose costly mandates on school systems. Ironically, the "gridlock" so frequently decried by pundits and politicians is inseparable from institutional developments that have produced rapid and unexpected policy change.

The Politics of Rapid Legal Change:
Immigration Policy in the 1980s

PETER H. SCHUCK

Conventional wisdom maintains that the structures of American politics make rapid policy change unlikely. This proposition is confirmed by much political science. Our institutions are designed to bridle and domesticate reform impulses; the separation of powers establishes numerous veto points; the political culture's commitment to participation and due process places a much higher value on consultation than on decisiveness. Special interests tolerate only incremental changes, while the major parties clothe themselves in the familiar, moving toward the political center and its embrace of the status quo. New ideas are of only marginal importance, their transformative power routinely blunted by one of America's oldest ideas, pragmatism. Stability, not innovation, is the master theme of our politics.

There are exceptions, of course, but they tend to prove the rule. Progressive Era reforms occurred only after a long period of resistance. Implementing the New Deal required an unprecedented economic collapse, a national crisis, and a presidential campaign against the Supreme Court. It took the assassination of a president, important demographic changes, and the conjunction of the civil rights, environmental, and consumer movements to produce the Great Society. Watergate and Vietnam spawned congressional policy initiatives in the 1970s. The deregulation project of the Reagan era completed initiatives begun in the Ford Administration.

This historic pattern makes all the more interesting the innovations in immigration policy that were adopted during the 1980s. By 1990, the new immigration policy was quite different from its predecessors. It also contrasted sharply with the restrictionist, xenophobic immigration policies then being instituted by many other Western nations.

The decade's reforms will expand legal immigration to the United States for years to come. While conscripting employers into the campaign against illegal immigration, the new laws establish a process that will eventually confer legal status on millions of undocumented workers and their families. They diversify the ethnic composition of the immigration stream, jettison Cold War principles of exclusion, liberalize asylum policies, and establish the possibility of safe haven for hundreds of thousands of dislocated individuals ineligible for asylum. They make the status of citizen and alien more equal, and they strengthen enforcement against criminal aliens.

These outcomes contrast sharply with the aims of previous immigration laws, which were restrictive rather than expansionist. Even the 1965 law, which eliminated the national origins quotas, was restrictionist in important respects, and subsequent reform proposals were stalemated. What produced immigration policies in the 1980s that are remarkably liberal and expansive by historical standards? And why did commentators in 1980 fail to predict such changes?

These questions challenge the leading causal paradigms advanced by most political scientists. Interest group liberalism, incrementalism, rational choice, and "the new institutionalism" can explain rather well the small policy shifts that are so familiar in American politics. But because they expect political conflicts to yield fairly stable equilibria while allowing some change around the edges, they are far less successful at explaining major policy innovations that occur suddenly in areas of high political visibility.

Most of these theories view political interests and preferences as largely exogenous. Groups organize around these interests and bargain to a solution. The theories seldom acknowledge the political importance of difficult-to-quantify variables such as happenstance, creativity, sharp changes in values, persuasion through rational argument, statesmanship, self-sacrifice, and passions (as distinguished from interests). When these factors are mentioned, their roles are ordinarily of the "black box" or *deus ex machina* variety. Perhaps because such factors are elusive, evanescent, and unmeasurable compared to votes, rules, formal institutions, and other "harder" phenomena, the leading theories tend to treat them as residual and marginal or to use them as a dumpster for large, unexplained variances.[1]

Immigration policy changes during the 1980s fit rather uneasily into these theoretical paradigms. If these policy shifts had taken many years or if they had culminated in profound social upheaval or regime change, the fit might have been less awkward. In fact, the long-stymied movement to a much more expansive immigration policy occurred with remarkable speed.

Why did this happen, and why at this time? To a considerable degree, my answer accords with standard pluralistic and rational choice explanations. Mass migrations, international crises, and other events in the late 1970s and early 1980s set the stage for the subsequent debate, raising the political salience of immigration policy and deepening the broad public concern about illegal aliens. As the decade wore on, the perceptions, strategies, and influence of the major interest groups changed, shifting the political equilibrium toward more expansive policies. Political entrepreneurs reshaped the issue agenda. They logrolled, manipulated public symbols and ideals, and mobilized elite and grassroots support. Institutions structured this activity, bringing Congress, party leaders, interest groups, the immigration bureaucracy, the courts, the media, and other political actors into a complex series of negotiations. Between 1980 and 1990, then, external events, political entrepreneurs, and group interests all played essential parts in the decade's immigration reforms.

But these factors, while necessary to explain recent immigration politics, are insufficient for at least three reasons. First, they fail to explain why long-stalemated immigration reforms were finally enacted. The decade, after all, was dominated by conservative politics, the conservative administrations showed little commitment to more expansive immigration. No national crisis or social convulsion generated pressures for sharp policy changes. Instead, "normal politics" prevailed.[2] Congress, traditionally the dominant player in immigration politics, was fairly stable in both its partisan and its ideological composition, and the White House was in Republican hands for almost the entire decade.

Until late 1986, the prospects for *any* meaningful immigration reform, restrictive or expansionist, seemed decidedly bleak. Experts viewed immigration policy as the Vietnam of domestic politics, an arena of bitter, protracted warfare from which no one could emerge unharmed. No enterprising politician, it seemed, would invest much time or capital in immigration reform. The interests most directly affected—growers, business, organized labor, ethnic groups, and human rights groups—had long been at loggerheads. The cast of characters in the House and Senate had changed very little. A less propitious time for ambitious immigration reform could scarcely be imagined.

Second, even if events, entrepreneurs, and interests could adequately explain why Congress addressed immigration issues when it did, these factors cannot explain why it *expanded* immigration benefits—and not just for legal aliens but for illegal aliens as well. One would have predicted precisely the opposite. If historical patterns had continued, the main public concerns driving immigration politics during the 1980s—especially the tide of illegal migration and the recessions that struck the economy at the decade's beginning and end—should have generated powerful pressures to *restrict* immigration. Indeed, Senator Alan Simpson of Wyoming, perhaps the most influential politician on immigration legislation during the 1980s, began the decade by proclaiming his strong restrictionist leanings.

Interest group pressures should also have pushed in the same restrictive direction. In the late 1970s, an aggressive alliance of environmental activists, population control champions, English language advocates, and labor interests joined the fray, and the newly formed Federation of American Immigration Reform (FAIR) argued that immigration was adversely affecting the quality of life. By 1980, then, the smart money would have bet that this new coalition would bolster the existing anti-immigration forces to produce a more restrictionist policy equilibrium.

Finally, events, entrepreneurs, and interests fail to explain a striking aspect of the decade's immigration politics: xenophobia and racism retreated to the margins, leaving relatively few traces on the new laws. The Haitian and Marielito migrations in the early 1980s did produce considerable anti-immigration sentiment. Little of it, however, evidenced the widely shared animus against foreigners or racial minorities that had marked earlier immigration politics. Such attitudes became even less prominent as time went on and were notably absent from the congressional campaigns and prepresidential debates of the late 1980s and early 1990s, at least until Patrick Buchanan entered the race for the Republican presidential nomination in early 1992. The 1992 campaign was remarkably free of anti-immigration rhetoric—or even much discussion of the issue—despite domestic economic distress, high unemployment, and the North American Free Trade Agreement. At a time when events, entrepreneurs, and interests were causing some of the leading Western democracies to close their doors to immigrants, often harshly, with openly xenophobic rhetoric proclaimed by strong parliamentary parties, American politics was producing just the opposite behavior.

If the standard pluralistic model fails to predict the historically unique expansionist policies that the decade produced, we must seek a more complex explanation, one that acknowledges another causal factor: the power of the *ideas* that frame our understanding of the world. Ideas, I argue, were crucial to the triumph of expansionist immigration reform.

The political role of ideas has not gone unnoticed by positive political theorists. Their theories, however, tend to view ideas as epiphenomenal rather than causal, instrumental rather than normative. These theories note that innovative politicians use agendas, voting, and issues strategically and that these resources may include new ideas. But ideas in this view are little more than additional tools in the politician's kit bag. From the theorist's perspective, ideas may even be *less* than this—if they obscure the "real" interests that lie beneath them.

I do not propose to challenge these theories; indeed, my account provides much evidence to support them. But ideas can *precede* interests as well as *promote* them. They not only help political actors fulfill their existing political agendas; they also affect how those actors construct their agendas in the first place. Ideas can alter how people perceive the world, how they decide what to value, and how they organize to attain their goals. In this way, they redefine ends and means and may even supply new ones. Immigration politics in the 1980s exemplifies this independent role of ideas. Certain distinctive notions about immigration and its effects propelled the reform impulse in directions that were more expansionist than interests, entrepreneurship, and events alone would have dictated.

Few of these ideas, of course, were really new. None of them, however, had previously been effectively mobilized to support an expansive immigration policy. Even the most familiar ideas became more salient to the immigration debate as conditions changed. Some ideas—the constitutional principles of due process and equal protection are perhaps the best examples—were well established in other areas of public law but had not generally been applied to immigration. Policy intellectuals and advocates forcefully advanced these ideas, and the media brokered them, helping to galvanize a consensus around an expansive immigration policy and to influence the specific forms of the new policies.

There are pitfalls in emphasizing the causal role of ideas in politics. Compared with votes, institutions, interests, events, and the other palpable phenomena that political analysts can observe and even measure, ideas are elusive and their effects on outcomes are hard to gauge. Ideas may simultaneously alter what political actors perceive and what they pursue. At the same time, actors may deploy ideas rhetorically and instrumentally. Thus, ideas' independent causal force in politics must be revealed through inference and the testimony of those most intimately involved. We are wise to be skeptical of such evidence, but we would be foolish to ignore it simply because it is less tangible and quantifiable.

The Pressure of External Events

The present era of immigration reform began with an epochal event: the Mariel boatlift, which brought 125,000 Cubans to the United States early in 1980. In that year other crucial immigration-related developments occurred in Central America, Iran, the Soviet Union, Poland, and elsewhere, and a conservative Republican administration entered the White House. The reform era ended with the enactment of the Immigration Act of 1990.

The significance of this decade for immigration politics can best be grasped by comparing the prospects for reform as they appeared in 1980 with the reality of reform in 1990. In 1980 the Carter administration was in its final death throes, struggling with double-digit inflation, high unemployment, and a hostage crisis in Iran. Politicians and their constituents were edgy, cautious, and inward looking. When boatloads of Haitians and Cubans sought refuge in South Florida early in the year, the authorities greeted them with initial hospitality followed by undisguised hysteria and hostility. In the 1970s, after all, the United States had accepted a very large number of refugees from Indochina, Cuba, the Soviet Union, and elsewhere. The total refugee cohort reached a historic high of 350,000 in 1980.

At the same time, illegal migration across the southern border was burgeoning. The growing volume of illegal crossings caused environmental and population control organizations to form FAIR in 1979 to lobby for restrictive immigration legislation. Some civil rights groups concerned about minority job losses shared FAIR's concerns, while usually spurning its rhetoric. In that same year, Senate Judiciary Committee Chairman Edward Kennedy, concerned that growing illegal migration could trigger a political backlash against immigration, persuaded Congress to establish a Select Commission on Immigration and Refugee Policy (SCIRP) to propose new, prudent solutions. Father Theodore Hesburgh, then president of the University of Notre Dame, chaired the commission for most of its life.

When the Reagan administration assumed office in 1981 and the Republicans gained control of the Senate, reform seemed imminent. Except for the 1965 abolition of the national origins quota system, Congress had paid little attention to immigration policy since the early 1950s. With illegal migration now recognized as a national issue, a new administration determined to "regain control of our borders," widespread concerns about public service budgets, and ethnic conflict becoming a staple of TV evening news programs, reformers on Main Street and Pennsylvania Avenue geared up to do battle. Restrictionism was in the air.

In 1981, Senator Alan Simpson appended an avowedly restrictionist statement to the SCIRP report. In response to that report, the Reagan White House proposed its own restrictions on illegal migration, emphasizing that an "immigration emergency" existed. In August 1982, Senator Walter (Dee) Huddleston of Kentucky, FAIR's chief advocate in the Senate, mobilized considerable support for a decidedly restrictive bill. It would have capped all legal immigration (including refugees and "immediate relatives," neither of which categories was capped at that time) at 425,000, a level far below the almost 600,000 immigrants and refugees admitted that year. With the economy sliding into a deep recession, representatives of organized labor redoubled their traditional efforts to preserve American jobs for American workers.

Less than a decade later, however, Congress had substantially liberalized immigration policy. In 1986 it enacted the Immigration Reform and Control Act (IRCA), a measure widely but misleadingly billed as restrictive. In one very important respect, it *was* restrictive: IRCA for the first time penalized employers who hired illegal aliens. But many of its other provisions were remarkably generous to illegal and temporary workers. In addition, it reserved 10,000 visas for "diversity" admissions,[3] a harbinger of a new strategy for expanding legal admissions that would become firmly embedded in the Immigration Act of 1990 (hereafter referred to as the 1990 act).

The 1990 act was generous to both legal and illegal aliens, especially the former. The new law, which FAIR strongly opposed, will eventually increase annual legal immigration totals by about one-third.[4] It bestowed work authorization and possible citizenship upon an estimated 250,000 close family members of amnestied aliens. It also conferred protected status upon almost 200,000 undocumented Salvadorans and, by codifying the previously discretionary practice of "extended voluntary departure," created the possibility of protected status for members of other nationality groups illegally in the United States. The new statute also embodied a firm commitment to ethnic diversity in admissions, expedited naturalization, and for the first time *narrowed* the power of the Immigration and Naturalization Service (INS) to exclude aliens on ideological grounds.

Any remaining doubts about the political and legal forces propelling the new expansionist ethos were dispelled only a few weeks after passage of the 1990 act. Litigation pressures forced the Bush administration to provide new asylum hearings under liberalized standards and procedures for an estimated 150,000 Salvadorans and Guatemalans whose claims (some dating back to 1980) had been denied or were still pending. The attorney general, who late in 1989 had permitted thousands of Chinese students to remain in the United States despite their visa restrictions, also granted temporary protected status under the new law to over 50,000 Kuwaitis, Liberians, and Lebanese aliens in the United States.

The 1990 act's expansionist character is even more remarkable when one considers the inhospitable political climate in which it was enacted. First, the 1965 reform had dramatically and unexpectedly shifted the source-country pattern toward high-volume Asian and Hispanic flows. Equally unexpected, the asylum provisions of the 1980 Refugee Act had further stimulated illegal migration by Hispanics. There was considerable sentiment, not all of it restrictionist, that an imbalance had developed and needed redressing. Second, successful implementation of IRCA's employer sanctions program was widely viewed as a political precondition for seeking to expand legal immigration, yet mounting evidence in 1990 indicated that, three years into the program, the "back door" of illegal migration remained wide open. Third, the restrictionists could also argue that IRCA's amnesty programs were all too successful, in contrast to the sanctions. They had already produced in 1989 *the highest legal admissions total (almost 1.1 million) in seventy-five years*, an increase of 70 percent over the previous year. (The 1990 figure, not published until 1991, would soar to over 1.5 million, a record by far.) Perhaps most important, economic recession, which historically had spawned strong restrictionist sentiments and policies, was already under way. Despite these formidable obstacles, however, the 1990 act passed by lopsided margins.

These rapid and dramatic changes in immigration policy are particularly significant because immigration is a bedrock, traditionally divisive political issue. Immigration does not simply operate on the surface of politics, nor is it driven by transitory, faddish concerns. Instead, it engages the enduring economic, political, and cultural interests of powerful social groups in visible, often emotional ways. Politicians and citizens know that immigration defines who and what Americans wish their society to be. Understanding how we forged a new consensus on immigration may therefore reveal some of the forces that are reshaping contemporary American politics.

External Events

In the 1970s and early 1980s, international developments magnified the migratory pressures on the United States. These included political and economic upheaval in Southeast Asia and the Caribbean Basin, the Soviet decision to permit more Jewish emigration, the Iranian Revolution, and a new surge of illegal migration from Latin America. Although American foreign and economic policy certainly influenced these events, they were largely beyond our control.

Throughout the 1970s, congressional committees increasingly criticized the executive branch's response to these spasmodic, uncontrolled refugee flows, as well as its human rights record. By the end of the decade, the committees' leaders had mobilized support for a new refugee admissions system, one that would be more predictable—and that would also enhance Congress's policy influence. The Refugee Act, signed by President Carter in March 1980, was the result of this vision.

Most migration to the United States in the 1970s was gradual and largely invisible outside of the newcomers' enclaves. But when 125,000 Cubans—many from Castro's prisons and mental hospitals—arrived from Mariel by boat less than a month after the Refugee Act was signed, they immediately became front-page news not only in South Florida, but also throughout the country, severely embarrassing the Carter administration. Coming so soon after other refugee crises, this new incursion triggered public anger at the government's fecklessness and weariness at the seemingly endless line of people knocking at or clambering over the gates. A neologism—*compassion fatigue*—was coined to describe the popular frustration. The United States had become a major first-asylum country for the first time in its history.

The torrent of Cuban and Haitian asylum claims drew additional migration. Other groups followed suit, and the asylum backlog soon reached almost 200,000 claims. The United States, it seemed, no longer controlled its own destiny; its fate was now inexorably linked to upheavals elsewhere. Taking various forms, this theme would become a central political preoccupation of the 1980s.

Political Entrepreneurship

As has often been noted, the same Chinese ideogram denotes both crisis and opportunity. In the 1980s, shrewd politicians in Congress seized upon these external events and the anxieties that the events aroused, magnifying an already acute fear of change into a deep sense of crisis. By defining the crisis in ways that invited certain policy solutions that lay near at hand, they succeeded in creating political opportunity.

"We have lost control of our borders." This slogan fueled deep concerns about the erosion of economic security, national autonomy, and the "social contract" that legitimates the modern welfare state. An immigration policy designed to preserve customary ways of life now seemed unable to do so. As welfare burdens on taxpayers grew, immigrants became easy scapegoats.

Employer sanctions bills had been proposed at the behest of organized labor in the 1960s and then again during the Nixon and Ford years. In 1977, the Carter administration, politically vulnerable due to the wide currency given to an earlier exaggerated estimate of twelve million illegals, again broached the idea. Hoping to deflect growing restrictionist pressures and passions, the White House and congressional leaders agreed to create a blue-ribbon panel, the Hesburgh Commission, to study the problem of illegal aliens, shape a consensus, and recommend policy changes to solve the problem.

This was not the first time that political leaders had established a study commission to help resolve an impasse over immigration legislation. The Dillingham Commission, which urged literacy tests in its 1910 report, set an infamous precedent with its racist rhetoric and restrictionist policy recommendations. The Hesburgh group, however, was very different in composition, staffing, and processes. Its members and staff were highly sympathetic to immigration and ethnic diversity; half of its members were descendants of the very groups that the Dillingham Commission, comprised entirely of men with English and Scottish roots, had stigmatized. And the new commission was preoccupied with a new problem: illegal migration.

The Hesburgh Commission would play a central role in the immigration politics of the 1980s. Some of its congressional members became the leading protagonists in the decade's struggles over immigration. The commission staff deliberately emphasized ideas that could appeal across partisan, ethnic, and economic lines; as SCIRP Director Lawrence Fuchs later put it, "the central strategy was to take xenophobia, race, and even economic conflict out of the debate." The policy agenda laid out by the commission in its 1981 report—linkage between control of illegal migration and expansion of legal admissions; a three-track system of admissions (family-related immigrants, independents selected for economic reasons, and refugees); adherence to civil rights and civil liberties values—set the terms of the subsequent debate. Indeed, IRCA and the Immigration Act of 1990 can be viewed as having largely fulfilled the agenda advanced by the commission a decade earlier.

Senators Kennedy and Simpson, two strikingly different politicians, played especially significant roles. Of the two, Kennedy's position favoring a liberalized immigration and refugee policy was the more predictable. As a freshman senator, he had managed the 1965 reform bill. During the 1970s he had chaired the Judiciary Subcommittee on Refugees, and he had steered the Refugee Act of 1980 through Congress.

Simpson was another story entirely. Nothing in his personal or political background prepared him for his decisive role in the immigration debates of the 1980s, much less for his sponsorship and management of legislation that would substantially expand and diversify legal immigration. Even his appointment to the Hesburgh Commission had been fortuitous, occurring only after Strom Thurmond declined to serve.

Immigration reform was a political quagmire, conventionally viewed by politicians as a "no win" issue, a lost cause, the domestic equivalent of Vietnam. This was especially true during the pre-IRCA period, when the focus of legislation was on illegal aliens who aroused negative feelings even among otherwise pro-immigration Americans. Immigration, moreover, was an issue that primarily excited people in Florida, Texas, California, New York, and a few cities in which residents felt inundated by undocumented workers, wanted more of their ethnic compatriots admitted, or both. In the rest of the country, there were even fewer political points to be scored by immigration reform. Simpson's devotion to this cause over the course of a decade, then, is simply inexplicable in terms of the traditional careerist goals that animate most legislators.

Simpson plunged into the commission's work with gusto as soon as he was appointed to it early in 1979. His earlier views on immigration had been relatively unformed. But he learned quickly. In 1981, when the Republicans took control of the Senate and just before the Hesburgh Commission was to issue its final report, he convinced the new chairman of the Judiciary Committee, Strom Thurmond, to recreate an immigration subcommittee—with Simpson as chairman. From this perch, he would orchestrate the legislative politics on immigration during the decade.

While the leadership on immigration issues in the Senate remained stable during the 1980s, the roster of influentials in the House changed after IRCA's enactment in 1986. Before that, Peter Rodino and Romano Mazzoli were the key players. Rodino, Judiciary Committee chairman since 1973, was an urban liberal who had helped secure the 1965 immigration reforms. Rodino was ardently pro-immigration. Mazzoli, who became chairman of the immigration subcommittee in 1981, was a moderate Democrat from Louisville, Kentucky. Like Simpson, he began with amorphous views on immigration issues. Also like Simpson, he was under few constituent pressures on immigration and was not thought to harbor higher political ambitions. Simpson and Mazzoli, then, were uniquely situated to rise above narrow electoral interests in seeking reform, should they be motivated to do so.

Simpson and Mazzoli developed a close working relationship and decided to pursue an unusual joint legislative strategy. Early in 1981, the Hesburgh Commission had issued its report proposing (among other reforms) employer sanctions linked to a secure employee verification system, a legalization program, and some relief for the growers whose labor supply would be reduced by sanctions and legalization. This package, the commission hoped, would break the political logjam that had long blocked reform, although the three special interest members had not budged from their initial positions. Although Simpson generally endorsed the commission's approach, he advanced a more restrictionist position on several specific policy issues.

Simpson and Mazzoli decided to use the commission's proposals, ignoring the White House "immigration emergency" package, as a starting point for their own bill. In practice, the White House failed to give Simpson any meaningful political support on immigration legislation. This lack of significant presidential involvement in the legislative struggles over immigration would continue throughout the decade.

The two legislators introduced identical bills in May 1982 and held joint hearings. Simpson skillfully steered his bill, containing a generous legalization program, through a conservative, Republican-controlled Senate; it carried by a lopsided vote, 80–19. Here, as in immigration reform legislation throughout the 1980s, Kennedy's political contribution was crucial to the bill's success, especially in the Senate, where most Democrats looked to him to signal what was and was not acceptable to liberals.

As Congress neared adjournment, however, the House bill got stalled in the crush of other closing business. Although there was a postelection session, the House bill seemed doomed. The Rules Committee yielded to Hispanic groups that opposed both employer sanctions and rigorous identification requirements and allowed virtually unlimited floor amendments. Speaker Tip O'Neill said that he had scheduled the bill for floor action only as a courtesy to the White House. The bill died with the 98th Congress, the House having considered only two of some three hundred pending amendments. The House nevertheless gave Mazzoli a standing ovation, an extraordinary gesture recognizing the heroic effort necessary to bring immigration reform even that far.

In 1983, Simpson and Mazzoli decided to try again, this time with separate bills containing the provisions supported in their chambers the year before. The prospects for reform, however, seemed dimmer than ever. The main problem was not in the Senate, which again (with Kennedy's blessing) approved Simpson's bill quickly, adding a transition period for the growers. As always in immigration legislation, the politics in the House was more complex. No fewer than five different committees—Judiciary, Agriculture, Education and Labor, Energy and Commerce, and Rules—held hearings and proposed amendments. As the election approached, the Hispanic caucus and the growers whipsawed the proponents. Each of these groups (albeit for altogether differ-

ent reasons) opposed sanctions; the growers opposed legalization; and
both groups would wield influence during the impending primaries.

A deeply fractured House approved the bill 216–211, only after additional concessions to the growers and bitter division over sanctions and
legalization. Time ran out, however, when the conference became
embroiled in disputes over federal payments to the states to cover
legalization-related costs and, to a lesser degree, over remedies for
sanctions-related discrimination against Hispanics. Congress adjourned,
requiring the proponents to start all over again in Reagan's second term.

The tortured progress of immigration reform in Congress from 1981
through 1984 revealed several clues to the evolving pattern of immigration politics. First, politicians would not seriously consider expanding
legal immigration until they felt that the problem of illegal immigration
had been addressed. The back door must be closed before the front door
could be opened.

Second, a reformist majority would be exceedingly difficult to assemble. It might perhaps be cobbled together by designing a package of
interconnected and somewhat incompatible measures: sanctions, legalization, a generous farmworker program, antidiscrimination remedies,
and federal subsidies to state and local governments. But this package—
by pitting Hispanics against blacks, urban areas against rural, Washington against state capitols and city halls, unions and environmentalists
against ethnics, and interest group leaders against their own rank and
file—would be riddled with policy inconsistencies and would further
divide a Democratic party already severely weakened by another presidential defeat. The Hispanic caucus and the growers were essential to
any viable reform package and must be appeased to pass a bill, yet their
interests conflicted on many points. The legalization proposal had become increasingly generous with respect to both eligibility and federal
subsidies, yet more liberal amnesty provisions would threaten state and
local government support and might prompt a presidential veto.

Third, and more encouraging, the immigration debate was being
conducted at a higher level than ever before. Few traces of racism or na-
tivism could be found. Indeed, the nation's opinion leaders—politicians,
editorial writers, interest groups, and academics—seemed determined
to transcend traditionally parochial concerns about immigration. They
seemed genuinely committed to finding a path to reform.

Still, the prospects for reform in the new Congress that convened in
1985 were hardly rosy. The proponents, especially in the House, were
reluctant to bloody themselves once again in what seemed like a hope-
less struggle. Indeed, some of the obstacles had grown more formidable,
especially the political influence of the growers of perishable crops, who

were determined to maintain their supply of cheap labor. This was apparent when Simpson, who was now assistant majority leader, was obliged to accept a large temporary worker program in order to get his bill through the Senate. Characteristically in immigration legislation, this addition served only to complicate matters in the House, where further increases in the illegal population had fueled restrictionist sentiment and where the Hispanic caucus opposed the farmworker program as well as sanctions. Amnesty was the major attraction for Hispanics and many liberals, yet polling evidence indicated that public support for it, which had never been significant, was now eroding.

The only way to forge a majority coalition would be somehow to persuade the growers to accept a farmworker program that met liberal demands for worker protection. Charles Schumer, a very junior member from Brooklyn, devised such a proposal with Rodino's blessing and began to negotiate with the growers and the California delegation. This provision would grant illegal farmworkers temporary legal status on quite generous terms, allowing them to go on to become legal residents and ultimately citizens and with no obligation to remain in agriculture, while assuring growers a future supply of imported "replenishment" workers should the need arise. The Schumer amendment passed the Judiciary Committee in late June on a close vote, 19–15.

Simpson did not like Schumer's proposal or indeed any legalization not preceded by credible, enhanced enforcement, but he favored compromise. The bill's supporters from both chambers convened a preconference meeting and worked out a deal even before House passage. After diluting the Schumer provision somewhat, the embryonic conference announced that, if the House would approve a bill, the House and Senate could reach agreement. Encouraged by these developments, the House voted 278–129 to bring the bill to the floor, along with fourteen amendments. After a fatal amendment to eliminate legalization was narrowly defeated, 199–192, the House approved the bill, 230–166. Simpson told the press: "I guess we just jump-started a corpse."

Because Congress's adjournment had been postponed, there was time for the conference, which Simpson effectively controlled. He hammered out an agreement on the key issue that troubled the White House: the cost of funding benefits for legalized aliens. The Schumer provisions largely survived as a generous amnesty for illegal farmworkers. With editorial opinion in the media strongly favorable to the compromise, the conference bill passed the House. After an attempt to prevent its consideration in the Senate was defeated, 75–21, the Senate also passed the bill. It was opposed by many conservatives, including

Phil Gramm, and by some liberals, including Ted Kennedy, who echoed the Hispanic caucus's argument (which was actually rejected by its leaders in the House vote) that the antidiscrimination safeguards were inadequate. When the president signed the legislation on 6 November, IRCA became law.

For present purposes, there are two important things to be noted about IRCA. First, its passage was anything but inevitable. The key votes were remarkably close in the House, and any of a number of possible circumstances could have brought about its demise. There was plenty in the compromise for anyone to dislike, and its enactment said as much about the members' exhaustion as it did about the bill's political support. If it had not passed then, it is not at all clear that Senator Simpson and other key sponsors would have tried again in the next Congress, especially since the legislative struggle would take them into a presidential election season.

Second, it was on balance a law that would expand immigration. This is most apparent, of course, in its legalization provisions. These granted the opportunity for amnesty to workers in general, to agricultural workers, and to Cuban and Haitian immigrants. IRCA also updated an earlier, general amnesty provision to protect other aliens who had been in the United States since 1972. These provisions, moreover, were fairly liberal, especially for farmworkers—with respect to eligibility criteria, time periods, and access to benefits, permanent legal status, and citizenship. But the law's pro-immigrant character is also evident in its antidiscrimination provisions (despite Senator Kennedy's doubts), which were designed to protect legal Hispanic workers; in its raising of the quotas for the colonies of foreign countries; in its expanded program (H-2) for agricultural workers; and in the special provisions making five thousand extra visas available to immigrants from countries (the Irish were the intended beneficiaries) "adversely affected" by the 1965 repeal of the national origins system—the precursor to the diversity provisions that would be such a striking feature of the 1990 act.

The pattern of interest group views about IRCA likewise confirms its generally pro-immigration tenor. Perhaps most telling was the lament by the head of FAIR, the leading restrictionist lobby: "We wanted a Cadillac, we were promised a Chevy, and we got a wreck." Groups seeking more legal immigration and generous treatment of undocumented workers tended to support IRCA. Even the employer sanctions, the principal provisions restricting immigration, were solicitous of employers' interests.

The Changing Balance of Interests

Immigration politics had obviously changed by 1986; IRCA was compelling evidence of this. And it would change even more in the same direction by 1990. But why? The *dramatis personae* were much the same (although control of the Senate would return to the Democrats in 1987), and no immigration crises comparable to those at the beginning of the decade occurred in the late 1980s. The combination of political entrepreneurs and external events can explain just so much. A successful merchandiser, after all, must have something to sell that people want to buy.

A fuller answer can largely be found in two broad changes that occurred or culminated during the decade: a shift in the relative strength of interest groups and the prominence of ideas capable of galvanizing a new cultural consensus favoring expanded immigration. These two developments, of course, are linked: interests both promote and reflect values, and interests and values are both redefined through the political process.

During the decade, the terms of trade among the crucial organized interests with high stakes in immigration policy—Western growers, labor unions, business, ethnic groups, and human rights advocates—changed. As a result, the political equilibrium, the compromises that were struck, moved in a sharply pro-immigration direction. This change strained an already fractured Democratic party coalition in Congress. As the power of the ethnic and human rights groups waxed and the power of organized labor waned, restrictionist influence in the party declined. FAIR had a staunch advocate on the Senate floor in Dee Huddleston—but after Huddleston's defeat in 1984, FAIR's influence steadily declined.

In addition, immigration advocates hoped to neutralize the main institutional centers of restrictionist sentiment. These were the state and local governments that would be saddled with most of the costs of the public benefits and services claimed by the new immigrants or by the workers they displaced. These governments did not oppose increased immigration in principle; their growing Hispanic and Asian populations, buttressed by the willingness of most black leaders to support these groups' family unification claims for expansion, would have made restrictionism politically suicidal. Instead, their chief concern was simply to defray the immigration-related costs, which might be accomplished with federal subsidies. (The amount of the subsidies, of course, remained subject to much haggling.)

Why is this not just another story about the political strength of organized business and the weakness of organized labor? In one view, business (which generally favored expanded immigration) won, while labor (which generally sought to restrict both permanent and temporary skills-related admissions) lost. There is certainly some truth to this explanation, as we shall see. During the decade business did gain politically at the expense of labor in many policy areas, not just immigration, and this change affected political outcomes. But this account elides an inescapable fact. Business interests have *always* been powerful and have almost always favored increased immigration. Yet restrictionist policies have been the rule for the last seventy-five years; the triumph of restrictionism, in fact, came during the 1920s, when business was in the saddle and the influence of labor was negligible.

Factors other than the power of business and labor, then, must have affected the political equation in the 1980s. One such factor was the changed status of nativist and racist arguments for restriction, arguments that had become largely illegitimate and irrelevant. Another was the new role of ideas in immigration policy debates.

Inasmuch as the interest groups concerned with immigration policy interacted constantly in the legislative process, I risk some artificiality by discussing them separately. This is especially true of labor and business; I therefore treat those two together after discussing the growers.

THE GROWERS

The agricultural interests, especially the growers of perishable commodities, exercised enormous influence over IRCA. As they have so many times in the past, the growers hoped to defeat employer sanctions and institute a large guestworker program that would guarantee their labor supply. Although they did not get their way entirely, they did achieve enough of their agenda that little remained at stake for them in the post-IRCA legislative debates over legal immigration policy. The growers' interests were well represented in the California, Florida, and Texas delegations in Congress and after 1981 in the White House as well. This representation placed their goals within reach, but the growing public indignation over undocumented workers during the pre-IRCA years forced them to compromise on sanctions. As other enforcement efforts proved ineffective, some sanctions program came to seem inevitable.

Growers were also met with alarming reports on Europe's experience with guestworker programs. These programs invited Third World workers to come without their families when the labor supply was tight, with no hope of permanent residence or political rights. When labor needs slackened, however, the guestworkers refused to leave, even when their "hosts" offered them large subsidies. Living as single men in enclaves of poverty, crime, and hopelessness, the guestworkers aroused strong nativist backlash among voters, which simply increased their isolation. This experience, coupled with vehement opposition by Hispanic groups and their allies, generated congressional resistance to such a program.

The growers were therefore obliged to adopt the more limited goals of weakening the sanctions and assuring that they would not shut off the supply of cheap labor. Coupled with an enlarged H-2 program negotiated between grower interests and Congressman Howard Berman, the Schumer plan satisfied these goals by giving the growers an amnestied work force and a guarantee of "replenishment agricultural workers" if their supply of labor became tight. In exchange, Berman extracted a concession—generous legalization terms for agricultural workers— that was vitally important to the Hispanics and liberals while costing the growers little so long as amnestied workers and, if need be, replenishment workers could be relied upon.

LABOR AND BUSINESS

Organized labor's hold over immigration legislation gradually weakened during the 1980s as the number of union members continued to decline and labor's reputation for political effectiveness lost its luster. Still, labor succeeded in protecting its vital interests in immigration policy throughout the decade, including the 1990 act. For a century, the unions, like most of their rank and file, had favored restrictions on immigration. During the 1970s, most unions had opposed increased admissions, amnesties for illegal aliens, and importation of temporary farmworkers, while favoring employer sanctions and stepped-up border enforcement.

In the pre-IRCA period, organized labor's position was clear and long established, and it usually got its way. In 1964, the AFL-CIO had succeeded in engineering the termination of the Bracero program, which had permitted seasonal farmworkers from Mexico to enter to work on American crops without much protection, undermining domestic wage levels. During the 1970s, labor had been the principal force propelling the employer sanctions proposals that surfaced in Congress and passed the House only to fail in the Senate. As the 1980s began, the Hesburgh Commission member representing the AFL-CIO expressed the unions' continued, uncompromising hostility to any guestworker program, however protective it might be of American workers.

In IRCA, however, organized labor enjoyed only modest success. It did obtain its long-sought goal of employer sanctions, but the sanctions were widely viewed as weak. After IRCA, labor's influence in Congress generally continued to wane, as revealed in its declining membership base and its defeats in its high-priority battles on common-situs picketing, plant-closing legislation, and fast-track authority for the U.S.-Mexico free-trade agreement.

The post-IRCA politics of immigration, however, were quite different. With the rancorous debate over illegal migration behind it, Congress could now turn to the question of legal immigration. Having closed the back door, it would be easier to pry open the front door. Pre-IRCA, illegals were the target and so restrictionists had the upper hand. Thus, expansionists had to use up all of their political capital seeking to soften the effect of sanctions through an amnesty, which was unpopular with the general public. After IRCA, expansionists had more valuable things to trade, and a logrolling strategy of granting more visas to favored groups became attractive.

In this setting, even a weakened labor movement was better situated to protect and promote its positions. Senator Kennedy had assured Lane Kirkland and other labor leaders that he would protect the unions' vital interests in any immigration legislation. Labor defined those interests as protecting domestic jobs and wage levels, and it sought to advance them primarily by limiting temporary labor visas. Significantly, labor did not seek to limit family-oriented admissions; to the contrary, it sought to expand them despite the fact that those entering under family visas are more likely to compete for the jobs that the unions covet than are those entering under employment visas, who are (especially after the 1990 act) more highly skilled workers. Refugee admissions, which Kirkland personally favored, were also endorsed by organized labor.

During the 1980s, industrial, commercial, and professional organizations exercised growing influence over immigration policy. As in some other areas of public policy, business dissatisfaction with the inefficiencies of the status quo spurred it to become a leading advocate of reform. The Reagan and Bush administrations were decidedly attentive to business interests, which converged with more general public anxieties about U.S. competitiveness and the increasing globalization of labor markets.

These interests, of course, were not monolithic. Employers of low-skilled workers in the garment industry, hotel and restaurant services, and other sectors dependent upon illegal labor lobbied to preserve their access to cheap labor. Many other employers had a more complex agenda. IRCA might affect the status of their highly skilled employees who came to the United States on temporary visas but then violated their terms and became just as illegal as the clandestine border crossers.

Nonetheless, many firms were less concerned about IRCA's employer sanctions and legalization provisions than about the anachronistic system of employment-related visas. This slow, rigid system often prevented them from hiring and moving their employees about efficiently.

Reform of legal immigration, however, would pit business directly against two forces: organized labor, which sought to restrict temporary labor visas, and the coalition of ethnic, denominational, and human rights groups, which sought more visas for family unification and humanitarian reasons. Business interests hoped that, with IRCA and illegal immigration issues out of the way, Congress would turn next to urgently needed reforms of legal immigration, but neither Mazzoli nor Rodino nor the administration was anxious to move on these issues. Before opening the front door, they insisted on assessing IRCA's effect to see whether it had indeed closed the back door.

In 1988 the Democratic-controlled Senate overwhelmingly passed a Kennedy-Simpson bill after only seven hours of debate. This bill established the baseline for all future negotiations on immigration reform. It began its long legislative journey with three major agenda items, reflecting a compromise between Simpson's and Kennedy's views. First, it sought to limit chain migration by restricting the existing law's fifth preference (for citizens' adult siblings and these siblings' spouses and children) to include only never-married siblings of citizens and by limiting the second preference (for resident aliens' spouses and unmarried children) to only those children under twenty-six years old.

The bill also added a new category of "independent" workers, who possessed skills needed in the United States but had no employer to file for labor certification on their behalf. This category combined two themes: emphases on skills-based admissions and on source-country diversity. The new "independent" admissions policy was designed to favor English speakers; Irish and Western Europeans would have benefited, as well as Indians, Filipinos, Nigerians, and English-speaking natives of the Caribbean. Another provision, admitting those willing to invest $2 million here (reduced on the Senate floor to $1 million dollars) and to employ at least ten Americans, was similar in its emphasis on immigrants' economic contributions.

Finally, the bill imposed the first-ever overall numerical ceiling on legal immigration, although one exceeding then-current levels. Kennedy had accepted the cap as a necessary price for obtaining Simpson's support for higher overall numbers. Kennedy knew that a cap was particularly important to Simpson, who viewed it as a symbol of the nation's sovereign power and its willingness to control immigration in the face of relentless demographic and political pressures for expansion.

This bill, however, was not enacted. Mazzoli and Rodino were simply not interested in pressing reform on a reluctant Congress, and there was substantial opposition to a cap—even a generous one. Instead, Congress responded in a less contentious way to the growing ethnic group pressures for more admissions. Embracing the diversity slogan, it passed a law enlarging the special IRCA-created preference for "adversely affected" countries (primarily Ireland) and adding a new one for "underrepresented" countries, which would turn out to favor the Indian subcontinent.

None of this, however, seriously addressed business's concerns; indeed, several personnel changes in the new Congress that convened in 1989 dimmed the prospects for business-oriented reforms. Jack Brooks, a Texan with little immigration policy expertise, had replaced the retired Rodino as chairman of the House Judiciary Committee. Bruce Morrison, a liberal Democrat from New Haven with strong backing from organized labor, had taken over the chairmanship of the immigration subcommittee from Mazzoli. Morrison was a highly partisan activist and a quick study. Some of his congressional colleagues, however, found him mercurial and difficult to deal with, especially as he began to maneuver toward a tough race for governor of Connecticut in 1990. Although junior in terms of service in the House, on the full committee, and even on the subcommittee he now chaired, he itched to take the lead. It was a sign of the times in Congress that he was able to do so.

By 1989, Morrison had begun to focus on three main areas for reform. First, he viewed the limits on visas for the spouses and minor children of resident aliens as inhumane and foolish, simply encouraging illegal migration. Second, he echoed the complaints, confirmed by a congressional consultant's report, that temporary employment visas were being abused and converted into what was in effect permanent employment. Third, he saw the political appeal of diversity admissions; indeed, he viewed them as politically essential to immigration expansion. Morrison was convinced that ethnic groups must feel that their members had access to the United States or else they would simply circumvent the system. Sensitive to both the merit of greater federal support to defray local immigration-related costs and the political value of using cash payments to mute local government opposition to wider reforms, he advocated "immigration emergency" subsidies.

While Morrison was fashioning his strategy, Kennedy and Simpson—whose own bill had been close enough to Kennedy's to enable them to combine forces—again moved their bill swiftly in the Senate. It was almost identical to their joint bill of the year before, with one important alteration: this time, it increased the number and proportion of employment-based visas. Senate passage, however, was not as easy as it had been in 1988. Simpson was forced to drop his proposed changes to the preference system, through which he hoped to limit chain migration. The provision valuing English-speaking skills as part of an "independent" visa point system, which Kennedy had also strongly favored (partly as a boost to Irish applicants), was deleted in the committee. Perhaps most important, Simpson was decisively defeated when the Senate approved a Hatch-DeConcini amendment placing a floor under the immediate relatives category. This would make the cap "pierceable"; in effect, the cap would be nonexistent. The Senate also raised the number of scheduled visas from the bill's proposed 590,000 to 630,000 and approved a stay of deportation for close family members of aliens legalized under IRCA. In addition, the final Senate version, approved in July 1989, placed some restrictions on federal benefits for illegal aliens.

Kennedy, who was determined to win passage of the Senate bill in the House, made a politic gesture of deference to the other chamber by paying a visit to committee chairman Brooks and subcommittee chairman Morrison. Kennedy confided that he had no more time to waste on unsuccessful immigration bills and that reform would be achieved either now or never. Brooks agreed to move legislation through his committee as soon as Morrison's subcommittee completed its work. As it turned out, however, this took a long time.

The Senate bill had avoided a politically explosive issue: temporary (nonimmigrant) visas, which the unions wanted to restrict and business wanted to expand. In addition, the Senate, as in 1988, dealt only indirectly with the issue of diversity visas. Business wanted more numerous and flexible employment-related visas; elimination of employment preference backlogs, which had increased sharply since IRCA; and the use of immigration policy to serve labor market needs, as it did in other countries competing with the United States. The AFL-CIO attacked the numerically unlimited aspect of temporary employment visas. The union also challenged the notion that immigration could be used to reduce particular labor shortages, pointing out that efforts to do so in the areas of nursing and agriculture had failed. The problem could only be solved, it claimed, through better wages and working conditions.

Morrison's approach had little in common with the Senate bill. Opposed to a cap, Morrison wanted instead to expand immigration. He believed that the climate for liberal reform would not persist; a recession was widely predicted, and Kennedy seemed unlikely to try again if this effort failed. He therefore fixed on a new strategy. Rather than responding to what people feared about immigration, which Morrison saw as the politics of the pre-IRCA era, he would seek to institutionalize what each particularly constituency liked about it. He hoped to logroll his way to a majority with an omnibus bill built around a coalition of intense, pro-immigration special interests. This was a familiar political device, but it had not previously been used in immigration bills because restrictionists were too strong. It was also dangerous, especially in an election year, because it threatened to increase the number and intensity of opponents.

Central to this strategy was Morrison's effort to attract and meld labor and business support. He launched this effort with a bold but politically risky tactic, announcing that he favored reforming *both* permanent and temporary employment visas. In consultation with labor, he floated several new proposals. These included a cap on temporary employment visas and a tax on employers importing workers under permanent visas, the proceeds to be used for retraining domestic workers. Under no illusions that he could get such a tax through the Ways and Means Committee, Morrison hoped to use the idea as a way to open a debate about employer-financed worker retraining.

When Morrison introduced his bill (H.R. 4300), it contained provisions that would produce substantially higher admissions, which organized labor opposed but which everyone also knew would have to be reduced if the bill were to be politically viable. But Morrison's bill also contained two other new elements that labor ardently supported: a cap on temporary employment visas and a labor recruitment test as a precondition for temporary skilled worker visas. When business protested, Morrison neutralized their opposition by increasing the number of permanent employment visas and relaxing the labor recruitment requirement. Simpson, who had done little to secure business support for his immigration proposals in the past, did not really address them in the pending Senate bill either. Thus, Morrison's concessions were important in attracting business support for his approach when the crucial conference stage was reached.

ETHNIC GROUPS

Ethnic groups made up the other crucial component of Morrison's coalition. To a considerable degree, immigration politics is and has always been ethnic politics. In the struggle for preferred access to limited immigration benefits, some groups have fared much better than others. Hence, the cooperation among different ethnic groups is by no means predestined; they often make uneasy coalition partners. Deep differences in ideology, perceptions, interest, organizational skills, and other political resources may also divide them. Even within particular groups, class and generational divisions may impede cooperation on specific political issues.

In the immigration reform context, the ethnic groups did not lack for political advantages. They could invoke themes like family unity, ethnic or source-country diversity, redress for past injustices, and foreign policy goals that resonated deeply with the public and Congress. Their geographic concentration in a few politically important states gave them especially great political influence in the House. And as their newly naturalized members joined the voting rolls, their growing numbers swelled the chorus of voices demanding more immigration.

For purposes of understanding the politics of immigration reform in the post-IRCA period, it is useful to divide ethnics into two groups: the Irish and the others. The Irish, of course, were not alone in seeking favored access to the United States for their fellow ethnics. But because family reunification would not bring over many Irish, they *were* unique among ethnic groups in their downplaying of the importance of family-related visas. Instead, they emphasized education, English competency, knowledge of U.S. history, and other requirements that putative Irish immigrants could readily fulfill.

The Irish also held some unusually strong political cards in the House. Since many of them had come after IRCA's 1982 amnesty deadline, they could claim special hardship in the prospect of deportation. They also formed an important constituency in Connecticut, where Morrison had launched an uphill campaign for governor against an incumbent named O'Neill, a member of his own party. Morrison thus needed to play the "Irish card" for all it was worth. The Irish viewed the "independent" admissions approach, adopted by the Senate in 1988 and again in 1989 with them in mind, as too limited and uncertain to help them much. The Irish recognized that they would often be "outskilled" by other English-speaking workers from India, Pakistan, Jamaica, and Hong Kong. They naturally preferred a sure thing: a "diversity" program defined to favor the Irish. This was also a viable option in the Senate. Although Simpson opposed it, his deep commitments to an overall cap on admissions and to the provisions strengthening enforcement and making it easier to deport criminal aliens made him willing to make major concessions to obtain them. And higher Irish immigration was among Kennedy's key policy goals.

The term *diversity* seems a bit curious when one considers the historical context and beneficiaries of the new provisions. More than 75 percent of the so-called NP-5 visas under IRCA went to four countries whose emigrants were already very well represented in the United

States: Ireland (41 percent), Canada (18 percent); Great Britain and Northern Ireland (9 percent), and Poland (9 percent). A special program for "underrepresented" countries—the OP-1 program—was more generous to Third World countries: Bangladeshis, for example, received 22 percent of the OP-1 visas in 1990.

In the debates leading up to the 1990 act, proponents of such diversity programs commonly sought to rationalize them by invoking civil rights rhetoric, arguing that the 1965 law had "discriminated against" or "disadvantaged" Europeans and other "old seed" groups. One could make this argument, however, only by ignoring the history of pre-1965 immigration. In enacting the 1965 reforms, Congress had intended to favor these same northern and western European groups, which had been previously advantaged by the national origins quotas jettisoned in the 1965 act. As it turned out, however, the new system was exploited most effectively by immigrants from Asia, the Pacific region, Latin America, and (to a far less extent) Africa, who had been obliged by the national origins quotas to languish on endless queues but who now quickly turned the tables using the family-based admissions categories to bring in their relatives.

This wholly unexpected turnabout sparked the political interest in diversity programs during the 1980s. Congress had responded to these pressures in IRCA and in 1988. It was especially responsive in the 1990 act. It knew full well, of course, that the new provisions would disproportionately favor Europeans, especially the Irish. Congress appreciated that these groups are already well represented in both the legal and the illegal U.S. population and that they are well represented precisely because of their advantaged pre-1965 immigration patterns. Indeed, much of the "disadvantage" cited by the beneficiaries of the new provisions actually reflects the fact that they, like the Italians, had been in the United States for so many generations that they could no longer gain much help from the 1965 law's preferences for immediate family members and siblings.

Other ethnic groups also demanded special relief, marching under the banners of diversity, human rights, and family unification—depending upon their particular circumstances. Morrison promoted legislation in 1989 protecting Chinese students after Tiananmen Square. He and Senator Frank Lautenberg had won an amendment giving Soviet Jews special advantages under the Refugee Act. Steven Solarz was actively promoting the cause of Hong Kong residents.

Hispanic organizations lobbied vigorously to protect and increase family preferences. They found an eager advocate in Morrison, who proposed a thorough revamping of the preference system. Among other changes, he followed earlier reformers in seeking explicitly to separate the immigration flow into distinct streams, one for family members and one for independent workers, and allot visas to each stream. At the same time, he recognized family unity as the dominant norm in immigration politics. He proposed a higher allotment for the existing second and fifth preferences, which Simpson hoped to limit. He also favored backlog reductions and "family fairness" admissions (for immediate relatives of IRCA-legalized aliens). There was little support for an overall cap in the House, and Morrison did not propose one. In addition to the increase in numerically limited visas, he would maintain the unlimited admission of citizens' immediate relatives.

As Lawrence Fuchs has noted, the willingness of the older immigrant groups, notably the Jews and Italians, to support higher Asian and Hispanic immigration levels was a remarkable feature of the politics that produced the 1990 act. These groups endorsed expansionist principles even though they could anticipate that Asians and Hispanics, rather than their own fellow ethnics, would be the main beneficiaries of those principles. At least in the short run, there was little prospect for Soviet Jews coming here after the invasion of Afghanistan in 1979, and by 1990 most of those who got out were being diverted to Israel, not the United States. Italians could no longer gain many admissions through the family-related preferences precisely because they had been here so long. Yet these groups helped to prevent a reduction of the fifth preference, which was now as important to the Asian and Hispanic groups as it had been to the Italians at an earlier stage. In part, this may have reflected more long-range considerations; should there be a new influx of Jews and Italians, that preference would be available to bring their siblings here. More fundamentally, however, the behavior of these groups was one more sign of the emergent expansionism, a new politics that reflected the interplay between a growing consensus on pro-immigration ideas and a broader coalition mobilized by ethnic logrolling.

HUMAN RIGHTS GROUPS

The human rights groups—the American Civil Liberties Union (ACLU), Amnesty International, religious groups, and others—were concerned about several other policies: the protected status for those Salvadorans (and, they hoped, other groups) who did not technically qualify as refugees but who would face danger if they returned home, the repeal of the ideological exclusion provisions enacted during the Cold War, a softening of the Procrustean marriage fraud provisions enacted in 1986, and the fate of Tibetans displaced by Chinese oppression. The last three concerns were easily accommodated. Some of the ideological exclusions had been temporarily repealed earlier as related to nonimmigrants, and it was hard to imagine why permanent residents should be treated less generously. Only the INS and Senator Simpson seemed committed to the existing marriage fraud provisions; here, as elsewhere, the INS's agenda enjoyed little credibility with Congress. The Tibetan's plight appealed to the entire political spectrum, diehard anti-Communists as well as militant liberals.

In contrast, the issue of protected status for Salvadorans implicated fierce partisan struggles over American policy toward Central America, not just immigration. Congress was bitterly divided over it. Although the House had passed some version of the Moakley-DeConcini bill, which would protect Salvadorans, on four occasions, Simpson adamantly opposed it and had always killed it in the Senate. This time, however, Moakley was chairman of the House Rules Committee. Since his committee regulated the process of floor amendment, which could make or break an immigration bill by fracturing the fragile coalition supporting it, Moakley had to be reckoned with and mollified. Simpson and the White House tried to ignore this fact, but Morrison, who favored the human rights agenda anyway, did not. Morrison therefore proposed to Moakley the packaging of a generic safe-haven provision along with a specific designation of protected status for the Salvadorans and Chinese.

Morrison's larger coalition-building strategy took a long time to put together, and Kennedy, who provided important help by keeping Brooks on board and by getting the Senate to adopt specific pieces of Morrison's package, was becoming nervous and impatient as the end of the Congress approached. Morrison's omnibus bill was not approved by the full committee until 1 August, and it elicited the Justice Department's "fundamental opposition" and a presidential veto threat, primarily because of the high immigration levels that the bill would authorize. The committee report was not issued until after Labor Day. When it reached the floor for debate, however, its supporting coalition was broad and powerful. The only serious complaint lodged against it there was business's concern about the restrictions on temporary workers, which Morrison promised to address in conference. Congressman John Bryant, a Texas Democrat on the immigration subcommittee, proposed an amendment to delete all provisions of the bill except those relating to family reunification. His position, however, was decisively rejected, 257–165, and the House passed the committee's omnibus bill on 3 October.

Still, there was great cause for concern. First, the margin of victory was a slender thirty-one votes, a sign that Morrison's bill could be vulnerable to amendment during the forthcoming conference. Second, the

House bill bore little resemblance to the Senate version. Finally, time was running out. The leadership planned to adjourn within a few weeks, and the power of opponents increases geometrically at the end of a Congress. Kennedy, on the Senate side, was particularly worried about the time factor because it could encourage any senator, including Simpson, to demand concessions on controversial issues and thereby derail the legislation again.

The White House had signaled its support for the Senate bill and its opposition to Morrison's. Beyond this, however, it had played no significant role in lining up votes or shaping the legislative process. The INS, a long-troubled agency under relatively new and shaky leadership, deferred to the attorney general's initiative, which was seldom forthcoming. In this negative posture, the administration would neither negotiate nor even discuss compromises between the two bills. It indicated some flexibility only after the *Wall Street Journal* praised Morrison's bill for its higher ceilings for skilled workers. The *Journal* also criticized the administration's silence, eliciting a letter to the editor from Michael Boskin, the chief White House economist, indicating his support. Two days later, the chastened Simpson also responded. Roger Porter, the president's domestic policy adviser, concluded that the administration was on the wrong side on the issue and should support the enactment of a bill.

The negotiations leading up to the Senate-House conference were delicate. Simpson was adamantly opposed to many of the provisions in the highly expansionist House bill, so much so that he might have preferred to see the legislation die—indeed, he threatened to filibuster it to death—rather than accept those provisions. He wanted to reduce the proportion of family visas; eliminate the family backlog reductions; retain the increases in permanent employment visas but reduce or eliminate visas for unskilled workers; eliminate or raise any cap imposed on temporary worker visas for entry-level professionals; make it easier for employers to obtain Department of Labor certification of domestic worker unavailability; adopt an earlier cutoff date for the family fairness relief; drop Moakley-DeConcini; and—most important to him because of their symbolic value—adopt an overall cap and strict border enforcement and deportation provisions to close the back door to illegal immigration.

Kennedy, however, was also resolute. Fearing that the next Congress, which would extend through the presidential election, would be unable to agree on immigration reform, he was not prepared to give up the present opportunity in the vain hope of passing a more liberal bill later on. Kennedy promised that, if Simpson did not try to block the conference, Kennedy would not sign a conference report embodying legislation that Simpson found unacceptable. Simpson accepted Kennedy's proposal and then confronted the House conferees with his demands. He began the negotiations by asking the other key conferees whether they too had "bottom lines" for the bill. Morrison insisted on provisions favorable to the Irish. Moakley demanded asylum for the Salvadorans. Berman required generous treatment of Asian and Hispanic family groups. Schumer insisted on the new diversity programs. The negotiations were delicate and rancorous.

Faced with the challenge from Simpson, who was supported by Kennedy, the House surrendered on many fronts. On the issue of a cap, however, it held fast. The ceiling, set at 700,000 visas for the first three years and dropping to 675,000 thereafter (not counting refugees and asylees), remained pierceable whenever the number of admissions of citizens' immediate relatives exceeded 226,000 a year. Even without piercing the ceiling, the bill authorized an increase of 40 percent over current levels, which was well above the increase in the Senate bill. Indeed, even at that high level, the cap did not include refugee/asylee admissions.

The House conferees were obliged to make important concessions in exchange for this substantial increase in legal admissions. The family fairness cutoff date was moved back to 1988. Restrictions on temporary workers were retained but diluted. Employer attestation was permitted on an experimental basis. Finally, Simpson obtained both beefed-up border enforcement measures and stronger (some would say Draconian) provisions restricting the rights of aliens who commit crimes, limiting their appeals, and accelerating their deportation. In focusing on drug-related offenses, of course, Simpson was riding a wave of drug-war rhetoric deployed by the administration and Democrats alike. To achieve these gains, however, Simpson was obliged to accept provisions that he opposed but Kennedy and the House conferees favored: a transitional and permanent diversity program (the former reserved 40 percent of its visas for the Irish); another year's extension of the period during which IRCA legalization applicants could apply for permanent status; and other provisions providing special relief for the Tibetans, Hong Kong residents, and (again) the Irish.

The last obstacle to a conference agreement was the Moakley-DeConcini provision establishing a safe haven for Salvadorans. Simpson opposed any country-specific relief, making the long-familiar argument that Salvadorans were only economic migrants, not refugees. Moakley, who controlled crucial votes on the Rules Committee, insisted that he would kill the bill unless it provided specific relief for the

Salvadorans. At that point, Simpson decided to relent in the interests of getting a bill passed, and the White House quickly fell into line. When the conference reconvened, there was movement. Moakley proposed a thirty-six-month temporary protected status period for the Salvadorans; he compromised on eighteen months. Simpson extracted promises from Moakley that deportation notices would be sent out to Salvadorans at the end of the eighteen-month period, that neither Moakley nor DeConcini would seek to legislate legal status for them at that point, and that it would take an extraordinary majority (three-fifths of the Senate) to pass such legislation. In return, Simpson accepted a generic safe-haven provision that Moakley, with specific protection for Salvadorans now in hand, very much wanted.

It was, as Simpson said, an "anguishing compromise," but the Senate immediately ratified it, 89–8. As usual with immigration legislation, House approval posed more of a problem. At the eleventh hour, the Hispanic caucus, led by Ed Roybal, challenged a Simpson-sponsored provision in the compromise report that would establish a pilot program in three states to test a more secure driver's license as an identification document—a proposal that the caucus claimed was the first step toward a national identification card. Although the unions and others in the expansionist coalition also opposed ID cards, they did not feel strongly enough about it to view it as a possible deal breaker. The Hispanic groups, however, pressed the coalition hard. Perhaps most important to the political fate of the bill, they convinced the black congressional caucus, which few politicians wished to offend, to support their position. The eagerness of the black leadership to cement ties with the Hispanics is an especially striking feature of the politics of the 1990 act. Black leaders had sought in earlier immigration debates to mobilize their supporters around opposition to expansion. Now, however, they were willing to mute this traditional restrictionism in the hope of mollifying a group with whom they were increasingly competing over redistricting, patronage, access to housing, control of public schools, representation on the Supreme Court, and other issues. Armed with black support, the Hispanic caucus could kill the bill if its demand was not met. At this point the bill was much closer to being a corpse than IRCA had ever been.

If the Hispanic caucus was bluffing, it was not at all clear that the bluff would succeed. Simpson, after all, had already made many concessions. Unable to get his overall cap and displeased with many of the provisions that had been logrolled into the bill, he might be tempted to let it die, especially since the caucus, which was often at odds with him politically, would probably end up bearing public responsibility for its death.

Barney Frank, a liberal Democrat from Massachusetts, saw this mortal danger to a bill that he desperately wanted to pass and moved to break the impasse. Frank argued to Simpson that the bill could be saved if Simpson would drop his drivers' license proposal, in return for which Frank would try to convince Senate liberals to consider the proposal in the next Congress. Simpson now found himself in an oddly familiar position. During the final act of the IRCA drama, he could have defeated the liberals' move to broaden amnesty. Now he again held the fate of immigration reform in his hands. And, as he had done in 1986, Simpson decided to yield in order to secure a bill. Agreeing to Frank's plan, he allowed the pilot program to be deleted. With this resolved, the House proceeded to approve the conference report, 264–118.

Ideas

The Immigration Act of 1990 was a pastiche of many influential groups' policy agendas, but it was also considerably more than that. The immigration debate of the 1980s revolved around ideas as well as interests. One cannot adequately account for IRCA and the 1990 act without understanding the role of these ideas.

It is not easy, even in theory, to distinguish ideas from interests. We can hardly conceive of our interests without drawing upon ideas, and we often use our ideas to advance our interests. In another sense and in certain contexts, however, we *can* readily distinguish them. Voters, for example, are aware both of their own interests and of public interests that transcend their own interests, and they know—and routinely act on—that difference.

Ideas perform at least five functions in politics: they help build coalitions, change beliefs, mobilize symbols, reinforce existing regimes, and reduce dissonance. These functions, of course, are only separable at an analytical level; in practice, particular ideas may perform several of them simultaneously. This was certainly true of ideas about immigration in the 1980s. The exogenous force of ideas, moreover, is greater for some of these functions (belief changing is the clearest example) than for others.

COALITION BUILDING

Ideas are the glue of a pluralistic politics. Appealing to general ideas is necessary if groups with disparate conceptions of self-interest and public interest are to form coalitions. And since politics must invariably be justified in public interest terms to win broad support, ideas can supply the necessary language in which that discourse of justification is conducted. In this respect, an idea's ambiguity may contribute to its power to facilitate coalition building.

The idea of *diversity*, which played such a crucial role in the enactment of the 1990 act, is an example. Although this notion might have been defined exclusively, as it was under the national origins quota system, its usefulness in fashioning and maintaining an *expansionist* coalition depended upon it being defined so that a large number of countries could qualify and their supporters in Congress could be placated. Much the same may be said of the idea of international human rights. In a world in which the number of refugees vastly exceeds the willingness of receiving nations to accept them, admission of one group on the basis of human rights principles can be viewed by others as little more than favoritism. The idea of *universal* humanitarian principles, although violated in many cases, helped to contain this favoritism and thus maintain the coalition.

Perhaps the most influential coalition-building idea during the 1980s was the Hesburgh Commission's emphasis, echoed by many of its members, such as Senators Kennedy and Simpson, on the need to control illegal migration as a precondition for expanding legal immigration. This linkage enabled liberals and conservatives to join forces to "close the back door" and "open the front door" at the same time. The wedding of employer sanctions to legalization in IRCA and of tougher enforcement provisions to expanded immigration quotas in the 1990 act must be understood in terms of the moral force and political logic of this linkage idea.

BELIEF CHANGING

Ideas can affect how policy intellectuals and other experts who influence decision makers think about an issue. Ideas call attention to new empirical relationships and alter the weight accorded to different values. For example, ideas about the benefits and costs of a policy and how they are distributed among individuals and groups fuel all politics, immigration included.

Certain ideas that gained sway during the immigration debates of the late 1980s encouraged many decision makers to believe in the existence of a mismatch between job skills needed in the evolving economy and those that new immigrants are bringing with them; some also came to believe in a looming labor shortage. Labor economists testified that the existing system of legal admissions was highly inefficient, aggravating these conditions, and that a restructured system expanding admissions of the "right" kind of immigrants could create immense social benefits while imposing few social costs. Although many business interests had long embraced these ideas, the general hostility to immigration evident at the beginning of the decade had pushed them to the margins of the debate. But the decade's free-market, libertarian *zeitgeist*, nurtured by prominent academics, influential mass media, and conservative think tanks, succeeded in grounding and sharpening these notions. Influential conservatives such as Alan Simpson and liberals such as Bruce Morrison came to accept them and to incorporate them into their policy proposals.

SYMBOL MOBILIZING

In the immigration debate, the fund of pro-immigration ideas was not confined to the efficiency-oriented calculations of neoclassical or labor economists. Ideas can also evoke the symbolic dimension of politics, linking workaday policies with our deepest emotional and normative commitments.

The civil rights movement supplied immigration advocates with a powerful imagery of struggle and a rhetoric of egalitarian ideals. During the 1980s, Americans' tolerance for ethnic differences continued to grow. The celebrations of the Statue of Liberty's centennial and the Constitution's bicentennial also imparted strong emotional, even romantic, resonances to the connections between ethnic diversity and national pride and strength, to the image of the United States as a haven for the persecuted, and to the idea that aliens should not be excluded because of their political speech.

Not all of the symbolism evoked by ideas, of course, carried pro-immigration connotations. The notions that the United States was unable to control its borders and that immigrants took jobs away from American workers aroused deep fears about both waning sovereignty and economic decline. These ideas competed vigorously for public allegiance with the more optimistic ones.

REGIME REINFORCING

Ideas, even those that call for policy changes, can reaffirm and thus support elements of the status quo. Ideas, as Peter Hall pointed out, are more warmly received to the extent that they converge with existing governmental institutions, policies, and implementation capacities and are consistent with social norms concerning the appropriate role of the state in society.[5]

Immigration policy debates during the 1980s provided many instances of this kind of reinforcement. Employer sanctions, for example, were adopted out of a widespread recognition that the INS's limited enforcement capabilities must be augmented with the enforcement resources of the private sector. The notion that alienage raises fundamental equal protection issues, which led to IRCA's antidiscrimination provisions, drew upon an explicit analogy to civil rights and fair employment principles that had long been established for the rest of the population. Similarly, the idea of restricting ideological exclusions reaffirmed the First Amendment protections applicable to the rest of society. These examples also suggest that ideas, by appealing to social continuities and legal traditions, often have the considerable political advantage of masking the extent to which change is in fact being effected.

DISSONANCE REDUCING

Ideas can give eloquent voice to a previously inarticulate sense among members of the public that social values and ways of thinking are changing and that policies therefore need to be brought into harmony with these new practices. By engendering a kind of cognitive dissonance, ideas can underscore tensions in our political life, stimulating the search for new modes of behavior or governance.

There were many examples of this dynamic in the immigration debate. The perceived economic inefficiency of the existing immigration regime prompted a demand for the admission of more highly skilled workers. The new limits on ideological exclusion reflected the idea that Cold War attitudes had become anachronistic. The adoption of liberal safe-haven policies was an acknowledgment that the traditional "refugee" definition was inadequate to deal with contemporary migration flows. Due process safeguards long withheld from aliens were included at many points. Generous protections for the close relatives of amnesty applicants sought to accommodate the conflict between family values and enforcement imperatives.

If ideas have different political functions and their autonomy from interests varies, they also shape policy at different levels of normativity. In the immigration debate of the 1980s, we can distinguish three such levels. The most foundational is that of the *rule of law*. The courts during the 1980s infused immigration decision making with certain transcendant principles of equal protection and due process that had long been conventional in virtually all areas of public policy except immigration. These principles obliged the government—"the potent, the omnipresent teacher," in Brandeis's phrase[6]—to treat immigrants more like citizens than ever before, in both substantive and procedural terms. At a second, more pragmatic level, the new ideas shaped *policy purposes.* The most important example was the conviction, shared by most policy elites during the decade,[7] that the United States was engaged in a high-stakes global competition spurred by the drive for economic efficiency and that expanded immigration could help us win it at little or no cost to other social values. At the third, most operational level, ideas shaped *policy design.* Here, ideas about immigration helped to forge a consensus on techniques for implementing new and old policies.

The Rule of Law

The Marielito incident drew the federal courts into the vortex of immigration policy as never before. To discourage illegal migration and asylum claims, the Reagan administration in the early 1980s adopted harsh, often arbitrary policies of exclusion and incarceration. These policies starkly raised the issue of whether and how the rule of law would apply to undocumented aliens. The courts, moreover, had to resolve this issue at a time when other trends in public and private law called into question the legal rules that had traditionally governed aliens.

The principle of rigorous court review of immigration policy was not widely accepted in 1981. Before then, judges had upheld almost all federal immigration policies, viewing them as expressions of U.S. sovereignty to which ordinary constitutional principles simply did not apply. They accorded the Congress and its agent, the INS, "plenary power" to regulate immigration and protect national borders pretty much as they saw fit. Policies that in other contexts would have been flatly unconstitutional easily passed judicial muster.

In the early 1980s, however, something had begun to change. The courts were especially responsive to the influence of the ideas of equal treatment, due process, and social integration. Drawing upon constitutional and administrative law norms long established in other policy areas, the courts invalidated key INS policies and practices, barred the states from denying public education to undocumented alien children, limited the federal government's power to bar controversial figures from entering on purely ideological grounds, and enlarged the procedural rights of aliens resisting expulsion.

To protect asylum claimants, for example, the courts eased the standard of proof, upheld claims by those who had been politically neutral, and pressured the INS into granting a work authorization—the brass ring in the immigration merry-go-round—to any alien presenting a "nonfrivolous" asylum claim. The INS's policy of confining thousands of undocumented aliens under conditions resembling criminal punishment obliged the courts to devise legal norms to control agency abuses. In still other areas, the courts reduced the gap between the (nonpolitical) rights of citizens and of aliens almost to the vanishing point. A particularly dramatic example of this occurred in 1989, when a federal judge held that a statutory ground of deportation was unconstitutional, the first such holding ever.

Coming when and in the form that they did, these principled thrusts helped to transform the political issue in Congress and in the country. The courts' insistence on protecting the procedural and constitutional rights of aliens during this period affected how politicians and citizens viewed them. By exploiting the deference to judicial ideals that marks American political culture, the courts helped to guide the normative debate in universalistic, human rights–oriented, pro-immigration directions.

Policy Purpose

Global competitiveness and labor market efficiency were important political touchstones during the 1980s. The rhetorical power of these slogans was stoked by the spectacle of rapid economic growth along the Pacific Rim and in West Germany at a time of recession in the United States. Policy elites raised alarms about looming shortages of high-skilled workers in the United States, the reluctance of many low-skilled Americans to do the menial work that a modern society required, the decline of our educational system, and the need to compete internationally.

These alarms were reinforced by the writings of free-market economists and libertarians. Their theories were supported and disseminated by a network of academic institutions, think tanks, and prominent media, which included the Heritage Foundation, the Cato Institute, and the *Wall Street Journal*. These writers argued that recent immigration policy had been deeply misguided and that our preoccupation with undocumented aliens and generous family-oriented admissions had diverted us from more important issues: How many aliens should we admit? Which kind should we seek? What should be their role in the economy? How should we go about encouraging them to come?

Although these commentators' specific answers to these questions often differed, they usually agreed on a set of decidedly pro-immigration ideas: immigrants tend to be especially productive and entrepreneurial, immigration promotes economic growth and makes almost everyone better off, it neither reduces the wage and employment levels of domestic workers nor consumes significant welfare benefits, and immigration policy should be carefully tailored to our economic needs. Some

economists—Julian Simon was perhaps the most notable—came peril-
ously close to saying that open immigration, like free trade, would
provide us with a free lunch! These ideas flooded TV and radio talk
shows, congressional hearings, and the editorial pages of major newspapers.

Even those who reject this remorselessly Panglossian view of immigration agree that these ideas seemed to soften the bitter *distributional*
conflicts that lie just beneath the more placid, cooperative surface of
American life. It was somehow reassuring to think that the important
zero-sum game was an international competition between the United
States and other nations for investment and jobs, rather than a domestic
conflict among low-income groups in America's cities—an assurance
belied by the smoldering political struggles between native-born blacks
and recently arrived Hispanics.

The new emphasis on global competition and resource mobility had
another resonance: it made the old idea of national sovereignty seem
anachronistic, perhaps moribund. If a nation's policy independence increasingly connotes isolation and irrelevance, if our fate is inexorably
linked with the policies of other nations, than a pragmatic people would
feel impelled to use immigration policy to shape its destiny, rather than
having outsiders and events thrust that destiny upon it.

But, although the new ideas made remarkable headway by the time
Congress completed its work, they did not displace all the old ideas. In
particular, they failed to dislodge family unification as the core immigration policy value; it continued to trump all others as it had for over a
quarter-century. An affirmative case could be (and was) made, of course,
that economic and family goals were in harmony because family links
would actually advance labor market efficiency by providing valuable
social, emotional, and economic supports to immigrants, helping them
to produce and succeed. Thus was an old idea pressed into new service.
Any competition between family-based and employment-based visas,
moreover, was muted by Morrison's successful logrolling strategy,
which sought to increase the numbers in *all* admission categories, making the pie large enough so that it would no longer seem worth fighting
over the relative size of the various slices. Morrison's strategy was evident in the title of his version of the immigration bill: the Family Unity
and Employment Opportunities Act of 1990.

Still, a strategy of conflict-suppressing expansion clearly has its political limits, and the 1990 act may reach those limits, especially if
illegal migration continues to grow. The tradeoff between family unity
and skills, for example, probably cannot be ignored forever. Recent evidence suggests that U.S. income is considerably lower—$6 billion a

year lower, according to a recent estimate—than it would be if immigrants' skill levels had not declined as a result of the family unity preferences.

The 1990 act continued to accord primacy to family unity goals but did give labor market concerns somewhat more weight. In 1990, 20 percent of the legal immigrants admitted under numerical quotas (54,000 out of 270,000) were admitted under skills-related visas, and although the 1990 act increased the number of such admissions to 140,000, their share of the new total (675,000 for the first three years plus citizens' "immediate relatives" in excess of 226,000) remained at 20 percent. However, the allowance for 55,000 diversity visas, which also carry a skills requirement, does increase that share to as much as 28 percent. (To the extent that immediate family admissions grow and pierce the cap, of course, these proportions, although not the numbers, of skills-based visas will decline.) In addition to increasing the numbers, Congress also placed a much stronger emphasis in the employment-related visa categories on higher-level skills. More flexible labor certification procedures were also added. Still, the family category's share accounts for two-thirds or more of the visas.

Policy Design

As the ideas of the rule of law, free labor markets, more selective admissions, diversity, and human rights joined family unity in shaping the decade's immigration debates, they helped to generate and rationalize specific policies, adopted in the 1990 act, that were designed to implement these more general goals in a major way. Five of these policies, already discussed, are particularly important: (1) higher overall immigration levels, (2) more skills-oriented admissions criteria, (3) the continued primacy of family-based admissions, (4) enhanced enforcement against documented aliens, and (5) the elimination of certain grounds for exclusion that raised serious constitutional questions.

One additional policy—the use of presumptively universalistic criteria for source-country and humanitarian admissions—merits separate discussion because of its highly contested status. No firm consensus in favor of universalism in admissions has ever been established, as demonstrated both by the pre-1965 national origins quotas and by our country-specific refugee policies during the entire postwar period. Yet the universalistic ideal did prompt Congress to repeal the national origins quotas in 1965 and adopt the 1980 Refugee Act, which regularized refugee and asylum criteria and procedures in the interest of equal treatment while preserving discretion to favor some countries and regions over others.

During the 1980s, even this ambivalent universalism was thrown into a headlong retreat. In the refugee area, where pre-1980 policies had targeted certain areas and ideologies for special protection, favoritism was extended through administrative practices and statutory changes. Soviet Jews and Pentacostals, Salvadorans, Tibetans, and a few other groups with powerful patrons in Congress received special preference. Some favoritism is to be expected, of course, in any political system in which well-organized, cohesive interests enjoy special access and influence, and a properly constrained favoritism may even be a legitimate instrument of a sound and moral foreign policy. Yet the facts remain troubling: 74 percent of those approved for admission in 1990 came from two areas (the Soviet Union and Indochina), most of these had remained in their own countries rather than having crossed international borders (an exceptional situation for relief under the Refugee Act), and the vast majority of the world's refugees live in areas that are disfavored.

The source-country bias represented by the new transitional and permanent diversity programs and other country-specific benefits under the 1990 act also demonstrates the continuing power of well-positioned special interests to shape policy on legal immigration. These programs may fairly be viewed as affirmative action programs for the favored groups, programs in which admission, social welfare benefits, and the power to bring family members here are the valuable prizes. Perhaps some members of Congress view source-country favoritism as a form of indirect compensation for those who claim to suffer "reverse discrimination" in domestic programs. If the history of immigration policy teaches us anything, it is that *any* system of limited admissions discriminates against *some* nationality groups. The playing field cannot be made perfectly level.

Conclusion

An important political question remains: what is the relationship between the beleaguered universalistic ideal and the durability of the political coalition that produced the 1990 act? If the 1990 act was a marriage of convenience among a broad array of special interest advocates in which the diversity provisions were politically essential, as Bruce Morrison thinks, its enactment may not in fact demonstrate any long-term public commitment to increased immigration. Instead, the 1990 act may simply reflect a unique resolution of conflicting forces, a temporary truce owing more to logrolling than to a broad consensus in favor of increased immigration.

Few things in American politics, of course, are settled forever. Most settlements are precarious, established by coalitions whose political fortunes wax and wane. Immigration policy is no exception. Because it arouses powerful emotions, is linked to economic conditions, responds to the flux of ethnic group politics, and continually infuses into the polity newly naturalized voters seeking more immigrants like themselves, immigration engenders constant pressures for change. The events of the 1980s, culminating in the 1990 act, demonstrate just how rapidly these pressures can affect immigration politics and policy.

But the power of the immigration reform impulse during the 1980s only deepens the mystery of why these pressures produced a highly expansionist result by 1990. The restrictionist road, along which American immigration law had traveled for over sixty years, beckoned once again—yet this time it was the road not taken. Interests advocating restriction exerted countervailing pressures, and the political environment was in some ways quite favorable to their cause. IRCA had not really closed the back door. Many Americans believed that the 1965 and 1980 reforms had opened the front door *too* wide and that the immigrants passing through it added relatively little economic value to society. A recession had begun, and the Persian Gulf war impended. But, in the end, the restrictionists lost. The values of expansion and diversity prevailed over those of restriction and homogeneity. Although some existing policies were reaffirmed (especially family unification), policy innovation was the order of the day.

And two years later, when the electorate had had an opportunity to assimilate these changes and could either repudiate or ratify what the politicians had done, it seemed to take the latter course. The expansionist immigration policies of the 1980s raised hardly a ripple during the 1992 presidential campaign.[8]

Few political commentators in 1980 would have predicted such an outcome within a decade. Indeed, it is no easy thing to explain even after the fact. The phenomenon of rapid and radical policy change adopted by institutions and actors that ordinarily prefer continuity remains a fascinating intellectual puzzle. Important clues to that puzzle, I have argued, can be found in new and renovated ideas about immigration and its role in American life.

That the political entrepreneurs and special interests exploited these ideas for their own policy ends is hardly remarkable, but this did not render the ideas epiphenomenal; they were not simply markers in a game in which the "real" stakes were elsewhere. Rather, these ideas helped to form an agenda, define the terms of debate, and structure the conflict. They possessed independent political significance—and, for us, explanatory power.

Whether all of these ideas prove to be sound and whether the policies they produced will endure are of course questions for future historians. What today's scholar can say with some confidence is that the course of U.S. immigration politics in the 1980s reveals a society and a policy-making system that take new ideas ever more seriously.

Adversarial Legalism and
American Government

ROBERT A. KAGAN

In 1988, international shipping lines launched a new generation of fuel-efficient, $40 million containerships. The new containerships are part of a transportation revolution that dramatically increased the efficiency and reliability of transoceanic, transcontinental cargo movements. Osaka residents nowadays eat Florida grapefruit, shipped in refrigerated containers. A moving inventory of Toyota parts, stowed in containers, flows from Japan via ship and train to an assembly plant in Kentucky. On both sides of the ocean, local monopolies and stodgy oligopolies are threatened by distant competitors, spurring productivity and innovation.

Now the bad news. The big new containerships draw thirty-eight or forty feet; the harbor at the Port of Oakland, a major West Coast seaport, was only thirty-five feet deep, on average. Port of Oakland officials, anticipating the problem, first sought congressional approval of a harbor-deepening project in 1972. In 1986, Congress funded the project and the U.S. Army Corps of Engineers, in charge of dredging permits, pronounced the plan economically desirable and environmentally acceptable. But then, for month after month, a seemingly endless series of regulatory actions and lawsuits blocked any authoritative decision about dredging and disposal of harbor floor sediments, a small portion of which contained potentially toxic chemical wastes.

While lawyers, judges, and regulatory officials debated the adequacy of sediment samples and environmental impact models, the powerful hydraulic dredging equipment stood idle. To call on Oakland, the big ships had to carry reduced loads and wait for high tides, which in turn disrupted the schedules of containertrains and consignees. Shipping companies, facing higher costs and customer complaints, began to abandon Oakland. The port lost money, the municipal government lost revenues, and port-related employment—the city's major economic hope—was adversely affected. In the fall of 1992, six years after the project had been poised to begin, a compromise plan was implemented, providing the big containerships additional but still suboptimal clearance and postponing the full project pending further regulatory study.

The dredging of Oakland Harbor foundered on what might be called *adversarial legalism*. Unfortunately, the same kind of costly, drawn-out legal conflict recurs in many spheres of American public policy, transmuting political responsiveness and good policy ideas into bad outcomes. This chapter examines adversarial legalism as a mode of governance, tracing its origins to fundamental features of the American political system.

Adversarial Legalism

Derek Bok, when president of Harvard University, complained that every year America's educational system turns thousands of bright students into lawyers, who work at redistributing pieces of the economic pie, while Japan's best and brightest become engineers, makers of a bigger pie.[1] An administrator of the U.S. Environmental Protection Agency (EPA) estimated that more than 80 percent of EPA's regulations have been challenged in court and that each year litigation consumed 150 person-years of EPA program staff and lawyers' time.[2]

Social scientists who study the legal system, on the other hand, tend to denigrate these complaints. Surveys show that *most* people confronted with a problem don't sue or raise legal defenses.[3] Some scholars conclude that current litigation rates, viewed cross-nationally and historically, are not unprecedented.[4] Complaints about too much law and litigation, therefore, are often dismissed as misguided or as the laments of conservatives who resent legal changes designed to empower the disadvantaged.[5]

I'm not inclined to dismiss the "too much litigation" perspective quite so quickly. Yes, I would agree with the scholars, law is a good thing, a barrier against official arbitrariness, a check on economic rapaciousness, a force for tolerance and healthy social change. But the scholars seem to have a parochial view of law. Focusing on legal practices in the United States over the last twenty or thirty years, they say, "This is modern law. Take it (with all its excesses) or leave it (and throw away its far more important social benefits)."

When one views the American legal system from a cross-national perspective, however, a different set of possibilities emerges. Western

European polities, for example, also care about justice, environmental regulation, and the prevention of professional or governmental malpractice. In some areas of policy, such as land use regulation and worker protection, many European countries have "more law" than the United States. Japan has a more detailed and extensive set of product standards and testing requirements.[6] What is different about the United States, according to an accumulating body of cross-national studies, it is not the amount of law it tries to enforce but the unique legal style that characterizes the American approach to public policy.[7]

Of course, national legal styles are not monolithic; they vary within nations and even across offices of the same legal institution. Nevertheless, for one social problem after another, the American system encompasses, on balance, (1) more complex legal rules; (2) more formal, adversarial procedures for resolving disputes; (3) more costly forms of legal contestation; (4) stronger, more punitive legal sanctions; (5) more frequent judicial review of and intervention into administrative decisions; and (6) more political controversy about (and more frequent change of) legal rules and institutions.

Searching for a handy rubric for these legal propensities, I label them *adversarial legalism:* a method of policy making and dispute resolution characterized by comparatively high degrees of

— *formal legal contestation:* disputants invoke legal rights, duties, and procedural requirements, backed by the threat of judicial review or enforcement;
— *litigant activism:* the gathering of evidence and articulation of claims are dominated or profoundly influenced by disputing parties, acting primarily through lawyers;
— *substantive uncertainty:* official legal decisions are variable, unpredictable, and reversible; hence, adversarial advocacy can have a substantial effect.

This definition might be clarified by suggesting its opposites. Table 4.1 displays two dimensions along which legal or administrative decision making varies. The horizontal dimension involves the degree of legal formality—that is, the extent to which contending parties invoke formal procedures and preexisting legal rights and duties. The vertical dimension concerns the extent to which decision making is hierarchical —dominated by an official decision maker, applying authoritative norms or standards—as opposed to participatory—influenced by disputing parties and their lawyers, their normative arguments, and the evidence they deem relevant. Taking each of these dimensions to its extreme form produces four ideal types.

TABLE 4.1 Modes of Policy Making and Dispute Resolution

Decision Making	Informal	Formal
Hierarchical	Expert or political judgment	Bureaucratic legalism
Party-influenced	Negotiation/mediation	Adversarial legalism

1. *Negotiation/mediation:* A decision process in the lower left cell of table 4.1 is adversarial in the sense that it would be dominated by the contending parties, not by an authoritative governmental decision maker. And it would be informal and nonlegalistic, in that neither procedures nor standards would be dictated by law. The purest cases would be dispute resolution via negotiation without lawyers and policy making via bargaining among legislators representing contending interests. The cell would also include mediation, whereby an "official" third party attempts to induce contending parties to agree on a policy or settlement but refrains from imposing a settlement in accordance with law or official policy.

2. *Expert/political judgment:* The more an official third party controls the process and the standards for decision and the more authoritative and final the third party's decision is, the more "hierarchical" the process is. Hierarchical processes can be legally informal, as suggested by the upper left cell in table 4.1.

European disability and workers' compensation systems, for example, follow a "professional treatment model";[8] decisions concerning eligibility are made by a panel of government physicians or social workers, without significant probability of judicial review. Consider also Badaracco's description of regulatory rule making concerning occupational safety and health in Great Britain, France, West Germany, and Japan.[9] A government ministry, with final authority to promulgate a rule, conducts a series of informal, closed-door discussions with industry, labor representatives, and scientists; in contrast with rule making on similar issues in the United States, participation and assessment of evidence is not organized in a "judicialized" manner, and the agency's decision is not subjected to judicial reversal. Rather, faith is placed in the agency's political judgment and its ability to forge acceptable compromises.

3. *Bureaucratic legalism:* A process characterized by a high degree of hierarchical authority and legal formality (the upper right cell of table 4.1) would resemble Weber's ideal-typical bureaucracy, staffed by carefully trained, apolitical, rule-guided civil servants. The more hierarchical the system, the more restricted and controlled the role for legal

representation of and participation by affected citizens or contending interests. In contemporary democracies, this is an ideal systematically pursued, for example, by tax collection agencies or the U.S. Social Security Administration. Tending toward this cell, too, would be German and French courts, where bureaucratically embedded career judges—not (as in the United States) the parties' lawyers and not lay juries—dominate both the evidentiary and the decision-making process.[10]

4. Adversarial legalism: The lower right cell of table 4.1 implies a process that is formal, but in which hierarchy is weak and party influence on the process is strong. American civil and criminal adjudication provide vivid examples. Complex legal rules govern pleadings, jurisdiction, pretrial discovery and testing of evidence, and so on, but the gathering of evidence and the invocation of rules is dominated not by the judge but by contending lawyers.[11]

At the same time, as comparisons of American and British "adversarial systems" make clear, hierarchical imposition of legal rules is relatively weak in the United States.[12] From a comparative perspective, American judges are more political, their decisions less uniform.[13] Law is treated as malleable, open to parties' novel legal arguments and pleas of extenuating circumstances. Lay jurors, whose decisions are largely shielded from review, still play a large and normatively important role in the United States, reducing legal certainty and magnifying the importance of skillful advocacy by the parties.

Similarly, when compared to policy making in European democracies, regulatory decisions in the United States entail more legal formality. But hierarchical authority is weak. Policy-making and implementing authority in particular realms is often shared by different agencies at different levels of government. Agency authority is checked by numerous legislative oversight committees, and agency decisions are frequently challenged in court and reversed by judges. Lawyers, scientists, and economists hired by contending industry and advocacy groups play a large role in presenting evidence and arguments. Overall, the clash of adversarial argument, rather than the imposition of official norms, is the most important influence on decisions.

No legal system falls entirely into any of the cells in table 4.1. Different programs tend toward different policy-making and dispute-resolution methods, and variation also occurs within programs. Adversarial legalism can and does occur in cooperative nations such as The Netherlands and Japan.[14] Americans, conversely, often refrain from adversarial legalism, resorting to negotiation or submitting to bureaucratic or expert judgment. But, viewed in the aggregate, adversarial legalism is more common in the United States than in other democracies and is more common today than in the America of thirty years ago. Adversarial legalism, often latent but always easily triggered, circumscribes virtually all contemporary American political and legal institutions.

The Costs of Adversarial Legalism

Adversarial legalism is deeply intertwined with American ideals of limited government and pluralistic democracy. Americans value the right of ordinary citizens to pursue legal claims against anyone, including powerful corporations or government officials, who unfairly harm them or infringe their interests. Adversarial legalism encourages and facilitates the articulation of new justice claims and ideas. Ready recourse to a politically responsive judiciary enables dissenters to challenge the dogma and defenses of highway planners, school administrators, and corporate toxicologists. Repeatedly, adversarial legalism has enabled political underdogs to demand justice from the government, first and foremost in the cause of racial equality, but also in the quest for more equitable electoral districts, more humane prisons and mental institutions, and more compassionate welfare administration. Focusing on these shining victories, many legal scholars tend to celebrate the institutions that support adversarial legalism.

Without intending to dismiss these social benefits, I suggest that it may be useful to attend to the other side of the ledger. The distrust of authority that underlies adversarial legalism can be directed against trustworthy public officials as well as against scoundrels. An equal opportunity weapon, it can be invoked by the misguided, the mendacious, and the malevolent as well as by the mistreated, and its procedures make it possible to use the law as a weapon of extortion.

No comprehensive account of the social and economic costs of adversarial legalism is readily available. This brief survey can only suggest some of the principal categories, referring to scattered data or examples drawn from several legal subfields.

LAWYERING COSTS

The law for settling international cargo damage disputes, derived from an international treaty, is the same in The Netherlands and the United States. Nevertheless, shipping company officials maintain that, if a claim is processed in New York rather than in Rotterdam, their attorneys' fees will be far higher. The New York lawyers charge a lot more, but they also do more. They handle the claim in a far more aggressive, adversarial, and labor-intensive manner.[15] This reflects one of the hallmarks of adversarial legalism—its heavy reliance on lawyers in resolving disputes, conducting litigation, structuring transactions, and implementing governmental programs.

One obvious, direct cost of adversarial legalism, therefore, is the cost of lawyering. American expenditures on legal services are approximately $100 billion a year. In terms of value added (an industry's gross receipts minus its purchases from other economic sectors), the American legal industry was larger in 1987 than the U.S. steel industry, textile industry, and even the domestic auto industry.[16]

In tort cases, lawyers for both sides absorb an astonishing 40 or 50 percent of the sums that insurers expend on claims.[17] A more wasteful method of income replacement and compensation could hardly be imagined.[18] In the federal Superfund program, litigation and related transaction costs, public and private, account for as much as 44 percent of the funds expended on actual waste site cleanup.[19] And, although dollar estimates are hard to come by, there is little doubt that American business executives engaged in negotiating sales franchises, acquiring other companies, floating stock issues, and launching new products are surrounded by larger phalanxes of expensive attorneys than are their counterparts in France or Switzerland or Japan.

LIABILITY INSURANCE

Then come the less visible costs. In states such as California, automobile liability insurance costs are so high that an estimated 20 to 25 percent of motorists do not carry compulsory insurance, and an equal number (burdened by a fee to cover the uninsured motorists) do not carry enough insurance to pay fully for the losses they inflict.[20] American manufacturers, obstetricians, day care centers, and municipal governments pay far higher liability insurance premiums than do their counterparts in other countries.[21]

Money spent on liability cannot be spent on other things. In fiscal 1991, New York City paid out $229 million to settle lawsuits for medical malpractice, auto accidents, sidewalk falls, and the like—more than the city spent to operate all its parks and libraries. Huber estimated that liability insurance adds $300 per birth to the cost of maternity and obstetrical care in New York City and accounts for 30 percent of the price of a stepladder, 95 percent of the price of certain childhood vaccines, 25 percent of the cost of a Long Island tour bus ride, and over one-third of the price of a small airplane.[22] Unless one imagines a world with no liability costs, it is hard to say how much of these figures might be deemed "excessive." But these insurance costs are far larger than those incurred by comparable producers and consumers in Western Europe.

LEGAL RESISTANCE

Prosecutions and lawsuits demanding heavy legal penalties induce many defendants to wage an all-out defensive legal battle. Thus, the United States, unique among developed nations in not abandoning the death penalty, is also unique in the extended, redundant, sometimes frantic round of legal appeals that precede virtually every execution. American regulatory enforcement evokes more legal appeals than does enforcement in England and Sweden because American regulators are far more likely to seek legal penalties against violators.[23] Pretrial adversarial hearings concerning American police practices are stimulated in large part by an especially punitive (and largely ineffective) approach to the control of narcotic drugs.

DEFENSIVE BEHAVIOR

The heavy legal sanctions and unpredictability associated with adversarial legalism also can lead to excessively defensive behavior. Most notorious are the unnecessary hospitalizations, lab tests, Caesarian sections, and other procedures designed to ward off malpractice suits.[24] Clozypine, a promising antipsychosis drug, costs four times as much in the United States as in Europe, solely because liability fears have induced the supplier to insist on expensive patient-monitoring systems for clozypine sold in America.[25] When corporations seek to raise money by selling public securities issues, they pay enormous sums to high-priced lawyers for drafting lengthy prospectuses and "due diligence" letters in hopes of staving off the class action lawsuit that often follows a significant decline in stock prices. To forestall litigation challenging port expansion, port authorities spend tens of thousands of dollars on environmental "mitigation projects" (such as man-made marshes and wetlands) that often fail to achieve their ecological objectives. Manufacturers of some generally safe but easy-to-misuse products—such as child-care equipment, contraceptive devices, and small aircraft—have withdrawn their wares from the market to avoid the threat of tort suits.[26]

INEFFECTIVENESS AND INJUSTICE

Because it costs so much, takes so long, and entails so much uncertainty, adversarial legalism undercuts the law's most basic aspirations for effectiveness and justice. The American jury trial, for example, epitomizes adversarial legalism's faith in legal institutions that respond to the arguments of contending parties and that are only weakly subject to hierarchical review and control. Early in this century, 25 to 30 percent of civil cases actually resulted in a jury trial. In recent years, however, that figure has dropped to less than 5 percent in many jurisdictions; as Albert Alschuler explained, "few litigants can afford the cost of either the pretrial journey or the trial itself."[27] The resulting out-of-court settlements are distorted by the parties' unequal ability to deal with the costs and delays of litigation. Jury verdicts for similar injuries vary significantly.[28] Experimental studies indicate that settlements negotiated in the uncertain shadow of the jury verdict are glaringly inconsistent.[29] Because insurers concentrate defense efforts on large damage claims, the most severely injured claimants, on average, are undercompensated, while small claims tend to be overcompensated.[30]

Adversarial procedures for picking jurors and controlling evidentiary presentation have also bloated felony trials. Prosecutors must therefore restrict the number of cases they take to trial, reducing charges and penalties in return for guilty pleas. Defendants who insist on a trial, meanwhile, receive heavier sentences if convicted than do similar defendants who plead guilty before trial.[31]

In other spheres of policy, too, the delays and costs of adversarial legalism induce individuals and organizations to abandon meritorious claims and defenses. School administrators not infrequently accede to unjustified parental demands concerning education of handicapped children simply to avoid repetitive hearings and litigation (see chapter 2). In debt collection and consumer protection cases, any show of adversarial resistance commonly results in the abandonment or compromise of just claims and defenses.[32]

GOVERNMENTAL PARALYSIS

Adversarial legalism provides wider access to the policy-making process, but it also breeds legal deadlock and inertia. For example:

— Government regulations often are delayed by lengthy judicial appeals, sometimes mounted by regulated entities complaining that the regulations are unreasonably strict, sometimes by pro-regulation groups complaining that they are too lax.[33] Protective measure concerning workplace health risks, hazardous air pollutants, and motor vehicle safety features have remained bogged down in the bureaucracy for years while administrators conduct further analyses in hopes of avoiding judicial reversal.[34]
— Procedures for involuntary commitment of mentally ill individuals have become so demanding and complex that many police and hospital personnel refrain from initiating the commitment process even when they think that it is fully warranted.[35]

— The Superfund program generates so much time-consuming litigation to allocate responsibility among former chemical waste disposers that, "after 10 years of operation, only sixty-three of the more than twelve hundred National Priorities List sites had been cleaned up."[36]

DIVISIVENESS

Adversarial legalism has a corrosive effect on personal and institutional relationships. Physicians inevitably come to regard certain patients as potential medical malpractice claimants. When a regulatory inspector and a regulated enterprise become locked in an adversarial posture, the cooperation and exchange of information so essential to effective regulation is cut off.[37] When regulatory rule making is only a prelude to litigation, contending interests are more prone to exaggerate or minimize risks and to suppress or distort information that weakens their position.[38] Steven Kelman argued that "adversary institutions fail to create any relationship among the parties to a policy disagreement. Participants in adversary institutions remain separate individuals, physically proximate only in order to argue before a third party. They do not talk to each other."[39]

Finally, adversarial legalism, by making legal processes costly, complex, uncertain, frustrating, and threatening, probably tends to alienate citizens from the law itself, eroding respect for lawyers, courts, and active government. Empirical attitude data are lacking, but it is noteworthy that, during the 1992 American presidential campaign, candidates easily could elicit enthusiastic applause from general audiences simply by criticizing the American legal system.

ON THROWING OUT THE BATHWATER AND KEEPING THE BABY

Yes, the reader might think, adversarial legalism does entail significant costs in some settings. But isn't that a necessary by-product of the controls needed to achieve justice? One could argue that complex rules, tough penalties, legal rights to challenge administrators, and adversary procedures are quite appropriate for a society like ours—where citizens are more mobile, individualistic, and culturally diverse than in Western Europe or Japan; where informal social controls are weaker; where citizens are less deferential;[40] where entrepreneurs resist regulatory restrictions[41] and where sluggish, politically divided legislatures and bureaucracies often fail to address social problems and injustice. From this perspective, isn't adversarial legalism just an unfortunate but relatively minor side-effect of a generally desirable system, like the pollution emitted by an electrical power plant?

It is difficult to answer such questions definitely, just as it is hard to know precisely when the emissions from scores of power plants add up to a serious environmental problem. Yet one can try to imagine responsive governance without so much litigation. One way to do so is to look more closely at both the mechanisms and the causes of adversarial legalism—as in the following case study.

Dredging Oakland Harbor: Adversarial Legalism in Action

Until recently, seas and harbors were used as free disposal sites for sewage sludge, garbage, and chemical wastes. Regulatory officials and environmentalists had little input into port expansion decisions, even though dredging and disposal operations often destroy the habitats of bottom-dwelling mollusks and crustaceans and have other harmful environmental consequences.[42] In response to these concerns, during the late 1960s and early 1970s, important environmental protection and land use laws were enacted. Today, the legal structure governing harbor expansion is as follows:

1. *The environmental impact statement process:* The U.S. Army Corps of Engineers is the permitting authority for harbor dredging. Pursuant to the National Environmental Protection Act (1969), dredging projects cannot be initiated until the Corps has written and circulated a comprehensive analysis of all potential environmental impacts as well as methods of mitigating unavoidable adverse consequences.

2. *Focused environmental laws/specialized regulatory watchdogs:* The Corps, in turn, is regulated by other governmental bodies. Before issuing a dredging permit, the Corps must consult with the U.S. Fish and Wildlife Service, the National Marine Fisheries Service, the relevant state department of fish and game, the U.S. Environmental Protection Agency, the state agency charged with protecting water quality, and the relevant state coastal zone management agency. Each of these agencies is expected to object to or block dredging projects that fail to meet the legal standards in the specific environmental statute the agency is bound to enforce.

3. *Public participation:* Most of the relevant studies and plans must be made available for public review, and the Corps must conduct public hearings in which the voices of locally affected interests—including municipal officials, commercial fishermen, neighborhood groups, and environmental advocates—can be heard.

4. *Judicial review:* To ensure that the Corps and the relevant regulatory officials will conduct comprehensive, factually accurate, environmentally sensitive analyses, judges are given a powerful "fail-safe" role.

Citizens, local politicians, or environmental advocacy groups who think that the Corps or any of the other relevant agencies have not fulfilled their statutory responsibilities can seek judicial review before any additional steps are taken.

NEGOTIATING THE LEGAL MAZE

In November 1984, the Corps of Engineers completed a cost-benefit analysis and an environmental impact statement (EIS) concerning the Port of Oakland's proposal to deepen the harbor; in 1986 Congress authorized funding. However, California regulatory agencies suggested that fisheries and water quality would be harmed if the seven million cubic yards of dredged sediments were dumped at the planned site— near Alcatraz Island in San Francisco Bay. The Corps of Engineers prepared a supplementary EIS that disputed the agencies' arguments. But the state agencies had legal power to block bay disposal; hence, the Corps selected an ocean disposal site (designed 1M), fifteen miles from the Golden Gate; the added distance would double dredging costs to $39 million. The EPA, however, refused to authorize use of the 1M ocean site. Citizens for a Better Environment threatened a lawsuit challenging the Corps' supplementary EIS and demanding disposal beyond the edge of the Continental Shelf, 50 miles out to sea.

In January 1988, Port of Oakland officials brought together representatives from the various regulatory agencies, environmental groups, and fishing organizations. Compromise was elusive. The Corps argued that, since there were no demonstrated environmental problems associated with disposal at 1M, it could not endorse disposal at more remote and more expensive ocean sites. EPA and U.S. Fish and Wildlife officials said they were legally precluded from accepting 1M without further research showing that it was environmentally preferable to more distant, deeper ocean sites. In March 1988, EPA and Corps of Engineers officials in Washington, D.C., made a political decision: since fishery interests were likely to sue and delay the project if 1M were used, a different ocean site (B1B) should be used for the first 500,000 cubic yards of dredged material (except for material from a clearly contaminated area); this phase I dredging scheme would make the channel just deep enough to accommodate the larger ships. Citizens for a Better Environment and the Pacific Coast Federation of Fishermen endorsed this solution. Port of Oakland officials made arrangements for the dredging and transport of sediment to the B1B site, which was twice as deep as 1M but also twice as far—and hence 50 percent more costly.

Where access to court is easy, however, compromise is unstable. In mid-April 1988, the Half Moon Bay Fishermen's Marketing Association

(HMBFMA), alleging that dumping at B1B would disrupt a valuable fishery, brought suit in federal court, arguing that the Corps' supplementary EIS concerning B1B was inadequate; that using B1B would violate the Marine Protection, Research and Sanctuaries Act; and that HMBFMA had not had adequate notice to request a public hearing. On 5 May, the federal trial judge denied HMBFMA's request for an order prohibiting dredged. HMBFMA immediately appealed. The Ninth Circuit Court of Appeals first issued a restraining order but on 12 May, despite its expressed misgivings about the quality of the EIS, dissolved the stop order. Port officials ordered the dredging to commence; harassed by fishing boats, barges dumped the first loads of sediment at B1B.

On 16 May, Half Moon Bay fishermen dumped a ton of fish heads at the Port of Oakland.[43] On the same day, a San Mateo County Superior Court judge, acting in a suit filed by the HMBFMA and the County of San Mateo, ordered a halt to the dredging. The dredging permit had been issued, the court held, without a requisite certification from the California Coastal Commission that the project was consistent with its coastal development plan, which included enhancement of fisheries. (Actually, the Coastal Commission long before had been given notice of the project but had not informed the Port of Oakland or the Corps that it thought "consistency review" was legally required.) But on 15 July 1988, a state appellate court rejected the Port's appeal of the lower court's restraining order.

Port of Oakland officials, under increasing pressure from shipping lines, were still paying for rental of expensive dredging equipment in case the injunction should be lifted. They had expended huge sums enlarging train tunnels in the Sierra Nevada, buying larger cranes, and building new intermodal transfer facilities, all in order to handle large ships as efficiently as did competing ports. In August 1988 the Port announced a plan to barge the first 440,000 cubic yards of sediment to a Sacramento River Delta site, where local reclamation officials were eager for diking material. Disposal there would be 50 percent more expensive than taking sediment to B1B. It also would require an environmental impact report (EIR), mandated by state law.

The 400-page EIR was completed in February 1989; it included test data indicating that the project would not significantly lower water quality or adversely affect the environment. Then the public hearing and comment process began. On 12 July 1989, the Central Valley Regional Water Quality Control Board, from which a "waste discharge permit" was needed, accepted the plan, provided that the Port of Oakland would undertake additional protective measures and postdisposal environmental monitoring. But the Contra Costa Water District, downstream from the disposal site, asserted that the EIR contained "incorrect dilution calculations" and expressed concern that heavy metals and salts in the sediment would run off into the delta waterways, violating water pollution discharge regulations. In early August 1989, the Contra Costa Water District and the Port of Oakland each filed a lawsuit against the other, seeking a judicial determination of whether the Port's EIR was legally sufficient. Not until July 1990 did the court decide. It upheld the legal sufficiency of Oakland's plan.

By then, however, Port officials calculated that, after all new regulatory conditions had been met, it would cost $21 a cubic yard to use the delta site, compared to $2 for Alcatraz, $4 for B1B, and $7 for an off-the-continental shelf site. They decided to try again to gain access to San Francisco Bay or an ocean site for Phase I dredging spoils. But the Bay Area Water Quality Control Board prohibited disposal anywhere in the bay. And EPA, fearful of legal challenges by fishing and environmental groups, declined to approve even a temporary ocean disposal site until it could complete a laborious multiyear research project assessing impacts at various alternative ocean sites.

Meanwhile, large container ships could enter and leave the port only at high tide, only partly loaded, with small margins of safety. Shipping lines using Oakland sustained millions of dollars of extra operating costs, and tide-induced delays disrupted the schedules of waiting containertrains and consignees. Oakland began to lose business to competing ports, diminishing port revenues. Employment in local warehousing, stevedoring, trucking, ship supply, dredging, and other port-related businesses was adversely affected. Shipping companies scrubbed plans to expand terminals in the Port of Oakland. In short, *certain* economic costs to the community and to the shipping industry accumulated, while regulatory regimes operated to prevent *possible* harm to aquatic environments.

Finally, in the fall of 1992, six years after the original EIS, state and federal regulatory agencies, under mounting political pressure, authorized partial phase I dredging, deepening Oakland's ship channel to thirty-eight feet—barely enough to accommodate fully loaded larger ships, provided that they waited for high tide. Dredged material found to be contaminated, some 4 percent of the 500,000 cubic yard total, was deposited in a lined upland site. The rest, as the plan returned full circle, was dumped at Alcatraz, probably the least environmentally desirable choice.[44] An EPA decision authorizing ocean disposal for the bulk of the dredging (over five million cubic yards) finally emerged (after President

Clinton publicly urged the EPA to "get on with it") in 1994, but the final, complex disposal plan (which included some disposal in the delta) still could be further delayed by litigation.

THE PATHOLOGIES OF ADVERSARIAL LEGALISM

The legal procedures that structured the Oakland harbor story reflect widely held legal and political ideals—that public policy should be based on rational analysis, attentive to the precise factual circumstances of each case; that meaningful attention should be given to the claims of those who are not politically powerful (such as the Half Moon Bay fishermen); that environmental protection should be given special weight in planning development projects that might cause future harm; and that, to vindicate those values, a variety of interest groups and agencies should be able to scrutinize and challenge official assumptions and judgments.

But in the Oakland case, the procedures designed to protect those values seemed to fall into the hands of the Sorcerer's Apprentice, multiplying themselves beyond control. Consider the operative characteristics of the process, for they provide a full-blown catalogue of the pathologies of adversarial legalism.

1. *Irresolution:* After seven years of debate, there was no authoritative determination about where to put the bulk of the sediments to be dredged or about their likely effect on the environment.

2. *Institutional fragmentation:* Instead of combining their concerns in one comprehensive forum, a cascading jumble of regulatory agencies, private interest groups, and courts were legally enabled or compelled to take *sequential* whacks at the problem.

3. *Legal complexity, uncertainty, and inconsistency:* The process was constrained by a sequence of separate statutory reviews, certifications, substantive specifications, and scientific standards. But for all its detail and complexity, the law afforded no certainty. Three compendious, expensive environmental impact reports, scrutinized through the lenses of adversarial legalism, were stripped of legitimacy; *they resolved nothing.* When one court upheld a regulatory decision concerning ocean disposal, another could be found to overturn it on a different legal argument. One water agency approved a delta disposal plan, but another blocked it in court for a year.

4. *Instability of compromise:* Negotiated agreements, when reached, were unstable. Any interest dissatisfied with the compromise could sue in court, relying on the uncompromising language of the law. Adversarial legalism thus limited the ability of government agencies to build consensus.

5. *Procedural extortion:* Simply by preventing definitive resolution of the issues, adversarial legal conflict shaped the outcome. For more than five years, no dredging occurred. Repeatedly, the Port of Oakland was compelled to accept more expensive disposal plans in hopes of avoiding crippling procedural delays. Until the Port finally dug in its heels, the extortative pressures engendered by litigation and regulation bulked larger than rational economic and environmental analysis in determining where the dredged material would be dumped.

6. *Economic inefficiency:* For more than five years, notwithstanding the law's apparent intent, the social and economic benefits of more efficient transportation and trade were not balanced against but were totally subordinated to concerns about the environment. Adversarial legalism seemed to enable virtually any claim of potential ecological harm, no matter how minimal or remote, to take precedence over development, no matter how beneficial to human beings.

7. *Defensiveness:* Governmental authority and conviction collapsed as officials retreated to a position of litigation avoidance. A Corps of Engineers official asserted that, in harbor-dredging matters, the Corps no longer wants to "get caught in the middle" or "to tell state agencies what to do." The Corps wants local entities—that is, port authorities—to "carry the ball."[45] As if hoping the problem would go away, the EPA refused to designate an ocean disposal site based on the best current evidence, since it was safer to await completion of a multiyear research effort.

8. *Diversion of attention:* In April 1990, the *Exxon Long Beach*, a sister supertanker to the infamous *Exxon Valdez*, laden with fifty million gallons of Alaskan crude oil, ran around on a "high spot" in Long Beach Harbor. Fortunately, no damage occurred; the ship was moving very slowly.[46] In other recent harbor accidents, tons of petroleum did foul the environment. The message should be clear: shallow harbors pose a far larger danger to water quality and marine habitats than do properly "capped" dredging spoils. But adversarial legalism tends to focus attention on only those problems raised by the claimants' legal briefs.

The Oakland case is not unique.[47] A 1989 LEXIS search turned up 123 *reported* cases in the federal courts alone involving dredging and disposal issues.[48] The Port of New York's urgent dredging needs were delayed three years by interagency sparring and a lawsuit over standards, testing, and disposal methods for a portion of the sediment that was tainted with dioxin.[49] In other cases, port authorities, fearful of the costs of further delay, have quickly acceded to any plausible (i.e., not easily rebuttable) claim of environmental harm, investing in expensive mitigation measures to help the project move ahead.[50] Thus, litigation and deadlock are not the only manifestations of adversarial legalism; equally notable are its extortative effects and the resulting increase in the costs of development projects.

The sediments in Oakland's harbor are akin to the New York City garbage that was barged from state to state in search of a dumping ground, encountering in every port the same chorus—"not in my back yard" (NIMBY). The disposal of dredged material, like the creation of a chemical waste storage facility or a halfway house for narcotics addicts, may provide large benefits for the public at large, but also imposes risks or concentrated costs on residents of the neighborhood (or ecosystem) adjacent to the operation. In the United States, proposed highways, solid waste disposal sites, and housing developments often are tied up by lawsuits brought by neighborhood and environmental groups. Frequently, as in the case of the Seabrook, New Hampshire, nuclear power plant, the development project never really loses on the merits, but repeated administrative hearings, research projects, and court appearances drive up the project's costs enormously—and sometimes induce the financially exhausted sponsors to give up.[51]

The Roots of Adversarial Legalism

Must the decision-making process in NIMBY cases be as legalistic, protracted, costly, and insensitive to economic values as it was in the Port of Oakland? The answer, I believe, is "No." Adversarial legalism is a product of a particular way of articulating and implementing public policies—one that invites and exacerbates legal conflict—but it is not the only way to run a government.

FINALITY VERSUS FRAGMENTATION

One can easily imagine another way of handling problems like the Oakland port dredging. Suppose, for example, that the Congress had established a few regional port-planning agencies with broad discretionary authority. Each agency's governing board could include representatives of recognized environmental groups. Agency officials would be expected to meet, in private, with local advocates of port expansion, environmental agencies, conservation groups, and fishermen's associations. They would commission research, taking into account both the seriousness of environmental risks and the social costs of delaying port expansion. The regional agency would attempt to build consensus around the plans it deemed best, but if no consensus could be reached, agency officials would be empowered to make a final decision, not reversible in court unless demonstrably arbitrary or corrupt. Such *discretionary administrative authority to make final and binding decisions* would almost certainly encourage serious efforts by participating interests to reach a negotiated accommodation.

In contrast, the numerous congressional statutes and state laws that structured decision making in Oakland created a *legally constrained, fragmented decision-making system.* The Corps of Engineers, the so-called lead agency, could not make binding decisions about the severity of the environmental harm threatened by dredging or whether it was worth the time and money to undertake additional research. As in numerous other policy arenas, the lead agency's analysis and permit decisions were subject to legal vetoes by other environmental agencies, each bound to give primary consideration to the stringent standards of its own statute.

In addition, as in other areas of American public policy, each agency's authority was weakened by the prospect of *judicial review.* Because the relevant statutes are complex and because judges do not respond uniformly,[52] there is always a chance that a court will decide, *post hoc,* that the agency has not met its legal obligations.

The result has been characterized by Richard Stewart as "a self-contradictory attempt at 'central planning through litigation.'"[53] Indeed, legal constraints virtually prohibit the informal, binding compromises that are essential to planning. In the Oakland case, each law demanded formal legal and scientific findings for each project, viewed in isolation; hence, a California regional water quality agency had no incentive or authority to trade a concession in the Oakland case for a more urgent environmental protection measure in another harbor.

In contrast to the Port of Oakland, the Port of Rotterdam has dealt with far larger volumes of far more seriously contaminated dredged material in an expeditious and environmentally responsible manner.[54] The deadlock in Oakland, therefore, stemmed from a particular institutional structure characterized by fragmented authority, complex and constrictive rules, and high risks of judicial reversal.

Some might object, of course, that a policy-making system that rests on administrative discretion, closed-door negotiations, and administrative finality is not politically or legally feasible in the United States, where governmental authority is so deeply mistrusted. Environmentalists mistrust the Corps of Engineers. Industrial engineers mistrust the EPA. American practice, therefore, is to disperse governmental power among separate, mutually suspicious agencies; to subject administrative bodies to regulation and review; and to guarantee that citizens can challenge the bureaucrats in court. And that is precisely my point: the

legal traditions and structural features of American government create
the conditions under which adversarial legalism flourishes.

SOMETHING CHANGED

As Tocqueville observed, there has always been a tendency in the
United States for political issues to become judicial issues. Still, adversarial legalism of the type seen in the Oakland harbor case did not
become common until late in the 1960s and the 1970s. Before then,
standing to sue the government was limited. Public interest groups
rarely appeared in court. The regulatory statutes of the Progressive and
New Deal eras typically granted administrative agencies broad discretion; detailed "agency-forcing" statutes did not appear until the
mid-1960s.[55] Before then, courts generally deferred to the decisions of
federal administrative agencies and of local zoning boards, universities,
school boards, and prison administrators. Massive class actions against
business corporations and welfare departments were rare. So were malpractice claims against physicians and damage suits against police departments.[56] Both civil and criminal trials were shorter and less costly
than they are today.

Between 1960 and the 1980s, contract and other types of litigation
among businesses became the most rapidly increasing category of federal lawsuits.[57] National expenditures on lawyers exploded, growing
sixfold (in constant dollars) between 1960 and 1987 and more than
doubling the share of gross national product (GNP) devoted to legal
services.[58] In the 1980s, some 20 percent of the approximately ten thousand state supreme court decisions per year involved constitutional
issues, more than double the rate in the 1905–40 period. The federal
courts of appeals in 1980 decided an estimated two thousand cases
involving apparently serious Constitutional issues, compared to perhaps three hundred in 1960.[59]

The period before 1965 was not a Golden Age, of course. It was harder
to challenge governmental and economic power, and power was not
always benign. Regulatory agencies, neither monitored nor pressured by
public interest groups, were often soft on the industries that they were
supposed to control. Citizens, especially poorer citizens, often had little
recourse when highways were thrust through their neighborhoods,
when chemical waste sites were located near their homes, when schools
discriminated on grounds of race, when policemen or welfare bureaucrats treated them arbitrarily. The point is descriptive, not normative:
before the 1965–70 period, adversarial legalism was far less common.

Moreover, adversarial legalism persisted—and in many ways continued to grow—through the more conservative 1980s. It persisted even

as conservative presidents sought to dampen "excessive regulation" and liberal judicial activism, appointing political conservatives to the federal bench and to federal regulatory agencies. It persisted in the face of dissatisfaction among many segments of bench, bar, and public with judicial restructuring of school systems, extension of liability to parties who don't seem principally at fault, high insurance costs, and due process rules that seem to restrict police powers. It might be useful to consider why it persisted.

LEGAL AND POLITICAL CULTURE

Arguably, the increase in adversarial legalism mirrors changes in American attitudes and capacities. Since the 1940s, people have become richer, better educated, and more adept at organizing. Perhaps citizens, especially the less powerful, have become feistier and more legally demanding—quicker to translate grievances into demands for rights, readier to fight city hall and corporations in court.

Lawrence M. Friedman argued that American legal culture has shifted its center of gravity, manifesting a widespread expectation of "total justice." Most Americans, Friedman suggested, no longer accept injury, ill treatment, environmental degradation, or poverty as acts of God or as the inevitable by-products of capitalism and modern technology. To the contrary, they see that capitalism and modern technology create the means to prevent or remedy misfortune—insurance systems to alleviate suffering, sophisticated methods to test for carcinogens, double hulls for oil tankers, better education and nutrition for poor children. If those techniques *exist*, it is unjust not to *use* them. The law, therefore, should require them and establish individual rights to insist in court that the law be obeyed.[60]

Such ideas, Friedman argued, have come to dominate the thinking of many members of the governmental elite—law professors, judges, legislative staffers, lobbyists, and journalists. Hence the expansion, beginning in the 1960s, of legal rights and remedies for people harmed by accidents, pollution, discrimination, economic misfortune, and official unresponsiveness.

While popular demands for "total justice" help explain the demand for more *law*, they do not explain increases in *adversarial legalism*. European governments have led the way in establishing social insurance schemes for victims of misfortune.[61] European "Greens" have campaigned effectively for laws regulating pollution, waste disposal, and nuclear power. But the expansion of legal entitlements and regulation in Western Europe did not produce American-style adversarial legalism. In European countries, fierce controversies sometimes erupt concerning development plans,[62] but they usually are resolved in political and administrative forums, not in the courts, and outcomes rarely are shaped by the manipulative use of legal procedures and standards.

Aaron Wildavsky argued that in modern societies three political cultures contend for influence. Believers in *hierarchy* value authority. They care deeply about order, traditional morality, balanced budgets, national defense, and effective government control of social instability. Economic *individualists*, on the other hand, favor freedom from government control, low taxes, and policies that promote economic efficiency. *Egalitarians* mistrust authority but also believe in economic and social equality, even if it takes governmental coercion to achieve it. Hence they favor redistributive tax, regulatory, and welfare programs, along with expansion of the legal means to compel governments and corporations to ameliorate injustice.[63]

From this perspective, if adversarial legalism has grown in the United States, it is because American egalitarians enjoyed a period of remarkable political success, penetrating the legislatures, judiciaries, law faculties, and news media more fully than did their political antagonists.[64] In Western Europe, in contrast, believers in *hierarchy* presumably are stronger, influencing European egalitarians toward *corporatist* rather than toward litigational strategies.

Wildavsky's argument might help explain why the 1960s and the early 1970s represented a turning point. It was then that the populist, egalitarian spirit had one of its powerful periodic outbursts in American political life.[65] The street demonstrations and the civil disobedience of the civil rights and anti-Vietnam War movements overwhelmed the incremental processes of "normal politics." They spilled over into environmental, consumer protection, and feminist movements, spawning similar advocacy organizations, inspiring ambitious politicians to seek their support through a moralistic, entrepreneurial brand of politics.[66]

It was precisely in these years that strict, "technology-forcing" environmental, health, and safety laws first proliferated and that detailed enforcement programs were mandated.[67] It was then that administrative rule making was "judicialized,"[68] that the Supreme Court most aggressively extended the "due process revolution" to local criminal justice systems, and that many states extended tort liability for malpractice, defective products, and injury caused by government.[69] It was then that judges began to issue injunctions requiring bussing to achieve racial balance in the schools, the deinstitutionalization of mental patients,[70] and the relief of crowding in prisons and jails.

Still, it is not quite clear why legal measures that encourage adversarial legalism have *persisted* even in the face of conservative presidential opposition—and as public concern for social transformation has declined relative to its concern for such matters as oil shortages, inflation, declining productivity, trade imbalances, and international competitiveness.

POLITICAL STRUCTURE

Adversarial legalism in the United States has been stimulated by a fundamental mismatch between its changing legal culture and its fragmented political structure. Americans have attempted to implement the socially transformative policies of an activist welfare state through a reactive, decentralized, nonhierarchical governmental system. It is largely because the United States has always lacked a respected and powerful national bureaucracy that proponents of change have insisted on citizens' rights to challenge and prod governmental and corporate bodies through litigation.

This argument is inspired by Mirjan Damaska's *The Faces of Justice and State Authority*. Damaska formulated a typology of legal processes built on two dimensions. One concerns the organizational structure through which administrative and legal processes flow; the other concerns contrasting visions of the proper role of government.[71]

Hierarchical versus Coordinate Authority

One mode of organizing authority Damaska labeled *hierarchical*, an ideal type toward which continental European legal systems incline. It features a limited number of strong, highly professional, national bureaucracies topped by a central ministerial authority responsible to political leaders. Fidelity to official policies and uniformity of case-by-case decision making are the reigning ideals. Officials are relatively insulated from the potentially corrupting influence of local politicians and politically assertive citizens.

American legal and administrative processes, on the other hand, lean toward what Damaska calls a *coordinate* organization of authority. To limit the potential for tyranny or political bias inherent in central authority, power is fragmented among many governmental bodies, often staffed by locally selected officials. Control is exercised horizontally, through one governmental body's capacity to check another and through citizen's rights to challenge governmental decisions in court.

Thus, in the American criminal justice system, there is no national ministry of justice with powers to direct and discipline front-line criminal justice personnel. Instead, thousands of separate municipal police forces are responsible to local mayors and city councils. Most prosecutors are elected or appointed at the county level and remain free from hierarchical control. Most judges owe their selection to local political party organizations and not to high grades on a civil service exam. Public defenders and correctional officials work in still other, semi-autonomous organizations. Control is exerted by each organization's ability to reject a case pushed forward by another. Juries can reject the prosecutor's view of the facts or even the trial judge's statement of the governing legal standards, for they deliberate in private, free from the prospect of hierarchical appellate review. In hierarchical systems, the dominant role is played by judges; in coordinate systems, the dominant role is played by lawyers, who control the course of factual investigation, evaluation, presentation, and testing of evidence.

Activist versus Reactive Government

Damaska next turned to variations in political culture. At one pole is the *activist state,* dedicated to the aggressive management of economy and society. At the other pole lies a political culture that supports a *reactive state,* expected only to provide an orderly framework for private economic and social interaction; it formulates and implements public policy primarily by resolving conflict among competing interests.

Through the nineteenth century, the United States blended a reactive state and coordinate authority. The central government never developed the large, high-status national bureaucracies created by European states before the advent of mass democracy. Courts shared power with legislatures; they did so both through common law adjudication and through Constitutional decision making that erected individual and states' rights as barriers to governmental regulation.

Activist Policies, Coordinate Structures

In the twentieth century, however, American government, like government in other industrialized democracies, has experienced powerful political pressures to become more activist—to steer and stabilize the economy, to bring about the "total justice" Friedman described. But in the United States, those political demands were channeled through political structures designed for reactive government and decentralized conflict resolution, not for centralized, top-down social engineering. That meant trouble. As Damaska wrote, "a state with many independent power centers and a powerful desire to transform society can be likened to a man with ardent appetites and poor instruments for their satisfaction."[72]

Consider, for example, the 1960s "due process revolution" in criminal procedure. Advocates of this strain of "total justice," appalled by abusive police practices in segregated southern states and crime-ridden northern ghettos, could not readily exert reform pressure on the federal government. Congress and the Department of Justice did not have clear Constitutional authority to impose reforms hierarchically on local police departments. The only viable strategy for change seemed to be a further elaboration of *coordinate* controls. Thus, the Warren Court extended the terms of the Bill of Rights to state and local police forces. It elaborated rules to regulate pretrial detention, interrogation of suspects, searches for evidence, station-house line-ups, and jury selection. Simultaneously, the Court mandated *adversarial* mechanisms for enforcing those new rules. It required states to provide free defense counsel— before, during, and after trial. It required local judges to exclude evidence obtained via searches or interrogations that violated the Court's rules—freeing the criminal, if necessary, for lack of reliable hierarchical control over the blundering or biased constable. The Court also expanded the federal courts' powers to review state court decisions, thus opening multiple appeal routes. The result has been a surprisingly effective but unusually adversarial, expensive, and often confusing way of regulating local criminal justice officers.[73]

Similarly, in the 1960s, explosive political movements demanding transformative civil rights, environmental, antipoverty, and consumer protection policies led to enormous increases in centrally formulated legal norms. Federal legislation preempted less protective state and local laws. At the same time, however, movement leaders were intensely suspicious of centralized legislative and bureaucratic power, which they saw as potentially (or even inherently) corruptible by conservative interests. They wanted governmentally engineered social change but wished to check enhanced governmental power by further dividing it and subjecting it to law. They worked to realize a "judicial model of the state."[74]

Fragmenting Authority

In the late 1960s and early 1970s, political movements and their legislative, academic, and journalistic allies splintered authority in the legislature and in the Democratic party. The power of congressional committee chairmen was decentralized to subcommittees.[75] Campaign finance reforms intensified each legislator's search for independent sources of funding and support. Hence, political party leaders were stripped of a considerable measure of control over their members and over policy formulation.[76]

Advocates of governmental activism also sought to further restrict and fragment *executive* authority. After 1968, the implementation of socially transformative legislation was in the hands of an executive bureaucracy headed by President Nixon's Republican appointees. And bureaucracy, in the coordinate tradition, was open to pressure from regulated businesses, lawyers, and tight-fisted budget office officials. So reformers demanded *additional* coordinate controls—expanded rights for citizens and advocacy groups to participate in, challenge, and seek judicial review of administrative decisions. Statutes began to include more detailed restrictions on administrative discretion, enforceable in court.

In addition, advocates of transformative *federal* legislation faced a decentralized political order that reserved a large policy-implementing role for potentially recalcitrant state and local governments, school boards, environmental agencies, and welfare departments. The reform strategy, once again, was to extend coordinate controls. The Supreme Court required state and local governments to provide due process hearings before cutting off welfare benefits or suspending unruly students. Congress gave citizens and advocacy groups rights to sue state and local government for half-hearted enforcement of federal laws, to sue the feds for inadequate oversight of the states, and to sue regulated businesses that had not been adequately controlled by state and local governments. To sustain such "private attorneys general," government was ordered to pay the lawyers' fees for advocacy groups that won in court.[77]

Conservatives and Adversarial Legalism

Liberal and egalitarian reformers did not have the field entirely to themselves. Conservatives lacked the political power to block or alter the basic goals of liberal legislation, but they too could insist on further legal checks on administration and on the substitution of litigation for governmental bureaucracy. For example:

— Regulated businesses were given the right to appeal Occupational Safety and Health Administration (OSHA) fines to an administratively independent review panel.[78]
— Administrative regulations were subjected to coordinate review by Republican appointees on the federal Courts of Appeals.[79]
— Because conservatives were reluctant to fund European-style public works methods of waste site cleanup, the Superfund statute encouraged a "first-let's-sue-the-polluters" approach.[80]
— Conservative senators' reluctance to fund a federal enforcement bureaucracy led liberal sponsors of the federal Truth in Lending Act to propose an enforcement strategy that relies on financial incentives for private lawsuits against lenders.[81]

Why Adversarial Legalism Continues to Grow

The resulting institutional and legal structure helps explain the persistence of adversarial legalism in the 1975–90 period, when the transformative impulses of the 1960s ran up against stubborn economic realities, budget deficits, and conservative political successes.

The legislation of the newly activist state demanded strict top-down enforcement of centrally formulated standards. In the United States, however, hierarchical administration is repeatedly subjected to lateral legal challenges. Regulated enterprises and municipalities complain to local legislators and hire lawyers to take their cases to court. Local administrators and judges often respond to local demands for more accommodative regulatory decisions[82] or for more restrictive social benefit program decisions.

But then enormous gaps appear between the ambitious law on the books and the law in action. Advocacy organizations and disappointed entitlement seekers file lawsuits and appeals (a coordinate model strategy) alleging administrative infidelity to law (a hierarchical model principle).[83] Legislatures then impose tighter legal deadines on administrators, mandate larger financial penalties for violations, and encourage private enforcement actions.[84] Hence, adversarial legalism grows rather than diminishes.

Similarly, because authority in Congress remains fragmented, legislation becomes more prolix and procedurally complex. Individual senators and House subcommittee chairs add hastily drafted last-minute amendments, further reducing statutory clarity and coherence.[85] Fearful that statutory standards will be eroded by Republican administrators or judges, liberal legislators add amendments articulating more exalted rights and heavier penalties. Conservative legislators add amendments enabling regulated entities to raise technical defenses. Laws end up resembling elaborately constructed arms control treaties between mutually suspicious nations, laden with convoluted but substantively unclear provisions that one side or another can invoke in court to challenge administrative decisions it dislikes.[86] Like multisubject omnibus appropriations acts, impenetrable tax and pension law provisions, and the 400-page Clean Air Act of 1990, statutes become longer but more opaque[87]—and hence more likely to generate uncertainty and litigation.[88]

Interpreting poorly drafted statutes, judges shape and reshape the law according to their own political judgment.[89] Decisions vary from court to court and even across panels of a politically divided federal court of appeals,[90] further encouraging litigation. As laws and special purpose agencies proliferate, so do elaborate interagency review processes (as in the offshore oil and harbor-dredging policy areas), giving rise to more legal disputes. Hence, again, adversarial legalism grows rather than diminishes.

POLITICAL STRUCTURE AND "PRIVATE" ADVERSARIAL LEGALISM

Litigation in the business sector, some studies indicate, has been stimulated by international competitiveness, higher levels of financial instability, and the growing frequency with which business is transacted among firms that do not have longstanding relationships.[91] But there are political-structural forces at work in this realm as well.

The mistrust of concentrated power that fragments American government has long worked to fragment economic power as well. A broad array of governmental policies—embodied in antitrust law, legal restrictions on multistate banking, and legal limits on corporate stock ownership by banks, insurance companies, pension funds, and mutual funds—has banned the industrial cartels and the interlocking, bank-dominated corporate families that dominate the private sector in countries such as France, Germany, and Japan.[92] Such overarching financial and corporate organizations provide hierarchical, nonlegalistic mechanisms for resolving business conflicts and for responding to economic losses.[93] Similarly, American business corporations, inhibited by antitrust laws, are not bound together in the industrywide employers' associations and multiindustry federations that play a large political governance and conflict management role in many European countries.

The American economy, therefore, is generally more open and more competitive than are European (and Japanese) capitalist systems. There are many more small—and financially vulnerable—banks and other financial intermediaries. Corporate finance is more dependent on public stock offerings, more open to new financiers—and more vulnerable to opportunistic, litigation-triggering behavior. American corporate finance and governance are pervaded by arms-length contractual relationships, negotiated by lawyers. Compared to hierarchical corporate systems, disagreements (and declines in earnings) in the United States are more likely to be dealt with by "exit" rather than "voice," and relationships ended by exit are more likely to result in litigation.

Consequently, in recent years, when intense international competition and volatile capital flows hit the American economy, there were fewer hierarchical structures to absorb and manage them. America experienced more hostile takeovers, more innovative and risky modes of financing, more radical and rapid corporate restructurings—all of which could (and did) lead to financial trouble and hence to conflict. New forms of litigation emerged or became more prevalent—barrages of law-suits designed to foil hostile corporate takeovers or leveraged buyouts;[94] class actions, based on claims of securities fraud, against virtually any corporation whose new stock issue declined in value;[95] antitrust law counterclaims against parent corporations seeking to terminate a fran-chise; fraud suits by disappointed real estate investors; trade secret suits against departing employees and their new employers.[96]

Private sector adversarial legalism also has been stimulated by the "mismatch" mentioned earlier: the confluence of (1) rising popular de-mands for security against misfortune and (2) a fragmented, decentral-ized governmental system that is more attuned to the style of a limited, "reactive" state. In Western European democracies, injured persons and their families turn to social insurance programs. Their medical bills are taken care of by national health care systems. Their lost earnings are taken care of by generous disability programs mandated or paid for by government. There is usually not much left to sue for.

In the more reactive American state, however, the provision of medi-cal care and disability insurance is entrusted to a highly decentralized private sector.[97] It is plausible to suspect, therefore, that the willingness of American judges and juries to expand tort liability in the 1960s and 1970s reflected the absence of a government program to compensate accident victims for their medical expenses and lost earnings. And, because loss replacement through the liability system is based on proof of fault (and promises potentially large payments for noneconomic suf-fering as well), it triggers hard-nosed resistance by insurers, exaggerated claims, and adversarial legalism. Similarly, because of the country's reliance on competitive, private insurance markets rather than on *so-cial* insurance, there are far more controversies about the limits of in-surance coverage and more lawsuits about alleged fraud or bad faith by insureds and insurers.[98]

This same disposition toward decentralized institutions also helps explain the prevalence of adversarial legalism in American labor rela-tions. Compared to the United States, Western European governments generally provide much stronger legal protections for workers—restrictions on dismissal without demonstrable just cause; high mini-mum wages; generous retirement pensions, termination pay, holidays, and personal leave allowances; and, in some countries, extension of the wage levels established in union-negotiated labor contracts to all work-ers in the industry, union members or not.[99] Consequently, differences in wages, benefits, and protections between union members and non-members and between "unionized" employers and "nonunion" em-ployers are far smaller than in the United States.[100] Labor markets in

Europe tend to be more sluggish, payroll taxes are higher, and unemployment often is higher, too. But there is less occasion for adversarial legalism.

American workers desire security as well. But American employers, since they are not uniformly bound by centrally formulated laws or nationwide agreements, have greater incentives to curtail benefits in order to compete more effectively. Thus, despite declining union membership in the United States, adversarial legal contestation concerning union elections has increased dramatically. As union membership has plunged, workers' demands for security, difficult to realize through national legislative action, have found expression in new *judicial* doctrines limiting dismissal without "just cause" and in increased civil litigation alleging unfair firing or discrimination.[101] Moreover, since the United States relies far more heavily than do European countries on a decentralized system of company pension plans to supplement the Social Security system, the American retirement regime is characterized by financial instability, mismanagement, and complex regulatory rules—and hence by more legal contestation concerning pension security—than are the more centralized, tax-funded retirement regimes of other countries.

Conclusion

Adversarial legalism arises from a vicious circle. Americans want government to do more. But government is mistrusted. So Americans seek to achieve their goals by demanding more of government while controlling it still further—and suing for damages when they don't get what they want. Legislatures and courts mandate new goals, new benefits, and new protections. Yet bureaucracies are constrained by formal requirements and buffeted by threats of litigation and judicial review. And litigation, as a mode of policy implementation and dispute resolution, is costly, slow, and erratic. Courts are clogged. To avoid the costs of litigation, valid claims and valid defenses must be foregone or compromised. Many violations of law go unpunished.

In this harried condition, government seems doomed to fail—incapable of living up to the demands imposed on it, bogged down in costly disputes or in legal defensiveness. Perceiving governmental failure, public cynicism grows and governmental authority is diminished even further. Meanwhile, those seeking to achieve their ends through government feel compelled to arm themselves with lawyers, simply because the opposition is likely to do the same.

Increasingly, scholars are calling for less litigious ways of solving problems, making public policy, and resolving disputes. Many of the solutions discussed suggest the need to reverse the antiauthority spiral: if we want less adversarial legalism, we will need to find ways to reconstitute governmental authority.

Some legal scholars, for example, call for an administrative process based on discussion and debate, a search for shared values, a spirit of compromise and cooperation. They criticize a body of administrative law that squeezes policy making through a courtlike litigational mold. Instead, they call for decision-making methods that foster "public deliberation" and informal negotiation of regulatory rules among contending interests.[102] In social benefit programs, some scholars suggest, the adversarial assertion of due process rights should give way to mechanisms designed to support a "dialogic community" between administrators and beneficiaries.[103] Administrative law, Mashaw argued, should focus less on judicial review and more on building and supporting administrative competence.[104]

Cross-national studies of administrative rule making and implementation point in the same direction. Western European regulatory agencies, Badaracco demonstrated, avoid adversarial legalism because they have the final say. The laws give them broad discretion. Their decisions, absent major misfeasance, are not usually reversible by courts. They meet informally, privately, and repeatedly with a relatively small network of interest group representatives who, to retain influence, must develop a reputation for integrity and reasonableness. The participants, lacking any escape route to the courts or to individual legislative allies, know that the agency's decision, if the interest groups cannot agree, will be final; hence, they are compelled to bargain seriously, to reach compromises on scientific issues, and to balance regulatory values against compliance costs. The "dialogic community" arises because the law fosters, rather than undermines, "administrative finality."[105]

Corporatist policy-making structures have their own deficiencies, of course, Compared to adversarial legalism, they are less powerful guarantors of some important values—contestability of expert opinion and official plans, openness to a wide array of opinions and intersets, sensitivity to individual rights. But in the United States, merely to *discuss* corporatist models stimulates great suspicion. If administrative discretion and closed-door negotiations are to supplant legal constraint and review, Americans ask, how can we be sure that discretion will not be abused? How can we be sure that the politically weak will not be overwhelmed by the politically or the economically powerful, or that the Army Corps of Engineers will not revert to environmental insensitivity, or that regulators will not be captured by the regulated? In a disbelieving age, the diminution of adversarial legalism seems to require magic: the generation of faith in the competence and public spiritedness of governmental authority.

Similarly, scholars have begun to propose radical surgery on the extravagantly costly and often unjust tort law system. European social insurance models again provide an interesting perspective. Thus, some American scholars have argued for comprehensive "no-fault" self-insurance plans (as contrasted with the watered-down versions enacted by lawyer-dominated state legislatures) and for replacing tort actions with public programs; basic losses would be compensated without regard to the injured person's or the injuror's fault.[106]

Here too, however, many Americans (led by, but not limited to, members of the Trial Lawyers Association) are skeptical.[107] Isn't it likely, they warn, that government compensation will be eroded by budget pressures? (Workers' compensation benefits in many states often have been capped at very low levels). If the tort laws threat is diminished, can we expect that dangerous activities will be deterred by government regulators (or government-set "injury taxes")—especially since regulatory agencies often are weakened by budgetary and political pressures? Again, reducing coordinate controls, to use Damaska's terminology, seems to require greater faith in governmental reliability—and more willingness to fund and train a truly professional civil service—than American citizens and their legislative representatives have ever been able to muster.

But this need not always be the case. Deadlock sometimes generates institutional changes, designed to make progress on particular problems. Learning from the Port of Oakland's experience, Port of Los Angeles officials have built a multiagency, multicity forum for negotiating port expansion plans. To avoid the delays of litigation, regulatory agencies constantly try new ways of forging consensus on particular regulatory standards and methods of implementation. It would be risky to wager that twenty years from now American procedures for compensating injured motorists will be as litigious and wasteful as the current tort system. And increasing awareness among policy analysts and policy makers of the costs and causes of adversarial legalism may lead, here and there, to a conscious effort to find a less costly and more effective system of policy making and implementation.

Taxing and Spending

Policy Models and Political Change: Insights from the Passage of Tax Reform

TIMOTHY J. CONLAN
DAVID R. BEAM
MARGARET T. WRIGHTSON

One of the most enduring criticisms of American government has been its seeming inability to respond quickly and responsibly to important policy issues of the day. Reflecting an eighteenth-century commitment to limited government and based upon an elaborate system of checks and balances, our government seems designed to encourage caution and delay. That certainly was the concern of critics in the early 1960s, when James MacGregor Burns warned about the dangers of "deadlock and drift."[1] More recently, charges that the government is in a condition of "stalemate," "delay," and "gridlock" have grown even more frequent, leading some analysts to renew calls for constitutional reform.[2]

The enactment of policies that pit the interests of the broad, unorganized public against those of concentrated, highly organized special interests is deemed particularly difficult. Tax policy seemingly exemplifies this problem, as the tax-writing committees of Congress have presided over a massive proliferation of credits, deductions, and exemptions thought to benefit such interests at the expense of both the taxpaying public and the integrity of the tax code itself.[3]

This pattern of tax policy making seemed so deeply entrenched that enactment of comprehensive income tax reform was almost universally considered impossible before the passage of the 1986 Tax Reform Act (TRA). In early 1985, political scientist John Witte rightly declared that "there is nothing, absolutely nothing in the history or politics of the income tax that indicates that any of these [contemporary tax reform] schemes has the slightest hope of being enacted in the forms proposed."[4] Reform proposals were "doomed to failure," economist David G. Davies concurred in 1986.[5] Yet the TRA passed both houses of Congress by wide margins and was signed into law by Ronald Reagan on 22 October 1986.

This unexpected outcome offers insights into recent changes in the political system that have made such nonincremental policy reforms easier than is generally recognized. The 1986 tax bill was not a typical case of legislative enactment, but it was a "hard" case—an archetype of the institutionalized barriers to fundamental policy change. Its adoption suggests that American government has become less rigid and less prone to the Madisonian stalemate that has long worried political commentators.

The tax reform story also has important implications for two conventional theories that structure so much of our understanding of political behavior and policy making. In particular, acceptance of this far-reaching legislation in the face of powerful organized opposition clearly contradicts the view that policy making is chiefly a process of adjustment among contending groups. The basic structure of tax reform did not reflect the balancing of group pressures, nor did it demonstrate the cautious, incremental changes of law that normally accompany such pluralist politics.

Neither did the TRA's adoption exemplify the standard model of presidentially led policy reform. Politically, this sweeping legislation was not the result of a powerful president's success in mobilizing a partisan majority on behalf of a popular cause. On the contrary, its enactment was propelled by a process of interparty competition, in which leaders in both parties sought to outbid each other for the right to claim the mantle of reform.

Equally important were a trio of actors who have come to play an increasingly prominent role in contemporary American politics. These include experts and professionals, who are able to craft persuasive policy ideas that alter the terms of political debate; political entrepreneurs, who are adept at hawking such ideas in the political marketplace; and the news media, whose sustained attention to issues can transform the audience, scope, and terrain of political contests.

In short, the enactment of the Tax Reform Act challenges scholars and critics to reconsider conventional theories of politics and policy making. The politics of tax reform offers insights, not only into tax policy, but also for the adoption of other unanticipated policies from environmental protection to immigration reform to deregulation. Collectively, the enactment of such nonincremental policies helps to illuminate evolving changes in the policy process itself.

Explaining the Adoption of Tax Reform: Two Traditional Models

POLITICS AS USUAL: THE PLURALIST-INCREMENTALIST PERSPECTIVE

In Washington, interpretations of "politics as usual" typically employ a "pluralist-incrementalist" perspective. Pluralism views policy making as a process of adjustment among contending organized interests. Politicians assume the role of brokers, and legislatures essentially "referee the group struggle," ratifying interest group victories and defeats in statutory form.[6]

The theory of incrementalism, to which pluralism is often wedded, emphasizes outcomes as well as processes. It recognizes that most new policies involve only small departures from their predecessors, in part because no individual can rationally evaluate all the means to multitudinous ends. Incrementalism also has a strong political rationale, however, as incremental change is normally the path of least resistance when there is a pluralistic distribution of power. Because the existing allocation of benefits should conform to the allocation of political influence, any attempt to revise policy dramatically would spark heated opposition.

The traditional pattern of U.S. tax politics has been a variant of this pluralist-incrementalist model.[7] Although the federal income tax has grown enormously in fiscal importance and complexity since 1913, it has not changed in basic structure, and proposals to alter it fundamentally have never advanced far. Further, the creation and expansion of tax preferences, which is the most obvious trend, is typically attributed to the influence of organized groups.[8]

Traditional interest group politics can hardly explain the TRA's enactment, however. Indeed, the anticipated and actual opposition of organized interests was a principal source of the pessimism about its political prospects. According to the familiar logic of the "free rider" problem, only narrow interests find it economically profitable to organize and expend significant resources to influence policy. The public interest tends to be underrepresented because, as Davies argued, "taxpayers remain rationally ignorant of tax matters" owing to the high costs of participation. For this reason, he stressed that small but powerful organizations hold tax-writing committees as "virtual prisoners."[9] Other observers, noting that committee members were recipients of unusually large political action committee (PAC) contributions, agreed that the bill "is likely to go no place, and the reason is that all the groups that benefit from the current system are all big contributors."[10]

Such predictions proved wrong. Though the TRA was heavily lobbied for almost two years, the combined efforts of thousands of well-
organized, well-heeled opponents failed to block or even greatly alter
the outlines of this landmark legislation. "This tax bill is really a testa-
ment to the limitations of special interest groups," observed Ways and
Means Committee member Tom Downey, expressing the view shared
by virtually all of those engaged in the process. "They were annihilated.
They took a beating the likes of which I could not have imagined before
it occurred."[11]

Rather than dominate the politics of tax reform, interest group politics and pluralist bargaining were confined to secondary or supporting
roles in the tax reform drama. Even when provisions affecting large
constituencies or well-organized groups emerged relatively intact, tax
reform gave new meaning to the concept of "winning." Whereas past
legislative victories earned expansions of tax benefits, winning on the
TRA mostly meant reducing the anticipated damage.[12]

At certain times, a pluralist bargaining strategy was employed by
institutional leaders to move the process along. For example, then-
Treasury Secretary Baker made interest group accommodation the hallmark of the administration's second draft bill, dubbed "Treasury II."[13]
Baker thought instinctively in terms of coalition building and opened
the doors of the once-secret Treasury process to groups of every stripe.
The initial proposal, Treasury I, "was probably very good tax policy," he
acknowledged, "but it had little if any chance of being enacted."

Congressional leaders, too, blended reform ideas with group demands to produce legislation uniquely structured to pass their respec-
tive committees and chambers. After a near brush with failure, Ways
and Means Committee Chairman Rostenkowski made key concessions
on provisions crucial to House Democrats and allowed committee
members to carve up portions of the pie to their own liking. Similarly,
Senate Finance Committee Chairman Packwood's unsuccessful first
attempt to develop a reform bill testified to the power of committee
members' alliances with various constituencies and interest groups.
After pluralistic politics collapsed in failure, Packwood successfully
gambled on a radical reform plan—but only on the individual side of the
tax code. The committee still deferred to powerful interests on the
corporate side.

In such instances, pluralist bargaining assuredly helped move tax
reform forward and restricted the scope of legislative change. However,
this bargaining was different in scope and character from that observed
in ordinary tax bills or predicted by pluralist-incrementalist theories. It

did not provide the motive force behind reform legislation, nor did it define the act's contours. Pluralistic coalition building simply offered side payments designed to make congressionally unpopular legislation passable. Furthermore, many of these group victories did not survive: thanks to scathing press criticism, the excesses of group bargaining and accommodation often to led to their undoing. The fiscal requirements of the conference committee process also left little room for accommodating interest groups. What was devised as final legislation was not as kind to Democratic constituencies as was the House bill nor as kind to corporations as was the Senate's.

In overall character, then, the TRA was neither pluralist in tone nor modest in its departures from existing law. As one major accounting firm observed, "the magnitude of change cannot be overstated."[14] Most notably, corporations lost tax benefits totaling an estimated $120 billion over five years. The losers comprised a virtual "Who's Who" among the economic interests that traditionally shaped tax policy, including real estate, heavy industry, large banks, casualty insurance, defense contractors, and multinational corporations. In contrast, the clearest "winners" in the tax reform process were the poor, six million of whom were removed from the rolls. Though benefiting from the TRA, this large and poorly represented interest in no way was responsible for it.

How, then, to account for these unexpected outcomes? In part, they must be attributed to unique characteristics of the tax reform process. The TRA was adopted during a period of concern about large and seemingly intractable federal deficits. The resulting need to produce a "revenue neutral" bill transformed the traditionally distributive politics of taxation into a redistributive battle royale. Gaining protection for a favorite preference meant robbing provisions that benefited some other group. This made coalition building far more difficult because it virtually guaranteed organized opposition. As then-Assistant Treasury Secretary Manuel Johnson said, "The whole strategy was to create a zero sum game between special interests and the average taxpayer."

At other key points, organized interests were shut out or kept off balance by a high degree of secrecy. This was especially true at the beginning—during TRA's initiation in the Treasury Department, when even the White House was left in the dark—and at the end—during the closed and highly centralized conference. Between these events, secrecy often prevailed as well. Ways and Means Committee members rejected their earlier experiments with writing tax law in the "sunshine" and closed markup sessions to the public. Key meetings of the Senate's "core group" excluded members' staffs as well. Although most major interests still had a supportive member on the inside, the scope of the legislation and the speed with which it proceeded limited the value of such connections.

Finally, reformers were assisted by a coterie of groups that supported tax reform. In addition to assorted public interest lobbies, supporters included corporations and industries—such as retailers and electronics —that received few tax subsidies and would benefit disproportionately from lower overall corporate tax rates. The Tax Reform Action Coalition (TRAC) helped inoculate reformers against charges of being antigrowth or antibusiness, and at times it played an important role in rounding up votes. But this coalition did not equal the strength or multiplicity of groups opposing tax reform. Had Congress been a mere referee, the TRA would have lost in a lopsided game.

OLD STYLE REFORM: THE PRESIDENTIAL-MAJORITARIAN PERSPECTIVE

Traditionally, the American system overcomes the obstacles and political inertia that block nonincremental policy changes only on those rare occasions when it resembles the ideal of responsible party government.[15] In what can be termed the *presidential-majoritarian model*, a strong president sweeps into office along with large party majorities in both chambers of Congress. He mobilizes the resources of his office to construct a coherent legislative program, rallying the public and party followers behind it.

Under such circumstances, the nation seems capable of speaking with a single voice and, in a few weeks or months, the legislative "backlog" of an entire political generation may be disposed of. But such periods are usually brief. The presidential party coalition typically succumbs to internal disunity or electoral losses, thereby returning the nation to an era of political stalemate and policy consolidation.

This presidential-majoritarian model might seem to offer a ready explanation for TRA's legislative acceptance. Viewed in broad historical perspective, tax policy has been shaped by intermittent party realignments.[16] Moreover, tax reform itself was placed firmly on the national agenda by a popular president after an electoral landslide. Finally, presidential politics shaped several features of the final legislative package. As in 1981, lower tax rates were Ronald Reagan's raison d'être for reform, and he warned that his "veto pen" was poised to attack any tax hike.

Considered more closely, however, the presidential model does not adequately describe TRA's enactment. First, the president's role was somewhat less grand than the honorific title "chief legislator" implies. Although substantial executive branch resources were committed to pushing the bill through Congress, neither the Democratic House nor the Republican Senate used the White House's official proposal, Treasury II, as the starting point for its own deliberations. And, although Reagan attempted to keep public attention focused on the issue, his personal involvement was episodic and only modestly influential compared with that of past "master legislators."

Second, and more importantly, Reagan never mobilized a partisan (or popular) majority in favor of reform. His party did not control the House of Representatives, and conservative control of that chamber was lost after the 1982 election. Moreover, it was congressional Republicans who were least enthralled with tax reform. In 1985, their mass defection in the House nearly killed the legislation. In the Senate, too, Packwood and most of his party colleagues initially viewed tax reform as a direct attack on their preferred style of government and their most supportive constituencies. For addressing social problems, many Republicans preferred tax incentives to government-provided services. Moreover, few in either chamber ever came to accept the administration's early argument that tax reform would shift voters from Democratic to Republican loyalties. Their own conversations back home indicated limited support and, indeed, growing doubts as the specifics of the proposal became understood. Thus, had the president been forced to mobilize a tax reform coalition primarily within his own party, he almost surely would have failed—as had Jimmy Carter in his own drive for tax reform in the 1970s.

What actually drove reform forward was not a solid Republican phalanx that overwhelmed Democratic resistance, but rather a process of interparty competition in which leaders of both groups first sought to win credit for enacting tax reform and later sought to avoid blame for killing it. Historically and theoretically, such partisan divisions within the government are expected to obstruct action. Sundquist observed that "when one party controls the executive branch and the opposing party [controls] one or both houses of Congress, all of the normal difficulties . . . are multiplied manifold . . . When the president sends a recommendation to the opposition-controlled Congress, the legislators are virtually compelled to reject or profoundly alter it."[17] Yet, divided party control not only failed to thwart the TRA's enactment, it powerfully advanced its cause. It forced Democrats in the House and then Republicans in the Senate to respond to the reform proposals of their partisan and institutional rivals in ways that would never have occurred had a single party possessed unified control.

This process of party competition began very early in the TRA saga. Key advisors in the Reagan White House believed initially that the negative effects of tax reform for Republican constituencies outweighed the economic arguments in favor of it. They consented to the study that produced the landmark Treasury I proposal only because "we were concerned that the other side would be embracing it and using it against us in the 1984 presidential election," as former White House Chief James Baker acknowledged.

When Treasury's study was completed after the November election, there was still no assurance that tax reform would be accepted as a major Reagan initiative. Baker and others in the White House were taken aback by the political audacity of Treasury's plan. In the end, however, the appeal of potential partisan advantage overcame such objections. When the Democratic candidate, Walter Mondale, pledged to raise, not reform, taxes, some Republican activists began to champion reform as a vehicle for party realignment. These political operatives hoped to strengthen the GOPs political base by granting a measure of tax relief to lower- and especially middle-income voters and by assuring that corporations and the wealthy did not escape their fair share of tax burdens. As presidential advisor Mitch Daniels argued, "Passage of tax reform . . . will erase the cartoon of our party as defender of the rich and privileged. The dramatic relief . . . would reflect very well on . . . all Republican candidates for the next generation."

In turn, the administration's eventual decision to make tax reform the centerpiece of the administration's political and policy agenda posed important challenges to Democratic leaders. In terms of policy, the president's proposal threatened to coopt a "Democratic" issue. Former Speaker Tip O'Neill recalled telling Dan Rostenkowski: "Danny, this is *our* issue. You know, Gephardt and Bradley started this, and whatever you do, don't let [the White House] steal [it] on us." His concern was intensified by the need to neutralize the Republican's electoral gambit. Congressman Jim Jones (D-OK) observed that "this whole tax reform measure was . . . driven by politics . . . The Republicans would like to be the majority party and they are going after a class of voters who vote a lot and they want to give them tax cuts. And Democrats have traditionally been for tax reform, and they obviously want to remain a majority party, so they're defensively protecting tax reform."[18]

Although tax reform began as a positive proposal to secure political credit and electoral advantage, the politics of reform soon degenerated into blame avoidance. By the time the Ways and Means Committee began to mark up legislation in the fall of 1985, it was clear that tax base broadening lacked political appeal. Opinion polls showed that the public's concern about losing tangible, specific preferences outweighed the promised gains from lower rates. This realization dampened enthusiasm for reform in Congress, but it failed to halt its partisan momentum. Neither party nor chamber wanted the proverbial "dead cat on their doorstep." Despite weak popular support for specific legislation, legislators feared that a skillful political opponent might turn the issue against them at some later date. As Congressman Tom Downey observed, "This was blame avoidance in part when we went into it . . . If [the Republican] party turns its back on tax reform and [it] loses . . . Democrats [will have] the opportunity to beat them about the head and shoulders saying, Your own president wanted it, it was fair, and you were too interested in worrying about big corporations . . . to help the American people." So it is largely a process of dodging political bullets. [The] party that dodges them best can turn around and use some of those bullets against their adversaries."[19] Such concerns helped sustain tax reform through both chambers, even though the cause never did become popular.[20]

The New Politics of Reform

The pluralist and presidential models are familiar ones. Both have frequently been applied in policy research. Yet neither of them adequately explains the enactment of TRA. Each accounts for some elements of the legislation but fails to capture the entire dynamic.

Instead, the political success of tax reform and its specific legislative features are largely the result of a quite different set of political conditions, actors, and forms of behavior. Some of these have been described above, including party competition, blame avoidance, and the enforcement of revenue neutrality throughout the process. However, other significant contributors include policy professionals and their ideas, political entrepreneurs, and the news media.

If these factors were important only in the passage of tax reform, the TRA would be an interesting but isolated historical curiosity. However, scholars throughout this volume have offered similar analyses to explain the enactment of other significant legislation that is difficult to account for on the basis of interest group politics or presidential party leadership. Like tax reform, many consumer and environmental regulations, as well as economic deregulation for air transportation and other fields, pitted the interests of broad unorganized publics against narrow, highly organized opponents. Given the seemingly unequal sides, "it may seem astonishing that . . . legislation of this sort is ever passed," James Q. Wilson has written. Yet "it is, and with growing frequency in recent years."[21] Viewed in this context, the TRA is simply the most recent, complex, and far-reaching example of what might be termed the the new politics of reform.[22]

THE POLITICS OF IDEAS

This new model of reform politics begins by emphasizing the significance of ideas. Perhaps because American politics has lacked the ideological passions of Europe, it has often been regarded as pragmatic and interest based. In recent years, however, more political scientists have come to emphasize the role of beliefs and ideas as an independent and influential force. Wilson argued that "a complete theory of politics . . . requires that attention be paid to beliefs as well as interests. Only by the most extraordinary theoretical contortions can one explain [recent statutes] by reference to the economic stakes involved."[23] Similarly, Deborah Stone argued that "ideas are the very stuff of politics. People fight about ideas, fight for them, and fight against them . . . Moreover, people fight *with* ideas as well as about them."[24]

Changes in politics, society, and the economy help explain the recent interest in developing this "ideational" model. Party loyalties have diminished, and increasing reliance has been placed on mass communications and "issue politics." Americans are better educated, and the work force has become more professionalized. This growing professionalization is important because experts of various kinds are natural generators and propagators of ideas. When experts and professionals are employed in and around government itself, they can influence policy quickly and directly. Daniel Patrick Moynihan traces much of the War on Poverty to what he termed "the professionalization of reform."[25] Similarly, Samuel H. Beer noted that, throughout the 1960s and 1970s, "people in government service, or closely associated with it, acting on the basis of their specialized knowledge . . . first perceived the problem, conceived the program, initially urged it on the president and Congress, went on to help lobby it through to enactment, and then saw to its administration."[26]

Ideas, Experts, and Tax Reform

The concept of comprehensive tax reform was "invented" decades before the TRA began moving ahead on Capitol Hill.[27] Its most touted features consisted of long-recognized solutions to often-considered problems.

The movement for tax reform rested above all else on the shared conviction of knowledgeable experts in and outside of government that the federal income tax system had grown indefensible from the standpoint of professionally salient values. Although economists continued to disagree about some issues, by the mid-1980s there was widespread agreement on the basic features of an ideal income tax system. It should be horizontally equitable, investment neutral, and administratively efficient. All three goals could be attained by broadening the tax base and lowering rates, as Joseph A. Pechman had demonstrated in the 1950s and as had been more recently emphasized by the "flat tax," Bradley-Gephardt, and Kemp-Kasten proposals.[28]

This professional consensus was especially important because, after the president requested that Treasury produce a reform proposal in his 1984 State of the Union address, there was virtually no further input from or contact with the White House, other members of the administration, Congress, or outside groups until Treasury I was released.[29] This insulation was reinforced by Secretary Regan's idealized approach to the reform process. "Political considerations were irrelevant," he instructed his staff, urging them "to disregard every factor except fairness, simplicity, and efficiency."[30] Consequently, the initial Treasury I plan was an astonishingly pure expression of expert views. Although never formally proposed as legislation, it—rather than current law—set the standard against which subsequent proposals were measured.

Despite all subsequent changes, the basic contours of the TRA—base broadening, reduced rates, revenue and distributional neutrality—were all fixed at this early stage.[31] Expert consensus also accounts for the removal of the poor from the tax rolls, a costly feature of Treasury I adopted without instructions from the president and also without controversy.

It was even choices made by Treasury experts that instituted the sharp business tax hike. Responding to Regan's request for a lower, simpler personal rate structure than the one first proposed by departmental estimators, Treasury lawyers recommended a rise in the corporate tax rate from 28 percent to 33 percent. Though unplanned at the start, the resulting revenue permitted overall individual tax cuts that were subsequently embraced by the president and then sold by the White House as tax reform's principal attraction.

As one would expect, professional ideas were less overtly dominant through the remainder of the legislative process. In Treasury II, the experts' handiwork was reexamined "through the lens of pure politics." Similarly, in the legislative arena, professional purity consistently lost out to the immediate needs of coalition building whenever the two came into direct conflict—whether it be fringe benefits and state and local taxes in the House or corporate provisions in the Senate.

Nevertheless, such politically motivated departures from the professionals' design overstates their influence. Most provisions did not engender overt conflicts between political demands and professional norms. Indeed, the vast scope and comprehensive structure of reform overwhelmed members, leaving an enormous number of issues to be decided by the Joint Tax Committee (JTC) staff. As a top House tax aide said, "Any one of these issue areas—the R & D credit, bonds, accounting, pensions—would be an enormous change . . . Weave them all together and the only way that people could feel comfortable dealing with it was to look at it globally."[32] Finally, by controlling the all-critical revenue estimates, JTC staff exercised life and death power over countless alternatives considered by decision makers. Revenue estimators were the invisible hands in the legislative marketplace, directing choices and often controlling outcomes. As one disillusioned member of the Ways and Means Committee remarked, "If I really wanted to influence the way the actual law was written, I would have applied for a job on the Joint Tax or Ways and Means staff."[33]

Values and Symbols in Tax Reform

In a field as complex as tax policy, it may not be surprising that the assessments of experts were quite important. But that is only half of the story. In the new politics of reform, ideas shape policy in a second, quite distinctive way.

Some have suggested that the power of ideas has an essential normative foundation. For example, Steven Kelman contended that "the wish to choose good public policy, evaluating options against a standard of . . . right and wrong" is "important in understanding the results of policy making in the United States."[34] Such a view suggests that tax reform was enacted because a majority of participants wished to do what was right, and they relied upon experts to define *right* for them.

For some of the participants, this public-spirited objective was paramount. Apart from the tax experts themselves, whose definition of good policy coincided nicely with their professional interests, certain legislators believed that tax reform should be enacted because it was "correct" and courageously chose to subjugate their own electoral interests to its pursuit. But for most, the power of the reform idea was more complex. If a commitment to "doing right" were all that was required, tax reform should have been enacted many times before.

In point of fact, opinions varied sharply about what constituted good policy. Those legislators who lacked the economists' faith in efficiency and neutrality granted a higher value to tax policies that benefited charitable giving, federalism, or economic competitiveness. Others believed that competing priorities, such as deficit reduction, were more important.

The political power of the ideas that propelled tax reform forward often emanated from their symbolic content rather than their intellectual rigor or moral commitment.[35] As Rostenkowski observed early in the process, "Those who are gathering to derail tax reform should recall [Reagan's] knack for dividing complex issues into two simple parts— good and bad, fair and unfair, givers and takers—and asking, "which side are you on?" . . . It's a devastating question that could unleash a potent backlash."[36] Symbolic concerns also shaped the substance of reform proposals, as some features were designed to suit the purposes of propagandists more than those of policy analysts. Regan settled on a three-bracket rate structure of 15-25-35 percent for Treasury I because the original 16-28-37 suggested by staff "sounded like a football signal" and would fail to grab the public imagination. Yet this slight change in enumeration had enormous fiscal consequences, forcing a sharp increase in business taxes and creating net tax cuts for many individuals. The symbolic power of a low, two-rate structure became even more important in the Senate. It was "magic," recalled Packwood; an idea that "intoxicated us," reported Senator John Danforth (R-MO). So strong was this magic that, when a higher third rate had to be created to maintain revenue neutrality, it was done in a hidden fashion, with quite perverse distributional results.

Tax reform is not unique in these respects. As Mark Moore observed,

> Many ideas that become powerful lack the intellectual properties that policy analysts hold dear. Most such ideas are not very complex or differentiated. There is no clear separation of ends from means, of diagnosis from interventions, or assumptions from demonstrated facts, or of blame from causal effect . . . Moreover, it is not clear reasoning of carefully developed and interpreted facts that make ideas convincing. Rather, ideas seem to become anchored in people's minds through illustrative anecdotes, simple diagrams and pictures, or connections with broad common sense ideologies that define human nature and social responsibilities.[37]

However, the case history of tax reform offers striking illustrations of these propositions. For example, poll data suggest that the public was dissatisfied with income taxation but that its understanding of the tax's operation and relative burdens was a caricature of reality. The public's imagination had been captured by lurid stories about wealthy corporations and individuals who paid no income tax, leading them to conclude wrongly that a majority of the rich paid no income tax at all.[38] Further, although the public and experts agreed on the need for action, there were sharp contrasts in their understandings of such key concepts as *fairness* and *simplicity*. The public at large would have preferred a stiff minimum tax that would prevent the avoidance of tax liabilities, rather than the elimination of popular deductions and exemptions for such things as state and local taxes, fringe benefits, and individual retirement accounts (IRAs). Experts, on the other hand, aimed to attain real horizontal equity, which threatened many popular deductions and exemptions which, taken to the extreme, implied such things as the taxation of the "imputed rental value" of owner-occupied housing—a result that surely would have astonished the general public.

Although the symbolic, emotional aspects of tax reform had more influence on the citizenry than on experts, one cannot help but be impressed by the extent to which key figures were won over to the cause by highly personalized representations of tax injustices. Reagan often recalled that, when his movie income placed him in the top marginal bracket of 94 percent during World War II, he and other actors simply stopped making films. For Bill Bradley, simmering resentment at being considered a "depreciable asset" as a professional basketball player fueled his early interest in reform. And one committee member recalled that "Danny [Rostenkowski] spoke very emotionally about his sick daughter and how she paid more taxes than the airline she worked for. He's rough and tough, but I thought there were tears in his eyes."

POLICY ENTREPRENEURS

On many specialized policy issues, particularly those in which the executive branch assumes leadership, professionals alone may formulate policy. But when it comes to nonincremental policy changes, where the formation and manipulation of symbols is important, a second set of actors—who specialize in placing ideas in the political arena—often help shape the agenda. The term *policy entrepreneur* has become the accepted designation for such champions of policy ideas.[39]

Entrepreneurs are not necessarily the originators of policy proposals. More commonly they act as middle men between professional experts, who formulate and perfect policy solutions, and the broader political arena. Entrepreneurs simplify and distill these complex ideas and link them to values accepted by and familiar to the broader public. This is frequently a vital role. Wilson has traced the enactment of much recent regulatory legislation favoring dispersed over narrow interests directly to such policy entrepreneurs. Enacting such laws, he writes, "requires the efforts of a skilled entrepreneur who can mobilize latent public sentiment (by revealing a scandal or capitalize on a crisis), put the opponents of the plan publicly on the defensive (by accusing them of deforming babies or killing motorists), and associate the legislation with widely shared values (clean air, pure water, health, and safety)." In such cases the entrepreneur serves as the "vicarious representative of groups not directly part of the legislative process."[40]

Policy entrepreneurs can be members of Congress, independent advocates, civil servants, legislative staffers, academicians, lobbyists, or writers. Typically, they do not occupy positions of great formal power or visibility. Instead, they gain influence largely because of their expertise, persistence, and skill, plus an ability to develop a symbiotic relationship with political figures who are hungry for action proposals.[41] Policy entrepreneurs also rely heavily on what Wilson described as "third parties," of which the media may be most important, to build support. Unable to steer events by exercising authority, entrepreneurs manipulate ideas and symbols to alter the behavior of others. Often, they seek to "expand the scope of conflict" from narrow, anonymous centers of decision to much larger and more visible political arenas.[42]

In tax reform, experts worked hand in hand with politically junior middlemen who packaged professional concepts for mass merchandizing and then marketed them to those who counted most. These entrepreneurs played a vitally important role in helping place tax reform on the political agenda. Indeed, during the early 1980s, the cause itself was almost indistinguishable from the names of its most noted congressional champions: Bill Bradley, Dick Gephardt, and Jack Kemp.

For such men, the cause was attractive because they could at once pursue their policy ideals and enhance their reputations. As Senator Bradley's tax counsel said, "We had nothing to lose and everything to gain." In contrast, tax reform was more problematic for institutional leaders, who by virtue of their position had much to weigh against quixotic causes. They acted only when circumstances dictated.

The role of these entrepreneurs was quite distinct from that of the tax professionals. None of these energetic merchandisers developed as much expertise as the latter possessed. Indeed, Charles E. McLure, who served as Deputy Assistant Secretary for Tax Analysis in 1984–85, later commented that, "having spent all of my adult life studying tax reform, I did not need to be taught the subject by Bill Bradley and Jack Kemp." But in the arena of political ideas, they contributed something equally important: a politician's ability to seize a useful idea and tie it to a politically compelling problem. They moved tax writing from C-Span to prime time by converting complex concepts like horizontal equity and investment neutrality into powerful populist themes like fairness and economic growth. Aided by groups such as Citizens for Tax Justice, they helped establish the notion that support for tax reform (in whatever incarnation) was synonymous with the general public welfare, while any opposition (even the most principled) could be considered selling out to special interests.

THE POLITICS OF THE MEDIA

The entrepreneur's least costly and most effective resource is publicity. For example, consumer activist Ralph Nader first attracted attention to the issue of auto safety through a dramatic magazine article. Such stories, insider "leaks," and other information disseminated by the press provided much of the foundation for the development of consumer protection programs. Furthermore, as analyst Mark V. Nadel has noted, information provided through the press was "always favorable."[43] Reporters tended to regard consumer advocates as more reliable sources of information than business groups or even government agencies.[44] But the tendency of journalists to favor the "little guy" has other attractions. Lichter, Rothman, and Lichter suggested that the media are increasingly "eager to unmask the hypocrisy and puffery of the [political] combatants . . . by deflating the claims of all sides that their own selfish interests represent the public interest, journalists . . . establish themselves as the final repository of the public interest, . . . [producing] a gratifying self-image."[45]

Without strong media support, the TRA would not have been adopted. At every step along the way, the legislation was prodded by intensive, mostly favorable, often page 1 coverage.[46] Only some of the credit for this media attention can go the entrepreneurs, however. Tax reformers had tried long and hard to enlist the press to their cause, with only modest success. The subject had been viewed as too arcane to merit prominent or extended treatment.

This had changed by the mid-1980s, with a variety of external factors contributing to its newsworthiness. Tax policy gained salience after the California-led property tax revolt of the late 1970s. The supply-side theory and the dramatic rate cuts of 1981 also brought tax issues to center stage, focusing attention on taxes and their relationship to economic growth.

In tax reform, the release of Treasury's proposals gave the media a new and sharper angle, a story in black and white, pitting special interests and the tax policy status quo against the public interest and tax reform. This theme, which Bradley and others had been sounding for years, was amplified first by the purity of Treasury I and later by the president's endorsement crusade. Indeed, the administration's own initial misgivings were countered in part by publicity favoring the Treasury plan, according to aide Eugene Steuerle. The proposal, he recalled, "received uncharacteristically strong attention from the press . . . It was the positive press reaction to the study in December that got [the White House] thinking, "Hey, maybe we *should* make this a political issue."

Treasury I's uncompromising application of economic principles gave the study credibility with the media, while Reagan's subsequent emphasis on "fairness, simplicity, and economic growth" gave journalists the prominent themes they needed for front-page news. Thereafter, ambitious reporters who might normally expect to find their articles relegated to the back sections of the newspaper continued the story, turning the TRA battle into an epic struggle between good and evil—the best political story in town.

This media attention turned tax reform into a "tar baby" for politicos inside the Washington beltway. As a Rostenkowski aide noted, "The press did its share, running pictorials of many of those who voted against us." Later, Bob Packwood became the most visible victim of media crusading when he was singled out as the Senate "bad boy" on tax reform.

Such lessons were not lost on wavering legislators. Thanks to press scrutiny, an infamous Ways and Means Committee vote that gave banks generous new benefits was reversed, resurrecting reform after many had given it up for dead. Similarly, the man unceremoniously dubbed "Senator Hackwood" by a merciless press became born again in a matter of days after he embraced sweeping reform. Thereafter, his committee reported a radical reform bill in less than two weeks as members considered the price for standing in front of a rolling train—or worse, being tagged as one who had derailed it. Populist rhetoric, bright lights, and the casting of tax reform as something members could only be "for" or "against" converted many who would not have been supporters under other circumstances.

LEADERSHIP: THE MISSING INGREDIENT

Tax reform was "the bill no one wanted," Dan Rostenkowski said at one point. And it may be fairly said that, in the beginning, hardly anyone important wanted it. With the exception of President Reagan himself, most institutional leaders came belatedly and with reluctance to the cause.

Yet, if *no one* wanted it, tax reform would not have been adopted. In fact, professional experts wanted it. Diligent but poorly positioned entrepreneurs promoted it, aided by good-government groups and sensation-hunting journalists.

But to attribute the legislative success of tax reform to the role of ideas, experts, policy entrepreneurs, and the press ignores a critical variable. When you ask participants in the reform process what single factor was most responsible for the TRA, they typically emphasize individuals with leadership responsibilities. "Ronald Reagan, pure and simple," said one House Democrat. "If it hadn't been for Rostenkowski, there would have been no tax bill," maintained a high administration official.

Such answers reflect more than Washington myopia. By every indicator, the efforts of leaders were absolutely critical to the enactment of tax reform. It was they who put reform so firmly on the agenda that it could not be ignored; indeed, they escalated the partisan and institutional stakes at every turn. Having decided for personal and political reasons to take action, they became converted to the cause, devoting themselves completely to its success and compelling followers to proceed down a path most resisted.

Tax reform, then, did not just "happen." Rather, this massive legislation was *willed* into effect by men in powerful positions—kingpins, not young turks—who concluded that moving tax reform forward at least *one more step* coincided with the best interests of their party, their institution, their career, or their country.

Beginning, of course, with the president. Reagan's stamp of approval alone made it worthy of serious consideration. Although never fully understanding the legislation he eventually signed and rarely fulfilling his expected leadership responsibilities once Rostenkowski picked up the legislation, his men continued working, mostly around the edges, but on occasion at the very center of congressional activity.

After the president put the issue on the government's action list, it would not have advanced without the backing of other skilled leaders, most notably Rostenkowski and Packwood. To achieve success, they creatively used all of the resources at their disposal. Traditional leadership tools of staff, timing, and distributive benefits were aggressively employed, but they brilliantly adapted the new techniques of entrepreneurial politics to serve their ends.

In the House, Dan Rostenkowski went public in response to the president, urging voters to "write Rosty" in a dramatic TV appearance. He manipulated symbols, seeking to make the House bill "fairer to the middle class." When his committee balked, he encouraged media criticism to bring members back into line. When necessary, he reconfigured his coalitions to build a majority. And finally, by producing a Democratic bill, he compelled the Republican Senate to respond in what had become a high stakes game of partisan oneupmanship.

Packwood, in turn, proceeded when only three of his committee members wanted to proceed. Failing first in an effort to use time-tested methods of coalition building, he aggressively changed strategies, joining forces with Bradley to win media acclaim with a startlingly pure reform bill on the individual side—while pacifying his committee members with old fashioned constituency politics on the corporate side. Like Rostenkowski, he appealed to committee pride and team spirit, as well as electoral self-protection, and used the symbols of reform and the vise of revenue neutrality to push a bill through the Senate floor with virtually no amendments.

This strong leadership role has implications that extend beyond tax reform to reform politics in general. The risks involved in legislation that pits dispersed benefits against concentrated costs mean that entrepreneurs are critically important in placing such issues on the policy agenda. And, on issues of limited scope or on individual provisions of omnibus bills, their efforts can be sufficient to win enactment. But on larger, more controversial legislation, formal leaders have often been central to the adoption of reforms.

Leadership behavior on tax reform had earlier parallels in consumer and environmental protection laws in the 1960s and early 1970s and in airline, trucking, and telecommunications deregulation in the 1970s and 1980s. Although deregulation, too, was built on an ideational consensus among experts and across parties, it was moved toward implementation and enactment by legislators in key committee posts, as well as by President Ford and the heads of the regulatory commissions. The seemingly remarkable willingness of such leaders to turn to embrace a variety of innovative reform causes seems to reflect the pressures of publicity and responsibility that are focused on them.[47] Moreover, in deregulation as in tax reform, leadership competition had a major effect on the scope and pace of legislation: "When numerous leaders in different parts of the government became involved and began competing with one another, policy change occurred very fast."[48]

Conclusion

Tax reform owes its existence to—and illuminates the dynamics of—a new model of reform politics that has appeared with growing frequency in recent years. Yet, although it has become more common, the outcomes of the process are no less surprising in each successful case. "It can't happen here" has been the usual forecast and, in truth, the legislative obstacles to legislation from federal aid to education to environmental protection seemed considerable. But, in these and many other cases, seemingly insurmountable political barriers were overcome.

Some of these achievements can be explained at least in part by the "old" reform politics: presidential leadership, an aroused public, and strong partisan backing. But others fit more closely what is described here as the new politics of reform, emphasizing the role of experts, entrepreneurs, and the media. What certainly seems established, by tax reform and other parallel cases, is that advocates of far-reaching policy shifts now have not one but two roads down which they may travel.

Why is the acceptance of such legislation still so surprising, then? In part, because the pattern of legislative victories appears only across varied policy fields. Within any single realm, historic patterns of behavior and the weight of the status quo typically remain stacked against far-reaching change. When the aggregate of important nonincremental changes is weighed, however, lingering images of "deadlock and drift" seem dated and incomplete.

Such outcomes also are surprising because they flow from a pattern of politics that is inherently less predictable. Traditional interest-based politics is stable because the underlying patterns of interests change only slowly as society, government, and the economy evolve. Ideas, on the other hand, come not only in the form of lasting ideologies but frantic fads. Public moods and intellectual commitments can come and go quickly. Entrepreneurs similarly may switch issues or fade from view.

To some extent, then, the unpredictability of the new politics reflects the increasing individualization of politics, the erosion of more stable political alliances, and the fragmentation of governing institutions. Highly atomized political structures are often erratic. With fewer mediating structures, they can move quickly from stagnation to rapid change and back again.[49]

Ultimately, the tax reform experience cautions against excessive reliance on any one model of the policy process. The TRA process had something to tempt every theoretical taste, as the politics of pluralist bargaining, of presidential leadership, and of entrepreneurial mobilization each contributed at different stages or to different aspects of the resolution of this complex issue.

Indeed, the goal of clarity is better advanced if these "models" are reconceptualized as distinctive *systems of power*, rather than deterministic patterns of action. There is in contemporary American government one system of power revolving around organized and constituent interests, another around presidential elections and parties, and a third around ideas. To some extent, each constitutes a separate "game" with its own rules, resources, umpires, and plays. Yet the nature of the dominant game can change in midplay, with new players added or dropped. Indeed, one test of effectiveness in the political arena is the ability of certain players to alter the prevailing game to their advantage.

Unpredictability is inherent in such a dynamic contest. Yet this more flexible image corresponds well with the character of contemporary power relations. We now have, as journalist Hedrick Smith has written, "a more fluid system of power than ever before in our history. Quite literally, power floats. It does not reside in the White House, nor does it merely alternate from pole to pole, from president to opposition, from Republicans to Democrats. It floats. It shifts. It wriggles elusively, . . . passing from one competing power center to another, . . . gravitating to whoever is daring enough to figure out the quickest way to make a political score."[50]

Because "normal" tax politics operates as a game among interests, involving few but the most attentive, tax reform seemed a certain failure. Here, the advantage lay with the best organized—and against isolated policy entrepreneurs—just as pluralists suggest. To this problem, most advocates and analysts saw only one clear solution: a change in the game to presidential and party politics. Success seemed to require a mobilized electorate, strong presidential leadership, and unified party control of the institutions of government. Past efforts of this kind had failed, however, leading to more pessimistic forecasts.

Nonetheless, tax reform was embraced by President Reagan, giving it a strong push ahead. In the end, however, it was adopted because the dominant character of the game shifted and changed once again. Experts, entrepreneurs, and the media all played important roles, but when a combination of factors led key legislative leaders from both parties to put their reputations and resources on the line, the highly publicized cause advanced from the unmovable to the seemingly unstoppable.

This is not to say that the politics of taxation has become an arena of perpetual reform. To the extent that any fundamental transformation has occurred, it is primarily the result of structural budget deficits and the perpetuation of zero sum fiscal politics. Otherwise, traditional interest groups still exist. Members of Congress still represent their individual constituencies. The use of selective tax incentives to stimulate savings, capital investment, and other forms of economic behavior continues to have political appeal in many quarters. Moreover, the overall levels and distributional characteristics of the nation's tax system continue to divide our political parties.

In short, the success of the TRA did not necessarily produce a fundamental change in the ordinary politics of taxation once the media spotlight was turned off and the entrepreneurs moved on to other issues. Rather, it reflected an important new pattern of politics that can and does reappear in other issue areas when conditions ripen.

Given this perspective, the main lesson of tax reform is clear: far-reaching policy change remains a real possibility in American politics. Without changes in Constitutional structure and despite the proliferation of organized interests, the system has developed sources of creativity and energy that make it capable of mounting seemingly insurmountable political obstacles and bridging apparently unbridgeable gaps of institution and party. These rest with the new model of "ideational-entrepreneurial politics," coupled with the commitment and legislative skills of established leaders. To understand more fully the character of these forces and to be certain that the costs as well as benefits of the political style they typify are recognized are principal challenges of this volume.

The Politics of the Entitlement Process

A A R O N   W I L D A V S K Y

All entitlements are not created equal. If they were, then all programs with entitlement status would keep growing, none would become smaller, and all would fare better than programs in similar policy areas funded by appropriations. But the facts belie such easy generalizations. Appropriations sometimes grow faster than entitlements; some entitlements decline, and some are abolished. Understanding the growth or decline of an entitlement calls for a closer examination of the history and the politics of particular programs.

Entitlements are legal obligations that require the payment of benefits to any person or unit of government that meets the eligibility requirements established by law. Budget authority for such payments may be but is not necessarily provided in advance. Thus, some entitlement legislation, such as the food stamp program, requires the subsequent enactment of appropriations. Examples of entitlements are Social Security, revenue sharing (now abolished), and unemployment compensation. Entitlements comprise the largest single part of the national budget.

Entitlements generally follow one of three trajectories: some programs have grown rapidly, some have stayed at approximately the same level of expenditure (adjusting for inflation), and some have declined significantly or have been abolished. Obviously, entitlements are not an automatic ticket to financial paradise (although entitlement status greatly helps) and being funded through annual appropriations is not necessarily a death knell.

Case studies demonstrate that three factors are involved in determining the fate of an entitlement program: (1) the institutional character of the political system, (2) attitudes toward the program and how these affect the program's treatment, and (3) the design of the program itself. Although the histories of specific entitlement programs differ, the cases are significant in that they offer evidence that government is not encased in frozen inaction. Not all entitlement programs expand, and some even die. Gridlock can be broken.

The first variable affecting program development is the institutional nature of the American political system: a weakened party structure and a decentralized institutional environment have encouraged certain kinds of government action and policy reform. This atomized institutional environment magnifies the role of individual policy entrepreneurs and increases access for interest groups. These factors, in turn, are enhanced by American federalism: by multiplying the number of government offices and officials, federalism increases access and multiplies the number of policy entrepreneurs, while creating complex programs administered jointly by the national and state governments. These characteristics allow incremental and often unrecognized growth in a program and hinder attempts at general reform. Obligation and commitment are not easily rescinded and are guarded closely by the public and by interest groups.

The second factor in the fate of entitlements is the opinion in which the program is held, both by the public and by individual members of Congress. Elements include whether the program is popular or unpopular, the degree to which it is seen as a moral obligation or a government commitment, and the image of the program (regardless of its original intent) as an entitlement. The importance of these attitudes is magnified by the institutional nature of the system. Fragmentation creates high visibility and thus the desire, among members of Congress, to appear responsive to public opinion or to interest groups. This increases the relevance of public attitudes toward programs, both among outside groups and among members of Congress. In effect, the vacuum created by the breakdown in centralized leadership and control becomes an opportunity for influential access by interest groups as well as by individual policy entrepreneurs.

The third factor is the program's design—for example, its linkage to other programs such as Social Security, its mechanisms for functioning and control, and the programmatic incentives that direct behavior. Linkage to popular programs, loose control structures, and incentives that operate toward inclusiveness or against cost control lead to program expansion.

All of these factors tend to work against the cutting of entitlements, but the case histories that follow demonstrate that these factors do not prevent the control of entitlements. Congress is not totally at the mercy of special interests or gridlock.

The significance of the three factors varies. No one factor is clearly more important than the others, and they are interrelated. A fragmented Congress institutes reform, yet these reforms often enhance a program design already open to expansion. Public opinion, reinforced by the access and influence of individuals and interest groups, takes advantage of a fragmented Congress. A program's successful design, in turn, can influence attitudes in Congress and in the general public. In the simplest case, a fragmented government, a widespread favorable opinion, and an incremental and open-ended program linked to another successful program may lead to a program's expansion. Medicare fits this model. Medicaid varies; although it is an unpopular program, its design encourages expansion and a fragmented Congress has been unwilling to take medical care away from poor people.

Other cases, however, demonstrate that reforms are enacted and changes made even when these three forces might seem to encourage expansion. The black lung and the end-stage renal disease (ESRD) programs demonstrate that the three factors, even in conjunction, can be overcome. The black lung program shows that a fragmented system allows a program to be controlled by shifting costs to other areas of government or onto the private sector—a policy that insulates Congress from the political penalties of directly cutting entitlement benefits. The black lung program also proves that Congress has leverage in dealing with powerful business interests and numerous potential beneficiaries.

Congress was also able to contain the growth in ESRD spending by exacting compromises from interests supporting the program. The ESRD program was structured in a way that created its own army of vested interest groups, including physicians and beneficiaries. Congress was able to bring these interests to the table and enact change by providing reform incentives for each interest, leading the participants to support a less expensive system of home dialysis care. It bears repeating: contrary to the popular impression, Congress can stand up to powerful lobbies in the interest of reform.

Some programs are cut or even eliminated. Congress was willing and able to enact significant cuts in social service grants, despite the fact that federalism and linkage to the popular Social Security system encouraged the program's expansion. Although these reforms have had mixed results, they belie the myth of gridlock. The elimination of general revenue sharing disproves the gridlock myth twice: first, an unlikely coalition acted to institute the program in the first place; second, that coalition disintegrated and Congress was able to kill the program. Both the original coalition and its demise resulted from a fluid and fragmented political system.

Popular and congressional perceptions of a program can be of crucial significance in a decentralized system. These attitudes are not limited merely to the program's popularity or unpopularity; an important element of public opinion is the degree to which a program is perceived as an entitlement. This perception may become more important than the program's original design. For example, the popular Head Start program is funded less generously than the unpopular Aid to Families with Dependent Children (AFDC) program. Head Start, as a result of budgetary incentives at its inception, failed to achieve status as an entitlement. AFDC, on the other hand, achieved that status long ago, despite its unpopularity with both the public and many members of Congress.

The food stamp program (FSP) and the women, infants, and children program (WIC) reinforce this argument. FSP's growth has led to skepticism in Congress and scrutiny of the program; WIC, which continues to be very popular, has escaped this scrutiny and continues to grow. Congressional fragmentation, embodied in the committee system, explains the difference in the treatment of the two programs.

Gridlock is not a necessary element of American government. To the contrary, there are many ways in which programs have been changed and even eliminated. Each of the cases discussed in this chapter will be analyzed in terms of the relationships among and effects of, three factors: (1) the institutional characteristics of Congress, (2) popular and governmental attitudes toward the program, and (3) individual program design.

High Risers: Medicare and Medicaid

MEDICARE

Medicare is a highly popular program that has grown incrementally, but the key factor in its expansion has been its design. Medicare's program design discourages attempts to cut or control costs and is marked by the goal of expanding inclusiveness. These design factors, together with popular support and a fragmented congressional system, seriously hamper attempts at reform.

Incremental and unrecognized program growth is a feature of a decentralized governing system. Without an overarching power organizing long-term development and overseeing trends, a program can expand while government officials sit unaware. The Medicare trust fund is a prime example of Martha Derthick's observation that "incremental enlargements" are capable of "obscuring their long-term consequences."[1] Table 6.1 shows annual increases over a five-year period; notice the relatively large total increases that occur over the five-year period and compare those figures to the relatively small changes that occur in any particular year. The maximum tax contribution, for example, climbed from $148.50 in 1977 to $421.20 in 1982, a compound annual growth rate of 23 percent and a total increase of 184 percent over that period. These figures would apply only to individuals whose incomes matched or exceeded the taxable wage base in each year. Nevertheless, for any individual, the annual increments in the tax contribution will have appeared small relative to the total change occurring over the five-year period.

Medicare has two components: part A provides hospital insurance, and part B—the Supplementary Medical Insurance Program (SMI)—covers physician services and other health care services. Like the part A payroll tax, the SMI (part B) premium gives enrollees the impression that they are paying for their benefits.

For SMI, however, general revenues are a significant funding source. When Medicare was enacted, it was expected that enrollees and the government would make equal contributions to the SMI trust fund. Premium rates were to be set annually by the Secretary of Health, Education and Welfare—the only instance at the time in which someone outside of Congress could change financing conditions under the Social Security Act. The Treasury and enrollees did make equal contributions until 1972, when Congress placed a limit on the extent to which SMI premiums could be increased. By this method any increase in the SMI premium was limited to the rate of increase in Social Security cash benefits, and Congress also made the federal treasury responsible for differences between the funds necessary to make SMI benefit payments and the size of SMI premiums.

Then the crisis came. The share of the budget taken by Medicare and Medicaid virtually doubled from 4.6 percent in 1970 to 9.1 percent in 1985. Though the increase in Medicaid spending slowed down by the end of the 1970s, Medicare's costs kept rising, from $6 billion in 1970 to $66 billion in 1985 (Medicaid came to "only" $20 billion in 1985. Before long, fears were voiced that the Medicare Assist Fund Part A would be depleted. In hearings before the House Select Committee on Aging's Subcommittee on Health and Long-term Care, Representative Vandergriff of Texas set an urgent tone for the debate: "I believe that we in the United States face a crisis of potentially catastrophic proportions . . . All too few Americans realize that the catastrophe is near at

TABLE 6.1   Annual Changes Add Up in Big Ways: Medicare Tax Base and Tax Rate, 1977–1982

Year	Taxable Wage Base		Individual Tax Rate		Maximum Tax Contribution	
	Amount	% Increase	Amount	% Increase	Amount	% Increase
1977	$16,500		0.90		$148.50	
1978	17,700	7%	1.00	11%	177.00	19%
1979	22,900	29	1.05	5	240.45	35
1980	25,900	13	1.05	0	271.95	13
1981	29,700	15	1.30	24	386.10	42
1982	32,400	9	1.30	0	421.20	9
(Total)		96%		44%		184%

Source: Figures for the taxable wage base and the tax rate are from Senate Committee on Finance (Staff Report), *Staff Data and Materials Related to Social Security Financing.*

Note: Percentages and tax contribution amounts were calculated from the taxable wage base and the tax rate. Yearly percentages reflect change from the previous year. Total percentages represent the total change from 1977 to 1982.

hand. Medicare is the fastest-growing expenditure in the Federal Budget. The Hospital Insurance Trust Fund will be depleted by 1986 or 1987 . . . Skyrocketing health care costs push the Medicare bill even higher."[2] At the same time, medical care inflation—part quality, part profit—outpaced the general increase in prices by a large margin.

Analysts and politicians alike attributed this inflation to the ability of patients and providers to pass on cost increases to others. Then-Representative Phil Gramm hinted at the problem inherent in a governing system ruled by policy entrepreneurs: "Nobody has a bottom line interest in making rational decisions on the basis of cost."[3]

Republicans and Democrats alike sounded warnings about this cycle of increasing costs. Coming together to enact reform, the usually decentralized Congress realized $2 billion in savings under the first-ever use of the reconciliation procedure in 1980, through such devices as lowering the rates that could be charged by skilled nurses. In addition to raising the deductibles paid by patients under Medicare, Congress slightly reduced payments to states in the 1981 Omnibus Budget Reconciliation Act, allowed states to set up rules that gave patients the ability to choose their source of medical care, and repealed the "reasonable cost" provision for reimbursements. In the 1982 reconciliation law, the

Tax Equity and Fiscal Responsibility Act (TEFRA), Congress further reduced hospital reimbursement for Medicare, cut the government's Medicaid contribution to states with high error rates, and allowed states to charge small fees for certain services in an effort to discourage frivolous use of services.

Within a month after President Reagan proposed prospective reimbursement in March 1983, Congress approved. No longer, it was thought, would hospitals and doctors pass on costs after they were incurred (i.e., retrospectively); rather, they would be paid a fixed price for patients who fit any one of the 467 diagnosis-related groups.[4] Yet costs continued to escalate.

Meanwhile, attitudes favored the program and its noble goals. The two eligibility requirements—those over sixty-five who have contributed to Social Security and any others who join voluntarily and pay a monthly premium—created a strong political base for the Medicare program.

Aside from the twenty-nine million people currently eligible for payments, Medicare also drew support from family members, who are protected against possible financial responsibility for the illness of a parent or relative, and of active members of the work force, who are current contributors to and future beneficiaries of the trust fund. Since medical care for the elderly has come to be generally recognized as the morally correct course, politicians talk about cutting Medicare only at the risk of sounding insensitive and uncaring.

Expansion of the program has, predictably, expanded its support. In 1972, for instance, disabled individuals younger than sixty-five became entitled to monthly disability benefits under the Social Security retirement program, and individuals under sixty-five suffering from kidney failure were made eligible for the Social Security retirement program and the spouse or dependent child of such an insured individual became entitled to hospital insurance benefits. Each of these groups was in some way a contributor to the trust fund and, accordingly, had some type of claim to payments from the trust. Yet other groups, such as the unemployed, have been unable thus far to work their way onto the Medicare rolls.

The program also gained support by being linked to another highly popular program, Social Security. Social Security, approximately four times more costly than Medicare and much older, takes a much larger share of the pie. Individuals tend to identify the payroll tax as "the Social Security tax," and many are more or less unaware of the portion being taken to finance Medicare. The relative attention paid to each of these programs shows up at higher levels as well. Congress usually considers Social Security funding problems to be much more important than whatever woes are suffered by the Medicare program.

The program's design has also played a role in its expansion. Cost-sharing rules, on which Congress was able to come together in the interests of reform, have not controlled demand. One reason is that Medicare's primary goal is to improve access to medical care. Consequently, rather than designing cost-sharing schedules to ensure that beneficiaries do not overuse services, schedules have been designed to ensure that no one who needs services hesitates to seek help merely because of cost-sharing arrangements. Another reason is that both providers and intermediaries have strong incentives not to control costs. For providers, like hospitals, lower costs would mean lower revenues. For intermediaries, such as insurance companies, the incentive is somewhat different. Their interest is to promote good relationships with providers, for insurers have to deal with providers to process their own claims. By facilitating Medicare reimbursement requests, intermediaries maintain positive relationships. Intermediaries certainly have no incentive to lower costs, since the government is paying the bills. Finally, Medicare payments often subsidize private insurance payments. If providers garner higher revenues from Medicare patients, they can afford to charge lower rates to privately insured patients. These incentives add fuel to the high rate of inflation in the health care sector, which, ironically, had been an early impetus for Medicare legislation.

Attempts at reforming the Medicare program have not been very impressive—in large part because of the fragmented institutional nature of the Congress. For example, although food stamp recipients or mothers on AFDC have been the targets of administrative efforts to reduce "fraud and abuse" in benefit provision, the *providers* have been the targets (and on occasion the perpetrators) in Medicare. In the old days, as I know from personal experience, some doctors provided care to poor people at much lower rates than they charged rich people (in my case $2 for the same doctor who charged $10 in his fancy Park Avenue office). It was a good thing, most people believed, for rich doctors to help poor patients. We still think so: Nowadays, the same logic requires doctors to accept reimbursements for poor patients that are far less than they would charge patients who are not on Medicare. Many providers, especially physicians, have left the Medicare program, and the results has been higher costs for the beneficiaries.

My own view is that Congress is looking at the wrong things—wicked providers and other bad actors—instead of probing its own system of financing. So long as huge flows of money continue to wash over the medical care system, costs are going to rise. Attempting to monitor trillions of transactions is futile. Will not hospitals diagnose patients into higher-cost categories? Won't workers choose higher-cost medicine (or pay no attention to cost) so long as insurance is "free"? It would be better to place limits on financial resources. With less money around, fewer or less expensive services would result. Those who dislike this prospect, whatever their other virtues, do not wish to control costs.[5] It is true, of course, that one step in this direction has been taken: tax deductions for medical care, used by middle- and upper-income groups, were substantially diminished during the Reagan administration. But fringe benefits, including comprehensive policies, were not.

The decentralized and fragmented nature of Congress, operating in the absence of an overarching authority to give reforms coherence and long-term attention, means that even congressional action for reform can lead to the continued growth of a program. Medicare demonstrates the simple case: given a fragmented Congress, a popular program, and a program design that encourages expansion and discourages reform, one expects to find growth in the program; we would be surprised not to find it. The central factor here is the interplay between the program's incentives and Congress' fragmentation. The former encourages growth; the latter precludes effective reform. Congress, once unified to *attempt* reform, failed because its own fragmentation crippled its ability to aim coherent reforms at the real sources of the program's problems.

MEDICAID

It is the fragmented nature of the American political system which stands at the center of Medicaid expansion. Federalism creates political confusion and encourages the shifting of blame. This interacts with congressional incentives and popular opinion to hinder reform. The combination of government characteristics and program design acted to overcome negative attitudes about the program.

It would be absurd to try to divorce the structure of the Medicaid program from the federalist structure of American government. These two factors are so closely interrelated that defining one element as the catalyst for Medicaid's growth only makes sense by noting that federalism came first. The nature of the American political system influenced the development of Medicaid, and thus its expansion, more than the design influenced the government.

Medicaid has never been as popular as Medicare. Two factors have made Medicaid an unpopular system: first, the discovery of "Medicaid mills" that provide bad or overpriced medicine, and, second, the belief that, although poor people are sicker than richer ones and should have more medical care, they do not need as much as they are getting. So it is necessary to begin by observing that many people too poor to afford medical care are being helped by Medicaid.

But why has the unpopularity of Medicaid not been translated into comparable cuts? The answer has two parts: first, the obvious alternative to increasing federal Medicaid costs—making states pay more—is very unpopular with state governments and, second, the federal government would rather shift the blame for high costs (to providers or to the states) than limit the spending.

Like Medicare, Medicaid grew incrementally, taking advantage of Congress's decentralization and lack of oversight. Its immediate precedent was the Federal Emergency Relief Act of 1933. Under this act, the Federal Emergency Relief Administration (FERA) was set up to make funds available to states for paying medical costs of the unemployed needy.

Although the FERA program lasted only two and a half years and was not uniform throughout all the states, it exercised great influence on subsequent medical care programs. FERA, for example, emphasized the role of governmental agencies as purchasers of medical care, in contrast to the traditional reliance on volunteer services of physicians and hospitals. And, of course, it set a precedent for increased participation of the federal and state governments in financing medical care for the indigent.[6]

At the state level, Medicaid is a vendor payment system, one of several federal-state welfare programs in which benefits are made available to eligible citizens. The benefits in this case are medical services; the eligible are welfare recipients and poor people; the mechanism is public payment to vendors. This vendor payment mechanism operates as third party coverage. State programs pay bills for services rendered to recipients by health providers. Payment is made directly to providers rather than to recipients.

Like Aid to Families with Dependent Children, Medicaid is a means-tested, residual welfare program. As a residual program, it is intended to pick up the slack when the market and the family do not meet the need. Medicaid requires individual applicants for benefits to demonstrate not only that they are poor but also that they meet certain other requirements (which vary with the state).

At the federal level, Medicaid is a grant-in-aid program; the federal government pays a portion of the cost incurred by states in providing medical care to the poor, the blind, and the disabled. The program is financed by payroll taxes and general revenues. Medicaid is therefore also a bifurcated program: the federal government pays half or more of the money but leaves development and administration of the program to the states. This makes Medicaid not just a single program, but fifty, since the decisions that states make within the federally established framework of laws and regulations determine the character of the program.

The Medicaid program has been able to take advantage of the political relationship between the states and the federal government, encouraging the program to grow. When President Reagan took office, for example, his interest in reducing federal spending carried over to Medicaid. In 1981 he proposed to end Medicaid's status as an entitlement program: that is, federal Medicaid expenditures, rather than grow as the number of eligible recipients increased, would be capped, regardless of how many recipients there were. Most state governors opposed the cap and lobbied against it in Congress. With a federal Medicaid cap, each marginal dollar would have come entirely from state revenues, creating intense pressure to cut state programs, raise taxes, or make up the difference in other ways. Not surprisingly, therefore, the states argued that it was unfair for them to bear the entire fiscal burden because state budgets were already stressed by the national economic recession and because past and continuing federal policies had contributed to the medical cost inflation that the national government was not taking action to curb.[7]

While the states and the administration battled, both the Senate and the House rejected the proposal. Congress took a different tack. It acted indirectly to promote cost containment by giving the states more flexibility to make targeted cuts in their own programs. In doing so, however, Congress did not impose cuts on the program as a whole. In addition, Congress gave states the freedom to offer varying amounts of services to different categories of individuals in the medically needy programs, although certain restrictions still applied.

The structure of the Medicaid program also hindered attempts at reform. Even in an unpopular program, there are constraints against cutting benefits directly. State governments and the federal government both operated under this restriction, and program incentives worked against other types of reform.

Because of the open-ended nature of Medicaid, new fiscal controls cannot be applied through budget limits. States can assert their own fiscal control only by changing their programs—eligibility standards, services covered, and the like. The federal government asserts fiscal control indirectly by enacting laws and regulations that increase or restrict states' options in designing and administering their programs.

States have relied primarily on *indirect* means of cutting benefits. Unemployed adults who still had financial resources were more likely to be targeted for cuts than were individuals who were poor enough to have been eligible for welfare if they had applied. States were reluctant to cut those eligible for welfare because such individuals would simply have applied for general assistance, thus increasing costs for which states were entirely responsible.

In general, taking direct action affecting existing beneficiaries was less popular than relying on inflation to effect cuts, although a few states did change eligibility standards. The most important argument against eligibility reductions was the fact that many of the medically needy are aged and institutionalized. Consequently, elimination of eligibility was extremely unpopular. The cost of treating such individuals (at least under Medicaid the federal government pays half) would have been shifted to country-run hospitals and facilities and ultimately to local taxpayers.

There are two main ways to affect eligibility: (1) reduce eligibility for AFDC or Supplemental Security Income (SSI) recipients or (2) restrict groups covered specifically and optionally under Medicaid itself. Some states restricted the number of AFDC recipients by lowering the income level and allowable assets people could retain while receiving AFDC. Many states failed to raise welfare standards to keep pace with general inflation. As poor people's incomes and assets rose and surpassed the unindexed eligibility ceilings, they were cut from AFDC and hence lost Medicaid eligibility. Automatic Medicaid eligibility for SSI recipients occurs at the state's option. Thus, some states decided to place SSI recipients in the optional category of medically needy rather than to cover them as medically eligible.

States have an incentive to obtain federal matching dollars. If they choose not to, there is an increased financial burden on counties and cities, since the need for medical care for the poor does not disappear if Medicaid eligibility is constrained. Experience has shown that broad Medicaid eligibility standards (and higher federal assistance) actually reduced overall medical spending by states, counties, and cities instead of increasing it.[8]

Congress succumbed to the pressure of its constituencies and also failed to adopt successful reform. As in the case of Medicare, Congress shifted blame for the program's increasing costs and aimed its reform in the wrong direction. Congress believed that it could not be seen to be directly cutting Medicare benefits, so it acted indirectly, encouraged by the lack of a central, accountable authority. By contrast, the Congressional Budget Office (CBO), when it was asked to tell Congress how to lower Medicaid spending, bit the bullet; it suggested that federal outlays could be reduced if the current formulas for calculating federal support for Medicaid and AFDC were modified or new formulas were adopted. One possible modification would be to remove the statutory 50 percent minimum federal share from Medicaid and AFDC. This would lower outlays by $3.3 billion. Under this option, the decline of the federal share of state Medicaid and AFDC expenditures in thirteen affected states would range from about 2 percentage points to about 33 percentage points. An alternative proposal, one that would affect all states rather than just those with the highest per capita incomes, would be to reduce the federal share under the Medicaid formula by 3 percentage points. This would save roughly the same total amount as removing the 50 percent federal minimum.[9] Such embarrassing directness, however, would put Congress in the position of cutting benefits—and, more importantly perhaps, of being *seen* to cut benefits. Caught between conflicting desires—less spending and more benefits—Congress never directly removed medical services. Rather, it cracked down on hospitals and doctors or let inflation eat away the benefits through freezes on payments.

In effect, the fragmentation of Congress exposes individual members to their constituencies; there is no cover to hide behind. This operates as a disincentive to cutting benefits. At the same time, fragmentation allows the shifting of blame because no central authority can be held accountable. Thus, Congress, state governments, and the administration can all shift the blame while an unpopular program continues to expand.

THE EXPANSION OF MEDICARE VERSUS MEDICAID

The end result is a paradox: the growth rate of Medicare has been reduced by 6.8 percent, despite its great popularity, while the growth rate of Medicaid has been reduced by only 2.8 percent, despite its unpopularity. Allen Schick provided a cogent rationale: (1) A dollar cutback in Medicare reduces federal costs by one dollar; the same reduction in Medicaid saves the federal government only about fifty cents. (2) Medicaid is seen by many members of Congress as a vital part of the safety net for low-income Americans. Moreover, as pressure has grown to curtail entitlements, there has been greater willingness to differentiate between means-tested and other benefits. (3) Medicare cutbacks have been spurred by financial crises in the hospital insurance and SMI funds. Since it is financed out of general revenues, Medicaid is affected only by the overall deficit. (4) States have been effective lobbyists against federal cutbacks in Medicaid. Their efforts have been motivated by concern that reduced federal assistance would compel them to pick up a larger share of Medicaid costs.[10]

TABLE 6.2 Federal Health Outlays

Program	Billions of Dollars Spent			% Change (Constant Dollars)[a]
	1978	1980	1983	
Medicare	25.2	35.0	52.5	+56
Medicaid	10.7	14.0	17.0	+10
Discretionary	7.7	9.1	8.6	−36

Source: David Blumenthal, "Right Turns, Wrong Turns and Road Untaken: The Discretionary Federal Health Budget," in Health Care: How To Improve It and Pay for It, Alternatives for the 1980s, no. 17 (Washington, D.C.: Center for National Policy), 61.

[a]Adjusted using medical CPI as reported in Statistical Abstracts through May 1983. Source: Budget of the United States, Fiscal Years 1975–85.

Under certain circumstances, in other words, strength can be weakness. Moreover, since Medicare is about three times larger than Medicaid, Medicare is the more tempting target every time there is a felt need to reduce the deficit.

As Medicare and Medicaid costs have risen, what has been happening to the discretionary (i.e., not entitlement) health programs (community centers, preventive medicine, high blood pressure control) of the federal government? Table 6.2 tells the tale. While Medicaid spending just kept even with inflation and Medicare spending jumped by 52.5 percent in five years (from 1978 to 1983), the purchasing power of discretionary programs eroded by 36 percent. Again we see that one of the hidden effects of entitlements in times of stringency is to squeeze out appropriations, not necessarily because they are undesirable, but simply because they are more readily controllable.

Medicare and Medicaid both have expanded, but the dynamics have been different. In both cases the cornerstone is the nature of the political system, but that system is in turn subject to different combinations of influences. Medicaid overcame a lack of popularity through the fragmentation of the American political system. In spite of its unpopularity, the federal nature of the program, the dynamics of federal politics, and the program's design weakened the ability to reform the program or to attack it directly.

Medicare, on the other hand, expanded as a result of the political system, its popularity, and, most importantly, the goals and incentives of the program itself. The three variables—fragmented politics, popular attitudes, and program design—were present in both cases, in differing alignments, with similar results: both programs continued to expand.

Holding Their Own: The Black Lung and ESRD Programs

BLACK LUNG

Early expansion of the black lung relief program follows the pattern already identified: incremental and unrecognized expansion within the context of a fragmented political system, supported by attitudes favorable to the program and a program design that encouraged growth. In this case, however, fragmentation also provided an opening for reform through cost shifting—a reform that was additionally encouraged by strong presidential leadership.

Black lung disease (or pneumoconiosis) is produced by inhaled coal dust lining the airways of the lung. Federal participation in mine regulation and disease compensation was intended to be temporary and limited in scope, while the states and the coal mining industry were negotiating a compensatory mechanism for job-related disabilities—including, importantly, coal dust pneumoconiosis. Once these arrangements were settled, it was thought, the federal government could safety withdraw its administrative and financial involvement. Sixteen years later, the government is contributing nearly $1.8 billion a year to support disability payments to coal miners.[11] It was expected that by mid-1970 over 165,000 applications would be filed. In fact, over 183,000 were filed by June, and 250,000 were filed by the beginning of 1971.[12] The backlog of claims created innumerable delays for thousands of miners and their dependents.

The first expansion of the black lung entitlement occurred in May 1972 when President Nixon signed PL 92-303, specifying that inconclusive or negative x-ray examination could not be the basis for denial of benefits. The 1972 amendment also declared that surface miners would be eligible for benefits. In addition, the amendment strengthened the government's authority to specify the "last responsible operator" as being liable for benefits the government already had disbursed to an individual miner. The federal government would honor claims presented to it up to 31 December 1973; thereafter, claims would be paid by operators via state worker's compensation laws (or federal laws if state laws were inadequate). If no operator could be charged, benefits would be paid by the government. The operator's right to appeal remained intact.

The 1972 amendment liberalized the medical criteria needed to establish eligibility. This foretold a key development in expanding the entitlement. By accepting the eligibility of some miners who could not demonstrate radiographic evidence of coal dust pneumoconiosis, the amendment effectively expanded the definition of *black lung* to include dust-induced bronchitis and emphysema.[13] Expanding the number of compensable diseases under a generic category not only added financial responsibility for the government, but—through looser standards of medical criteria and administrative review—also greatly enhanced applicants' accessibility to the entitlement.

Further growth was encouraged by Congress's fragmented committee system. Action on eligibility standards by House and Senate authorization committees effectively bypassed the more conservative Appropriations Committee. In the Senate, eligibility provisions fell under the aegis of the Human Resources Committee, whereas trust fund details were the responsibility of the Finance Committee. Splitting the two key elements of the entitlement proposal among separate committees allowed for little leverage by expenditure control groups. Limitations imposed in one committee could be negated by the liberalizations passed by another.

Popular attitudes reinforced support for the program. The program was born in the late 1960s and was strongly influenced by a coal mine explosion at Farmington, West Virginia, in November 1968, that killed seventy-eight miners and sparked a nationwide outcry over working conditions in the mines. The television pictures of smoke, rescuers, and weeping families made such a powerful impression that the federal government was called to redress the miner's plight.

The black lung issue became a passion when, by early 1969, spontaneous walkouts at various mines exploded into a series of "black lung strikes" involving over forty-five thousand miners in West Virginia, Pennsylvania, and Ohio. Miners besieged the State House in Charleston, West Virginia, to clamor for inclusion of black lung as a compensable occupational illness. The coal companies opposed the bill, of course, and called for a series of diagnostic procedures beyond x-ray films to firmly establish the presence of pneumoconiosis. A compromise bill was arranged whereby a liberal definition of black lung was adopted along with acceptance of an array of diagnostic criteria to be considered as evidence of disability. West Virginia Governor Arch Moore signed the bill in March 1969 and effectively ended the strikes.[14]

The West Virginia law took on greater influence in Washington because it established a black lung entitlement framework that miners took to be a central tenet of their health care interests. As federal policy on the black lung issue evolved, a broad definition of black lung as adopted by West Virginia became a lever by which miners could establish and increase their federal benefits. The fervent demonstration of militancy by the miners, furthermore, instilled a popular notion of moral obligation by the federal government to ensure safety and compensation. The public image of the miner as an economic instrument of the coal companies put that industry—and the cost-control advocates in Congress—on the defensive for the coming decade.

Congressional fragmentation and popular attitudes combined to foster the program's growth. The usual financial myopia led legislators to believe that costs would be small and that they would be paid by the coal companies. Nevertheless, Congress pledged its general revenues. In the first decade, attention to black lung came from interested parties— the miners and their relatives, who wanted to get on the rolls, and the owners, who were happy to support their workers provided that the federal government paid all the bills. Talk of medical procedures introduced notions of bureaucracy and miserliness into what many legislators thought should be concern for human suffering. Only with evidence of cascading costs and the appearance of a new administration did a question, sidestepped in the past, rise to the fore—namely, why should the federal government be operating what was rapidly becoming another retirement program?

Several aspects of the program's design encouraged future growth. First, the irrefutability clauses (the cause of pneumoconiosis is defined by law as related to the amount of time spent in the mine) and the assumption of total disability upon demonstration of "complicated" pneumoconiosis, make it hard for the government to deny claims. Second, unlike most compensation programs (where there is an inherent adversarial relationship between worker and company), the black lung entitlement neutralizes antagonism by forcing the government to pay benefits without assessing responsibility upon the coal-mine operators. Although government reserves the right to recover from the responsible operator any monies paid to workers, the lengthy and costly appeals process available to mine operators makes such recovery a very expensive enterprise. Third, the appeals process available to unsuccessful applicants incurs additional legal and administrative expenses. Backlogs of cases add to the frustration of both worthy miners and claims adjusters and fuel political pressure to simplify the process by liberalizing eligibility criteria. Fourth, the very specificity of the entitlement—pneumoconiosis and disability derived from underground coal mining—entails substantial effort to document, review, and assess medical criteria (often incomplete) relevant to the benefit.

Nevertheless, in spite of political fragmentation, popular support, and a program design that encouraged growth, the government was able to achieve successful reform and control the program's expansion. As time passed and costs rose, words of warning were heard. First, Congress responded by dropping automatic eligibility—but it passed more lenient standards of disability and restricted governmental review of x-ray films in 1978. A new Black Lung Disability Trust Fund was to be financed through a federal excise tax on coal—fifty cents a ton on underground coal and twenty-five cents a ton on surface coal. Congress also gave tax preferences to companies that established their own fund to cover their obligation to miners. The industrywide trust fund was to pay miners for whom the government could not find an individual operator responsible.

Another key provision committed the Treasury to cover deficits produced by the trust fund. Unfortunately, the trust fund began to bleed almost immediately, committing the government to pay nearly $420 million after FY79, $1 billion after FY80, and $1.5 billion after FY81, with projections of a $9 billion deficit by FY95.[15] Lagging coal sales reduced income for the fund as operators continued to contest a high percentage of claims, thus transferring more cases to the trust fund's responsibility. The number of cases financed by the trust fund nearly doubled: from 69,500 in 1979 to 138,000 in 1980.[16]

Reform was also promoted by the White House. With the advent of the Reagan administration, the focus changed from increased federal participation to shifting costs. Reagan's FY82 budget proposals called for restricting benefits to the "truly medically disabled" and increasing the coal tax for the trust fund. The president's budget stated that "lax statutory and administrative procedures have expanded the program from its original purpose—to compensate people who are medically disabled because of the black lung disease—into a general coal miners' benefit program that approaches an automatic pension."

In exchange for a sharp reversal in benefit and eligibility standards, Congress transferred 10,200 unresolved cases to the fund, more than offsetting savings from benefits changes for the next five years. The bill doubled the coal tax until such time as the trust fund had fully repaid the government for monies paid from general revenues. The change in eligibility standards was even more striking: It ended the presumption that miners with fifteen years in the mines who were totally disabled due to respiratory impairment were in fact disabled from black lung disease, and it allowed the Labor Department to seek a second opinion in determining whether an x-ray examination showed pneumoconiosis. Survivor benefits were limited to cases in which the miner died from black lung disease, and black lung benefits were reduced for those who had earnings above the Social Security limit.[17]

By shifting costs, the government was able to overcome potential opposition from beneficiaries and from those who would condemn the government for abandoning its moral commitment. The black lung case illustrates that government, far from being gridlocked, can enact reforms to control the growth of entitlement programs.

END-STAGE RENAL DISEASE

The ESRD program, like the black lung program, enjoyed the benefits of a decentralized government, popular support, and a program design that created its own lobby. Still, it was possible to enact reforms to slow the program's growth. The ESRD program, like the black lung program, demonstrates the ability of Congress to negotiate successfully and effectively with vested interest groups to achieve reform.

End-stage renal disease describes the kidney in its dying moments, unable to filter and process the body's metabolic wastes and allowing the waste to accumulate to fatal levels in the blood. As early as 1963, the federal government had established a small ESRD entitlement program for veterans eligible for medical benefits. By 1972, dialysis units had been established in 30 Veterans Administration (VA) hospitals and maintained nearly 15 percent of all dialysis patients in the United States.[18]

When ESRD was enacted, there was hope that a cure for renal disease would soon be found. The entitlement then could be justified as a temporary, life-sustaining measure. But no medical or surgical breakthrough has freed patients on dialysis. Instead, there has been a steady increase in the patient pool and a continued rise in federal spending.

Another therapy that did not live up to expectations was transplantation. A successful transplant restores the recipient to an independent life with only regular immunosuppressant therapy needed to maintain the new kidney. It is the general rule in surgery that, as a procedure is carried out more often, the success rate increases. But for transplant surgery there has been a slight decrease in the success rate—down from a high of 54 percent to nearly 45 percent.[19] Thus, a greater percentage of patients who have unsuccessfully tried transplantation have returned to dialysis.

The appropriations committees moved cautiously in expanding access to renal dialysis and transplants by providing only limited support to the first fourteen community dialysis centers administered by the Public Health Service (PHS). The Senate Appropriations Committee in

1964 had explicitly limited the PHS's use of appropriated monies in renal treatment to "demonstration and training programs—not patient care financing. The overriding concern, obviously, was costs.

> The Federal Government has borne the cost of treatment for its legal beneficiaries and shared these treatment costs when it has been in connection with research investigation or demonstration. Traditionally, payment for illness has been the responsibility of the patient or the local community. If the Federal Government were to share the full costs of lifetime treatment for all who suffer from these chronic diseases and conditions, the financial burden would be excessive.[20]

This was the voice of the classic budgeter; the new budgeters were more concerned with alleviation of suffering than with collective financial burdens.

In 1970 community-based dialysis centers, threatened with termination by the Health Services and Mental Health Administration, were transferred through legislation from the Public Health Service to the Regional Medical Programs Service (RMPS). This transfer separated the dialysis and transplant program from the research orientation of the PHS and the appropriations committees, locating it within the more patient-oriented RMPS. It also allowed decentralized funding through the established regions of the service, although patient-care financing continued to be excluded.[21]

An existing entitlement framework (VA benefits), a growing cohort of clinically oriented renal physicians, and an expanded capacity for dialysis and transplantation—all of these brought federal kidney programs to the brink of entitlement. What supporters needed was a new framework within which the ESRD program could gain legitimacy as a therapy and thus eligibility for patient-care financing. The strategy chosen was to entitle people with kidney failure to medical benefits.[22]

This move took advantage of the committee system by ignoring it. As Allen Schick told the story:

> On the next to last day of its 1972 session, Congress completed action on an omnibus Social Security bill that (among its many provisions) entitled victims of kidney failure to Medicare benefits. The provision was added to the bill by a Senate floor amendment, without prior committee hearings or review and without any consideration of the issue in the House. When it adopted the amendment by an overwhelming margin, the Senate had no reliable cost estimates and only a fuzzy notion of how expanded Medicare cov-

erage would affect future budgets. During brief floor debate, Senator Vance Hartke, the amendment's sponsor, implored the Senate to put health care ahead of budgetary concerns: "How do we explain," he asked, "that the difference between life and death is a matter of dollars?" Hartke estimated that the new benefits would cost $75 million in the first year and perhaps $250 million in the fourth. Annual expenditures turned out to be much higher—about one billion dollars by the end of the 1970s. By then, however, the entitlement of kidney patients to Medicare was inscribed in law and the budget routinely labeled these expenditures as "uncontrollable."[23]

The sharp drop in the number of patients using home dialysis, a much cheaper mode of treatment than dialysis at a hospital or proprietary clinic, raised costs to the government. The 1972 ESRD amendment, while liberalizing provisions for care in a hospital or outpatient dialysis center, did not provide economic incentives for home dialysis. As a result, many patients who might otherwise have considered home dialysis continued to depend on hospital or proprietary-center dialysis.

ESRD enrollment grew from 11,000 at the start of the program to 63,200 at the end of 1980. More spectacularly, the total cost of ESRD rose from $283 million in fiscal 1974 to $1.8 billion in fiscal 1982.[24] In 1986 the federal government paid over $3 billion for 87,000 kidney patients. ESRD coverage now includes nearly 93 percent of all patients in the country who are in need of kidney treatment.

ESRD also benefited from popular support. In 1987, the Gottscholk Committee was drawn together to make recommendations on the dialysis, transplant, and therapy policy of the government. The group endorsed the VA use of dialysis and transplantation, but it also supported home dialysis. More significantly, it recommended financing through Medicare. The committee thus linked disability benefits with the treatment of end-stage renal disease—a linkage that provided the impetus for conferring Medicare benefits on the severely disabled.

Entitlements that are enacted on the coattails of a larger initiative and that have not been subjected to legislative scrutiny often can generate unanticipated costs in later years. Then again, vast cost underestimation is a feature of almost all entitlements.

This linkage was encouraged by policy entrepreneurs. The general discussion of federal support for medical care rested upon the issues of the quality of life and the inability to pay. Each of these issues influenced the chairs of key congressional authorization committees to favor ESRD as an entitlement. Senator Russell Long, chairman of the Senate

Finance Committee and a long-time advocate of health insurance for financially catastrophic illnesses, viewed kidney disease not only as a disability but also as a disease whose cure or amelioration few people could finance on their own. A demonstration of dialysis before a hearing of the House Ways and Means Committee apparently convinced the chairman, Wilbur Mills, to favor the inclusion of benefits under Medicare.[25]

Another significant factor favoring ERSD entitlement benefits was the growing number of clinically oriented renal physicians. As opposed to research physicians, the clinicians' primary concern was the advancement of therapy. Thus, the National Medical Care Corporation (NMC), a major national operator of dialysis clinics, became a potent lobbying force, able to call upon the most prestigious names in nephrology (the study of kidney disease) to testify about ESRD. NMC grew phenomenally after the 1972 enactment of ESRD. By keeping its costs low and opening centers in populous areas, NMC was able to reap substantial profits with government reimbursements. By 1980, NMC had earned over $20 million on revenues of $245.5 million, while its 120 dialysis centers treated nearly a fifth of the nation's dialysis patients.

The program's design helped nurture these vested interests. Although entitlements are generally thought of as benefits conferred upon individuals, a reimbursement mechanism can become a form of entitlement for the providers. In ESRD, the providers are guaranteed reimbursement for their services as long as they deliver treatment to the designated beneficiaries. Often more vocal in promoting the entitlement than are the beneficiaries, providers themselves then become a vested interest group.

As with black lung, however, reform attempts successfully fought this array of factors, and growth was slowed. A bill introduced incentives for home self-dialysis and additional support for transplantation. The bill also called for a national quota (50 percent) of all ESRD patients in renal disease networks to be on home dialysis or in self-dialysis training. All major groups who testified on behalf of eliminating disincentives, however, opposed the establishment of quotas—especially NMC, which opposed a federally mandated 50 percent home dialysis rate on the ground that the survival rates of home dialysis patients were lower than those of center dialysis patients, a controversial medical point at that time.[26]

The combination of a fragmented system and the pressure brought by patients and providers was a significant obstacle to reform. NMC, for example, successfully lobbied Senator Herman Talmadge, chair of the Senate Finance Health Subcommittee, to reject home dialysis quotas altogether in the final bill. In its place was the statement, "It is the intent of Congress that the maximum practical number of patients who are medically, socially and psychologically suitable candidates for home dialysis or transplantation should be so treated."[27] President Carter signed the watered-down bill on 13 June 1978.

Although NMC was successful in preventing a home dialysis quota, the reform effort to shift patients from clinics to home dialysis was not abandoned. The next battle in this war, however, was over a slightly different (but related) issue: whether all providers of dialysis should be paid the same rate.

NMC supported a single rate, a position that hospitals vehemently opposed. The hospitals claimed that their overhead for specialized personnel was higher and that hospitals care for sicker patients than do proprietary centers. NMC countered that the hospitals were simply inefficient and that a higher reimbursement rate for hospitals would subsidize that inefficiency.[28] The Carter administration could not make up its mind on the rate issue, but President Reagan proposed a single rate. The hospitals successfully lobbied the Congress, however, to adopt a dual rate. Still, the 1981 Omnibus Reconciliation Act did contain a complicated home dialysis incentive. The act directed the Health Care Finance Administration to create a higher federal payment for each patient trained to perform dialysis—whether that patient was trained by a hospital or by a proprietary center such as NMC. Although such a provision helped to ameliorate NMC's opposition to the multiple-rate structure, it was also meant to shift patients into a lower-cost form of therapy.

Meanwhile, the Department of Health and Human Services (HHS) sought to reform the reimbursement mechanism for physicians. Originally, there were two methods of reimbursement: the initial and the alternative reimbursement method (ARM). The initial method pays the doctor on a fee-for-service basis for work done either in a center or at the patient's home. The ARM paid doctors a fixed, monthly, per capita fee regardless of the mix of medical services provided—but the doctor received less for home care under ARM than under the initial method. HHS eliminated the initial method in favor of a consolidated prospective payment under ARM for home and center care ($184.60 per month for each patient).[29] The intention was to create an incentive for physicians to shift patients to home dialysis if medically allowable. The Reagan administration strategy was clear: Use prospective reimbursement for institutions and physicians, rather than reducing benefits, to foster the cheapest mode of treatment.

These strategies are clearly compromises—but they are compromises with a consistent aim, namely, to reduce costs. And they have been modestly successful: the strategy of enticing hospitals, proprietary centers, and physicians to make greater use of home dialysis has resulted in slower increases in spending on the ESRD program—although spending is still high.

Riding for a Fall

The black lung and ESRD programs demonstrate that entitlements can be controlled, despite political fragmentation, popular support, and program designs that encourage growth. Social services and revenue sharing offer good examples of how programs can be cut or even killed in the face of these same forces.

SOCIAL SERVICE GRANTS

Federalism and a linkage to Social Security encourage the growth of federal social service payments. Title XX of the Social Security Act gives the federal government authority to give grants to states for the provision of social services. For each state dollar spent on services defined by the legislation, the federal government would provide three dollars in matching funds to the state. The states give money to local governments, which give money to agencies that provide services to individuals.

Expenditures were stable until 1969 but grew rapidly between 1969 and 1972 because a few participants learned that certain provisions of the Social Security Act permitted the federal government to pay up to 75 percent of various costs that heretofore had been borne totally by state and local governments. A few federal departments and administrators actually encouraged states to exploit the program.

Illinois opened the door to huge increases in social service expenditures. As Schick noted, "Illinois in the early 1970's had $100 million overrun on welfare programs. The Governor rejected cutbacks in welfare assistance, and he and his budget aides turned instead to the Federal government in an effort to gain Federal funding of various social programs. After months of intensive political pressure, Illinois won the additional Federal assistance it sought."[30]

Once Illinois put this foot in the door, other states followed suit. Creative financing blossomed everywhere: "An example of how the states took advantage of the program would be an alcohol or drug abuse prevention program that the state had previously financed itself. By purchasing the same services from a private agency, the state would qualify for 75 percent Federal financing." In this manner, the federal government was asked, in effect, to "buy" Mississippi: in 1972 that state submitted claims for social services grants totaling over half of its state budget.[31]

Public support declined as media attention made social services into an object lesson in uncontrolled spending. When the cost of the program was estimated at $4.7 billion for fiscal 1973, Congress took action. Although the results of congressional reform were ambiguous, the case does not show gridlock. On the one hand, a consensus had developed by 1972 that limits would have to be placed on social services grants. Accordingly, the State and Local Fiscal Assistance Act of 1972 placed a $2.5 billion annual cap on social services grants and limited any state's share to its percentage of the national population. On the other hand, the ceiling was set higher than the previous year's expenditures to ensure higher funding levels and to grandfather in the existing elements of services provided; benefits once granted, it seems, are not to be taken away, even by cost-conscious reformers.

The Department of Health, Education and Welfare joined the reform action as well, with equally mixed results. HEW proposed restrictive regulations in 1973 and within two months received 200,000 letters of protest from private agencies and supporters. In the face of such public outcry, HEW softened the regulations to some extent, and Congress kept postponing the new regulations. Provisions were added that required a "maintenance of effort" on the part of the states, which meant that federal matching funds could be used only to supplement but not to supplant existing state programs.

In enacting the cap, Congress first established spending limits and then developed a formula for allocating funds among beneficiaries. Although this action suggests that Congress is both able and willing to control spending, part of the price for obtaining support for the social services cap was passage of the revenue sharing program that created over $4 billion in *new* benefits for state and local governments and corresponding new costs for the federal government.

GRS: THE ENTITLEMENT THAT FAILED

Unlike most entitlements, the general revenue sharing (GRS) program did not grow. After eight years of slightly declining budgets in real terms, the GRS program suffered a severe cutback in 1980, and it was terminated in 1986. For GRS, entitlement status not only failed to produce budget increases, but also could not even guarantee survival. Political fragmentation encouraged the creation of an unlikely coalition in early support of the program, but the coalition was itself too fragmented to survive. The case demonstrates, twice, that government can act and control programs.

Part of the State and Local Fiscal Assistance Act of 1972, general revenue sharing consisted of federal grants to state and local (city and county) governments with virtually no strings attached to the funds. A publication from the Office of Revenue Sharing labeled GRS an automatic entitlement, meaning that "no application is necessary to receive funds . . . To be eligible, governments must return a simple form which they automatically receive, certifying that funds will be spent in accordance with the law." In total, approximately thirty-nine thousand state and local governments received GRS funds.

Political fragmentation, which sometimes seems to encourage gridlock, also allows unexpected coalitions. When revenue sharing was enacted in 1972, different people assigned different purposes to it. The Nixon administration claimed that the primary aim of revenue sharing was the return of power to state and local governments. Although many Republicans agreed with this goal, they hoped that revenue sharing would also bring about the consolidation of other federal grant programs, thus reducing their overall costs. Still others felt that GRS would allow citizens more opportunities to affect the way their tax money was spent. Meanwhile, many Democrats hoped that revenue sharing would be a boon to financially strapped cities. As John Tomer wrote in the *Public Finance Quarterly* in 1977, "General Revenue Sharing . . . meant 'all things to all people.'"[32]

The program's design paralleled that of social services grants. A distinguishing feature of revenue sharing, though, was that its enabling legislation established annual budget ceilings first and only afterward determined individual benefits as a proportion of that ceiling. Entitlement expenditures, in this case, were not the sum of a set of relatively unforecastable individual benefits and were established through legislated expenditure appropriations that acted effectively as expenditure caps.

Although this design helped to control GRS, the dissolution of its coalition was the real key to the program's failure. Early in 1973 President Nixon submitted his budget for 1974, which proposed the reduction or termination of over 100 programs. Further, he stated his intention to renew his request for revenue sharing. Although Nixon claimed that the programs were being eliminated because they had failed, his budget clearly indicated that state and local governments might use revenue sharing funds to pay for these "failed" programs. Many local officials felt that they had been the victims of a bait-and-switch deception that would eventually saddle them with huge program costs and allot relatively limited revenue sharing funds to pay for them. Economist Walter Heller spoke for this view when he remarked that "the birth of general revenue sharing is being used to justify the homicide of selected social programs." Liberal support began to wane in Congress. As the date for renewal approached and opposition grew, supporters (namely, state and local government organizations) increased their lobbying efforts.

If GRS could be had only as a replacement for, rather than a complement to, categorical grants, then liberals wanted no part of it. They preferred categorical grants because these gave the federal government, where liberals had more influence, a greater degree of control over the funds than state and local governments, where liberals were weaker. Revenue sharing became an even better candidate for cutting once congressmen discovered that many states were enjoying enviable fiscal surpluses. Many agreed with the House Government Operations chairman, Jack Brooks (D-TX) when he stated, "[GRS] is a wasteful, illogical giveaway to the states when they're rolling in money."[33]

Assisting the collapse of the coalition was the unexpected weakness of the program's supporters, a coalition that had once appeared invincible. When the GRS program was enacted in 1972, Representative George Mahon predicted that "the passage of the revenue sharing bill will organize and galvanize the most powerful lobby group this country has ever known." This was an entirely plausible expectation. Yet, in 1975, just a year before the program would come up for extension, Senator Edmund Muskie summed up the paradoxical reality: "For the life of me, I can't understand how any program that is supported by thirty-eight thousand state and local governments could conceivably be in trouble in the Congress."[34]

There were two reasons for the unexpected weakness of the so-called Big Six coalition of state and local organizations supporting revenue sharing. (The Big Six were the National Governors' Association, the Council of State Governments, the National Association of Counties, the U.S. Conference of Mayors, the National League of Cities, and the International City Managers Association.) First, public opinion had turned decisively against uncontrolled government spending, especially of the sort that seemed wasteful or that smacked of pork barrel spending. Because revenue sharing supported visible local projects and programs all over the country, nearly every citizen was within shouting distance of something that could be considered wasteful.

A second reason for the Big Six coalition's vulnerability was its fragility. If Congress changed the distribution formula so that it favored cities over rural areas, for instance, rural areas would begin to fight cities in an attempt to secure a more favorable formula.[35] When the Carter administration proposed an additional $500 million in local revenue sharing for fiscal 1981, the squabbling intensified immediately. Meanwhile, on the sidelines, the groups that had always favored categorical grants over revenue sharing—groups like the League of Women Voters, the Urban League, the United Auto Workers, and the NAACP—joined a powerful iron triangle against revenue sharing. The other two points of the triangle were members of Congress and federal agencies that administer categorical aid. In addition, as Hagstron and Pierce pointed out, members of Congress have never been very enthusiastic about revenue sharing because it is difficult for House members, who represent local districts, to claim credit for state action financed with federal money.[36]

Another defection from the coalition occurred when many Republicans concluded that revenue sharing was actually strengthening the federal government rather than increasing the independence of state and local governments. Many local governments had obviously become dependent on GRS funds for their basic programs; in their view, this money was no longer discretionary. Dependency is not decentralization.

Spending on social services and general revenue sharing suffered from both moral doubts and an inability to identify constituents—the one flaw compounding the other. None of this was inevitable. Congress could have seen an opportunity in the ability to spend in previously unsuspected ways. Once deficit spending became marked as the culprit, however, to enable some states to do better than others became suspect. There's the rub: if benefits are widely spread, costs escalate; if costs are contained, it is difficult to find acceptable rationales for providing some states with more and others with less. The Big Six were wrongly regarded as powerful because a crucial condition for the exercise of that power—agreement among themselves—was elusive. The government capitalized on this weakness and acted.

Entitlement versus Appropriations

Although entitlement programs do not always expand faster than appropriations, they do more often than not. Since a comparison of entitlements with appropriations would require a separate volume, we must be content with a couple of comparisons—deliberately designed to point in opposite directions so as to make it hard to draw easy conclusions. Relating the popular Head Start program to the less popular Aid to Families with Dependent Children entitlement primes us to ask why, despite its difficulties, AFDC has grown faster. If the entitlement wins out over the appropriation in that pairing, why has the appropriation for women, infants, and children done better budgetarily than the food stamp entitlement?

The answer lies in the images of the programs and in the politics of how the programs are cut. Head Start takes a larger share of cuts because reduction there does not increase other programs. Adding a few children to a class, moreover, is not as visible as a reduction in AFDC payments. Better one way—in accomplishment—is not necessarily better in another—holding the line of spending without raising too much fuss. AFDC has to be attacked directly; Head Start can be eroded indirectly by inflation. Whether or not AFDC is an entitlement, its budgetary status has protected it against a worse fate.

HEAD START

The Head Start program began so rapidly because the Office of Economic Opportunity (OEO) had a major incentive to spend. In the spring of 1965, OEO officials realized that they had several hundred million dollars to spend before the end of the fiscal year on 30 June. They could hardly expect much support for further appropriations in Congress if they failed to spend their 1965 appropriation. Head Start provided an opportunity to spend money and at the same time win favor in the nation's communities. Sargent Shriver gleefully explained how he used the opportunity.

> I increased the funding by myself! I didn't have to go to Congress; I didn't have to go to the President; I didn't have to go to the Bureau of the Budget. Congress had appropriated the money, and if I wanted to spend it on Head Start, I could spend it on Head Start . . . I felt we had a gigantic breakthrough, so I pumped in the money as fast as we could intelligently use it. It was really quite spectacular.[37]

With this political incentive went a popular attitude that would seem to encourage future program growth. "In our society," Shriver explained, "there is a bias against helping adults . . . but there's a contrary bias in favor of helping children." So he decided to launch a nationwide program of OEO-sponsored preschool education as a way to "overcome a lot of hostility in our society against the poor in general and against black people who are poor in particular, by going at the children." Community Action Program (CAP) organizers considered Head Start an opportunity to receive favorable publicity. They recruited Lady Bird Johnson to spearhead the publicity drive in the hope that, by receiving favorable coverage on the society pages, the CAP would seem more respectable.

When Sargent Shriver had taken his proposal for Head Start to Lyndon Johnson, the president had responded, "That's such a magnificent idea, triple it." Shriver did not need to work very hard to expand the program. In March, the OEO requested funding proposals from local communities and received such a massive response that it decided to fund 2,500 applications that proposed to serve 530,000 children. By the end of the summer, Head Start had in fact served 561,000.

Entitlement status was implicit in the rationale of the Head Start program, which makes its failure to expand all the more significant. For example, Head Start was conceived of as a compensatory education program; as such, it had both the social utility and the moral legitimacy characteristic of entitlements. Furthermore, Head Start regulations required that 90 percent of its participants be children of families who were below the official poverty line; it therefore shared the eligibility criteria of entitlement programs. Yet, despite concerted efforts during the late 1960s and early 1970s to establish an entitlement for child development services, Head Start failed to cross the threshold into genuine entitlement status, apparently for two major reasons. First, it was always easier to cut Head Start appropriations because such cuts did not automatically trigger increases in other spending programs (AFDC, for example). And second, Head Start was a *program* rather than a direct income transfer; budget cuts therefore did not have the immediately visible effect of cuts in the food stamp program or AFDC; if a Head Start class had to crowd in a couple more children, few people would notice.

AID TO FAMILIES WITH DEPENDENT CHILDREN

AFDC, by contrast, *did* come to be viewed as an entitlement, *despite* its unpopular status. AFDC grew slowly at first, as did other programs we have seen. It began, as Daniel P. Moynihan wrote, "almost as an afterthought." It was tacked onto higher-priority components of the Social Security Act and the need for it was expected to fade as the Depression came to an end. As with many Depression-era programs, AFDC was not designed for the poorest of the poor but rather for the temporarily submerged working and middle classes, such as the wife and children of a factory worker killed on the job. The legislative record indicates Congress's expectation that the program would wither away as the economy improved and as such programs as Social Security (which was a contributory social program rather than a poverty program) became established.[38]

With time and despite the fact that the economy was steadily improving, the AFDC rolls steadily increased—from 803,000 families in 1960 to 1.1 million families in 1965. Although this growth was disturbing, it was nothing compared to what came next. Between 1967 and 1971, the number of AFDC recipients literally doubled, reaching 3.2 million families by 1974. State and local officials (who had to pay much of the bill) were shaken and angry.

Between the mid-1960s and 1976, the cost of all antipoverty programs tripled to $81 billion (in 1983 dollars) and then grew more slowly, reaching $103 billion in 1984. The proportion of the population in poverty traced a less optimistic path. Over the 1960s and early 1970s, it fell more or less steadily, reaching 11.1 percent in 1973. It then remained constant until 1979, when it began rising again, and by 1983 it exceeded 15 percent.

This contradiction—a rising poverty rate in the face of rising antipoverty expenditures—led to the argument that the expenditures themselves had caused poverty by fostering dependence. As chairman of the Ways and Means Committee, Wilbur Mills (D-AR) asked, "Is it in the public interest for welfare to become a way of life?"

Nevertheless, cutting AFDC is not as attractive as it otherwise might be, because the states and the federal government would be expected to make up through other programs, such as general welfare and food stamps, for reductions in AFDC benefits. Food stamp program outlays are especially sensitive to changes in other programs. Attempts to reduce expenditures in a program such as AFDC will lead to increased food stamp expenditures. It was estimated in 1984 that roughly 82 percent of AFDC households received food stamps, a third received housing assistance, and 95 percent received Medicaid. Provisions in one program that confer categorical eligibility to participants in other programs create financial connectedness that make it difficult to cut either program. For these people approximately one-third of any cut in AFDC benefits will be offset by increased food stamp benefits.[39]

Head Start and AFDC indicate the strength of a program's budgetary status—how it is viewed—over purely political or other forces. The same political forces are still at work behind the scenes, however. Indirect cuts in Head Start are made possible by the cost shifting opportunities inherent in a fragmented political system, allowing government action to overcome widespread popular support. AFDC, the incremental growth of which was a result of that fragmented political system, is resistant to direct cuts and thus expands in the face of disapproval. Head Start, influenced by the politics of the appropriations process, never achieved status as an entitlement; AFDC, not clearly an entitlement in nature, grew into that status.

WIC VERSUS FOOD STAMPS

The women, infants, and children program and the food stamp program reinforce the idea that a program's image and reputation are central to its treatment. The program design of FSP encouraged its growth, which in turn resulted in congressional scrutiny, which resulted in a limited degree of control in spite of the program's design. WIC, like many other programs, has grown largely unnoticed from an initial, temporary program. Congressional support, maximized as a result of institutional fragmentation, has maintained the program's gradual expansion. Both cases demonstrate the importance of Congress' attitude toward a program and the effect of decentralization and fragmentation. Both cases also argue against the gridlock theory as government action has controlled FSP and has promoted WIC.

THE FOOD STAMP PROGRAM

The food stamp program and the special supplemental food programs for women, infants, and children share some important characteristics. Both are specifically intended to help prevent the occurrence of problems associated with undernutrition and malnutrition by helping low-income people obtain an adequate diet. Both programs are administered at the federal level by the Office of Food and Nutrition Services within the U.S. Department of Agriculture (USDA). Both provide 100 percent federal funding of actual benefits provided to recipients (in the FSP, however, states share in the cost of administration). Both provide benefits in the form of vouchers that are exchanged for food. These similarities reduce the number of factors that might be expected to result in differences in growth rates, such as differences in state funding commitments.

FSP is the largest federal food program, with a total outlay of about $11 billion in fiscal year 1982. It is intended to fill the gap between the amount of money low-income households are expected to use for buying food, based on a standard share of total income (currently 30 percent), and the amount of funds USDA determines is necessary to purchase an adequate diet.[40]

The food stamp program grew throughout the 1970s—and then Congress acted to slow its growth. The food stamp program first became an entitlement because of changes made between 1969 and 1971. During those years the purchase requirement—the amount of money recipients must spend to buy a given allotment of food stamps—was reduced, and allotments were increased. These changes greatly expanded both program benefits and expenses.

The next significant program change came in 1977 when, with the support of President Carter, legislation eliminated the purchase requirement completely and at the same time terminated eligibility for some relatively high-income recipients. The aim of these changes was to better target benefits to those most in need, since the purchase requirement was thought to be burdensome for those with very low incomes. The administration claimed that the cost of the proposed changes would offset each other. Congress remained concerned about the program's rising costs, however, and included yearly authorization ceilings. Two years later, the Carter administration acknowledged that eliminating the purchase requirement had resulted in a bigger caseload and indicated that large increases in food costs were driving the program over the authorization limits. The administration asked for and received an increase in these limits.[41]

In 1981 and 1982, as part of a general effort to reduce domestic expenditures, President Reagan requested major cutbacks in the food stamp program. The Congressional Budget Office estimated the cumulative effect of the 1981–82 legislation to be a 13 percent cut in FSP expenditures relative to the projected "base" and a 4 percent decline in the number of recipients (representing about a million people).[42]

These changes hint at a change in Congress' attitude toward the program. In 1980 Congress created a sanction system that held states financially responsible if they provided benefits to ineligible recipients (above a "normal" error rate). In 1982 Congress made the error-rate targets more stringent. This move suggests that the attitude of Congress is shifting from a belief that all who are entitled to food stamps should get them to a view that those who are not entitled should not get them. The change in perception is important. In administering any large program, there will be a normal error rate, or "waste." The trade-off is obvious: if the emphasis is on reducing ineligibles, there is a greater chance that some eligibles may also be acut from the program. Although Congress does not wish for the deserving to be cut from the program, the point is clear: The food stamp program is on probation.

FSP's status with Congress is significant. The entitlement status of FSP becomes especially important in what happens after legislative guidelines are established. Because funding is not fixed but is a function of the indexed benefit level and because of the number and characteristics of recipients, expenditures may vary from what is actually appropriated.

THE WIC PROGRAM

WIC is designed to provide food as well as nutrition information for low-income pregnant, postpartum, and breast-feeding women and for children up to the age of five who are determined to be at special health risk because of inadequate nutrition. The determination of nutritional risk is made by a health official such as a nutritionist or public health nurse. The program is administered regionally by state health departments that distribute funds to local public and private, nonprofit agencies (e.g., clinics, local health departments), which in turn supply the actual benefits to recipients. These benefits consist of food vouchers for items tailored to the particular family's needs, such as infant formula, as well as nutritional counseling and pamphlets. The average monthly value of the coupons per recipient is about $29, and the total national caseload is about 2.2 million.

WIC grew out of a special commodity distribution effort begun in 1968. It grew slowly at first and then increased rapidly. A smaller ($1.2 billion in total expenditures in fiscal 1982) and more narrowly targeted program than FSP, WIC was first authorized for two years in 1972 with an annual ceiling of $20 million. No funds were actually expended until 1974, when USDA was forced to do so by court action. Then the program took off.[43] "After more than quadrupling in size during the late 1970s, the program grew by more than 40 percent during the Reagan years. This growth shows every sign of continuing. In theory, WIC is part of the so-called discretionary budget that Congress can easily fiddle with from year to year. In practice, however, it is politically off limits."[44]

Attempts at reform demonstrate some of the effects of a multibranch government and a readily accessible, fragmented Congress. During the Reagan years, several unsuccessful efforts were made to reduce WIC expenditures. In 1982 Reagan proposed combining WIC with an existing maternal and child health block grant and reducing the total level of funding by $356 million. Congress rejected this proposal, actually adding $100 million in extra funds for WIC as part of the 1983 employment and emergency poverty relief legislation. As a result, WIC grew during the Reagan administration. Indeed, the Congressional Budget Office noted (in its study of the effects of 1981 and 1982 legislation of twenty-six programs) that WIC was one of only two such programs to have increased expenditures as the result of laws enacted over this time.[45]

Interest groups have taken advantage of their access to protect WIC, as well as FSP. Support for both programs has been led by a few nonprofit organizations dedicated to antipoverty advocacy, such as the Food Research and Action Center; liberal church organizations, such as Bread for the World; and also by recipient organizations. None of these groups can offer support to legislators in the form of campaign contributions or ready-made campaign workers. Activists for these groups, however, can help to highlight issues and inform legislators (this may be particularly important to sympathetic representatives and senators in need of "ammunition"), generate support or opposition to particular policies, and indicate to their own members and the press which legislators have "good" or "bad" records in the area of hunger programs. Legislators have at times paid backhanded compliments to the political effectiveness of these groups, as did Senator Carl Curtis of Nebraska who complained on the Senate floor about the pressure they brought to bear for eliminating the FSP purchase requirements. So popular is WIC that Representative George S. Miller, chairman of the Select Committee on Children, Youth and Families and a member of the Budget Committee, wanted the program to become an entitlement.

This support is reinforced by favorable attitudes in Congress. WIC has benefited from very strong congressional support. In conversations with legislative staff members, program administrators, and interest group activists, it was clear that all emphasized the program's "great popularity" with members "on both sides of the aisle." Why is WIC not merely popular but expanding in a restrictive environment?

Favorable implementation reports apparently have been important in congressional support for WIC. According to one influential comparison of WIC recipients to a similar population not receiving program benefits, WIC leads to such desirable results as increases in childbirth weight, fewer difficult pregnancies, and reduced health care costs generally. Another study showed three dollars in health care savings for every one dollar invested in WIC. Some of the claims made on behalf of WIC have been challenged, but the bulk of the literature and of professional opinions available to policy makers remain highly supportive of the program.[46]

The behavior of congressional committees helps account for the differences in treatment of WIC and FSP. One area in which we might expect to find differences between FSP and WIC on the basis of entitlement status is in the action of appropriations committees, even though the rules as to who receives benefits are set by the authorizing committees. The FSP is the type of entitlement that requires appropriations committees actually to provide funding. Nevertheless, the role of appropriations is more technical than substantive, suggesting that Congress considers the program to be an entitlement. As a result, hearings focus on administrative issues such as eligibility error rates and fraud prevention.

With regard to WIC, it would be possible for appropriation committees to play an active role in reducing spending. Thus far, however, they have not shown the inclination to do so. In 1982, for example, both House and Senate appropriations committees rejected the administration's block grant proposal, and both committees praised the program's "effectiveness." Congressional staff members indicate that there is a tendency for the appropriations committees to provide enough funding to maintain a certain caseload level, such as the year-end level, which means that this program is moving toward something of a hybrid status: Appropriations committees retain formal control but base their decisions on caseload considerations. What matters most is how you are treated—not what you're supposed to be.

Conclusion

Taken together with economic and demographic changes, entitlements as a class are buffeted by so many factors that it is vain to search for a common denominator. A full explanation-cum-prediction of the trajectory of entitlements, including comparison of appropriations in similar fields, would be equivalent to comprehending most of American national public policy. Since entitlements make up a good half of noninterest spending and related appropriations add to the proportion, asking for an explanation of entitlements is like asking for an explanation of domestic spending.

We have, however, learned a few things worth knowing. One of these is that, despite an image of invincibility, entitlements are modified all the time: Congress and the executive *do* act and *can* control or even kill programs. This belies the oft-heard claim that the government is locked into inaction.

Designs and support differ with each case, and the ties that each program has to political institutions vary. The cases suggest, however, a clear conclusion about the new politics of public policy. A government that is fragmented and decentralized, that has multiple points of access for interested parties and many opportunities for individual influence, can and does act to reform or even kill entitlement programs. Coalitions may shift, but their rise and fall results in action on policy. The dynamics of these actions, of course, vary with the specific constellation of institutional factors, attitudes, and program designs. The fact of action in these cases, however, argues against the theory of congressional impotence and suggests that Congress can stand up to powerful lobbies.

The stories about these entitlement programs suggest that Congress is both willing and able to attempt reform.

This conclusion is bolstered by another consideration. Congress's major weaknesses (as far as expenditure control is concerned) are its fragmentation and its dependence on public opinion. When we compare American with Western European experience, we learn, first, that most European governments do not do better in controlling entitlements. Second, unlike the United States, the most highly centralized European governments, whose proposals cannot be altered in their parliaments, do exert greater control over the direction and logic of spending. In no country are citizens much inclined to cut entitlements. Perhaps, if we the people want not just vague "reform" but lower levels of spending, we should worry less about our politicians and more about ourselves.

Elusive Community: Democracy, Deliberation, and the Reconstruction of Health Policy

JAMES A. MORONE

On the political surface, health policy has suffered from a particularly acute case of gridlock. After all, Americans have been debating national health insurance since the Bull Moose Progressives proposed it in 1912. Moreover, we are well into the third decade of a health care cost "crisis"—marked by steadily rising costs and a growing roster of discredited remedies.

Other nations seem, in contrast, to organize their health care more effectively. Elsewhere, as James Q. Wilson put it, "government . . . can say 'yes' or 'no' and make it stick."[1] While we turned over an additional percentage of the economy to health care every forty months through the 1980s, our partners in the Organization of Economic Cooperation and Development (OECD) averaged no rise at all; we let tens of millions go uninsured, while other nations cover all of their citizens.[2]

Gridlock, however, is the wrong metaphor. On the contrary, American health care politics has undergone a powerful transformation. Traditional American health policy long offered a textbook case of interest group liberalism: the medical profession dominated medical politics. During the past fifteen years, the profession has lost much of that authority. Power over health policy is increasingly wielded by the bureaucracies that oversee payment for health services. Those bureaucracies range from the federal Health Care Financing Administration (HCFA) to state Medicaid offices, from Blue Cross plans to corporate benefits offices. Together, public and private officials have begun to reshape medical politics, medical markets, even the practice of medicine itself.

In this chapter I trace the political transformation, showing how, beneath the apparent deadlock, Americans rearranged authority over health policy—breaking the "legitimacy barrier" to action in this policy realm. The process, however, offers a cautionary tale regarding democratic deliberation.

The most reflexive American strategies for empowering citizens and fostering communal deliberations are grounded in myth: implausible hopes of direct democratic participation and community consensus.[3] As we shall see, the democratic idyll offers powerful opportunities for change but limited prospects for sustained governance.

I begin by tracing the longstanding patterns of interest group liberalism. Medicare induced a policy crisis in the traditional political arrangement. The deadlock that followed was eventually broken by a democratic wish—an odd program that organized citizen participation in health care planning agencies across the nation. The visible result was a chaotic scramble for power, self-interest, and proper citizen representation; on the surface, the medical profession continued to get more or less what its members demanded.

The underlying result, however, was an important realignment of medical politics. The agencies described below took their great democratic aspirations and paltry political authority and organized unprecedented conflicts into local health policies. As it engaged in the controversies, the medical profession lost its trusteeship over medical policy. At the same time, entirely new political actors were mobilized into the health care fray. A new policy paradigm has emerged—both in health care and, more broadly, in public policy making. Despite frequent laments about stalemate, Americans have developed a new political pattern that sharply contrasts with both their own policy-making traditions and the experience in other nations.

Traditional Health Politics

A single pattern dominated American health care politics for most of the twentieth century: public power was ceded to the medical profession. Health care providers acted as trustees of health care policy. Legislation they opposed was generally defeated; programs that were legislated were placed in their hands. In many ways, the profession's power constituted an exaggerated case of interest group liberalism—government authority wielded by an industry, generally for the benefit of its members.

Physicians exercised three different kinds of authority, each resting on a different source. At bottom lay their politically uncomplicated claim to professionalism: physicians acted on the basis of technical expertise acquired through prescribed training, guided by internalized norms, and accurately evaluated only by colleagues. Medicine's link with scientific progress made its claim to professional authority particularly persuasive; physicians, not their patients, were the best judges of appropriate therapy.

Second, professional command over the content of medical treatment was extended to state-supported control over the health care industry. Almost every business—from barbers to egg checkers—has used the cover of professional expertise to seek government limits on potential rivals. Medicine enjoyed what might have been the paradigmatic case for self-regulation. Physicians met the progressive regulatory ideal of skilled professionals protecting the public from abusive practices. In the first two decades of the twentieth century, physicians appropriated public authority to take charge of the health care field. They defined the content, organization, and even financing of acceptable medical practice. By the end of World War I, physicians had consolidated their domination over a wide array of potential rivals—osteopaths, chiropractors, midwives, homeopaths. In theory, professional power would extirpate unethical practitioners such as alcoholics, charlatans, or abortionists. In practice, sanctions protected professional dominance. Southern medical societies barred black physicians; throughout the country, societies punished rebels who introduced new forms of medical organization or financing.

The ideal of professional autonomy—free from controls originating outside the profession—was won and forcefully maintained. The American Medical Association and its constituent state societies used both public and private power to extend the primacy of medical judgment into a professional hegemony over the American health care system.

Third, physicians sought to control health care politics. Government programs that enhanced their professional authority were frequently won; those that threatened their autonomy were, until the 1960s, generally defeated. For example, almost every industrial nation eventually sponsored a national health care system. In the United States the reform was repudiated whenever it was proposed. The political outcomes are usually ascribed to raw interest group muscle. By the 1920s, the American Medical Association had developed a reputation for political influence that would grow for almost fifty years. The association was unhampered by serious internal schisms, well organized, and richly financed. The *New York Times* judged it perhaps "the most powerful [lobby] in the country," explaining in unabashedly pluralistic terms, "The American Medical Association is the only organization in the country that could marshall 140 votes in Congress between sundown Friday night and noon on Monday."[4]

The AMA's ability to mobilize on short notice was undeniable. However, simply ascribing medical dominance to interest group power misses the underlying structure of American politics. The state's legitimacy to take on new tasks is always open to question. Moreover, through much of the twentieth century, Congress and the president divided over social programs. The political pattern rarely varied: public officials (usually northern Democrats) proposed a program like national health insurance; reformers cheered; as public opinion polls came into fashion, they generally indicated that the public concurred.[5] However, less liberal public officials opposed the extension of government authority. Health care reforms were sacrificed for other programs and the maintenance of political coalitions—victim of the American system of checks and balances as much as the dreaded AMA. Parliamentary institutions with stable coalitions between executive and legislature would probably have won the reform many times over.

The shrillness of AMA politics can be reinterpreted within the framework of a weak state. Each threatened encroachment of professional dominance triggered not debates about policy but uproars about tyranny. In 1918, the AMA house of delegates denounced "compulsory" social insurance as a "dangerous device . . . announced by the German emperor from the throne the same year he started plotting to conquer the world." Over the next five decades, the rhetoric remained unchanged, except for its growing stridency. Even before Roosevelt took office, the AMA warned the nation of the "forces representing . . . public health officialdom, social theory, even socialism and communism—inciting to revolution." By the late 1960s, national health insurance had evolved into Lenin's "keystone to the socialist arch."[6] The relentlessness of the theme, which has alternately baffled and amused political analysts, is clear in the context of a weak state; the AMA responded to the threat of public incursions into the physician's domain by underscoring the limits of governmental legitimacy.

The AMA's influence derived, first, from the ability to provoke a deep-seated American dread—to politicize the boundaries of legitimate public power—and, second, from its willingness to sponsor alternatives. Politicians eager to legislate popular health care programs were given uncontroversial options that reinforced the power and autonomy of the industry. The result made it easy to ascribe power to the industry and its lobbyists. Even a cursory history of American health care policy demonstrates the uninterrupted repetition of a single political pattern: the ceding of public authority to the medical profession.

Medicare: The State Articulates an Interest

Although liberals fought long and hard for national health insurance, they never challenged the model of professional dominance. Instead,

the liberal slogan—"removing the financial barriers to medical care"—
cast the reform as, somehow, outside the scope of actual medical practice. Reformers would pose no threat to professional autonomy or
power, they would simply deliver the patients to the physician's door.
Medical leaders perceived—quite accurately, it turned out—that massive federal funding would introduce new governmental incentives for
managing their sector.

The Medicare debate quickened when the Democrats captured the
Senate in 1958 and rose to its peak after John Kennedy's election. It was
an astonishingly exaggerated, almost hysterical, dispute.[7] In perhaps its
most delicious moment, the AMA sent every physician's spouse a recording with which to convince friends and neighbors to write Congress
opposing Medicare. The final words of the exhortation crystallized the
antistatist imagery of the day.

> Write those letters now; call your friends and tell them to write
> them. If you don't, this program, I promise you, will pass just
> as surely as the sun will come up tomorrow. And behind it will
> come other federal programs that will invade every area of free-
> dom as we have known it in this country. Until one day . . . we
> will awake to find that we have socialism. And if you don't do
> this, and I don't do it, one of these days you and I are going to
> spend our sunset years telling our children and our children's chil-
> dren what it was like in America when men were free.

The voice, clearly recognizable thirty years later, was Ronald Reagan's,
weighing in against big government in 1962.[8]

The great, often overlooked, irony is that the rhetorical pyrotechnics
did not matter. A dispute about the legitimacy of governmental action
turned almost entirely on the preferences of public officials. The debate
dragged on with little variation for decades. The actual reform awaited a
confluence of political will in both Congress and the presidency. When
Lyndon Johnson was elected with the largest Democratic majority since
1934, the public sector stalemate was broken.

In the new political setting, the AMA put aside antigovernmental
rhetoric and proposed an alternative to Medicare, a welfare bill that
would be administered by the states. Led by Wilbur Mills, chairman of
the Ways and Means Committee, Congress promptly passed both: Medicare for the elderly, Medicaid for indigents who fit into the American
patchwork of public assistance categories.

The liberals' long-sought triumph did not alter the traditional contours of American health care politics. Authority over the new programs was promptly ceded to the industry. The statute itself broke with

legislative tradition; rather than promising everything to everybody, this law began by promising to change nothing. Its first three sections all denied the charges of government intrusion that had been repeated for five decades: "Nothing in this title shall be construed to authorize any federal official or employee to exercise any supervision or control over the practice of medicine." The next five passages embellished the theme, forbidding state control over medical personnel or compensation or organization or administration or choice of provider or selection of insurer.[9] The implementing details were all of a piece, reflecting the unorthodox protests that had introduced the legislation.

The method for paying health care providers was set loosely. Shunning payment schedules or other controls, Medicare reimbursed providers their "reasonable costs"—essentially, whatever they charged. To avoid the stigma of government bureaucracy, the act provided that private insurance companies would process the payments; hospitals were permitted to select their own fiscal intermediaries, a potent guarantee against overly zealous scrutiny of reimbursement claims.[10]

The usual deference to providers may have been exaggerated by the sheer burden of implementation. Sixteen million elderly would be eligible for benefits in a year. Provider cooperation was uncertain. However, the deference with which the liberals' followed up on their Medicare victory had far deeper roots than implementation timetables or physician boycotts. Public and private officials, liberals and conservatives, all shared the same biases. Their approaches to medical politics—even their conceptual categories—were shaped by six decades of deference to the medical profession.

Costs, Crisis, and Citizens

The state had helped to finance a technologically sophisticated medical system and then assumed the responsibility for those least able to afford the rising costs. Payments without controls sent health prices soaring. In 1954, the health sector claimed 4.4 percent of the gross national product, a figure that had held roughly steady for a decade. The health care system grew to 5.3 percent of GNP by 1960, 5.9 percent in 1965, and—with the implementation of Medicare and Medicaid—reached 7.3 percent by 1970.[11] Rising prices radically redefined the health policy agenda.

A NEW POLICY DILEMMA

The discovery of a "cost crisis" followed fast on the implementation of Medicare and Medicaid. President Nixon declared "a massive crisis in this area" in 1969. *Business Week* ran a cover story on the $60 billion dollar crisis. *Fortune* judged American medicine to be "on the brink of chaos."[12] For the next decade, the crisis of rising costs became the major issue of American health care policy. Corporations, insurance companies, labor unions, and consumer groups joined politicians in calling for solutions. Even a cursory look at the health policy journals of the late 1960s and 1970s demonstrates both the unwavering focus on costs and the English language's wealth of synonyms for *rising*.

The usual interpretation is simple: the government passed Medicare and Medicaid; costs exploded; both public and private sectors scrambled to frame a response. The political reality was more complex. The cost crisis trumpeted by Nixon, *Business Week*, and almost everybody else was not an uncomplicated reflection of some objective economic reality that followed Medicare. Prices had already been rising for a decade. In the five years that preceded the program, total health costs jumped 13 percent as a percentage of GNP; in the five crisis years that followed, 20 percent. To be sure, the inflationary pace quickened, and there was a cumulative effect. More important, however, was the fact that the national government had suddenly socialized a large part of the bill. Federal health care outlays rose fast: from $9.5 billion (1965) to $25.4 billion (1970) and then to $41.5 billion (1975).[13] By nationalizing a significant portion of the cost, Medicare made health care inflation a public sector problem and placed it on the policy agenda. Shifting the uncontrolled spending from private pockets to the public tax system is what made a crisis out of rising health costs.

For six decades, medical politics had turned on spreading the undisputed benefits of medicine to more Americans. When the issue was recast as one of constraining costs, professional expertise was no longer the critical skill for the problem at hand. The redefinition of the issue turned professional judgment from the solution to the source of the problem. The AMA's anti-Medicare campaign made it easy to cast the profession as mean and narrowly self-interested, just another self-seeking group. All of the celebrated features of American medicine could be reinterpreted in the new political context. The system was now said to be too technical, emphasizing sophisticated (and expensive) tertiary care over (inexpensive) prevention and health maintenance. The former was cold and unfeeling, the latter humane and ultimately more effective. Medical treatment was provided in a haphazard pastiche of institutions (hospitals, high-tech nursing homes, low-tech nursing homes, physician's offices) with no logical flow from one to the next. "The American way" of financing care was now perceived as an irrational patchwork of public and private programs, often stitched together in a way that left families vulnerable to ruinous bills. At the same time, by covering most people most of the time, public and private health insurance encouraged inflationary overuse of medical services. The entire health care "empire" concentrated itself in urban areas, leaving many rural Americans with inadequate coverage.

Even the sources of medical professionalism were challenged. Consumers demanded an accounting, inverting the traditional norm of answering to professional peers rather than clients. Previously subordinated providers challenged physicians; midwives, osteopaths, acupuncture specialists, and a host of others staked their own claims to professionalism in a more sustained fashion than they had done since the Progressive Era. On the fringes, popular books claimed that the profession did more harm than good; they marked the resurgence of what Paul Starr termed *therapeutic nihilism,* an antiprofessional sentiment that had been dormant since the nineteenth century. Suddenly, more was less in medical practice.[14]

In short, the new crisis challenged every level of professional authority: The physicians' trusteeship over public policy, their control over the health care industry, and even the professional definition of proper medical practice. And yet the new skepticism did not lead immediately to new politics. Instead, the widely perceived crisis produced political stalemate. The next decade would vividly demonstrate how difficult it is for American government to reassert authority it has ceded to organized minorities, even when the changes are made in the name of broad majorities. The legitimacy of professional authority may have come under fire; it did not follow that the American state enjoyed a legitimacy of its own.

The programs that followed the discovery of crisis were bounded by the limits placed on the American public sector. Each new effort sought a source of legitimacy outside the government—reverting to the old patterns of professional dominance, searching for free economic markets, redefining the problem. More direct solutions than any the Americans tried are not hard to imagine. Indeed, the Canadians faced the same crisis in the same period, nationalized their hospital financing, and promptly got health care costs under control. Within fifteen years, the Canadian health care sector would consume 3 percent less of their GNP, although their prior cost experience had been precisely the same as the American. The Canadian solution was not seriously considered in the United States, for it involved unabashed state power over the hospital sector. Instead, the United States, caught between a widely perceived crisis and an inability to mobilize public power, ticked through the standard reform repertoire of American liberalism and then turned to a great experiment in deliberative democracy.

PAINLESS PRESCRIPTIONS

The first responses to the cost problem operated within the established rubric of provider dominance. The uncontroversial Comprehensive Health Planning (CHP) Program, passed in November 1966, funded voluntary planning agencies. Community leaders would coordinate "public, voluntary, and private resources" to meet local health needs. A series of amendments (in 1967, 1970, and 1972) pushed the agencies to focus on containing costs. However, the haphazard network of agencies was generally organized by hospital administrators who had neither the incentives nor the power to limit the expansion of their industry.[15]

A slightly bolder step followed in 1972. Legislation mandated Physician Standard Review Organizations (PSROs) to monitor the utilization and quality of local medical services, ostensibly with an eye to unnecessarily costly treatment patterns. The agencies were organized locally and then designated and overseen by federal officials. However, the cost-cutting effort remained firmly in medical hands. The legislation— after some agitation in Congress—forbade anybody but physicians to participate in PSRO decisions, banned the promulgation of national norms, and refused to permit federal officials to claim data generated by local agencies. In fact, local physicians were far more apt to dwell on the pricey matter of improving medicine than to take on the controversial task of criticizing professional peers for "inappropriate utilization." Nevertheless, physician leaders bitterly resented the legislation, "the most dangerous government intrusion into medical practice in American history, judged one AMA leader."[16] He was not far wrong. Although physicians had captured the regulatory effort, some congressmen had been seeking to promote lay judgments about essentially professional choices. Still, the first responses to the new problem did not break with the old political logic: the federal cost-cutting programs—CHPs, PSROs—ceded public authority to local medical elites in the hope that they would solve the problem themselves. The approach had been better suited to the industry's expansion than to its retrenchment.

A third political reflex was to redefine the problem. The Nixon administration along with many congressional leaders tried to dislodge the difficult new issue of rising costs and restore the old one of ensuring adequate medical coverage. Rather than grappling with inflation itself, they would protect individuals from catastrophic costs. Socializing the most expensive cases would only exacerbate overall medical costs (and the state's fiscal obligation). However, it returned public officials to comfortable political ground—removing financial barriers without meddling in the profession itself. Furthermore, the proposal offered the congressional ideal, providing concrete benefits to identifiable constituencies. Ultimately, public officials were trying to return to a debate they had already won. Rather than grapple with the limits of state power, they would pass Medicare again. In distinct contrast to the Canadian approach, the leading American proposal expanded financing without asserting cost controls. The Senate Finance Committee approved the legislation; the National Governors' Association endorsed it. In the end, the proposal was buried in the political wreckage of Watergate.

A fourth approach invoked an entirely different source of legitimacy. If state authority was suspect and professional autonomy caused difficulties, free-market competition offered an alternative solution. Certainly, it addressed the antistatist strain in American ideology. Furthermore, the providers themselves had inadvertently promoted the approach by cloaking their long struggle for autonomy as a defense of capitalism and "the American way" against incursions from government bureaucracy and state socialism. The Nixon administration embraced the powerful market symbols (as would the Ford, Carter, Reagan, and Bush administrations, each in a slightly different fashion). In 1973, a program promoting health maintenance organizations (HMOs) was enacted. HMOs are prepaid group health plans, widely touted as a way of disciplining the profession by injecting market forces into the health care sector. The government role would be to stimulate and protect the markets in a manner roughly analogous to antitrust policy; competition would do the rest, vitiating the crisis through the inexorable forces of supply and demand. The potency of the symbol led some Nixon administration officials to make widely extravagant claims: 90 percent of the nation would be enrolled in competitive health plans by 1990. (A prediction that would fall short by a factor of six.) Whatever the merits of the market claim—and they have been fiercely debated for twenty years— the HMO legislation briefly staggered the HMO industry, leaving it one of the most heavily regulated elements of the health sector until adjustments were made. Fifteen years of steady growth in prepaid group plans would achieve few of the promises that attracted five consecutive administrations. The market ideal always promised results for some distant future; the pressure of medical inflation on government budgets impelled political actors to search for more concrete and immediate results.

In short, the traditional patterns of American health policy did not square with the new definition of the problem, yet policy makers found it difficult to create a new approach. American public officials were caught between pressures for action and the lack of authority to undertake it. Their first responses carefully avoided governmental meddling in professional judgments. Public officials sought to turn the problem back to the profession. They tried to avoid government altogether and framed a policy based on the symbols of free-market competition. They sought to restore the old definition of the problem and to extend publicly sponsored insurance, a form of action whose legitimacy they had already won. (Predictably, direct government action was the only alternative that failed to win approval.) And, *mutatis mutandis*, they legislated a democratic wish.

REGULATION BY COMMUNITY CONSENSUS

In 1974, Congress passed the National Health Planning and Resources Development Act. The planning act pressed together what seemed to most observers an odd amalgamation of notions. It mixed minute specificity and vague generalities and was marked by colloquies in Congress that flatly contradicted passages in the bill. Immediately before the vote, Republican Senator Pete Dominick of Colorado rose to declare that "I for one am confused."[17]

The planning act established a national network of agencies (about 205, known as health systems agencies or HSAs) which would coordinate existing public and private resources. When the incoherent American state faces vexing problems, public officials often muster up this hope of rationalization without fundamental change.

The local health agencies were required to devise voluminous health planning documents (three-year plans, annual plans, and so on). Like coordination, planning is an abstraction that is easy to legislate. The health agencies were not given much guidance about what to plan *for.* The legislation proposed every health system desiderata that its authors could imagine. For example, planners were encouraged to foster better care for more people at lower prices; to overcome "geographic, architectural and transportation barriers"; improve competition; upgrade hospital management; help develop multi-institutional systems; and educate the public about their health habits.[18]

Proponents deflected criticism about the vagueness of the planning goals with a neo-Progressive nostrum: science. They distinguished this planning effort from failed predecessors, not by claiming to avoid industry dominance, but by touting the benefits of the latest planning technique. Ten technical assistance centers were to be established; each local agency would be staffed by planning professionals. The failure of "whiz kids" in both the Pentagon and the War on Poverty, less than a decade earlier, was forgotten. Scientific planning—a phrase endlessly repeated—would discern the public interest that had eluded health policy makers making narrowly political calculations.

The images of consensus, coordination, planning, and science all surrounded a controversial task, the regulation of capital expenditures in hospitals and nursing homes. Construction or expansion of health care facilities had to be certified as necessary by the planning agency regardless of who was paying. The agency, presumably measuring proposals by its scientifically derived health plans, would approve or deny a certificate of need. After all, reasoned the reformers, health care professionals made the decisions about health care consumption: physicians ordered tests and filled hospital beds. An expansion in health care facilities would be followed by an increase in demand for them. The planning act left plenty of loopholes. Physicians' offices were not included; neither were existing facilities or anybody's operating expenses. The new regulation addressed only the institutional supply side of the future.

The key to the entire health planning effort lay in direct community participation. In distinct contrast to the generalities about planning and regulation, citizen participation was specified in painstaking detail. All meetings were to be open to the community, advertised (in at least two newspapers, forty-eight hours in advance), and designed to allow plenty of opportunity for public comment. More important, the HSA governing boards were organized to reflect the community. In a sharp break with past American health policy, providers were limited to a minority of the seats; the rest were to be filled by consumers of health care, "broadly representative of the social, economic, linguistic, [and] racial . . . populations of the area."[19] The agencies were largely private nonprofit corporations funded by the federal government and, at least formally, independent of local political control.[20]

Just seven years earlier, Daniel Moynihan had prefaced his account of the community action agencies with *donna nobis pacem*, grant us peace. Yet here was a program organized along precisely the same lines (even the requirement for "broad participation"—apparently inadvertently—repeated the language of an old War on Poverty memo) promising nonpartisan consensus. The imagery of community was powerful enough to deaden the memory of recent efforts to achieve it.[21]

True to its civic-republican form, the program offered the community agencies no real power. Liberals pushed to invest the program with "teeth," significant regulatory authority. "Health planning without regulation to enforce it just doesn't work," insisted Congressman William Roy, a physician from Kansas. Senator Edward Kennedy (D-MA) would have had the citizen boards decertifying hospitals they ruled redundant.

Many members of Congress imagined the HSAs as an infrastructure for future national health insurance efforts. However, the program eventually emerged from Congress with virtually all of its teeth missing. Most HSA decisions were reduced to recommendations to be passed along to the proper authorities. In a larger political context, the weakness of the program was predictable: It was exactly the stalemate of public action that had led political officials to invoke images of community in the first place.

In sum, the program reflected an old American faith: direct citizen deliberation in local community agencies where—with the assistance of scientific technique—the people would form a consensus about the public interest without resorting to narrow power politics (or politicians). Health care elites opposed the programs, still struggling to maintain a trusteeship grounded in professional skill. "Consumers who insist on flying airplanes are called hijackers," said Russel Roth, an AMA vice-president; "a dangerous intrusion of the federal government into the practice of medicine," added Richard Palmer, chairman of the AMA Board of Trustees. However, if public officials were not able to challenge professional dominance with significant state powers, conservatives were hard pressed to turn back a program that invoked democratic mythology.

A FRAGMENTED POLICY

Facing a cost crisis, public officials legislated a regulatory program legitimated by a democratic wish. The pattern of ceding public authority directly to the medical profession was finally broken, at least in a formal sense. However, the HSAs operated in a fragmented policy environment, surrounded by hostile private and public institutions. They had almost no real power. And they were hobbled by the implausible organizational design that came from trying to regulate via community consensus.

Social scientists were not impressed by the prospects for change in health care policy: "Impossibly flawed." "A fatuously implausible construct." "We designed it backwards," judged one official. "Upside down," corrected a critic. "The awesome list of goals . . . strained the limits of credibility." Frank Thompson exposed the troubles simply by specifying the cost-cutting logic of the program.

If the community representatives picked economy from among the many regulatory goals; and they planned in a way that restricted expansion (forgoing the obvious benefits of more local facilities); and they said "no" to local institutions whose expansion did not fit the plans; and the state agency accepted the negative recommendations; and it all summed to less construction; then (assuming that less construction would lower costs) some diminution in costs might occur.[22]

Of course, if public officials could have designed a more coherent policy they would not have needed to resort to neo-Jeffersonian machinations in the first place. The American state was articulating a policy that it was not powerful enough to achieve. The citizen boards faced a multitude of checks to any regulation they might try.

First, the HSAs were immediately plunged into the tumult of American federalism. The program alarmed state, county, and local officials. They feared that HSAs might become health care power brokers within their jurisdictions but beyond their political reach. The governors won considerable control over the agencies as the program was being implemented. They won the power to draw HSA boundaries and to review HSA decisions—effectively reducing the agencies to advisory bodies. Finally, Congress tried to induce the states to legislate the authority for certificate-of-need regulation. Some flatly refused (at the cost of losing federal funds); most, lobbied hard by the medical industry, drafted weaker laws than Congress had intended. By 1978, only eight states had secured legislation that met federal standards. In typically American fashion, cost-cutting intentions in Washington were immediately diffused amid the cross-cutting cleavages of local politics.

Local turf wars were matched by clashes within the Washington bureaucracy. A new unit in the Department of Health, Education and Welfare (the Bureau of Health Planning and Resource Development) was formed to oversee the program. The bureau merged the staffs of three programs superseded by the planning act. The standard organizational confusion—murky lines of authority, more personnel than formally approved slots—was exacerbated by mixing staff members from programs with very different missions and outlooks.

Furthermore, by moving into areas that had previously lain beyond the scope of federal authority, the planning program provoked even more than the usual rush of litigation. The AMA contended that the act violated state sovereignty (citing the Tenth Amendment), due process, and equal protection (the Fourteenth Amendment). The National Association of Regional Councils, the National League of Cities, and various individual states and counties filed challenges of their own. When officials began to delineate the boundaries of local HSAs, the politics of gerrymandering triggered another set of suits. Longstanding local disputes were fought out over the health planning boundaries. In the end, roughly one-third of the local agencies operated with special waivers from the guidelines in the planning act. Naturally, when the program began to make regulatory choices, a third batch of suits was filed by local institutions who were denied expansion or aggrieved by the plans or disgruntled by the process.

In short, health care elites were offered a profusion of institutional opportunities to protect themselves from the program. They lobbied federal officials about regulations (one proposal elicited more than fifty thousand complaints), state legislatures over the certificate-of-need laws, governors and local officials about the agencies' boundaries, the HSAs themselves about specific projects, and state health authorities (and governors and legislatures) over adverse decisions by the HSAs. Those who exhausted the political sources of appeal turned to the courts. However, most observers agreed that the weakest link in the chain of public authority lay in the HSAs themselves.

First, the health professionals constituted a large minority of the governing boards (between 41 and 49 percent). Although mandating a consumer majority was a clear break with past policy, it did not seem enough to break with past politics. Here was the most elementary failure to distinguish between regulator and regulated. If long-established independent regulatory agencies could be captured by the industry they monitored, what hope would there be for the HSAs? The experts from the industry would be balanced by inexpert citizens.[23]

Second, local consumer interests did not seem to clash with those of the health professionals in any politically significant way. What could possibly induce HSA board members to fight against the expansion of medical services in their neighborhoods? Communities generally seek more facilities rather than fewer. Certainly, rising costs were a problem. However, Blue Cross premiums and Medicare taxes were set by distant bureaucrats; they were not obviously connected to any decisions a local board might make. The entire bias of the HSA enterprise seemed distinctly distributive. Local agencies were not allocating benefits from a fixed allotment. When they regulated, they judged proposals from individual hospitals whose funding had already been arranged, and they did so one case at a time so that different proposals did not directly compete with one another. Surely, this was the essence of pork barrel politics—highly individualized choices about distributing benefits, each made without reference to any other, none of them taxing any fixed budget. Consumers, it was widely believed, would share the providers' interest in encouraging the expansion of local institutions.[24]

Finally, even if citizens could overcome the limitations of ignorance and apparent self-interest, they still faced the lobbying of the professionals. Consumer board members were being asked to apply preformulated rules impartially (e.g., no new hospital beds where there were already more than four per thousand citizens) despite enormous political pressure. Larry Brown pictured the details of the process.

> Many hours of negotiation; the recurrent cycle of justification and critique; the charges of lay ignorance on the one side and provider dominance on another; the endless fiddling with formulas and ratios no one understands; the contrived public hearings at which a hospital displays its audio visual aids to testify to the urgent needs of a venerated community institution; the community in attendance (three fourths of it employed by . . . the hospital) rises in long winded support; the 4–3 vote finally taken at one AM in committee; the endless buttonholing and handholding; the threat of appeal and legal redress; all of this . . . raises the personal and organizational costs of nay saying very high.[25]

It would take confidence, knowledge, and perhaps even courage to turn down local projects. But what were the incentives to do so?

The Health Planning Act signaled a change in policy that the state was too weak to assert definitively. Most observers predicted that the HSAs would scarcely constitute a policy change of any sort. However, by legitimating the effort with the trappings of communal democracy, Congress subordinated disputes about political control to debates about representation within the program. The actual behavior of the health care boards would be shaped, at least in part, by who they answered to, by who selected representatives and how. Across the country, local agencies struggled to determine who qualified as a "consumer" of health care "broadly representative" of the community and how they ought to be chosen.

THE STRUGGLES OVER REPRESENTATION

Political reform had been propelled by an image of the people, of community consensus. Citizens would meet, deliberate, and define their health service needs. In political practice, the community turned out to comprise many conflicting interests; legislation that invoked consensus offered no principles by which to sort out the different claims for representation. Nor was there a clear constituency to come forward and seize the program (as African Americans had done with the similarly structured community action agencies of the War on Poverty). What, after all, was a health care consumer? The law and its implementing regulations seemed, at first blush, to offer little help: a health care consumer was not a health care provider (and not married to someone who was).

Across the nation, HSAs struggled to fill the governing boards with consumer representatives who would satisfy the federal funders in HEW. The only guide was the legislation's requirement that consumers be "broadly representative of the social, economic, linguistic . . . racial and geographic . . . populations of the area." (The implementing regulations simply repeated the phrase.) The local agencies all scrambled to meet the hazy ideal of "broad" representation.

The phrase was no more than a legislative circumlocution for *the people*. The unarticulated assumption was that, somehow, the entire community could be mirrored by the demographic characteristics of the twenty or so consumers selected for the governing board (or the executive committee, when governing boards began to run to a hundred or more members). Agencies developed extensive checklists of demographic types—religion, sex, education, age, income, and so on. Any group that sued or lobbied for a place would be added to the list. "There's one slot left," a staff member in central Illinois is reported to have said, "if we can find a retired Roman Catholic nun, we'll have [complete] representation." Clearly, chasing after examples of social groups— representations rather than representatives—was an inadequate model of consumer representation. The vagueness of the mandate gave standing to a large number of groups who claimed that they merited representation under the formula. Indeed, who did not? Suits were entered across the country. Left-handed Lithuanians never mobilized. But, within the rubric of the legislation, they could have made a case.[26]

Though several years of often confusing and sometimes bitter conflicts followed from the apparent ambiguity, the legislation defined exactly what public officials were groping for. Health providers had dominated health policy through out the twentieth century. This law, responding to a new kind of health policy dilemma, sought to break the pattern. The ideal of broad representation, of community, pushed aside health professionals with a symbolic constituency whose legitimacy was beyond question. What officials in Washington were struggling to define was a new constituency for health policy programs. For all the apparent ambiguities packed into "broadly representative consumers," Congress had defined precisely what it wanted: consumers were not providers. Beneath the philosophic confusion lay political simplicity.

Within this broad political rubric, many interests staked a claim for representation. Most understood that the key was not merely winning an ally on the board but winning the right to make selections. A broad range of interests competed for control of the boards within the context of fighting over representation. Underlying the disputes about who should be represented was a debate about what the agencies ought to do.

In many places, black Americans mobilized. The promises of participation sounded like a revival of the War on Poverty. After all, black neighborhoods suffered from dreadful health problems. The infant mortality rates for black Americans would rank thirtieth in the world, just behind the Sultanate of Brunei.[27] Here, said the civil rights challengers, was the health crisis HSAs should be addressing. Passages in the ambiguous Health Planning Act supported their claim that the program should focus on racial inequity and better access to health care.

Other groups came forward. Spokespeople for the mentally ill, native Americans, migrant farmers, and many others staked claims for representation on HSAs. In some places, rival social groups fought bitter conflicts; the Los Angeles agency was decertified when the clash of minority groups grew too intense for federal officials.

Far more quietly, an entirely different type of interest mobilized: corporate financial officers, Blue Cross vice-presidents, union officials, insurance company representatives (the latter trumpeting HSA participation in their advertising campaigns). They defined their claim to participation under both the vague aegis of "community service" and the more concrete claim to be major purchasers of health care. Of all the groups that came forward, their political object was closest to the problem that had been defined in Washington—the control of medical inflation.

The different claims for representation were adjudicated by officials in Washington. They forced the local agencies to embrace a wide range of mobilized interests. The various interests shared only a single significant trait: they were not providers. For a time, the different agencies took off in different programmatic directions, depending on the profile of the board members and the pressures of the local political environment. There was, at first, no distinctive national pattern. It was the next step in an old American reforming cycle that defined the agencies and the task they pursued. After the invocation of community consensus, the mobilization of previously quiescent groups into a new policy arena, and the conflicts over representation comes organizational retrenchment. Once the hot participatory issues are won and lost, political institutions generally focus on maintaining themselves. For the HSAs, this final phase defined the program's agenda and its overlooked political legacy.

The Decline of the Doctors' Power

The competing claims over the HSA agenda were ultimately settled by the demands made on the local agencies by officials in Washington. Throughout the 1970s the HEW bureaucrats pressured the HSAs to control health care costs. The agencies were, of course, not well organized to do so. However, they were the only national policy instrument available to federal officials increasingly consumed with the issue. HEW cajoled, threatened, regulated, and lobbied the agencies into emphasizing certificate-of-need regulation at the expense of other programmatic alternatives. The federal officials wielded a power over the HSAs that no other interest could match: organizational survival. The fate of the programs that preceded the Health Planning Act, the occasionally defunded agency, the accumulation of criticisms made by the agencies' many enemies, and the regular congressional calls for ending the program all granted verisimilitude to HEW's constantly reiterated threat: either the HSAs cut costs or they would be terminated.

The agencies could not miss the signals. Their utility to the federal funders turned on a single issue. As the members of the agency in Atlanta were fond of saying, "We bite the cost cutting bullet or we're gone." Across the nation, HSAs responded to the incentive and internalized the message. Other goals—like the reduction of infant mortality in black neighborhoods—were organized out of the process. Regardless of their background, ideology, constituency, or professed health care interest, consumer representatives struggled to work the unlikely regulatory apparatus. Across the country, they tried to control health care costs through certificate-of-need regulation. They did so to maintain the organizations to which they volunteered their time, for organizational survival hung in the cost-cutting balance.[28]

Despite almost universal expectations of provider domination, HSAs asserted their independence and struggled to control the health care industry. By the late 1970s, the media had discovered "the planners' new muscle" in Honolulu, Dayton, San Francisco, Pittsburgh, northern Indiana, and many other places. Two studies of New England HSAs found that almost all of them were fighting regulatory wars. My own case studies found the same result; despite often fiercely antiregulatory sentiments when the agencies first organized, HSAs across the nation eventually took up the weak cost control cudgels at their disposal.[29]

Prior analyses of the HSAs all focused on the same question. Did they succeed at controlling health cost? The answer is clear: no. It is, however, the wrong question. The actual outcomes in all those agonizing sessions where 4–3 votes were cast at 1:00 A.M. were irrelevant. For, in those late-night disputes, the medical profession lost its trusteeship over American medicine. In every community, groups of lay people were casting judgments on proposals submitted by medical professionals. As they did so, they transformed the way Americans think about health care policy. The hospitals may have won the 4–3 votes (or the appeal to the governing board, or the state agency, or the courts). However, in the process—in having to appeal at all—they had lost their hegemony over medical policy.

In sum, federal officials confronted a difficult new problem—uncontrolled growth in health care costs—without the political authority to assert an effective solution. The state had long ceded its authority over health care politics to the health care professionals. Both the strength of Americans' antistatist ideology and the weakness of their political institutions make it extremely difficult to strip control from private interests and place it in government hands.

Public officials overcame the limits of their authority by abjuring public power and calling instead on the people. The program that followed had all the trappings of democratic myth: community, participation, a consensual public interest (to be derived by a combination of representation and science), all coupled with the absence of authority and an ill-defined mission. The participatory reflex was not a conscious strategy—liberals had sought far stronger legislation. However, the invocation of community without any real power was all they could negotiate through the American shibboleths of antistatist ideology and democratic faith.

Once the program was operating, all kinds of groups mobilized, demanding representation. Local communities were plunged into conflicts that were unprecedented in the health care sector. However, the goal that eventually emerged was the one that federal officials—read, federal funders—cared about: health care cost control.

In the end, the lack of power which secured the legislation doomed the agencies. They did not have the political authority to achieve their policy goals. However, it is the process that mattered. The simple repetition of the HSAs' regulatory circus, year after year in community after community, stripped the medical profession of its authority over medical politics.

By the early 1980s, the agencies had been swept from the political limelight to the bureaucratic periphery. A host of newer programs took their place, operating with an authority that the HSA board members had unwittingly won. In many communities, lay interests that had entered health politics through health planning remained active. Business coalitions, Chamber of Commerce groups, corporate insurers, public officials, and consumer advocates who had sat on HSA subcommittees debating the need for a new nursing home or hospital wing maintained their interest in local health care politics. In addition, the state itself had developed a new legitimacy and new capacities. The claims of professional judgment which had once dominated medical politics were no longer trumps.

The Consumers' Legacy: A New Health Care Politics

By the early 1980s, a wide variety of new health policies had begun to emerge. For example, a half-dozen states appropriated the authority to set all hospital rates for all payers—an extraordinary intrusion into the most sensitive area of hospital management. In some cases, the government not only set the rates but also allocated the costs of uninsured patients among corporate payers—a complicated, hidden form of socializing medicine as intrusive as anything the AMA might have imagined when it was distributing the Reagan encomium to freedom in the early 1960s.

Even the Reagan administration, caught between its free-market rhetoric and its budget deficit, introduced powerful new controls on Medicare payments to hospitals. Once set by the providers with scant oversight, they are now computed on a basis that profoundly penetrates the boundaries of professional authority. Rather than paying whatever hospitals charge, Medicare pays a fixed rate for each procedure, based crudely on the average charge for that treatment. Hospitals are reimbursed the fixed amount, termed *Diagnosis-Related Groups* (or DRGs), regardless of the care they actually provide. Ultimately, the change is designed to alter the practice of medicine. Rather than deferring to physicians over proper medical treatment, Medicare sets unambiguous incentives for them to do less to hospitalized patients. In the historical sweep of American health policy, this is a profound assertion of public authority. In 1983, twenty years after affirming the sanctity of medical judgment (in the first sections of Medicare), Congress empowered the bureaucrats in the Department of Health and Human Services to reshape it.[30]

The discourse of health care policy has been reconstructed. The health industry, far from articulating a single perspective, is fragmented into competing interests. The corporate payers—insurance companies, large employers, labor unions, state governments, federal officials— now exert more influence on health policy than do the physicians or the hospitals.

Public officials have broken the "legitimacy barrier" in health politics. But this does not make broad-scale reform any easier to secure. The

American state remains fragmented, weak, biased against political action. Indeed, health care inflation has persisted, and even quickened, through the early 1990s.

Predictably, public officials used their new legitimacy to cope with rising costs in a piecemeal and haphazard way. The pieces, however, have summed into a consistent pattern. A growing list of complex, technical, formula-driven cost control programs have emerged. They are complicated to describe, hard to understand, offer the illusion of precision, and are not easily transformed into symbolic issues. (Resource-based relative value scales—RB/RVS—just don't sound like "socialized medicine.")

These technical methods rely on the traditional strengths of bureaucratic administrators: the precise coordination of highly specialized information. The process may be fundamentally political. However, the costs of entering the negotiations have grown very high and distinctly skewed. Participants must be ready to argue statistical models, assumptions, and formulas.

The result is not just a waning of professional political power. The bureaucratic politics also challenge underlying professional claims. The U.S. regulatory apparatus has begun to penetrate the offices, clinics, and hospitals of the profession itself. The search for cost control now challenges the essential nature of professional autonomy, of medical professionalism itself.

In 1989, Congress established the Agency for Health Care Policy and Research (AHCPR) to determine "how diseases, disorders and other health care conditions can most effectively be diagnosed and treated."[31] The expectation is that research teams can determine what is appropriate medicine under what conditions. The deeper faith is that inducing physicians to practice differently will produce higher-quality, lower-cost medicine. (An unidentified, endlessly repeated estimate is that 25 percent of the health care delivered in the United States is unnecessary.)

The AMA fought hard to keep the new research effort out of the hands of the Health Care Financing Administration. HCFA, asserted the medical association, would swiftly convert new findings into payment formulas for Medicare and Medicaid. The skirmish over which bureaucracy oversees medical outcomes research is part of the larger battle: reshaping the practice of medicine from outside the profession.

The managed care movement, championed in both public and private sectors, already judges medical practice in an extraordinary number of ways. In this new world, a Blue Cross (of Illinois) program sends monitoring teams into physician offices to judge everything "from appropriateness of primary care to the cleanliness of the office." And when physicians ask what criteria HCFA uses to trigger investigations for unnecessary care, the responses vary from "Can Doctors be Trusted?" (the *Washington Post*) to that's "like telling drug dealers when you're going to carry out a raid" (Congressman Pete Stark) to a $40,000 study to determine the costs of telling (HCFA).[32]

What is happening? The classic interest group liberal model is being transformed into a classic bureaucratic one. It is a profound break with both historical and international experience, one that puts U.S. medicine and U.S. public administration in distinctly uncharted territory.

The usual analysis of how we got here is different. Powerful secular trends have been reshaping U.S. medicine for decades: a huge growth in the number of physicians, a broad loss of faith in the profession itself, the apparently inexorable inflation in medical costs, the rise of medical capitalism, the splintering of the profession into subspecialties. These and other trends all put pressure on the medical profession and its political power. Never mind the bizarre law that called on American communities to negotiate complex policy problems without any real authority (but with plenty of participation). Rather, broad, deep trends within the profession and society led, inexorably, to the transformation of medical politics.

The flaw in this functionalist conventional wisdom lies in the uniqueness of U.S. developments. There is nothing inevitable about what has happened to our health regime. On the contrary, our OECD partners have all developed very different health systems. Elsewhere, stronger states created larger economic frameworks in which the medical profession continues to operate independently, with their medical authority largely undisputed. Our weaker, fragmented state, more narrowly bound by the preferences of clashing political groups, stumbled into a program that drew the actors together and—amid the complex politics described above—subordinated the medical profession. Naturally, there was a great deal more going on. And ultimately, the details of policy always reflect the deeper motions of political economy and social structure. But, in the end, American public officials extended their sphere of legitimate influence over the medical industry in a most round-about fashion—they did so under the cover of the people. The great irony of U.S. health policy is that, had the liberals succeeded and followed Canada to national health insurance, our medical profession might well have maintained the professional authority still maintained by the Canadian (and English and German) professions.

Conclusion: The New Politics

Still, the decline of interest group liberalism is hardly unique to health care. Many of the chapters in this volume note the same development in other spheres—our politics have grown "nationalized, judicialized, rationalized." Why?

In part, because the political landscape has shifted. We have moved away from a political setting that accommodated individualist, interest group–liberal arrangements to what I call a *dense political environment*.

The central feature of the traditional political establishment is, of course, weak and fragmented government—one not designed to focus national resources or mobilize the public for common projects. Political action is forged in a multitude of individualized agreements between public and private agents. Thus, a host of individual producers—fishing, lumber, tobacco, airlines, hospitals—negotiated their own benefits from public sector patrons. In classic interest group traditions, the state disperses benefits to individual interests without regard to other claimants or systematic effects. It is precisely what a loosely organized government is adept at doing.

In the increasingly dense environment of contemporary politics, large interests and organizations—public and private, domestic and foreign—have grown interdependent. The actions of one affect numerous others, often those that seem only distantly related. Problems in such a setting are not easily amenable to the simple striving of individual interests pressing ahead; there are too many consequences for too many others. Moreover, it is more difficult for government agents to assist one interest without repercussions for others. Decision making in such settings is far more complicated, marked by multiple and often unforeseen consequences. It requires policy makers to adopt longer time horizons and to weigh an expanded range of factors (and interests).

For example, consider the array of public and private institutions that are affected when hospitals dominate (or "capture," as political scientists used to say) the local rate review board and win large rate hikes for their services. Medicaid costs rise, creating problems in the state budget; Medicare costs increase (which probably means new federal cost control regulations). Private insurance companies pass the higher hospital costs to their corporate clients. Corporations, in turn, either self-insure (the large company response) or cut employee benefits (the small companies). When corporations self-insure, they scramble the insurance markets and move out of reach of state health regulators; when they cut benefits, hospitals face more patients with less insurance. In a dense political environment, even "capture" may rebound to the hospital's disadvantage. More generally, self-seeking behavior by each interrelated interest can yield disadvantages for all of them— precisely why health care competition has produced even higher costs and great gaps in health care coverage.

Consider a second illustration: Dams were once a pork barrel staple, a simple deal between public sector suppliers and private development interests. Now, antidevelopment forces (with their feared battle cry, "Not in my back yard") are likely to block these legislative boondoggles by taking them to the judiciary. More important, environmental concern—the essential illustration of dense politics—injects a wide range of new actors into the policy calculus. What was once a simple transaction is now complex and multifaceted.

American institutions are not designed to cope with such dense political conditions. What they produce is stalemate. The contemporary American dilemma lies in the disjunction between the bias of our institutions and the nature of contemporary politics. Ultimately, it is the conundrum that every chapter in this volume addresses.

Regulation and Deregulation

The New Politics of
Environmental Policy

M A R C   K .   L A N D Y

Environmental regulation is a major component of the new social regulation that has emerged since the late 1960s. Some aspects of the "new politics" that have forged this policy are relatively easy to explain. Environmental reform occurs because the public can afford it. In the United States (and in Western Europe and Japan as well), sufficient prosperity and economic and political stability have enabled politically active and powerful segments of the public to divert their attention from basic questions of survival to amenities like improving the quality of their physical surroundings.[1]

Affluence is catalyzed by scandal. The Santa Barbara oil spill, Love Canal, and Rachel Carson's exposé about the ravages of DDT were among the most notorious such policy-provoking events. In their wake came landmark environmental laws regulating water pollution, toxic spills, and pesticides.

As useful as the affluence-scandal model is, it leaves important aspects of the relationship between politics and environmental reform unexplained. It helps explain why environmental questions reached the public agenda when they did, but it has little to say about the scope and substance of the policy designs that were actually adopted to address those problems. More importantly, it cannot explain why so little learning about how to improve those designs has taken place over time. Why is there such a poor fit between the problems the laws are supposed to address and the policies devised to address them? Why have the initial mistakes embodied in these laws not been corrected when the laws have been revised, and why have these flaws been replicated in newer laws that address other environmental issues?

These peculiar and disturbing aspects of environmental policy are related to the common conceptual premise that they share—the premise of *rights*. The framers of these laws and of their subsequent revisions have persisted in posing key issues in terms of the people's right to a safe and healthy environment. In the words of Jay Hair, president of the nation's largest environmental organization, the National Wildlife Federation, "the right to a healthy environment is as inalienable as the right to free speech and freedom of worship."[2]

By defining environmental objectives in terms of rights, environmentalists were continuing the trend, begun by the Progressives, of supplementing the negative concept of rights contained in the Bill of Rights—meaning freedom from government intrusion—with a positive doctrine of entitlement. The New Deal presided over the extension of this notion of positive rights to matters of economic security. In the 1960s and 1970s, it was expanded to encompass rights for consumers, the handicapped, and aliens, as well as environmental health.[3]

Whatever the virtues or vices of conceiving of these other matters in terms of rights, the rights premise has proven particularly bedeviling with regard to the environment. Environmental quality is an inherently relativistic concept, at least when applied to questions of human health. People crave certainty. They want to know if the water is safe to drink or if inhaling a minute quantity of a particular chemical will give them cancer. At best, environmental health science can state such matters only in terms of probabilities. At the low doses in which most air- and water-borne pollutants are found in the environment, only a very small percentage of those exposed actually develop disease.[4] Thus, any given dose produces only the probability of disease, and this probability is itself uncertain. Also, probabilities vary among individuals in ways that are not well understood. On the one hand, no specific standard of air or water quality, other than zero, will protect everyone. On the other, it is by no means clear why very low risks stemming from pollution should constitute a rights violation when much higher risks stemming from driving a car, swimming, or even walking to work do not.

All but the most zealous environmentalists readily admit that they do not want to shut down all industrial output to achieve their goals; therefore, they tacitly acknowledge that the complete environmental purity needed to achieve environmental health for everyone is unattainable. However, key environmental statutes, such as the Clean Air Act, are worded as if this can and will be achieved.

Posing such inherently relativistic problems in absolutistic terms does not obviate the need to make choices, but it does obscure them. It deprives the polity of the very language required to make such choices rationally and coherently. To preserve the rights premise in the face of such difficulties, its proponents have been forced to reconfigure environmental laws in ever more convoluted and byzantine ways. This chapter examines this predicament with regard to two of the most important environmental statutes, the Clean Air Act and Superfund.

In an important sense, modern environmental policy began with the passage of the Clean Air Act of 1970. The rights premise had a seminal role in its passage, and a similar pattern repeated itself a decade later in the passage of the most important environmental reform of the 1980s, Superfund. An examination of the revisions of both the Clean Air Act and Superfund shows that, despite the many changes that have occurred in both, the key rights-based premises have not been reconsidered. As a result, the most important failings of these acts have been perpetuated and even exacerbated.

The Clean Air Act of 1970

The Clean Air Act, first passed in 1970 and revised in 1977 and 1990, is the single most important of all environmental laws. Its reach extends to virtually all U.S. smokestacks and tailpipes. The key to understanding the new politics that underlie its myriad provisions is the fact that it does not merely seek to improve air quality, it promises to establish a new right, a right to clean air. This new right is the fundamental premise upon which the act is built, and it remains the dominant factor in shaping subsequent air policy.

Before 1970, air pollution standards were set by the states, with the federal role limited to the reviewing of state plans. This system had been put into place in 1967 as a result of a law whose primary author was Senator Edmund Muskie of Maine.[5] The states proved slow to undertake their responsibilities under the 1967 act, and critics were calling upon the federal government to assume primary responsibility for standards setting. Muskie, however, felt that it was premature to judge the existing system a failure. His subcommittee prepared a revision of the act which sought to strengthen its enforcement provision but left its essential framework intact.[6]

Muskie's plan was derailed by the issuance of a report by a Ralph Nader study group which bitterly assailed the existing air law and Muskie's efforts to improve it and accused Muskie of selling out to business.[7] Also, the Nixon White House issued its own clean air proposal, which incorporated national ambient air standards and was therefore much more ambitious than Muskie's plan. Nixon's willingness to take the lead on air pollution control was strongly influenced by his desire to outflank Muskie, his likely rival in the 1972 election, regarding what he considered to be a popular issue. Muskie was identified in the public mind as the leading congressional environmentalist. It was therefore doubly embarrassing to be assailed by Nader and to have a conservative president take a stronger environmental stand.[8]

Muskie responded by scrapping his previous proposal and producing a new one endorsing national standards that were even more stringent than those Nixon had proposed. Muskie's proposal required that economic considerations be ignored in setting the standards. Human health alone would determine them. They would be set at a level "requisite to protect the public health, with an adequate margin of safety."[9] Muskie's proposal formed the core of the 1970 act.

Thus, the key political development in the passage of the Clean Air Act was Muskie's reversal on the issue of air standards. He simultaneously blunted Nader's criticisms and reasserted his position as the nation's leading pro-environment politician. In view of his interest in winning the 1972 presidential election, his motive was obviously political. But why did he deem it politically expedient to abandon a position that he believed in and adopt one that was so obviously flawed? After all, he was the nation's most prestigious authority on air pollution legislation. Why did he not try to convince the public of the superiority of his original position? The answer is once again a matter of rights.

In his foreword to *Vanishing Air*, Nader defines the pollution problem as the failure of the government to prosecute polluters for "harming our society's most valued rights."[10] Clean air is a right because it is necessary for preserving the essential nature of human beings. "The limits that must be imposed on social and technological innovations are determined not by scientific knowledge or practical know-how but by the biological and mental nature of man which is essentially unchangeable."[11]

To defend the existing program of state initiatives, Muskie would have had to question the rights premise as applied to air pollution. He would have had to explain that, since the decision about how clean to make the air is a political one, different states could well be left to render different verdicts about the standards they wished to achieve. Instead, he fully adopted a rights rhetoric. In his speech introducing his revised bill on the Senate floor, he proclaimed the right of every American to clean air. "100 years ago the first board of health in the United States, in Massachusetts, said this: We believe that all citizens have an inherent right to the enjoyment of pure and uncontaminated air . . . 100 years later it is time to write that kind of policy into law . . . Anybody in this nation ought to be able at some specific point in the future to breathe healthy air.[12]

Blame for this intellectual muddle should not be placed solely, or mainly, at Muskie's door. The late 1960s witnessed the flowering of what Melnick has termed the *rights revolution*, the extension of rights to a whole new bevy of claimants—students, consumers, aliens, and so forth.[13] The language of rights was in the air. For example, the Naderite appeal to human nature was echoed in the congressional testimony of the Sierra Club's Michael McClosky. "The parameters of ecological health are not negotiable. Nature has its law of limits. *Absolute results ensue when certain thresholds are crossed,* whether our political and economic institutions care to recognize them or not."[14]

Those who opposed the expansion of these entitlements seemed also to be unsympathetic with the grievances being made by blacks, consumer advocates, and environmentalists. There simply was no readily available repository of ideas that displayed sympathy for these claimants, proposed to help them, and yet rejected their claims to rights. In its absence, Muskie, as a working politician seeking to maintain his frontrunner status for the 1972 Democratic nomination, can hardly be faulted for adopting the menu of rights being dished up by his party's intellectuals.[15]

Richard Nixon faced no such exigency. His renomination was assured regardless of his position on clean air. But Nixon was a shrewd electoral politician. Nixon saw the appeal that environmentalism had for the middle-class suburban voters who were his core constituents, and he was determined not to cede the issue to the Democrats. Rather than strenuously objecting to the overblown rhetoric of the Clean Air Act, he adopted it as his own in the hope that, by appearing progressive on this issue, he could preserve his options with regard to a host of others.

Thus, three factors conspired to produce the distinctive version of pollution regulation that constituted the 1970 Clean Air Act. Two were narrowly political: (1) the existence of a policy promoter, Nader, savvy and aggressive enough to gain attention for his reform agenda and (2) a competitive electoral context in which two rivals strove to outdo one another in support of the reform agenda. But the underlying condition that gave life to the other two was the rights premise. The unavailability of a credible critique of that premise deprived both Nixon and Muskie of the political latitude to question the Naderite approach without abandoning their claims to leadership regarding this popular issue.

Perhaps the rights premises of the Clean Air Act would have been subjected to more skeptical scrutiny were it not for the particular policy design it incorporated. Despite its scale and scope, it required little in the way of public revenue. Instead, it employed regulatory mandates to force private parties to comply with its standards. At one level, this is a distinction without a difference. The real costs of the act are, for the most part, paid by consumers. It is really a sales tax. But, since the effect is experienced indirectly via higher prices, the public is unaware of the true dimensions of the price it pays for cleaner air and is inclined to treat it as a free good.

Superfund

The formulation of Superfund, the federal law governing abandoned hazardous waste sites, involved essentially the same political pattern as did the Clean Air Act. A policy promoter, in this case the Environmental Protection Agency (EPA) itself, was able to turn partisan competition to its advantage because of the reluctance of either Democrats or Republicans to challenge its rights-premised problem definition.[16]

At first glance, abandoned hazardous waste sites would seem to defy the need for federal intervention. Unlike air or water pollution, these sites do not move, and so they do not cross state boundaries. The problems they pose are local in origin and local in effect. Yet they came to be defined not as nuisances to be addressed by the surrounding community but as violations of basic rights to a clean and safe environment. Since rights are federally defined, perforce, they must be federally protected.

The initial impetus for Superfund came from a widely publicized environmental scandal, the discovery, in 1978, of a massive abandoned toxic waste dump beneath a suburban upstate New York neighborhood known as Love Canal. To make the case for federal action, the EPA first had to show evidence that similar problems existed nationwide. It created a task force of agency personnel whose mandate it was to uncover evidence that "ticking time bombs" were to be found across the land, in as many congressional districts as possible. Dutifully, the task force completed its mission. Sites were found and congressional offices were so informed.[17] No similar effort went into determining how great a risk such sites might actually pose and under what circumstances. Not for another seven years, after an even stronger version of Superfund was passed in 1986, did the agency come forward with a report admitting that the health risks of abandoned hazardous waste sites were overrated.[18]

Having made the case for federal action, the EPA framed its policy plan on a rights basis. Two key elements undergirded the rights approach. First, the proposal avoided the question of how much cleanup a given site should receive. To ask the question would imply that a trade-off existed between the degree of risk reduction to be achieved at a site and the amount spent on cleaning it up. At some point, the costs of further cleanup might outweigh the benefits of further reduction. Rather, the act implied that all sites would be cleaned up to a degree that guaranteed everyone's right to safety. Second, to ensure that this guarantee of protection did not impose great burdens on the taxpayers and thus cause them to inquire whether such a "right" was really worth creating, Superfund, like the Clean Air Act, kept the major responsibilities for funding the program off budget. It relied on liability law to impose the bulk of cleanup costs on responsible private parties.[19]

Neither of these two elements has functioned as intended. The EPA does, in fact, restrict spending on individuals sites below the level that would guarantee everyone's safety because, technically, total cleanup is impossible. And liable parties do not pay for most of the cleanup if one uses the commonsense meaning of liability (i.e., that one's contribution to the cleanup should bear some reasonable relationship to one's degree of responsibility for creating the problem).[20] Instead, the principles of strict joint and several liability and of retroactive liability have been invoked to ensnare parties who bare only the most indirect and tangential responsibility for the cleanup problems they are being forced to pay for. This broadening of the liability net is required to come up with sufficient revenues to pay the high costs of ambitious cleanup. Misleading though they may be, these principles are necessary to preserve the impression that rights are being protected at no great cost to the public.[21]

The EPA as Policy Promoter

The impetus for Superfund and the rights premise that undergirds it came not from outside advocates but from the government itself. To win its passage, the EPA adopted the posture of policy advocate and waged a brilliant legislative campaign. One might expect a federal agency, particularly one founded by Republicans, to be skeptical of rights claims and to try to place new policy initiatives on a firmer analytic footing. To understand why the EPA promoted such a dubious policy, one must understand how presidents Nixon and Carter conspired, inadvertently, to turn the EPA into an environmental advocate.

The original plan for creating an environmental protection agency, formulated by Nixon's advisory council on executive reorganization, was to combine pollution control with the resource development and conservation activities of the Department of the Interior and the Department of Agriculture to form a single Department of Natural Resources. The key virtue of this new department would have been that, because of the vast scope of its responsibilities, it would have had to consider the difficult tradeoffs between environmental protection and resource development. The idea was ultimately rejected because of opposition from Nixon's cabinet and because the logical choice to head such a powerful department was the incumbent secretary of the interior, Walter Hickel, a man Nixon mistrusted. Instead, the president accepted the council's alternative recommendation to establish a separate agency with a mandate limited to environmental protection to be located within the executive office of the president.[22]

Under the gifted leadership of William Ruckelshaus and Russell Train, the EPA successfully developed a strong constituency in the environmental community and in Congress, a constituency capable of sustaining it and protecting it against forces in the administration who felt it was betraying the pro-business orientation of the administration as a whole. Over the years, key congressional leaders, most notably Edmund Muskie and Henry Waxman, developed a proprietary interest in the agency and acted vigorously to create statutory means for warding off presidential efforts to exert greater control over it.

Thus, Nixon created an organizational Frankenstein. Because it does not have a mandate to consider the tradeoffs between the environment and the economy, it has not done so. Because it reports to the president directly, in practice it reports to no one. Except under the rarest of circumstances, the president is far too preoccupied with more pressing matters to spend the time it would take to rein in the EPA. Instead, the EPA's recommendations become the subject of adversarial maneuvering with other executive agencies who do not share its environmental preoccupation—Interior, Energy, the Council of Economic Advisors, Treasury, and, most especially, the Office of Management and Budget. Participation in such squabbles serves only to reinforce the EPA's own sense of itself as an environmental partisan that must exaggerate its claims to protect them from the equally exaggerated counterclaims of its bureaucratic enemies.[23]

President Carter aggravated the problem by appointing a top management team at EPA whose loyalties were more to the environmental movement and their congressional allies than to him. This was not so true of the administrator, Douglas M. Costle, as it was of the talented team of assistant administrators who served under him. For example, the assistant administrator for air was David Hawkins, who had been a staff attorney for the Natural Resources Defense Council and who returned to that organization when he left government. The team that wrote Superfund was led by two former Muskie subcommittee staffers.[24]

Superfund also provided an occasion for Costle to press his effort to reposition the agency strategically. He had made a conscious decision to create a new image for the EPA as a public health agency. This aim stemmed from his view (mistaken as it turned out) that general public support for the environment was waning and that the agency could only prosper by attaching itself to public concern about health.[25] He embarked on a series of initiatives all designed to demonstrate EPA's commitment to health.

Thus, the EPA promoted Superfund because it wanted to and because it could. The agency's insulation within the executive branch gave it sufficient discretion to redefine the agency's mission and then to promote a new policy initiative that would provide it with the authority and resources to pursue that mission.

The able public servants who made up that team were neither purposefully deceitful nor disloyal. But, as a result of their ties and their own outlook, the question they posed in devising Superfund was not Is this policy the most efficient means for addressing the relatively minor environmental problem posed by abandoned hazardous waste sites? Rather, it was How can we best make use of the extraordinary opportunity presented by Love Canal to expand EPA's regulatory authority and expand its resources?

An agency like the EPA has great power to influence policy change. It possesses a wealth of technical expertise not available elsewhere. Also, despite the prevailing hostility to government, it is perceived to be more impartial and trustworthy than a private party. Therefore, it is of enormous importance that it not be allowed to become the captive of special interests, be they pecuniary or ideological.

Placing the EPA within a Department of Natural Resources would have made such capture less likely. Because the department's mandate would have included both a concern for resource development and environmental protection, deliberation about the relationship between the two would have been encouraged and the temptation to enshrine either one as a right might have been checked. In the absence of such structural protection against capture, the best substitute would have been a senior management team committed to preventing it. The Carter EPA, which devised Superfund, embodied neither of these two attributes.

The 1977 Clean Air Act

Like the original Superfund, its 1986 reauthorization and the 1977 and 1990 revisions of the Clean Air Act failed to "learn" from the Clean Air Act. To protect the rights premise from political assault, these acts further contorted the original policy designs, exacerbating some of their worst flaws. As the time for reauthorizing the Clean Air Act approached, change became inevitable. The act had provoked consequences unacceptable to environmentalists, and these consequences threatened a serious and potentially devastating counterattack on the part of other powerful political interests.

Because regulation of nonattainment areas was more stringent than that of areas in compliance, the act seemed to abet the dispersal of industrial activity from highly populated Eastern and Midwestern metropolitan areas toward low-density areas in the South and West.[26] Although such dispersion might be defensible on strictly public health grounds, it was bitterly opposed both by environmentalists and by the congressional delegations from nonattainment areas. The former did not want pristine areas to be degraded. The latter were unwilling to obtain improved environmental quality at the price of decreased economic activity, diminished tax rolls, and higher unemployment in their districts. If the basic principles of the act, particularly the National Ambient Air Quality Standards (NAAQS), were to survive intact, some means would have to be found to diminish the incentive for firms to move from dirty to clean areas.

Also, the New Source Performance Standard (NSPS) as applied to coal-burning power plants threatened to drastically change the regional pattern of coal production in a politically unacceptable manner. Many power plants were finding that they could meet that standard more cheaply by importing low-sulfur coal from the West than by putting into place the scrubbing equipment needed to achieve it with the high-sulfur Eastern or Midwestern coal that most of them were currently using. Such a switch threatened to close vast segments of the coal-mining industry in West Virginia, Kentucky, Indiana, and Ohio.

The high-sulfur fields were the bastion of the politically influential United Mine Workers of America (UMWA). The union had shown little capacity to organize workers in the low-sulfur Western fields. Senate Majority Leader Robert Byrd and the chairman of the House Interstate and Foreign Commerce Committee, Harley Staggers, whose committee had jurisdiction over the act, were both from West Virginia. They could, and would, use their powerful positions to prevent the death of their state's most important industry.[27]

To preserve the rights-based fundament of the act, environmentalists had to address both of these objections. They succeeded in doing so, but at an enormous cost to both the economy and the environment. They were able to placate the nonattainment areas in two ways. First, they agreed to a delay of the deadlines for attainment. The 1970 act had called for the attainment of the NAAQS by 1975. As of that date, most nonattainment areas were still violating one or more of those standards, but, in anticipation of a major overhaul of the act in 1977, these failures were overlooked by the EPA. The 1977 revision stretched the deadlines out to 1982. Second, they fashioned a policy of "prevention of significant deterioration" (PSD), which made it more difficult and expensive for firms to degrade the air in areas that were in attainment. PSD won the endorsement of Ohio, the state with the most severe stationary source pollution problems in the nation, and of the National Association of Counties. The National League of Cities endorsed PSD as a way to address "the need to protect against massive industrial migration to clean air regions."[28]

Environmentalists placated representatives from the high-sulfur coal fields by amending the NSPS for coal-fired power plants to require that, in addition to meeting the standard, plants would have to achieve a percentage reduction in the sulfur content of the coal they burned, regardless of how clean or dirty it was to begin with. As interpreted by the EPA, this change in the statute required *all* coal-fired power plants to install scrubbing equipment regardless of what type of coal they burned. Since they had to scrub anyway, many plants would not have any incentive to buy low-sulfur coal. Thus, the economic position of high-sulfur coal was preserved.[29]

Whatever their political advantages, these compromises had very bad economic and environmental consequences. Extending the deadlines for another five years meant that, for that period, standards would continue to be flouted. It encouraged firms to adopt a cynical posture toward compliance. If failing to comply could succeed in obtaining a delay this time, why would not such a strategy work again and again, ad infinitum. In fact, the deadlines were stretched out continually throughout the ensuing decade.[30]

The PSD provision increased the cost of environmental compliance well beyond what could be justified on the basis of the NAAQS. Thus, it created a bias in favor of firms continuing to make use of older, dirtier equipment in highly populous urban areas where the risks of pollution-related illness were the greatest. Requiring scrubbers for everybody had the same perverse environmental consequence. Because it added greatly to the cost of building new power plants, utilities were encouraged to continue to use existing, dirtier plants. It also redistributed millions of dollars from the utilities' rate payers to certain coal companies and their employees.

The 1990 Clean Air Act

The political landscape surrounding the reauthorization of the Clean Air Act in 1990 was far different from that of 1977. Despite the onset of divided government, it was far more hospitable to the act's proponents. The political power of both the high-sulfur coal industry and the nonattainment areas had considerably weakened. Redistricting had reduced the strength of big cities in the House of Representatives. Moreover, the loss of manufacturing jobs during the 1980s meant that many urban congressmen had fewer jobs to protect and were therefore more willing to be influenced by the environmentally oriented segment of their constituency.[31]

In 1990, Byrd was no longer Senate majority leader. Although he continued to wield considerable power as chairman of the Senate Appropriations Committee, the new leader was one of the Senate's leading environmentalists, Muskie's protege, George Mitchell of Maine. Although the retirement of Harley Staggers as chair of the House Commerce Committee damaged coal interests, his replacement, John Dingell of Michigan, greatly strengthened the hand of the automobile industry.[32] As the 1980s wore on, the control over environmental matters of Dingell's committee came under greater challenge from the chairmen of its environmental subcommittee, Harvey Waxman from smogbound Los Angeles.[33]

The mounting congressional pressure for strengthening the Clean Air Act was checked throughout the 1980s by President Reagan's vehement opposition. The certainty of a veto dampened the ardor both of environmentally minded Republicans who were loathe to tilt swords with their president and of House Democrats, particularly members of the Commerce Committee, who did not want to risk the ire of Dingell in a losing cause.[34]

The election of George Bush did more than just remove an obstacle to passage. In the 1988 campaign Bush promised to be "the environmental president" and pledged to support clean air legislation.[35] Having pledged in advance to support a strong bill, he lost the leverage he might otherwise have had to shape it to his liking. This is not to say that the White House had no bargaining power vis-à-vis Congress. Senator Mitchell bargained intensively with the White House to gain its help in mustering enough Republicans to be able to overcome a threatened filibuster. But these negotiations were over details.

If, after promising a strong bill, Bush had tried to challenge the Clean Air Act's rights-based premises and the key policies that stem from it, he would have been attacked as anti-environment and been accused of reneging on his campaign promise. Having kept the bill intact during the Reagan years, both Waxman and his Senate counterparts would have preferred no bill to one that challenged its central tenets. Bush's pledge gave them the upper hand and ensured that the rights-based fundament of the act would remain intact and could even be extended.

The act takes up 314 pages of the *Federal Register* and is almost seven times as long as the 1970 version. It has many new and original features, including the use of alternative fuels and a marketable permit system for trading sulfur dioxide (SO_2) emissions. It is rife with mandates, deadlines, "hammers," and timetables, all geared to deprive bureaucrats and emitters of discretion and flexibility.

But these changes do not alter its essential standards-based command and control structure. NAAQS, PSD, and NSPS were not changed in any but trivial ways.[36] Rather, the changes represent a kind of perverse learning. The lesson learned from the EPA's twenty-year failure to provide people with their environmental rights is not that those rights are unattainable but that the agency has been insufficiently vigorous in pursuit of them. Therefore, the means for attaining those rights must be specified in greater detail, with stricter and more certain penalties provided for failure to adopt these means.

As Henry Waxman himself explained,

The specificity in the 1990 Amendments reflects the concern that without detailed directives, industry intervention might frustrate efforts to put pollution control steps in place. This could happen either directly, through EPA inaction, or indirectly, through interference with EPA rule making efforts by White House entities such as the OMB or, more recently the White House Council on Competitiveness. History shows that even where EPA seeks to take strong action, the White House will often intervene at industry's behest to block regulatory action.[37]

To an extent unprecedented in prior environmental statutes, the pollution control programs of the 1990 amendments include very detailed mandatory directives to the EPA, rather than the broad grants of authority that would allow wide latitude in the EPA's implementation of the CAA programs. In addition, statutory deadlines are routinely provided to assure that the required actions are taken in a timely fashion. More than two hundred rule-making actions are mandated in the first several years of the 1990 amendment's implementation.[38]

Perhaps the most significant change in the 1990 version was the virtual elimination of state discretion over how to bring nonattainment areas into compliance. For example, regarding ozone, the act establishes six different categories of nonattainment areas, ranging from moderate to extreme. The severity of the regulatory action required varies depending upon the designation. The more severe the problem, the more mandated actions are required. In the most severe problem areas, the act requires regulation of sources emitting as little as twenty-five tons, a level that might include gas stations, auto paint shops, and dry cleaners. The original act required that states make "reasonable progress" toward meeting deadlines, but the new act specifies the percentage of reduction that must be met each year.[39]

A similar decrease in flexibility pervades the changes in the regulation of toxic air pollutants. The 1970 act gave the EPA authority to list those chemicals that it found to be toxic and to establish emission standards for them at a level that provides "an ample margin of safety to protect the public health."[40] By 1990, the EPA had succeeded in listing only seven such substances. To show its dissatisfaction with this rate of progress, Congress declared 189 chemicals to be toxic, set emissions limits for them, and mandated the technology to be used to meet those limits.[41]

It is one thing to specify results but quite another to obtain them. The congressional drafters of the act had been continually frustrated by the failure of the agency to meet existing mandates, deadlines, and timetables. To overcome this frustration they made use of a device that they had used earlier in the 1984 amendments to the Resource Conservation and Recovery Act, the "hammer." Instead of waiting for the agency to fail to meet a deadline and *then* trying to get it to correct itself, the hammer specifies exactly what will happen if the deadline is unmet. For example, the 1990 act requires that in certain nonattainment regions the gasoline sold after 1 January 1995 must meet special EPA specifications. A hammer provision states that, if the EPA has not issued those specifications on time, the sale of all gasoline in the designated areas must cease.[42]

The act does contain one very important departure from the "command and control" approach, the acid rain provision. It allows power plants to trade rights to emit sulfur dioxide. If they can cheaply reduce their emissions below the 50 percent reduction mandated by the act, then it makes sense to sell the surplus at a profit. If it is too expensive to meet the target, they can buy additional allowances instead. Thus, the provision establishes a market in SO_2 allowances as a means to meet the overall goal of a 50 percent reduction at the lowest possible cost.[43] The most innovative provision in the law deals with a problem whose impact is on forests and streams, not human health. It seems that Congress is prepared to depart from its commitment to the cumbersome inflexibility of "command and control" only when it does not feel compelled to define the problem at issue in terms of human rights.

The Superfund Reauthorization of 1986

From its inception in 1980, Superfund's performance was dismal. Despite the "ticking time bomb" image that had been created, very few sites had been cleaned up. Instead, cleanups were being stalled as potentially responsible parties engaged in legal battle both to deny their own liability and to lessen their costs by dragging others into the liability net. Such non–cleanup-related "transaction costs" made up the largest percentage of the billions spent on Superfund by corporate America.[44]

As with the 1990 Clean Air Act, the perceived failure of the law did not lead to a rethinking of its rights-based objectives but rather to the adoption of more draconian means for attaining them. Because no formal standard existed for determining how much cleanup to do at a particular site, each site cleanup was done on an ad hoc basis. This lent credence to the charge that those sites with politically powerful constituencies received more cleanup.

Instead of responding to this perception by explicitly adopting a risk-benefit approach, the revised Superfund protects the right to safety by establishing uniform cleanup standards. All cleanups must meet all "applicable or relevant and appropriate" state and federal environmental air and water quality standards (ARARs).[45] To recognize how truly ambitious the ARAR requirement is, one must remember that virtually all of the standards to be met were not written with hazardous waste cleanup in mind. They demanded levels of quality that often required unbelievably expensive treatment at a site that had been degraded as much as many Superfund sites were. But the new law gave no real room for asking what possible benefits would be obtained from the tens of millions of dollars it could cost to insist that a site, which might well be in the midst of other dirty and smelly industrial workplaces, be restored to a pristine condition, a state that it may well not have enjoyed even before it became a hazardous waste dump.

To obtain these high levels of cleanup, the new law rejected the relatively cheap alternative of containment in favor of "permanent treatment." Containment may involve no more than capping a site, preventing the toxic chemicals it contains from spreading to adjacent land or leaching into drinking water supplies. Permanent treatment requires the use of chemical or biochemical agents to detoxify the hazardous material.[46]

Permanent treatment does offer palpable environmental benefits, at least if it is done on site and therefore does not require the toxics to be transported. But it does so often at a very high price. Since the liability regime has failed to supply adequate resources, Superfund cleanup does depend to a large extent on tax revenues. Because such revenue is in short supply, the permanent treatment requirement has perverse environmental consequences. Such expensive remediation can be performed on only a few sites. Therefore, fewer sites can be treated. The risk of leaving many other sites unattended may well be greater than that of providing a lower level of treatment to them all. Therefore, the net result of the more stringent cleanup requirements of the 1986 Superfund revision may well be to increase the health risks posed by abandoned hazardous waste sites.

Politics Old and New

As this review of environmental policy change indicates, the "new" politics of rights does not preclude an "old" politics of interests. Private firms have interests, government agencies have interests, even public interest groups have interests. The rights premise simply creates a new and perhaps more promising venue for each of these political actors to pursue self-regarding objectives.

In pressing for permanent treatment, environmentalists enjoyed the support of that segment of the environmental cleanup industry poised to provide this expensive remedial assistance. Companies that clean up toxic waste are represented by the Hazardous Waste Treatment Council (HWTC). This association severed itself from a broader contractors' organization because that group also represented landfill operators. The HWTC claims that landfills do not provide a "permanent" solution to the toxics dumping problem.[47]

The alliance between the HWTC and the environmentalists in support of permanent treatment is a classic "bootlegger and Baptist" alliance in which high-minded supporters of stringent regulations join forces with those who will profit from them.[48] A similar phenomenon occurred in the 1977 Clean Air Act debate as a coalition of coal miners, coal operators, and environmentalists formed to support "scrubbers for everybody."

The future holds excellent prospects for the bootlegger-Baptist liaison. The cleanup of hazardous and radioactive wastes at military facilities has the potential to provide a bootlegging opportunity of staggering proportions. This activity is virtually the only part of the defense budget that is experiencing growth of any real magnitude. Cleanup has been estimated to cost at least 100 billion dollars over the next several decades.[49] Faced with the loss of much of their current business, major defense contractors like Lockheed are gearing up to exploit this new business opportunity. These firms will surely call upon the same congressional allies who proved so helpful to them in their previous government contracting endeavors. Thus, the same coalition that undergirded what Eisenhower called "the military-industrial complex" now has a strong motive to turn toxic wastes into the Soviet menace of the 1990s. Its success in this effort will depend upon the willingness of the environmental "Baptists" to join in demanding that the very expensive cleanup requirements dictated by Superfund's rights-based approach be applied to federal facilities cleanup as well.

The EPA's involvement with Superfund was in many ways a classic story of self-interested bureaucratic politics. Fearing that ecology was an insufficiently strong foundation upon which to build, the EPA chose, in the late 1970s, to recast itself as a public health agency. The passage of Superfund did much to enhance the image of the EPA as a cancer fighter and to expand its budget despite the prevailing fiscal austerity.

The rights-based policy design embodied by both the Clean Air Act and Superfund also serves the political interests of the environmental movement. The repeated stretchouts of deadlines have deprived the NAAQS of much of their practical significance, but they still retain crucial symbolic value. The environmentalist and labor members of the National Commission on Air Quality opposed doing away with the deadlines for meeting the NAAQS because that "would legitimize the perpetual failure to provide healthful air quality."[50] Such failures may be tolerable for a considerable period, but they should never be made "legitimate." Thus, the key importance of deadlines, as Shep Melnick has argued, is political. Missed deadlines are emblems of government failure. They represent "another right violated, another promise unfulfilled."[51]

Perpetual failure to meet deadlines gives advocates of more air pollution control a key rhetorical advantage. Why is the government still refusing to do what is right? How can it condone this miserable situation? How long must we tolerate dirty air? The insistence on meeting all "applicable or relevant and appropriate state and federal environmental air and water quality standards" and on requiring permanent treatment performs the same rhetorical role vis-à-vis Superfund. The very inability to attain these often irrelevant standards and actually to achieve "permanence" provides the environmental movement with a continual supply of unmet promises and violated rights to decry.

Conclusion

This chapter presents a very grim picture of the consequences that stem from the rights-based approach to environmental policy. It is worth speculating whether such an approach is or was inevitable. Its success depended upon the ability of the environmental movement and its congressional allies to create the impression that it was the only legitimately pro-environment position. This victory was not the result of obtaining an expert consensus. Environmental economists and many environmental health scientists as well are committed to an alternative, utilitarian approach based upon the application of cost-benefit criteria to environmental decision making. But, unlike the case with transportation deregulation, these experts have been unable (with a few notable exceptions like the acid rain permits program) to exert much leverage on the environmental policy debate.

The transportation analogy may well prove instructive. In that instance, expert opinion proved most powerful after an apostle of deregulation, Alfred Kahn, was placed in charge of a key regulatory agency, the Civilian Aeronautics Board (CAB). He not only staffed the agency with deregulation disciples, but also used his position as a "bully pulpit" from which to preach the deregulatory gospel, garnering a measure of public attention unavailable to him when he was merely a college professor.[52]

As the CAB example demonstrates, the technical resources at the disposal of public agencies and the ability of their leaders to command the public stage may enable them to play a pivotal role in policy debate. Perhaps the key to a *new* new politics of environmental protection would be a reconstituted environmental protection agency capable of educating the public and the rest of the government about environmental issues, much as Kahn's CAB did about transportation questions.[53]

The CAB analogy is not perfect. In that case, reform was limited to a single piece of policy advocacy. Once that task was finished, the CAB no longer had a function and it was abolished. The EPA's duties are ongoing. The alternative to a rights-based approach would be a deliberative one in which all pertinent factual, political, ethical, and efficiency issues receive a full airing.

The mission of the EPA should be to provoke and lead such a sustained, comprehensive deliberation, which, of course, must involve all interested parties as well as the broader public and its elected representatives. Crucial to the success of such leadership is the ability to educate the public. The EPA's leaders should serve as champions of the technical merits, commenting publicly when a particular policy proposal, whether rights-based or otherwise, is infeasible, overly optimistic, or too costly. They should provide a scrupulous overview of what is known and what is not, illuminating both the empirical and the ethical import of alternative policy choices.

An agency like the EPA has many opportunities to engage in public education. It testifies before Congress, issues myriad documents that appear in the *Federal Register*, briefs the president and other executive officials, and holds press conferences. Its leaders make speeches. Each time the agency is obliged to respond to interest group comments or to hold a public hearing regarding a proposed standard or regulation, it has the chance to explain and to clarify the core issues raised by a proposed course of action.

The success of such a mission requires, first of all, that it be viewed as the proper one for agency officials to perform. This would necessitate a change in the prevailing climate of opinion within federal agencies which both abets and rewards the sort of policy entrepreneurship exemplified by the EPA's role in Superfund. As long as senior and middle level administrators believe that they are expected to be policy entrepreneurs, that is what they will be. They will seek out science and scientists whose findings justify the policy initiatives they favor.

If, on the other hand, they were to understand that their job is mainly to provide neutral competence for their politically responsible superiors, they would be far more likely to act that way.[54] The point is not to pretend that all politics and ideology can be wrung out of government to produce comprehensive "management," but rather that more or less disinterested behavior on the part of public servants is possible, depending upon their self-conception. And, further, that their self-conception will be strongly affected by the training they undergo and the incentives they receive.

It is a small but decisive step from discovering that bureaucrats often function as policy entrepreneurs to celebrating that development. Such a subtle but important shift has in fact taken place in the posture toward public executives adopted by the study and teaching of political science and public administration. Public executives are now referred to as "public managers" rather than "civil servants," as if to say that government agencies should pursue "lines of business" to be managed in order to produce a product for the public, just as private businesses do. The contrast with the earlier locution, which suggests a role subordinated to the polity and its needs, could hardly be more marked. Thus, the graduates of programs in public policy or public administration enter government service under the impression that their job is to know their line of policy and sell it.[55] They could be taught instead that their job is to be skeptical about policy initiatives, to provoke deliberation about those alternatives, and to publicize the fruits of those deliberations.

For such a change in orientation to be sustained, the reward structure within the bureaucracy would have to reinforce it. Promotions and raises would have to go not to the most successful policy entrepreneurs but to those who most effectively served their superiors by asking inconvenient questions of experts and by formulating reasonable criteria by which to evaluate competing policy proposals.

Difficult as such changes are to bring about, they would be well received by many segments of the EPA's public. Those members of Congress who do not view themselves as captives of the environmental movement nor of industry would benefit from a more disinterested source of information. That segment of the media that seeks to report environmental stories responsibly would find a better guide for posing their stories impartially and for highlighting key scientific controversies. A great deal of tension within the bureaucracy itself would be relieved. Many bureaucrats remain very uncomfortable with policy advocacy and long to become civil servants again. They would be quite happy to trade the job of salesperson for one that is both more public spirited and more intellectually demanding.

Most important of all, such a change would be of great assistance to the president. His educational needs are staggering. Buffeted on all sides by contradictory demands and statements of fact, he desperately needs dispassionate advice. Nowhere is this need greater than with regard to the environment. Except for Reagan, every president since Nixon has sought to portray himself as pro-environment. And yet none can escape the need to gain control of the federal budget and to improve economic performance, as the downfalls of both Carter and Bush bear witness. Therefore, the president's success in office is in no small measure dependent upon his ability to reconcile demands for environmental quality with the exigencies of economic efficiency. To do so he needs expert information and advice that he can trust. Political prudence as well as a concern for the public welfare should encourage a president to cultivate a climate among his subordinates that would enable such neutral competence to flourish.

Even a thoroughly renovated EPA could do little to improve environmental policy in the face of continued adherence to the rights-premise on the part of the wider environmental policy-making public, particularly those in Congress and the media who specialize in environmental matters. A broad shift in the climate of opinion within such circles is also necessary. The EPA's expertise and authority could enable it to serve as the linchpin of a broader coalition of academics, journalists, and philanthropists dedicated to placing the environmental debate on a sounder footing.

Policy Making in the
Contemporary Congress:
Three Dimensions of Performance

P A U L   J.   Q U I R K

By all accounts, the 1970s saw the development of a "new" Congress, different in important respects from the Congress of the several preceding decades. A reform movement produced sweeping change in the institution's norms, structures, and distribution of power. On the whole Congress became more decentralized, more individualistic, and more open. Even though Congress moderated some of these tendencies in the 1980s and 1990s, the main features of the reformed Congress have largely endured.

Many commentators have been uneasy about the consequences of these changes for the performance of government.[1] They assume that, without strong party organization or other forms of hierarchical control, Congress will be prone to stalemate and that, when it does act, it will have difficulty producing coherent, responsible legislation.

But, even after almost two decades of experience, the actual effects of congressional change on governmental performance remain unclear. There has been little careful analysis of those consequences. One reason is that we lack agreed-upon, operational criteria for assessing policy outcomes.[2] Another reason is that the effects of reform are hard to distinguish from those of other influences on congressional performance —such as the energy and inflation crises of the 1970s, the fiscal policies and budget deficits of the Reagan administration, and the divided party control of government during most of the period. Most of the variation in congressional performance, however defined, probably reflects the policy problems and political conditions of a given period.

In this chapter I seek to cast additional light on the effects of the structural changes in Congress. I offer a theoretical analysis of how the changes affect three dimensions of congressional performance: the representation of interests, deliberation, and the resolution of conflict. To illustrate the argument, I look for evidence of these effects in Congress's performance on two issues of economic deregulation in late 1970s and early 1980s: the 1980 Motor Carrier Reform Act, which substantially deregulated the trucking industry, and the 1978 Natural Gas Policy Act, which mostly failed to deregulate natural gas prices.[3] Because they differ in several respects, the two issues highlight important distinctions concerning the dimensions of performance and the circumstances of policy making.

The New Congress

Although the changes in Congress in the mid-1970s were complex and differed somewhat between the House and Senate, the predominant direction was toward decentralization and democratization.[4] The reforms took power away from the committee chairmen, who for most of the century had dominated the legislative process. In a few areas they gave power to party leaders or party caucuses. For the most part, however, they increased the independence of subcommittees and enhanced the participation of rank-and-file members, both in committee and on the floor.

Some of the reforms shifted power from full committees to subcommittees and reduced the autonomy of committee chairmen. In the House the method of appointing Democratic committee chairmen was changed from a strict seniority system, with essentially absolute security for sitting chairmen, to one of election by the party caucus. Committees were ordered to establish subcommittees with definite jurisdiction and to assign legislation to them. Subcommittees obtained their own staffs. And rank-and-file committee and subcommittee members were given power to force reluctant chairmen to call meetings or act on legislation. Subcommittees also gained power in the Senate—although only a modest amount, largely because full committees in that chamber were already small.

Other measures gave enhanced resources and opportunity for participation to individual members. In both chambers rank-and-file members were granted additional staff to help with their legislative work. They gained access to information through the creation or expansion of the congressional staff agencies, the General Accounting Office (GAO), the Congressional Budget Office (CBO), and the Office of Technology Assessment (OTA). And their influence was increased through rules changes that favored recorded votes on the House and Senate floors. Recording the votes encouraged floor amendments, and such amendments have given rank-and-file members, including those of the minority party, a larger role in making decisions. In the Senate, a loosening of informal norms led to more frequent exercise of the individual senator's power to put holds on legislation or filibuster against passage. In both chambers norms of apprenticeship, specialization, and reciprocity gave way to broader participation by individual members. To a great extent, the new opportunities for participation reflected the demands of the issue-oriented, independent members who won seats in the media-oriented and candidate-centered electoral campaigns of the 1970s.

Finally, Congress exposed more of its decision processes to public scrutiny. Both chambers required most committee meetings, including markup sessions, to be open to the public. They allowed television broadcasts of floor debate. The more frequent recorded floor votes have enabled important roll calls to be published in newspapers and exploited by challengers in election campaigns.

The tendency toward decentralization and democratization in the reforms of the 1970s was not uniform. Indeed, the 1974 Budget Reform Act concentrated considerable power over taxing and spending in a single committee in each chamber.[5] Moreover, in the so-called *postreform* Congress of the 1980s and 1990s, there has been some movement in the opposite direction.[6] For example, the Democratic leadership has become more active in setting the party's agenda. But, on most legislative issues, the decentralization, individualism, and openness of the reform Congress are still largely in force.

Structural Reform and Congressional Performance

To consider how the structural changes of the 1970s and 1980s are likely to affect Congress's capacities and performance as a policy maker, we begin with an analysis of what Congress must accomplish to act effectively and responsibly in pursuit of genuine national interests. Such a discussion presumes a set of normative criteria for evaluating congressional policy making. As a starting point in defining such criteria, I assume that Congress should adopt those policies that the public itself would adopt if it made decisions directly, under certain hypothetical ideal conditions. These conditions include (1) equality of power among citizens, (2) perfect information about the consequences of policy choices; and (3) efficient bargaining among citizens with conflicting interests. Of course, these ideal conditions cannot be met or even approximated in any real-world direct democracy, nor will the most satisfactory legislative process, so defined, necessarily have a high degree of citizen participation. But, corresponding to the ideal conditions, such a process must perform well on three dimensions of decision making: (1) the representation of interests; (2) the acquisition and use of information or, in short, deliberation; and (3) the resolution of conflict.[7]

THE REPRESENTATION OF INTERESTS

The dimension of Congress's performance most often discussed in the literature is the one I call the *representation of interests*. The issue in assessing this dimension of performance is whether Congress responds to conflicting interests in a reasonably balanced way. On some points the appropriate balance of power is a controversial political judgment; liberals and conservatives disagree, for example, about whether lower-income groups have too little influence or too much. On at least one crucial point, the main issue for regulatory policy, however, there is widespread consensus: Policy should serve general social interests, such as aggregate economic welfare, and not merely narrow functional or geographic interests. Relatedly, policy should respond to new demands and not merely "vested interests." These injunctions are often violated, and much of the literature on regulatory politics concerns the "capture" of regulatory policy by regulated industries or other narrow interests. Whether Congress can achieve balanced representation will depend largely on the distribution of resources in the political system. But it will also depend on features of the institution—for example, whether its procedures provide access to groups with limited resources.

The question of how congressional reform affects its response to broadly based interests is complicated by debate about the underlying dynamics of congressional decisions. One perspective attributes nearly all general interest response to centralized power and the "collective responsibility" of political parties.[8] On this view, individual members of Congress have little incentive to serve general interests. The electorate rarely knows how members vote and does not hold them individually responsible for national conditions. The impulse of the members, therefore, is to distribute benefits to interest groups and geographic constituencies. Moreover, members use the committees and subcommittees primarily for that purpose. In contrast, the president and the congressional parties are held responsible and have far stronger incentives to respond to broad interests. Accordingly, the ability of Congress to overcome particularism rests largely on presidential and party leadership.

This analysis, in my view, is overdrawn. Another perspective suggests that rank-and-file members often support general interest–oriented policies for reasons of their own.[9] They may perceive electoral incentives to serve broad constituencies and avoid identification with narrow interests, or they may support such policies without expecting electoral rewards, just because they prefer to do so. Accordingly, committees are not vehicles for delivering special interest benefits; they are also platforms for entrepreneurship directed toward broad constituencies and forums for deliberation about national interests. On the other hand, the support of presidents and party leaders for general interests is far from automatic. They may prefer to raise a few popular issues to a high level of salience while keeping other issues off the agenda by accommodating the existing balance of power. In many cases, the initiative in general interest policy change will come from entrepreneurial committee or subcommittee chairs or rank-and-file members. The response to general interests will not depend, clearly or consistently, on hierarchical control of the legislative process.

How, then, should the reforms of the 1970s affect the representation of interests? They should alter the mechanisms of general interest representation, and, overall, they should probably strengthen it. The proliferation of subcommittees with substantial resources and autonomy, what Davidson called *subcommittee government*,[10] should have no pronounced overall effect. It may actually increase the initiation of general interest–oriented policy change. But it should create obstacles to such policy change sponsored by presidents or party leaders. Entrepreneurship on the part of multiple leaders should tend to replace conventional party and presidential leadership. For the same reasons, the increased independence of individual members should also have mixed effects.

The most important structural change is probably the establishment of recorded votes on floor amendments and the growth of floor amending activity.[11] Because sponsoring and voting on floor amendments are quite visible activities—potentially significant in a reelection campaign—these developments should considerably strengthen general interests. The effect of open committee meetings, however, is ambiguous because the attentive audience for committee meetings is often dominated by organized groups. Committees have defended their increased use of informal, private negotiations and executive sessions largely on the grounds that secrecy permitted members to escape interest group pressure and decide issues on the merits. In addition, general interest representation has probably been reinforced by the changing recruitment patterns that have produced more issue-oriented members.

DELIBERATION

The second dimension of congressional performance, long neglected in the political science literature, is deliberation.[12] The issue is whether

Congress is reasonably thorough, accurate, and unbiased in identifying and weighing information relevant to decisions. To serve any interests effectively, Congress not only must want to do so; it also must consider a range of policy options and, within the limits of available information, must achieve an accurate understanding of their consequences.[13] In some cases an apparent failure to use information may in fact be more fundamentally a failure of representation; the dominant position of one interest makes information about another interest politically irrelevant. But sometimes inadequate deliberation can cause otherwise well-represented interests to be poorly served by congressional action.

Some have assumed, incorrectly, that effective deliberation in Congress necessarily involves extensive dialogue among members—on the model, say, of the Constitutional Convention of 1887. To ensure that Congress knows what it is doing, there must be a dialogue. Understanding develops through a process of exchanging claims, information, and criticism. But there is no compelling reason why the principal advocates must be members of Congress or why members must engage each other directly. In the contemporary Congress, most of the dialogue is contributed by private lobbyists, government officials, and various other experts and interested parties. Even though the advocates address the members, instead of each other, they are compelled to answer each other's claims.

In general, legislative deliberation is exposed to numerous threats. Some of the main ones are political demands or strategic temptations to act hastily, jurisdictional divisions that separate the consideration of related issues, political sensitivities that suppress the discussion of relevant subjects, the difficulties that laymen may have evaluating debate on technical issues, and the pressure on politicians to adhere to popular prejudices.

We can identify several plausible institutional conditions for effective legislative deliberation.[14] To deliberate effectively, a legislature should have norms and routines that elicit extensive information about policy choices. An example is the norm in Congress that legislative hearings on a major issue should be lengthy and include numerous witnesses on all sides of the debate. A legislature should have staff resources that permit the acquisition and transmission of a large volume of information. Some staff should play advocacy roles while others maintain a posture of neutrality—so that competing positions will be stated aggressively and yet tested for their credibility. A legislature should have a free flow of communication and regular liaison among committees or other subunits with related jurisdiction. It should have barriers to precipitous action. It should reward members for acquiring

specialized knowledge and concentrate authority where there is expertise, for example, in standing committees.[15] But within practical limits,
it should also ensure that information is broadly shared.

Purely from the standpoint of deliberation, a legislature should have
procedures that insulate discussion and decision making from public
view. This reduces the intrusive effect of uninformed public opinion. It
may also, however, reduce responsiveness to general interests. The only
fundamental solution to this dilemma is to improve popular political
discourse and understanding of public policy, but plausible means to
effect this solution are unfortunately lacking.

Considered in light of these conditions, the reforms of the 1970s
again have mixed consequences, but in this case the net effect is probably negative. As we have noted, Congress substantially expanded its
staff resources. The expansion included both partisan advocates (most
committee staff and members' office staff) and nonpartisan experts (especially in the congressional staff agencies). But it also shifted decision
making toward less expert members and increased the exposure of its
deliberations to observation by the public. Open committee meetings
are part of the increased exposure. The most important development,
however, is the new habit of making decisions through floor amendments with recorded votes. Thus, members who are less expert make
more decisions and do so under greater pressure of public opinion. Altogether, Congress has strengthened its capacity to use information but
has reduced its capacity to resist popular biases and stereotypes.

CONFLICT RESOLUTION

The final dimension of congressional performance is the capacity for
cooperative resolution of policy conflict. The issue is whether Congress
is able to work out agreements among the opposing factions in a policy
dispute, overcome stalemate, and adopt policies that exploit the opportunities for joint gain. This requires preventing the arbitrary exercise of
majority power. It also requires avoiding lowest-common-denominator
agreements, which merely minimize the need for difficult concessions.
The question, for example, is whether liberals and conservatives can
reach an agreement to achieve a mutual goal of reducing the budget
deficit or whether supporters of industry and environmental groups can
agree to reforms designed to increase the efficiency of environmental
controls.

In an earlier work, I defined this dimension of policy making more
precisely and set forth an analytic framework to address the conditions
for cooperative outcomes.[16] We can address the institutional conditions
for cooperative policy making in Congress by considering the circum-

stances that facilitate mediation or constructive negotiation. (1) Such negotiation is encouraged by features that level off differences in power and therefore militate against conflictual strategies. The Senate's rules have that effect, for example, because they permit a single member to block action. The House, in contrast, generally allows a partisan majority to act. (2) Because negotiation is labor intensive, staff capabilities are again a factor. A large and skilled staff can give detailed attention to numerous issues and solve many difficulties by agreement. (3) Cooperation is sometimes facilitated if negotiation can be confined to a small group and conducted in secrecy. Such negotiations are relatively free of constituency pressure, and participants tend to develop interpersonal trust. (4) Because an agreement may involve an exchange of concessions on unrelated issues and such issues may be in different committee jurisdictions, the capacity for cooperation is enhanced by procedures that can link issues in different committees. (5) Finally, cooperation is facilitated by the availability of powerful mediators. Several officials may play this role in Congress—presidents, party leaders, and committee chairmen—but there is no guarantee that any of them will.

Some of the changes in Congress have enhanced its ability to resolve conflict constructively. The expanded staff has been put to work in negotiations. One result has been more detailed and specific agreements—and longer bills. Such bills facilitate cooperation by reducing uncertainty for the affected interests.[17] The House has improved its handling of bills that span committee jurisdictions. The Speaker may refer such measures jointly or sequentially to multiple committees. Under a new Rules Committee procedure (involving "alternative substitutes"), those committees may then negotiate a single measure for consideration on the floor.[18] These arrangements aid competing interests in exchanging concessions on different issues. In some cases, the increased individualism of contemporary members of Congress should also promote cooperation. On issues that have largely partisan cleavages—which is to say, most issues—the arrival of members who respond weakly to party cues and who form unpredictable coalitions should provide an expanded base for negotiated outcomes.

Much as with deliberation, however, the changes in Congress have compounded the difficulties of cooperating on issues that are salient to broad constituencies or the mass public. To the extent that open committee meetings are actually used to make decisions, negotiations must take place in public, often a serious obstacle to successful outcomes. When committee decisions are revisited on the floor, compromise is more difficult. If a committee bill sets aside some claims of an important constituency as part of a negotiated agreement, some member will propose a floor amendment to restore them. To sustain the negotiated solution will then require rejecting the claims explicitly in a floor vote.

OVERVIEW

The contemporary Congress thus has both strengths and vulnerabilities as a policy-making institution. Compared with the pre-reform Congress, it is not especially prone to domination by narrow interests; the benefits that such interests receive are subject to broader scrutiny and more potential challengers than ever before. Neither is it incapable of significant policy change; its entrepreneurial subcommittee leaders and issue-oriented members allow it to respond vigorously to popular causes and widely shared policy imperatives.[19] However, the mechanisms of policy initiation and response to general interests have changed. Presidential leadership is no longer as central; more depends on responsiveness and leadership capability that is widely diffused among committees, subcommittees, and rank-and-file members. Congress has strengthened its capacity to analyze issues and transmit information among the members. Indeed, it probably makes very few policy mistakes that result, at bottom, from failure to obtain available information. It also has acquired procedural means to transcend jurisdictional boundaries in negotiations and put together complex packages of proposals.

The principal weaknesses of the new Congress are its relative inability to make use of responsible analysis or to resolve conflict constructively on issues that command widespread attention. Facing unprecedented exposure to public observation, members of Congress take unyielding stands on behalf of constituencies and defer even to biased or uninformed mass opinion.

Congressional Performance on Deregulation

We will now explore whether these expectations about Congress's performance were borne out in two of the major regulatory issues of the late 1970s and early 1980s—the extensive deregulation of the trucking industry and the limited deregulation of natural gas pricing.

TRUCKING DEREGULATION

In 1980 Congress passed and President Jimmy Carter signed the landmark Motor Carrier Reform Act, which relaxed or eliminated most economic regulation of the trucking industry.[20] Adopted during the Depression and administered by the Interstate Commerce Commission (ICC), economic regulation of the trucking industry reduced competi-

tion, imposed inefficiency, and raised rates in the industry. The deregulation act was expected to lower costs and increase efficiency to the
benefit of shippers and consumers; the evidence indicates that it has
indeed done so.[21] It was also expected, however, to produce instability,
reduce wages and profits, and destroy the value of operating rights in the
industry. The trucking industry and the Teamsters' Union, two heavy-
weights among American lobbying groups, violently opposed deregulation. On the other hand, there was exceedingly slight organized support.
To adopt deregulation thus required Congress to recognize the economic consequences of trucking regulation, respond to the widely shared
interests in efficiency and reduced rates, and either overcome the intense opposition of industry and labor or somehow secure their assent.

The fact that Congress responded to the general interests at stake
mainly reflected capacities of a decentralized and individualistic Congress and not traditional presidential or party leadership. Leadership
came from committees and subcommittees, and there was strong floor
support in both chambers. More than any other institutional unit, Senator Edward Kennedy's Antitrust Subcommittee put the issue on the
agenda through investigatory hearings in 1978. The Carter administration, although clearly sympathetic to reform, delayed a decision whether to support Kennedy's bill while it used the threat of deregulation for
leverage with the Teamsters on another issue—the union's demands in
contract negotiations with the trucking industry. (When, after embarrassing public prodding by Kennedy, the administration finally joined
the reform effort, however, it made the issue a high priority.) Congressional party leaders were not a major factor in support for reform. Speaker of the House Thomas P. O'Neill was understood to dislike the controversial bill and at one point threatened to block floor consideration.

In the Senate, the committee with jurisdiction over the bill was
highly responsive. Commerce Committee Chairman Howard Cannon
was initially skeptical, but eventually put the full power of the chairmanship behind the effort; ranking minority member Bob Packwood
was uncompromising in his support for reform. These leaders used the
committee as a vehicle not for distributing special interest benefits, but
for launching a general interest–oriented reform measure. Other committee members were divided, much like the whole Senate. Thus, when
a strong deregulation bill came from the committee to the floor it was
challenged, unsuccessfully, by both strengthening and weakening
amendments with substantial support. In the House, the Subcommittee
on Surface Transportation of the Public Works Committee—a noto-
riously client-oriented committee often allied with the trucking
industry—tried to obstruct reform but was unwilling to oppose it open-

ly. Under the spotlight of public attention, it eventually endorsed a strong bill that it had negotiated with the Senate and the White House and that the House proceeded to pass without amendment.

Congress in the trucking deregulation case exhibited a strong capacity to obtain and use information. In particular, it in effect accepted the economists' conventional wisdom, supported by extensive empirical research, that regulation of prices and entry in a structurally competitive industry produces few, if any, benefits and large costs to consumers and the economy. Congress rejected industry arguments, for many years the basis of regulatory policy, that regulation was needed to avoid the "chaos" of unstable service and prices, to prevent excessive concentration of control, and to ensure service in small communities. Considering that the ICC long had purported to require cross-subsidized service to such communities, the industry's claim about that service had a measure of plausibility. But Congress took account of evidence that the ICC requirement was not enforced, and even members from rural areas mostly supported deregulation.

The expansion of congressional staff in the mid-1970s was a factor in this strong response to information. The discovery that airline and trucking regulation was ripe for reform was the contribution of the Kennedy subcommittee's staff, headed by an economically sophisticated law professor on leave from Harvard. The Senate Commerce Committee staff worked with the Transportation Department to arrange studies to answer rural-state senators' concerns about the small-community service issue. The CBO, trusted as a source of nonpartisan expertise, produced reports reviewing the evidence about the economic effects of deregulation and its specific effects for small communities. On both scores, the CBO endorsed the reformers' claims. Much of what was learned undoubtedly made its way to individual members through their recently enlarged office staffs.

The response also owed a great deal, however, to some distinctive features of the case for reform. The support from economists was virtually unanimous. Perhaps most important, to accept the economists' arguments Congress did not have to resist pressure from the general public. If anything, deregulation fit the mood of a public concerned about inflation and big government. Although certainly encouraging, therefore, the trucking case does not suggest an ability of Congress to insulate policy making from rash or ill-informed public sentiment.

Nor does the case demonstrate a congressional capacity for cooperative policy making; rather, it revealed the limitations of that capacity. In principle, it should have been possible to obtain the industry's and the Teamsters' consent for deregulation by offering compensation for the loss of regulatory protection. Because the loss of consumer welfare caused by regulation was largely "deadweight loss"—sheer waste—a scheme of deregulation with compensation could have held the industry harmless and yet still provided large benefits for consumers. Early in the trucking debate, Gordon Tullock advocated that solution. As Dorothy Robyn pointed out, however, no such scheme was adopted or even seriously discussed. The reform forces simply defeated the industry.[22]

One obstacle to the cooperative strategy was that compensation through the tax system required the participation of another committee. Perhaps the device of multiple referral available in the new Congress would have helped overcome this difficulty if the compensatory approach had been pursued from an early stage of the debate. But it was not. For several reasons such a proposition could not be seriously considered: To discuss compensation would have required the industry to concede the impending failure of its effort to block deregulation. The pragmatism of a buy-out strategy would have made it hard for either side to rally its forces. And neither side wanted to highlight claims that deregulation would reduce industry profits: the industry because it proved that regulation produced excess profits; the reformers because it meant that deregulation would do harm. To have been politically viable, the compensation strategy would probably have required a very closed decision process, in which a resolution could be negotiated secretly and implemented without much further debate. The new Congress certainly did not provide a sufficiently closed process, but it is doubtful that the old Congress would have done so either.

NATURAL GAS PRICING

In developing the Natural Gas Policy Act of 1978, Congress conducted an often rancorous debate, was locked in stalemate for many months despite an atmosphere of crisis, and eventually produced a measure with provisions that were clearly inadequate to the main purpose of the legislation.[23] The act was part of Congress's response to the Carter administration's proposed National Energy Policy and was intended to relieve worsening shortages of natural gas. Federal regulation had held prices for gas transported across state lines far below market levels and even below intrastate prices, which were not subject to federal regulation. Much research suggested that the controls were largely responsible for the shortages, which had caused widespread school and plant closings and had cut off many residential users during the winter of 1976–77. Despite the sense of urgency, Congress took eighteen months to act on the president's proposal and then passed a bill that placed minimal emphasis on the one strategy—letting prices rise to market levels—that was likely to relieve the shortages decisively.

Although as a presidential candidate Jimmy Carter had promised to support the deregulation of natural gas, the administration's energy policy backed away from decontrol. Whether out of deference to congressional Democrats or because of its own recalculation of the political stakes, the administration instead called for extending regulation to intrastate gas while phasing out all controls very gradually. Both the House and the Senate were deeply divided on the administration proposal. The House passed it after narrowly defeating a strongly deregulatory floor amendment. The Senate, however, took up such an amendment and adopted it. The conference committee, with fundamentally different bills to reconcile and internal divisions within each chamber's delegation, was deadlocked for more than a year. Eventually, the conference committee reported and Congress passed a convoluted measure that created enormous administrative and economic complexity and provided very limited deregulation.

The challenge of policy making in this case was not primarily a need to represent unorganized, diffuse interests in conflict with well-organized, narrow interests. There were exceptionally salient diffuse interests on both sides of the debate. One side, in favor of price increases and deregulation, represented a diffuse interest in letting the market operate to increase supplies, reduce consumption, and end shortages. It also included the interest of the gas industry in higher profits. Judging from the voting patterns on floor amendments, however, the support for this side in Congress was strongly associated with conservatism and the Republican party and not with regional ties with the industry. The other side, in favor of maintaining controls and extending them to intrastate markets, represented a diffuse interest in keeping prices down and avoiding a massive transfer of income from consumers to the industry and, to some extent, from the poor to the wealthy. It also included the interests of industrial users of natural gas. But the support in Congress was largely associated with liberalism and the Democratic party. The principal affected interests were well represented as a matter of course.

The problematic dimensions of policy making were those of deliberation and conflict resolution. As Pietro Nivola's penetrating study demonstrated, congressional deliberation on natural gas pricing exhibited two kinds of distortion.[24] First, there was an unsophisticated or disingenuous discussion of how much an increase in prices would increase the discovery and production of natural gas. The answer to this question was by no means clear. Several reputable research institutions sponsored major economic studies, all four of the congressional staff agencies got into the act with studies of their own, but the results varied by orders of magnitude. At bottom, none knew how much natural gas was available to be found. (If they had known, someone would have found it already.) Congressional Democrats seized on the uncertainty to make utterly unsupported and implausible claims. For example, they argued that current shortages only reflected the gas companies' decision to hold back production in the expectation of higher prices in the future and that above a certain price—specified, completely arbitrarily, as $1.75 per thousand cubic feet—higher prices would bring forth no additional supply at all. Such assertions amounted to a thinly disguised rationalization for resisting deregulation; they were the kind of argument that would have been dismissed by sophisticated participants but would play well with the mass public.

Second and more important, the debate almost entirely overlooked what was undoubtedly the main advantage of deregulation: that by requiring users to pay full replacement costs, it would induce them to conserve natural gas. Research demonstrated that, in terms of capital expenditure, it was much easier to save fuel than to increase its production. Higher prices would eliminate shortages, therefore, mainly by encouraging reduced consumption. Even though much of the reduction would come from the development of more fuel-efficient practices, that sounded like sacrifice. It had no appeal to a mass audience. Even the market-oriented conservative politicians who advocated deregulation therefore refrained from appealing to it. As a result the most important argument for lifting controls was not a factor in the congressional debate. In short, the debate focused on the wrong issue (increased supply) and entertained absurd claims (the irrelevance of prices) about that issue.

Even with the sharp divergence of views between liberals and conservatives, there were opportunities for constructive, mutually beneficial conflict resolution, but Congress proved unable to take advantage of them. The most fundamental approach to such a resolution would have been to combine deregulation of natural gas prices with a program to recover excess profits and grant energy assistance to low-income families. Properly designed, this could have captured some of the supply benefits of deregulation and all of the conservation benefits while neutralizing most of the controversial effects on the distribution of income. Unfortunately, a similar arrangement (combining deregulation with an excess-profits tax) had been tried in the 1975 debate on oil pricing but had failed—the victim in part of difficulty coordinating the work of the commerce committee and the tax committees in each chamber. Senator Lowell Weicker suggested linking natural gas deregulation with a $100 million program of low-income energy assistance. But because of the small size of the program (compared with the amounts affected by deregulation) and the sad previous experience with such an exchange, liberals dismissed Weicker's idea, and no similar proposal was seriously discussed.

A less ambitious approach to a cooperative resolution, embodied in a proposal by Senator Bellmon, was to maintain regulation of natural gas prices but raise the regulated price substantially. A clean compromise, this would have ended the stalemate, produced a manageable regulatory program, and accomplished part of what both sides sought. But neither side wanted any part of Bellmon's proposal: Conservatives adamantly demanded deregulation, which had acquired symbolic value to them; liberals, equally adamant, refused to accept a significant price increase. An additional obstacle to compromise was that two powerful Senate committee chairmen, Henry Jackson of the Energy Committee, and Russell Long of the Finance Committee, had leverage in the debate but had radically different attitudes toward the energy industries. Interestingly, their ability to make trouble for any compromise proposal represented the vestiges of the traditional Congress, dominated by committee chairmen; in this case, powerful chairmen tended to obstruct a cooperative outcome.

The final bill, passed in the fall of 1978, was an incoherent, lowest-common-denominator solution; it undoubtedly was acceptable to majorities in both chambers largely because they otherwise faced the threat of failing to act at all. Although it deregulated new gas, it kept old gas regulated indefinitely. Indeed, because assembling a centrist majority coalition in a polarized ideological conflict depended heavily on granting special favors to narrow groups, the bill created a bizarre and implausible regulatory scheme. It had distinct pricing provisions for about twenty categories of natural gas and attempted to determine actual prices well into the next decade.

The deficiencies of performance that emerged in the natural gas case are ones that we suggested previously as likely attributes of policy making in the reformed Congress. Both deliberation and conflict resolution were apparently affected by the enlarged exposure to mass opinion. Mass prejudices (such as the doubts that higher prices would increase supply) played a large role in the deliberations; constituency pressures, and the rigidity and emphasis on symbolism that come with them, were prominent features of the negotiations.

Conclusion

The Congress that emerged in the mid-1970s is capable, at times, of surprising accomplishment and, at other times, of abject failure. But the differences in performance are not random. On the basis of our discussion and very limited case study evidence, it seems that the contemporary Congress has well-defined strengths and weaknesses as a policy-making institution.

Notwithstanding the absence of party government, the Congress is relatively successful in representing widely shared interests as opposed to narrowly based ones. The impetus to serve diffuse interests is not restricted to the president and party leaders; it is built into the incentives and inclinations of other leaders, such as committee and subcommittee chairmen, and even rank-and-file members of Congress.

The changes in Congress have diminished somewhat the ability of presidents and party leaders to direct general interest–oriented policy change. But they have strengthened the capacity of committees, subcommittees, and even individual members to initiate policy change; have made it easier to broaden the scope of conflict on an issue; and have increased the visibility of decisions between diffuse and narrow interests. Some of the effects were observable in our two cases. In the trucking deregulation debate, committee leaders preceded the administration in challenging the regulatory regime; the president at first temporized, although he later became committed to reform; and congressional party leaders never played a crucial role. The committee in one house, the Senate, and the both chamber floors responded favorably; indeed, the floors debated strengthening amendments as well as weakening ones. The natural gas pricing debate was intrinsically a conflict between diffuse interests. The members could have made it a contest of narrow, regional interests by focusing their attention on such interests. But they chose not to—at least until an ideological deadlock made congressional leaders desperate for ways to build a majority coalition. In short, the contemporary Congress represents general interests not because the parties constrain individuals, but because many members of Congress seek individual credit for or personal satisfaction from representing such interests.

The contemporary Congress is less successful, however, in deliberation and conflict resolution. As a result of the dramatic expansion of staff resources, the committees and even rank-and-file members have the capacity to acquire and take into account massive amounts of information. In the trucking debate, Congress not only was receptive to economic analysis and evidence on the general effects of trucking regulation; it also generated and took account of research on the specific effects for small communities. In the case of natural gas pricing, Congress debated a large body of research on how deregulation would affect production. If Congress overlooks significant information about a policy choice, it is probably because for political or other reasons it chooses to do so.

Rather, the difficulty with congressional deliberation is that Congress has difficulty discounting the biases and misconceptions of mass opinion. If a policy conflict is potentially salient to the general public, members of Congress have a hard time taking an independent view or deferring to appropriate experts, even on factual matters. Most likely, the pressure to conform to public sentiment is now greater, on significant issues, than is the pressure to comply with interest group demands. Because of public distaste for inducing energy savings by means of price, the natural gas debate overlooked the main benefit of deregulation and focused on the smaller and more speculative benefit of increased production. Congress entertained implausible claims by liberal opponents of deregulation, who questioned whether higher prices would bring forth any additional supply. There was no comparable distortion in the trucking debate. But the reason was largely that the economic case for deregulation, by good fortune, was reinforced by concerns and biases of the mass public.

Some of the same changes that have strengthened representation of general interests—especially recorded voting on floor amendments—have also increased the difficulty of sober deliberation about those interests. But an even greater source of such difficulty, quite likely, has been a widely remarked change in the methods of electoral campaigns. Because of the recent prominence and effectiveness of negative campaign appeals concerning issues, the dangers of being out of step with the mass public have risen considerably.

For similar reasons Congress evidently has lost some ability to resolve conflict constructively. In some mechanical respects, it has gained facility in working out complex negotiated solutions. In particular, the House has developed routines for using ad hoc committees and several kinds of joint referral, in effect, to tailor committee proceedings to the negotiating requirements of individual bills. This enhances the ability to reach negotiated solutions to difficult policy conflicts by linking measures that are substantively unrelated or fall in different jurisdictions—for example, deregulation of trucking and tax credits for the trucking industry.

However, because Congress has come to provide a more exposed and participatory environment for negotiation, it is now harder for leaders of congressional factions to negotiate constructively with opposing factions. It is easier for militant members to challenge and embarrass advocates of accommodation. And there are more rewards for posturing and extremism. In each of our cases, there was in principle opportunity for a cooperative resolution. But in neither case did it occur. It was impossible even to discuss making a deal to avoid opposition to trucking deregulation by compensating the industry for the loss of protection. It was impossible seriously to consider an agreement to satisfy liberal opponents of natural gas deregulation by using tax or benefit programs to neutralize the distributive effects of price increases. An agreement was eventually reached on natural gas after a year of debate in the conference committee. But the debate was so polarized and acrimonious, and the ability to cooperate so limited, that the agreement reached was an incoherent lowest-common-denominator compromise, enormously complicated by special interest provisions needed to assemble a winning coalition.

It seems, then, that the principal challenge for Congress and democratic politics in the United States is no longer how to keep special interests from dominating public policy. That certainly remains a problem, but it has receded in significance as Congress has represented general interests with increasing vigor.[25] The main challenges in our era are how to ensure sensible deliberation about public policy in an atmosphere of frequent, yet superficial public scrutiny and how to encourage constructive negotiation in a complex, open, and highly participatory institutional setting.[26]

Conclusion

New Politics, New Elites, Old Publics

J A M E S   Q.   W I L S O N

The United States has acquired a new political system that operates within an old constitutional order. We have witnessed over the last thirty years the emergence of a true national state within the confines of a constitutional system designed to ensure that no such state would be created. From the founding until the mid-1960s, a favorite theme of the proponents of a strong, activist central government has been that this country was ill-founded. Initially, such proponents were few in number (Alexander Hamilton was about the only one in the eighteenth century); by the early twentieth century, their ranks included Herbert Croly and Woodrow Wilson; by the mid–twentieth century their number had been vastly enlarged to include most New Deal and Great Society liberals and a growing fraction of business executives who wanted Washington to be their partner (read: protector) in managing domestic economic competition; recently, their ranks have been swelled by people of all political persuasions who think that government should have an industrial policy that would foster (read: subsidize) emerging industries and a protectionist trade policy that would level (read: tilt) the international playing field. To this group can be added the voices of millions of ordinary Americans searching for leaders who will make tough choices so that we can eliminate the national deficit, reduce congressional pork, and solve the problems of crime, drug abuse, illegal immigration, and poor schools.

These exponents of the virtues of a true state are frustrated by the apparent defects of a Constitution that was written not to make governing easy but to make it hard; not to facilitate choices but to impede them; not to empower leaders but to frustrate them. In a *real* state (Britain, France, or Sweden come to mind), the government is allowed to govern; somebody can say "yes" or "no" and make it stick. Abroad, legislators carry on meaningful debates; at home, they speak to empty chambers. There, politicians serve national goals and party policies; here, they serve their districts and personal reelection needs. Perhaps the American system was adequate when the nation was a semi-isolated, largely rural country, but in today's modern, complex, interdependent world, we need a modern, supple, and decisive political system.

This tension between political expectations and constitutional realities lies at the heart of the dramatic loss of public confidence in our governmental leaders and accounts for the increased popularity of certain constitutional changes (term limits, the line-item veto, quasiparliamentary institutions, and a balanced-budget amendment) and various "nonpolitical" politicians (first Lee Iacocca, then Ross Perot). To make sense of these beliefs, we must first understand what has changed and why.

The Shape of the New Politics

Over the last three decades, policy making in Washington has been nationalized, judicialized, and rationalized.

NATIONALIZED

Until the 1960s, much of the national policy debate was about whether the federal government had the right to pass a law addressing some problem. Despite the expansion in its powers during the New Deal and World War II, as late as 1962 Washington had an imperfect claim to wield legitimate authority over many aspects of our lives. There were spirited debates over whether Congress had the right to pass a civil rights law or authorize federal aid to education. Until 1965, any significant federal involvement in the provision of medical care (except for veterans) was suspect. There were federal clean water laws, but they relied for their interpretation and enforcement almost entirely on the states. Against any proposed expansion of federal power there was raised the doctrine of states' rights; as often as not, that objection was decisive.

The collapse of that argument—and the barrier it defended—can be dated with some precision: It fell in the twelve-month period in 1964–65 that witnessed the passage of the Civil Rights Act, the Elementary and Secondary Education Act, and the Medicare Act. When, a few years later, Congress voted in favor of a policy that before the 1960s would have been unthinkable—a national maximum speed limit that superseded all state laws on this matter—the cry of "states' rights" was scarcely heard. The legitimacy barrier had fallen; the authority of the federal government to intervene on almost any issue of public concern was assured.

State governments did not vanish nor fall silent, but the tone of their demands changed. Washington had for many decades been supplying grants-in-aid whereby federal dollars were used to serve state objectives (by financing local hospitals, highways, or airports). The states wanted more such dollars. But now these grants were increasingly given on the understanding that they would serve federal goals (empowering inner-city neighborhoods, facilitating access by the disabled to buildings and buses, and ensuring racial and gender integration in school programs). Moreover, even the old-style grants were now accompanied by a host of federal mandates and conditions. In this new era, governors were torn between lobbying for more money or fewer strings; rarely could they have both.

JUDICIALIZED

For most of American history, the courts deferred to agency administrators in implementing regulatory policies, deferred to state and national legislators with respect to a variety of "political questions" (such as legislative apportionment), kept litigants lacking a direct stake in an issue out of court altogether, and found new rights only in those provisions of the Constitution that, by tortured reasoning, could be said to yield something called *freedom of contract*. Today courts are often prepared to substitute their judgment of good policy for that of an agency head (a fact well known to, among others, the administrator of the Environmental Protection Agency) and are rarely inclined to acknowledge the existence of political questions (as was evident in their requirement that legislative districts be equal in population). The range of litigants who now can claim standing in court has broadened immeasurably: law students who like clean air were allowed to intervene in a proceeding to set railroad rates, people whose only stake in a church-state issue was that they were taxpayers were allowed to contest a proposed expenditure on behalf of church-related organizations. The Supreme Court has found a right of privacy in the emanations of various parts of Constitution, and some justices have claimed that the Constitution does not allow the death penalty even though that document refers in two or three places to procedures that should be followed in imposing it. When Congress creates a new agency or program, it often authorizes a variety of citizen suits against the agency or about the program as a way of ensuring that the legislative fight over purpose and power can be restaged in court by the allies of the congressional factions that initially did battle. As Robert Kagan at Berkeley, Shep Melnick at

Brandeis, and many other scholars have noted, our statutes and their interpretation are now suffused with the spirit of adversarial legalism.

Several decades ago the Supreme Court pretty much abandoned any effort to define limits to the powers of Congress over commerce and the economy or to restrain the delegation of legislative authority to administrative agencies. It turned instead to defining ever more sharply the limits to governmental powers over speech and conduct, expanding the opportunities for judicial review of administrative or executive decisions, facilitating (though not always consistently) the bringing of class action suits, recognizing individuals as private attorneys general, and perfecting structural injunctions and other court orders that would empower judges to supervise over long periods the management of schools, prisons, mental hospitals, and highway construction programs.

RATIONALIZED

Policy making has been rationalized in the sense that partial interests are now suspect and general interests are thought paramount. Business, labor, doctors, farmers, and particular localities are such partial interests; a political process that once unashamedly aggregated the preferences of those clients and distributed benefits among them is now embarrassed to do so and often refuses to do so. The underlying logic of industrial policy, environmental legislation, and consumer protection regulations is that there is a unitary, general interest, discoverable by reason and achievable by plan. Old-style client politics is everywhere on the defensive; even the redoubtable tobacco farmers of North Carolina and their champion, Senator Jesse Helms, have been forced to abandon any hope of large federal subsidies for their crops and to turn instead to a federally administered plan that is financed by the contributions of the farmers themselves. There are, of course, still clients making effective claims on government, but increasingly those clients are of a new type—not producer or territorial interests, but national, ideological or systemwide interests, such as those pressing for abortion on demand, the right to life, campaign-finance reform, the prevention of global warming, or the recognition of group entitlements in the allocation of jobs, school admissions, and federal contracts.

The old American political system paid off its clients with tangible benefits—cheap or free land, veterans' benefits, internal improvements, barriers to competition, agricultural subsidies. The new system still does a good deal of that, of course, but more and more the rewards accruing to political success are rules rather than funds: minority set-asides, constraints on administrative discretion, distributional formulas for state aid, and statutory protection for a host of new rights.

These changes can be overstated, of course, and I have probably done so. The states continue to play a significant role in national affairs, the courts devote most of their time to adjudicating ordinary disputes in accord with traditional understandings, and there are lots of old-style interest groups making demands. But some changes in degree are so large and numerous as to constitute changes in kind.

In the eyes of its supporters, the fundamental difficulty with this new policy system is that the institutions of government have not undergone corresponding changes. As a result, the political system does not match the policy system. Quite the contrary: The political system has become more decentralized, individualized, and constrained at the very time (and for many of the same reasons) that the policy system has become more centralized, rationalized, and ambitious.

Individual members of Congress are stronger than ever before, but Congress as an institution is weaker, perhaps not vis-à-vis the presidency, but in its capacity to deliberate carefully and act decisively. In the words of William Lunch, "The new Congress is less than the sum of its parts."[1] Subcommittees have proliferated; the power of committee chairmen over committee members has declined at the same time that the freedom of those chairmen from the influence of the House Speaker or the Senate majority leader has increased; House bills are often referred to several committees; and House-Senate conference committees sometimes have one or two hundred participants. Individual members are independent political entrepreneurs who can pursue careers with less attention to party or congressional leaders than once was the case.

The president now has a huge staff and a vast executive office, but he has acquired these at the price of creating his own personal bureaucracy with its own capacity for delay, obstruction, and the leaking of information to the press. These costs might be worth it if he had thereby gained the upper hand over Congress, but he has not. Congress has enhanced its powers by creating its own sprawling bureaucracy that includes not only large personal and committee staffs but also a series of new committees (the Budget and Intelligence committees) and specialized agencies (the Congressional Budget Office, the Office of Technology Assessment, and the General Accounting Office) that are designed to counter the president's organizational resources. What Senator Daniel Patrick Moynihan has called the Iron Law of Emulation has been at work: organizations in conflict with each other tend to acquire the characteristics of their rivals. As a consequence there is now more high-profile bickering than once was the case. Though this was probably exacerbated by twelve years of divided rule, with a Republican in the White House and Democrats in control of one or both houses of Congress, the struggle between the two ends of Pennsylvania Avenue is caused by fundamental differences in roles, powers, and constituencies that are not likely to be overcome by giving to each a common partisan identity.

The Sources of the New Policy System

Advocates of a strong state would explain its rise as the natural and desirable (albeit tragically postponed) working out of inevitable historical forces. Citizens want and require a strong state to serve their needs and manage their interdependencies. Less partisan observers might be inclined to explain its growth as the consequence of the competitive and self-interested struggle for votes: over time, politicians, seeking election, will offer benefits to voters who will accept them so long as the costs seem small, remote, or payable by others.

Since all governments grow in scope and power, it is hard to deny that there is an element of inevitability about it. But what is most striking about the growth of the U.S. national state has been its discontinuous quality. For many decades nothing much happens and then, in a brief period, a great deal occurs that raises governmental activity to a new and permanent level. One such leap occurred in the early 1930s, and another took place in the mid-1960s. One cannot be entirely satisfied with either of the more common explanations, since both imply a slow, steady, continuous enhancement of governmental power and reach. Of course, advocates of the historical necessity school may respond by arguing that institutional barriers or special interest opposition to change creates lags that must be overcome by a crisis. The Great Depression of the 1930s was one such, the Civil War another. But there was no crisis in the mid-1960s, yet the expansion of federal influence was probably greater then than at any other time. Franklin Roosevelt was a policy innovator, but most of the programs for which he is given credit did not require a constitutional revolution. By recalling his fight with the Supreme Court over the delegation of legislative powers to administrative agencies, a fight that had to be won before such programs as agricultural price supports could be put into place, we tend to exaggerate how bold his initiatives were. Most of his important programs were carefully crafted to adapt to existing understandings of Washington's powers. The old-age and retirement component of the Social Security Act was set up as a contributory "insurance" program, not a federal pension plan with a claim on the general revenues. Unemployment compensation and public housing were to be managed by the states, albeit with federal funds. Aid to Families with Dependent Children, already in existence, was continued as a state-run effort with the states setting benefit levels. The major regulatory schemes were directed at activities, such as air and truck transport, that were manifestly interstate in character. As Morton Keller has observed, one is struck more with the continuity than with the departures in most federal social and regulatory programs.[2]

Until the 1960s. Whatever Roosevelt or his advisers may secretly have wished, none would have been so bold as to suggest that the federal government supervise elections in districts with underrepresented racial minorities, pay directly for the health care of the elderly in ways that would require physician and hospital fees to be set in accord with federal guidelines, send federal funds and federal regulations directly to local school systems, use federal prosecutors to charge local elected officials with corruption, or require that any college receiving federal funds integrate all aspects of its educational and athletic programs along gender as well as racial lines.

Since the First Congress met, the voters have had an opportunity to demand of their representatives all manner of benefits, the costs of which could be deferred to later generations. Yet from Washington's administration through Eisenhower's, deficit financing rarely occurred except during wartime or acute domestic emergencies, and when it did occur in peacetime it took place amidst grave misgivings and after intense debate.

If people and politicians regularly exchange votes for programs, how can it be that voters never got large-scale social programs or peacetime deficits until quite recently? Is it that they only recently decided to want these things? Possibly. Yet it is odd that until the 1960s it never occurred to self-interested voters effectively to demand expensive new programs that their great-grandchildren would pay for.

I suspect that what has changed is what we believe and that the greatest change in beliefs has occurred, not among the public at large, but among political elites. American government is vastly larger and more complex than it was fifty years ago. A half-century ago no one would have imagined the extent to which liberties would be broadened (nude dancing now enjoys a level of constitutional protection once reserved for abolitionist editorials). Hardly anyone would have foretold the extent to which law would be mustered in support of rights. (In the 1940s one could have foreseen the day when schools would be desegregated, but no one could have foreseen that the courts would decide that children must go to school together even if it meant bussing them there.) Americans were accustomed to supporting the president in his military decisions, but hardly any American would have said in advance that sending troops to Korea, Vietnam, the Dominican Republic,

Lebanon, Grenada, Kuwait, or Somalia sounded like a good idea. Most people were quite prepared to see the federal government regulate big business, but very few were interested in seeing the government deregulate air travel, telecommunications, or financial institutions.

Many of the largest changes in this half-century have occurred, not because of popular demands, but because of elite interests. I have already mentioned some aspects of civil liberties, civil rights, deregulation, and foreign policy. Scholars are very good at explaining why Congress distributes material benefits to particular constituencies; they are not very good at explaining why it translates general ideas into new policy directions. Ideas are the currency of political elites, and elite ideas are always more volatile than popular ones. They may not be profound or well-thought-out ideas, but their power does not depend on their depth or feasibility; it depends, rather, on their being plausible and satisfying representations of a new way of looking at the world.

In this space I can only supply a caricatured account of the depth of those changes. But something can be learned from this oversimplification. Compare the views of a self-described liberal or conservative member of Congress (or editorial writer) in the 1950s with those of such a person today.

Then: The standard liberal believed in equal opportunity and a color-blind Constitution, was closely allied with and supportive of the union movement, gave unequivocal support to Israel, thought nuclear power was a blessing to mankind, opposed judicial activism because it had been used to block the New Deal, and took pride in the idea that the United States would be the world's policeman. A standard conservative was, at best, indifferent to civil rights, hostile to unions, in favor of judicial activism (because it protected "freedom of contract"), desirous of conserving the environment, and thought the country should adopt the posture of Fortress America, not Pax Americana.

Today: Many liberals believe in affirmative action (defined as group entitlements or, sometimes, equality of outcome), ignore or actively dislike union leaders, are equivocal about Israel, oppose nuclear power, like activist judges, and think that promoting human rights abroad is more important than promoting international stability. Many conservatives have very nearly the opposite of these views (and thus of the views that they had forty years ago).

Both liberals and conservatives have learned to live with large budget deficits. It was Richard Nixon who said that we are all Keynesians now. By that he meant, I think, not that deficits are always good but that they are often useful. Scarcely any politician can be found who will defend deficits as large as those we now have. But their objections to them are prudential, not principled. There is too much red ink, given our economic circumstances, but red ink is not inherently wrong under any or most circumstances. James Buchanan, the Nobel-laureate econo-mist, takes second place to none in his commitment to explaining polit-ical outcomes as the result of self-interested motives. Yet even he is convinced that one key explanation for the change in federal policy making has been the elite abandonment of the view that peacetime deficits are wrong. What constrained our natural desire to spend more federal dollars than we collect in taxes was, in his view, a kind of Victo-rian commitment to the idea of fiscal prudence.[3] It is a view that most Americans still share. They are self-interested enough not to let their dislike of deficits interfere with their support of politicians who incur them, but they are also other-regarding enough to be upset at the sight of those politicians making feeble and often insincere gestures at those deficits.

We cannot account for many of the most important shifts in public policy that mark—in many ways, define—the last half-century without close attention to changes in elite opinions. There is very little in mass opinion that would account for sustained budget deficits, the expansion of group entitlements and minority set-asides, the expansion of the rights of criminal suspects, the continuation of aid to foreign nations, the commitment to free trade, proposals for military intervention abroad, the maintenance of Aid to Families with Dependent Children, the Tax Reform Act of 1986, or airline and communications deregula-tion. These programs prevailed because strategically placed elites fa-vored them. That fact does not constitute an indictment of these poli-cies; the U.S. political system was not designed to operate on the basis of a national referendum or an electronic town hall. It was always under-stood that elected representatives would not simply reflect public de-sires, but would "refine and enlarge" them.[4] In my view, some of these policies are good, some are bad, and most are a mixed bag. But they are not the public's policies.

Elite views have always made a difference, but with the expansion in the scope and reach of the national government they now make a vastly larger difference. Political scientists have been slow to adjust to this new reality. As a consequence, our shelves are filled with books on public opinion but not with ones on elite opinion. Our journals have explored with great care the many ways in which members of Congress heed constituency desires but have neglected the ways in which some elites can ignore those desires. There is at least one conspicuous excep-tion to this neglect—studies of presidential nominating conventions. Since 1972, scholars and journalists have been documenting the widening gap between the beliefs of delegates and of voters. As is now well known, Democratic delegates are well to the left of most Democratic voters and Republican delegates are to the right of most Republican voters.

The institutional opportunities for elite influence began to widen during the New Deal but did not become significant until thirty years later. Though the Roosevelt era established the legitimacy of national social welfare policies and forged a new Democratic party coalition to support them, it did not alter fundamentally the way decisions were made. After the enthusiasms of the Hundred Days passed, states' rights were once again reasserted as a serious check on federal power. Though the Supreme Court abandoned its early opposition to new federal initiatives, it did not in the 1930s or 1940s take initiatives of its own by discovering new rights or providing new grounds for citizen action against the state. While business interest groups were thrown on the defensive and labor interest groups were nurtured into robust political life, the universe of groups was still narrowly bounded. For thirty years after FDR, it was still possible to write textbooks about pressure groups that did not venture much beyond the Chamber of Commerce, the AFL and the CIO, the American Medical Association, and the Farm Bureau Federation. Nobody talked about congressional staffers, issue networks, or beltway bandits; professional politicians existed, but a professional political class did not.

Today everyone is aware that such a class exists, composed not only of the members of the government but also of the national media, the countless Washington-based interest groups, and the consulting firms, political lawyers, and academic in-and-outers who swirl like fireflies in the conference rooms, dinner parties, and cocktail receptions of The Nation-State. Once, political debate was about what, if anything, the government should do; today it is about what the members of the political class are doing. Everything—that is, every human concern—is already on the agenda of official Washington, and most of these concerns are already the object of programs, grants, and projects. The essential political business, thus, is how these programs are managed and how, if at all, they should be revised or amended. The great political wars over purpose and authority have been replaced with tactical skirmishes over management and refinement. In these skirmishes, the traditional interest groups with a material stake in the outcome have been joined by the new interest groups with a symbolic stake in the result.

As a consequence, it is no longer as clear as it once was what, if anything, an election might settle. Benjamin Ginsberg and Martin Shefter, in their book, *Politics by Other Means*, argued that elections have lost their importance in the United States as we have become locked into a cycle of divided government that carries on its partisan and institutional wars by means of congressional investigations, media revelations, personal scandals, special prosecutors, and budgetary evasions.[5]

The factors that have contributed to these changes are thought to be well known: television, direct mail, the civil rights revolution, the decline of party loyalties in the electorate, and so forth. But it is not clear to me that what everyone knows, while true enough, is sufficiently true— that is, sufficiently fundamental—to explain a transformation that no one in FDR's cabinet or Congress could have foreseen, even if somebody had explained to them that television was about to be invented. In fact, after television had arrived and party loyalties had begun to decline, scholars such as James MacGregor Burns were writing books complaining of the "deadlock" of American democracy, by which they meant the inability of government to adopt large (and, of course, liberal) new programs.[6] It was an ill-timed message; the vast legislative outpouring of the 1960s and 1970s came right on the heels of these predictions.

Hedrick Smith in *The Power Game* has given us a portrait of the new American politics that might be summarized this way: The costs of political mobilization have been lowered in ways that permit more interests to be heard; make it easier for politicians to develop individual and personal, rather than institutional and partisan, relations with their constituents; and offer more opportunities for intervention in policy making.[7] The advent of direct mail solicitations, activist foundations, and easier access to courts has dramatically expanded the scope of influence on government and enhanced the power of ideological symbols as against pecuniary stakes.

But Smith's portrait is incomplete and, to a degree, distorted, a deficiency that is revealed by its title. Politics is not simply about power, it is also about purpose, and politics is not simply a game, it is a manifestation of a nation's institutions and beliefs. The costs of political mobilization may have been lowered, but the demand for such mobilization has risen and taken bold new forms. We now routinely expect the national government to do something about drugs, crime, AIDS, toxic wastes, and the homeless—matters that until very recently would not have been thought proper subjects for federal action. We all remember that until the 1960s Washington did not have civil rights on its agenda— it was a matter of "states' rights." But we forget that until the 1960s Washington also acted as if crime were a matter of states' rights. Many legislators were opposed to allowing the FBI to investigate prostitution and auto thefts, and J. Edgar Hoover's well-known aversion to FBI involvement in narcotics and organized-crime cases was in part a reflection of what he had learned about the limits of congressional tolerance for federal meddling in local affairs.

There has been a transformation of public expectations about the scope of federal action, one that has put virtually everything on Washington's agenda and left nothing off. If you doubt it, try thinking of a human want or difficulty that is not now defined as a "public policy problem." Moreover, the language by which that transformation was accomplished was that of individual rights—morally superior and legally defensible claims for protections and remedies. Ronald Dworkin may be incorrect in asserting that, philosophically, rights ought to be trumps,[8] but he is certainly correct in noting that, politically, rights have in fact become trumps.

One of the main reasons for the discontent Americans feel toward their political leaders is that American government has become more like European governments, in scope if not in procedures. As a result, Americans feel about their government much as Europeans feel about theirs: a conviction that it is run by people who do not have the true interests of the public in mind. The exuberance with which Americans fought and won a great war, the pride with which they took their place as the world's dominant nation, the confidence that intellectuals have always had in the power of reason to produce the good society—all these have been eroded by the daily frustrations of trying to manage the work of an activist government enmeshed in the countless details of everybody's business, by the recognition that America must share her position on the world stage with nations that fifty years ago either did not exist or were our supine enemies, and above all by the growing awareness that reason alone cannot create the conditions for a good life or sustain the spirit of those who try to live it.

The New Elites

How can political elites be more important today, when the system is more decentralized and participatory, than they were formerly, when it was less participatory—when, indeed, scholars called it *elitist?* At least three reasons can be suggested. First, the relationship between elites and masses has been altered. Formerly, those interests that were represented in government were largely based on pecuniary incentives. Though there were from time to time important social movements— abolitionists, suffragettes, and prohibitionists come to mind—the social groupings that had the greatest and most enduring day-to-day influence were economic in nature. Farm, business, labor, and veterans organizations represented the material interests of farmers, firms, unionists, and veterans. Many other sectors of society, or other ways of defining a sector, were omitted from politics. The leaders of the most powerful lobbies might speak only for a narrow segment of society, but the relationship between that segment and its leaders was not problematic. It was based on shared material concerns. A principal-agent problem existed in that some leaders might ignore the interests of their followers, but the followers had the motives and the means to correct the situation. Today, many of the most important leaders are the virtual, not direct, representatives of people for whom they claim to speak but who in fact are not organized, or at least not well organized, to supervise their spokesmen. Ethnic, feminist, consumer, environmental, and religious leaders represent important segments of opinion, but the segments they accurately represent are typically only a small fraction of the populations for whom they claim to speak. Most of us vaguely share some, but usually not all, of the goals of these leaders, but we have no organized relationship to them. To the extent that we get what we want from their efforts, we are free riders. But if we are free riders, then they are free agents, able to take positions and make claims that in a referendum might be endorsed by only a minority of the free riders.

Second, the political institutions to which elites enjoy privileged access have increased in power at the expense of those institutions in which they enjoy fewer prerogatives. The courts, media, bureaucracy, foundations, and think tanks have, I think, gained in influence relative to mass-based political parties, neighborhood associations, locally based business and labor associations, and even congressional committees. This has been partly the result of a successful effort to shift decisions out of arenas where public opinion is decisive and into those where it is relatively unimportant. Schools were integrated and abortions legalized by the courts as a result of suits brought by people who did not trust public opinion to make the right decision. But the shift has also been the result of the sheer growth in the complexity of public policy. Citizens can have a meaningful voice in a debate over whether to have publicly funded health care, but once those programs are created they involve such mind-boggling complexities that only full-time experts can hope to have much influence. Most people who wish to become players in Washington must become specialists.

Third, the expansion of the policy arena has required modern elites to make decisions on a variety of issues where constituency interests are unclear (e.g., foreign policy, foreign aid, space exploration), deeply divided (abortion, gun control), or insensitive to costs (environmental and consumer protection proposals). Elites are powerfully constrained by matters that directly and palpably affect the lives of ordinary citizens. No matter what the media or interest groups may say or judges and bureaucrats may do, people are keenly aware of unemployment, inflation, crime, school problems, and neighborhood disorder. Elites may not be able to respond well to these concerns, but respond they must. On other issues, however, including those listed in the first sentence of this paragraph, citizens usually have no direct experience with the problem and few ways of evaluating the merits of alternative proposals.

One of the striking anomalies of the new politics is that it has developed at a far more rapid rate at the federal than at the state level. Since both levels of government share similar constitutional systems and traditions, it is not obvious why political decentralization should today be so much more pronounced in Washington than in Albany, Austin, or Sacramento. State legislatures are on the whole under much more central leadership control than is the Congress. The media have less influence on state politics, I suspect, than they do on national affairs. The president has lost some of his powers, but many state governors have gained new ones. States that once boasted of having a weak chief executive confronting many elected rivals now boast of having replaced their Jacksonian constitutions with Progressive ones featuring a strong executive with few elected rivals.

I am not aware of many studies that explain the persistence of strong state legislative leaders in an era when congressional leaders have lost power. My conjecture is that those members of Congress who, in the late 1960s and early 1970s, challenged the leadership structure had available to them a motive and an appeal not equally available to insurgents in the state houses. That motive and that appeal was the desire to end procedural obstacles to civil rights legislation. The rights revolution was initially a federal phenomenon. Reinforcing this was the tendency of the national media to focus on national issues and to bring to bear on national arrangements the progressive impulses of most national journalists. Congress and the federal government generally was under heavier pressure than was the case in most state capitols to embrace the norms of openness, democracy, and due process. When the window of reform has been opened at the state level, the issues usually have involved increasing efficiency, delivering services, and reducing corruption. When the window has opened at the federal level, the issues seemed to be fairness and unmet needs. The state problem was defined in a way that made centralization and better management the obvious remedies, whereas the federal problem was defined in a way that made decentralization and due process the proper standards.

The New Politics and the Problem of Collective Choice

In every era, the American political and policy systems have faced a defining problem. For the first few decades of its existence—from the Founding to the Civil War—the key national political problem was to achieve legitimacy. Would the Union prevail against its rivals, the states, and would national elections permit the peaceful alternating in office of political opponents? From the Civil War through the New Deal, the key issue was power. With the federal government secure and legitimate, what limits on its powers would it be required to observe? In particular, how great a role could it play in either fostering or regulating the economy? From the New Deal to the Great Society and perhaps beyond, the key issue was representation. Given that Washington was secure in the exercise of expanding powers, were all segments of society appropriately represented in the making of decisions that now had become important to almost everyone? Among academic political scientists, this took the form of a debate over whether U.S. politics was truly pluralistic.

Today, the key issue is the problem of collective choice. The national government has unchallengeable powers and unquestioned legitimacy, and it is actively besieged by every manner of interest and faction. To a large degree (how accurately is another matter), every conceivable segment of society, broad as well as narrow, has spokesmen in Washington. Now that the government can do almost anything and is required to listen to almost everybody, will it strike a balance between costs and benefits that is in the long-term interest of the public?

The problem of collective choice is the problem of combining individual preferences into a policy that will command general assent over the long term. Some examples will make this clearer. Every opinion poll for the past several decades has made it abundantly evident that the U.S. public wants low taxes, no deficit, and more federal money spent on education, health care, the environment, and the control of crime and drug abuse. Now, it is obvious that one cannot simultaneously reduce taxes, spend more, and shrink the deficit. The public is not irrational in having such views. Everybody has partially inconsistent preferences. For example, most of us would like a higher income, more leisure, and no debts. As individuals we are forced to make hard choices, but as a collectivity we are not.

At one time popular desires for these inconsistent outcomes could be ignored either because the federal government had no authority to act on behalf of them (until recently, education, the environment, and health care were not on Washington's policy agenda) or because people who pressed for these things had no effective voice (the education, health, and environmental lobbies are no more than two or three decades old). Now these desires cannot be ignored.

The main way we have found by which to reconcile individual preferences and the common good has been to defer or ignore certain costs. We have funded many of our entitlements, subsidies, and grants-in-aid by borrowing from future generations. We have plans to fund more—such as health care—by shifting the cost to employers (but ultimately, of course, to consumers). We have dealt with the tragedy of the commons—that is, the incompatibility between the individual use of an environmental asset and its long-term maintenance—by opting for regulations that do not seem to be costly to most people. For example, we have tried to reduce auto pollution by regulating auto manufacturers rather than by increasing the costs of driving an automobile, as with a steep fuel tax.

During the Reagan-Bush administrations, these techniques for coping with collective-choice problems were supplemented by massive federal deficits that had the effect of persuading many people in Congress that no new programs could be adopted because there was no money for them. An interesting but unresolved historical question is whether the White House deliberately proposed budget deficits as a way of blocking the adoption of new programs or whether it supported tax cuts entirely out of its belief in supply-side economics.

Can Our Institutions Cope with Collective Choice?

I do not know whether we can rationally manage the New American State. Only time will tell. But I am convinced that most proposals for improving that management by altering the political system are flawed.

Electing as president a person who is "a strong leader with proven management skills" makes little sense because no person can be stronger than the (relatively weak) office he or she will occupy, and our fundamental problems are ones of choice, not management.

Congressional term limits would slightly shorten the average tenure in office, but would increasing the mean turnover rate in the House from 16 percent per election (which is what it has been since 1946) to 17 percent (which is what a twelve-year limit would mandate) make a real difference? Of course, the average change would conceal much bigger changes among some members, such as key leaders and other senior representatives, but we must have grounds for thinking that the benefit of the very real reduction in their terms would be worth the accompanying loss in knowledge, parliamentary skill, and personal relationships. I do not know on what grounds we can confidently make such a prediction.

Giving the president a line-item veto would surely enhance his power at the expense of that of Congress, but there is nothing in such a provision that enables us to predict how that power would be used. A fiscally conservative president might well use the line-item veto to cut spending, but a spendthrift president could as easily use it to increase outlays. Suppose Congress were reluctant to fund a large new program favored by the White House. Credible threats of a presidential veto of other, more cherished appropriations could well produce the extra votes necessary to carry the president's bill.

Moving toward a parliamentary system would certainly enhance executive power. Such moves have been advocated by thoughtful and responsible people such as Lloyd Cutler, C. Douglas Dillon, James Sundquist, and Senator Nancy Kassebaum.[9] Many of these changes are piecemeal and probably trivial (such as allowing the president to put members of Congress in his cabinet). But the spirit behind these changes clearly reflects an admiration for the British system, and so one must imagine our adopting changes sufficient to call something like that system into being. Of course, there is not the slightest chance of their obtaining the approval of enough Americans to sustain the necessary constitutional amendments. But if they were enacted, it is hard to picture the political system they would create. Our president (now in fact our prime minister) would be more powerful, and Congress (and especially its committees) would be weaker, but other things would change as well. In all likelihood we would have several political parties rather than two, and so a national government would often be a coalition government. Presumably, judicial review would survive, and so judicial activism and court oversight of executive agencies would continue. The states would, one imagines, continue to enjoy an independent share of political sovereignty. How this odd mixture might function is impossible to predict. Perhaps we would have a government akin to that of Australia or Canada, albeit one operating on a vastly more heterogeneous society. If so, are they the models we wish to emulate? These are also nations with large budget deficits and costly entitlement programs that are increasingly hard to sustain.

It is always tempting to assume that other democratic nations are managing their policy systems better than we. Clearly they operate differently than we. The absence of the separation of powers enhances the power of the chief executive and the national bureaucracy; the absence of judicial review increases the power of the political branches. This certainly increases the speed, secrecy, and flexibility with which foreign policy is conducted, no small gain in an interdependent and still dangerous world. But this is a gain purchased at the price of further empowering political elites whose views are not always congruent with that of the people they govern and whose incentives to consult with affected groups are rather weak. As I write this, French farmers are rioting, Italy is wracked by budget deficits even larger than ours and by revelations of vast and institutionalized political corruption, Great Britain is struggling to find its way out of a recession far deeper than ours, Sweden is wondering how to restore individual initiative and economic incentives to a populace that is paid not to work, Europeans are worrying that the Common Market threatens their interests, and the Japanese people are slowly awakening to the fact that the "Japanese miracle" was erected on the backs of consumers who have been saddled with artificially high land and food prices for decades.

The fundamental defense of the American political system is precisely that it *does* fit poorly with the new policy system. Events and ideas have combined to enhance the power of political elites, but their power is still checked by the same constitutional processes that the Framers invented to forestall the power of eighteenth-century elites. The popular impatience with the results of our sloppy, burdensome, inconsistent, decentralized, and individualistic political system reflects a popular desire for a leader who will set our house in order. Were they to get such a leader and were he to have the power he requires for making the hard choices, they would quickly recall to mind the virtues of sloppiness, burdens, inconsistency, and decentralization. *Given the fact that the views of both liberal and conservative elites are out of step with those of the average American, do we wish further to empower elites?* One example: the United States is likely to get a better (or less bad) health care bill as a result of congressional "bickering" than it would have gotten had President Clinton's plan been enacted as written.

We may wish, however, to create further barriers—not only to elite actions, but also to the short-sighted pursuit of our own preferences. A balanced budget amendment is the one proposal that is easiest to envisage and most consistent with the key problem of collective choice. If it were enforceable—a big *if*—it would require the president and Congress to make harder choices than those they are now disposed to make, and it would force us, the voters, to make harder choices in deciding which members to reelect to Congress. It would no longer be as easy for members to run for Congress by running against it, all the while concealing their own complicity in the fiscal mess by voting for every popular spending measure and against each unpopular tax. A balanced budget requirement would not be a strait jacket (it could always be overridden by an extraordinary majority), but neither would it be a panacea. There are many ways for ingenious legislators to move outlays off budget or shift program costs onto the private sector. But it would be a start, one that does the least institutional harm, draws on the greatest amount of existing political experience, and is most easily set aside when emergencies require it.

Two-Tier Politics and the
Problem of Public Policy

WILSON CAREY MCWILLIAMS

In my native California, observers have become accustomed to referring to the state as a "two-tier society," speaking of the distinction between the relatively comfortable, disproportionately "Anglo" sector that holds the upper hand in civic life and the economically embattled, largely nonwhite substratum, marginal in society and vulnerable in politics.[1] With appropriate variations, this description holds for more and more of the United States, as American society seems to be dividing into the unconfined and the caged.[2]

Here, I am concerned with a parallel but different phenomenon, our tendency toward a two-tier *politics*. On the one hand, the world in and around the centers of government is dense with organized interests and policy advocates caught up in intricate plans and maneuvers and inundated by data and detail. On the other, the mass electorate is weakly articulated and greatly baffled, far removed—or so citizens are apt to feel—from government and the effective discussion of policy. The first rarely addresses the second except in media campaigns, when it speaks in the language of sound bites and slogans or the garblings of the talk shows.[3]

Two-tier politics is a crucial dimension of "the new politics of public policy," the effort to combine strong government with a politics that grows more fluid, less structured, and, at bottom, less public, gradually slipping out of sight "into the body of the organization."[4] Yet, by weakening authorization, amorphous politics constrains government and policy in decisive ways: the foxes may be at large, but the lions are pretty much in chains.

In the first place, the decline of form does not result in general liberation but in a special kind of rule. Unstructured politics empowers insiders, the masters of detail who have their fingers on the pulse of change. It debilitates ordinary citizens, who find it difficult to keep track of a rule that is subtle and changing in appearance—"intricate and perplexed," in the old Antifederalist warning.[5] And contemporary Americans are only too aware that they can be led by "a government they do not see."[6]

The electorate is wary, and the upshot is a chronic and radical deauthorization that accompanies even the demand for active government and political change. In part, this is founded on doubt of government's *ability* to solve problems that matter to us. Recent history is littered with failed policies like Vietnam, the War on Poverty, and Supply Side Economics, as well as less towering but irksome failures such as the deregulation of the airlines. It has become commonplace to expect public policy to be badly designed and ineptly executed, combining self-defeating internal conflict with the inability to make tough decisions or use strong enough sanctions when applying policy to outsiders.

Temporarily, the liberation of Kuwait moderated these feelings— clearly, the Gulf War demonstrated that the government can mobilize and wield formidable powers effectively—so that, paradoxically, George Bush's greatest triumph encouraged the demand for economic intervention that was his undoing. But the Gulf victory, evidently inconclusive, has now lost its bloom, and the renewed doubt that government can succeed even when it wins, while it hurt Bush in 1992, also increases hesitancy about Clinton's activism.

Questions about government's technique, however, are less fundamental and less serious than doubts about its authority, its *moral* title to rule. An alarming number of Americans are convinced that their concerns are not voiced in deliberations or reflected in policy: 57 percent of the respondents in a 1990 Times-Mirror poll agreed that "people like me don't have any say about what government does."[7] Subtract an element of hyperbole and what remains is the conviction that representative government is radically defective, the belief that what say we have is too fractional or too muddled to imply our consent to what government decides, much less any active support for policy. On the contrary, voters are inclined to think of government as dominated by money and by organizational elites, so universally corrupt that, even where we can agree on the common good, public policy cannot be trusted to be fair in the sacrifices it asks of us.[8]

During the Reagan and Bush years, most Americans, by the measure of the polls, expressed concern about the deficit and tended to agree that it could not be reduced substantially without raising taxes. In equally impressive numbers, however, they declared themselves less likely to vote for any candidate who called for tax increases. Voters, in other words, virtually asked to be told what, in candid moments, they re-garded as lies or fairy tales about the public interest, sending the mes-sage that their overriding concern was to protect private well-being.

Opinion polls today show a greater verbal willingness to confront fiscal realities. In practice, however, the resistance to President Clin-ton's budget shows how marginal that change is and how reluctant Americans are to abandon the hope for a "no-pain politics," at least for their own and for themselves.[9]

Confronted with the electorate's "grumpy cynicism," political lead-ers tend to become contemptuous of opinion even as they bow to its restraint.[10] This strengthens the already lush charms of covert politics: the toleration of "disinformation" has now been extended well beyond matters of national security into the civil administration, as in the decision to leave the savings and loan rescue "off-budget" or in the routine use of a rhetoric of deception (i.e., "revenue enhancement"). In the same way, leaders are encouraged to champion, in public, only those policies that command very broad public support and then only at a very high level of generality. Such "consensus politics"—support for defense expenditures in the 1950s, for example, or for environmentalism today—is often only another mask, with the conflicts and costs trans-ferred off stage, into the administration.[11]

Covert politics is worrisome at best, and by reinforcing the sense that government is arcane and overwhelming, it tilts a great many Americans, across the ideological spectrum, toward political views that are recognizably paranoid.[12] But it also reflects a government that is severely limited, one that is extraordinarily vulnerable to scandal—since scandal publicizes policies whose condition often is that they not be noticed—and ruled by the maxim that the public must not be asked for much, nor expected to persevere. To an uncomfortable extent, the United States is a thin regime, able at best to pursue a politics of succes-sive improvisations and exposed to challenges from outside the Consti-tution and the laws.[13]

Still, the hallmark of the election of 1992 was the desire for change and for a government able and willing to address our common problems. The signs of that disposition were already visible in 1988, when most voters responded favorably to the candidate who promised, on any given issue, to use governmental power aggressively—Dukakis in relation to health care, for example, or Bush, in dealing with crime or foreign poli-cy.[14] And of course, the economy's woes and worries about the country's economic future have, for the moment at least, raised the current of activism to flood level.[15] Ross Perot suggested, in fact, that the Constitution's channels might be too narrow to handle the flow: disdainful of political institutions like Congress and the parties and impatient with democratic deliberation, Perot, like his movement, preferred to see politics as a kind of marketplace, requiring an entrepreneur rather than a tamed prince.[16] At the same time, however, great numbers of Americans showed some yearning for a more genuinely democratic politics, a justified frustration with the media, and a desire to hear public issues discussed in a more serious way.

Even in the midterm elections of 1990, there had been hints of a mandate for a modest sort of civic virtue. The returns suggested that it is a virtual kiss of death for a governor—or, as George Bush learned, for a president—to raise taxes after pledging not to do so. But while the most successful candidates were governors who had kept taxes down, others won in spite of increased taxes *if*, as candidates, they had indicated that taxes might have to go up. Enough voters to make a difference were expressing a desire to be told the truth, a hope for the kind of honorable deliberation that gives citizens the basis for reasoned choice. The strength of this impulse should not be exaggerated: Americans are pulled in two directions, and private interest is always the favorite in any tug of war. Nevertheless, the election of 1992 did demonstrate that, at least when allied with economic anxiety, the theater of democratic politics still can attract an American audience.

It is important to recognize, however, that the ambivalences of contemporary American politics are only partly due to problems of recent origin. To a considerable extent, after all, two-tier politics inhered in the decision to create a large republic, a regime that necessarily thins the ties of acquaintance between citizens and their representatives.[17] Constitutionally, many of us are represented in ways that are almost entirely formal: we reside and are entitled to vote in a particular district but share little else with those who "represent" us. This thinning and formalizing of representation was a crucial element in the design of the Framers, who valued the large state in part because—given its larger legislative districts and its relatively distant capital—it increased the measure of estrangement between citizens and their representatives.[18] They reasoned that such distance would encourage moderation: less tied to their representatives by feeling and friendship, citizens would tend to limit their enthusiasm and their commitment, holding their representatives closer to the safe ground of interest. At the same time, since merely local celebrity would be less likely to suffice for election, representatives would be more apt to be persons of "talent and virtue," combining technical skill and political foresight. These, in turn, would be afforded sufficient social, psychological and political distance from public opinion to enable them to pursue public interests more or less rationally and with an eye to the long term.[19]

A continuing problem was evident at the outset. The Antifederalist, "Brutus," pointed out that, since there is a necessary limit on the size of an effective legislature, as population expanded, districts would grow ever larger, and the bond of political friendship between representative and represented ever weaker. Citizens, consequently, would become increasingly suspicious of their leaders, disinclined to regard the laws as their own, and unwilling to listen to the reasonings of representatives whenever the broader good called for a sacrifice of immediate interest.[20] Like other Antifederalists, Brutus feared that the republic, combining formidable powers with attenuating allegiance, would turn more and more to force and deception, relying on its "misterious" institutions to evade oversight.[21] And those worries, of course, sound very up to date.

The bifurcation of contemporary two-tier politics, however, is starker than anything suggested by these earlier intimations. Against the Framers' plan, the mass media encroach more and more on the space for deliberation and discretion allowed to representatives, bringing opinion into constant contact with government. At the same time, the media aggregate opinion without the sense of participation and public deliberation that can strengthen and elevate popular judgment. In debate or discussion, Harvey Mansfield observed, individuals have to give reasons, even if prejudice or passion tips the scale in the end; in the politics of the media, "individuals do not have to state their opinions, much less defend them."[22] The media speak to and for an essentially *private* opinion, solicited and addressed in private places about predominantly private matters.

It makes matters worse that the media lack any organic connection to their audience: nothing—not even sloth, given access to a remote— keeps us from changing channels if we are bored or asked to exert ourselves intellectually. The media are driven by an anxious need to entertain that prompts them to appeal to the lowest common denominator, a strategy most evident in the ever-shortening sound bite.[23] Fitfully, in 1992, Americans felt nostalgia for a more substantial citizenship; constantly, the media conspire with our worst impulses to atrophy the skills and qualities that make such citizenship possible.[24] Moreover, in their eagerness to avoid giving offense, the media are reluctant to address questions of substance: John Tierney observed that, in response to President Bush's last State of the Union address, "the chief question raised by analysts on television was not whether his proposals made any sense, but how the Democrats would respond to his staff's strategy."[25] Change the names and the parties, and the same comment epitomizes President Clinton's encounters with the media. Words, in the media's exegesis, are only clues to covert forces and strategems. Political speech—and, for that matter, the whole public dimension of politics— is a ritual of deception, which can be interpreted only by the media's masters of the esoteric. Accentuating the distinction between "insiders" and "outsiders," in other words, the media virtually institutionalizes two-tier politics.

The early experience of the Clinton administration indicates the limits of any effort to bridge the gap between citizens and government. The face-to-face interaction characteristic of the "new news"— Clinton's forte in 1992—can provide a stage-set "town meeting," but one created and managed by media producers and talk-show hosts. These "new political bosses"—the phrase is Ellen Hume's—can be held accountable only by the private, voiceless act of turning off the TV; although the "new news" may provide a better show, it does not change the relationship between the audience and the players.[26] The media still must play to the public's resentment and its demand for simplification: almost necessarily, Walter Goodman wrote, television is "the policy maker's nemesis."[27]

Reconnecting the two tiers of our politics calls for more truly republican links between governors and governed and, hence, for the refurbishing of our representative institutions. Thus far, however, the prospects are not cheering: the major proposal on the public agenda, term limitation, is at best a thin echo of the founding debate, a fragment— and not a helpful one—of the more comprehensive Antifederalist case for strong representation.

That older view began with the demand for a "more numerous representation," reflecting the conviction that representatives, under the Constitution, would be "too far removed from the people, in general, to sympathize with them, and too few to communicate with them."[28] A district, Antifederalists argued, is representable only to the extent of its commonality of "acquaintance, habit and fortune," and every step away from political friendship and deliberative community undermines a representative's authorization.[29] Districts of thirty thousand—the smallest allowed on the standard of Article I, section 2—already seemed too large, and fifty thousand, apparently, was the upper limit, for Antifederalists, of republican acceptability.[30] Such ideas seem quaint today, since even partisans of "numerous representation" might balk at a

House with upwards of forty-five hundred members. Still, Brutus' words have the quality of prophecy:

> The confidence which the people have in their rulers, in a free republic, arises from their knowing them, from their being responsible to them for their conduct, and from the power they have of displacing them when they misbehave: but in a republic of the extent of this continent, the people in general would be acquainted with very few of their rulers: the people at large would know little of their proceedings, and it would be extremely difficult to change them.[31]

Second, Antifederalists contended for a representation that included all social orders, the "several classes of the people."[32] This aim, too, argued against large districts, since the larger the electorate, the greater the advantages of position, money, and celebrity—of elites and those who depend on elites.[33] "The great easily form associations," Melancton Smith observed, "the poor and middling class form them with difficulty."[34]

Finally, Antifederalists argued for rotation in office (as well as very frequent elections), both to bring the representative back into the people—minimizing any tendency to create a governing class—and to encourage ordinary citizens to hope for and hence to try to fit themselves for public office.[35] (In passing, it is worth noting that rotation in office entailed a limitation on *successive* terms, but not on the *number* of terms: quite the contrary, the term *rotation* suggests a coming back into office as well as a leaving of it.) Taken as a whole, the Antifederalists offered a blueprint for legislatures that would be very large and very talky, quite amateurish and dead slow, but capable of speaking with great force on behalf of the community as a whole.

In urging term limitations, contemporary advocates have fixed on what Antifederalists probably saw as the least important part of their program, promising very different results. Proponents of term limitation, for example, show no interest in increasing the size of legislatures to some upper limit of practicality. This is especially striking in a state like California, where the legislature is very small and could easily be several times as large. (There are eighty members of the Assembly and forty in the Senate, so that a State Senate district is larger than one for the House of Representatives.) Term limitation in California, in other words, preserves a legislature shaped, on the Progressive model, for efficient rule at considerable distance from local communities, an anathema to Antifederalists. And, of course, to the extent that it lessens the power and expertise of legislators, term limitation is compatible with and even enhances the power of organized interests, legislative staffs, and public bureaucracies. The upshot of the movement for term limitation is likely to be disillusionment and even greater estrangement.

Rebuilding political parties holds more promise. In a large republic, partisanship is the closest possible approximation of Antifederalist ideas of political friendship and strong representation, and over the years the parties have afforded the United States a second system of representation based on locality, memory, and conviction. Formally, we are represented by the legislators from our districts, but even in these latter days, the champions of our party are more likely to *speak* for us, just as they are more able to persuade us to accept unwelcome measures. Similarly, in parties, the "poor and middling class" finds its best hope of organizing "countervailing collective power" against those who are "individually—or organizationally—powerful."[36] "There is a sense," Woodrow Wilson wrote, "in which our parties may be said to have been our real body politic."[37]

But parties have been beset by nearly a century of debilitating reforms—particularly the direct primary and various attacks on patronage—that have sapped their local and affective foundations.[38] The reform tradition, moreover, has worked in silent alliance with economics, public policy, and technology to create a "nationalized" electorate and a politics increasingly shaped by the media and by money.[39] Necessarily, parties and candidates are engrossed with fund raising, and the campaign reform laws—eviscerated by the Supreme Court as any real limit on the power of money—require an emphasis on a broad base of donors, directly and actively solicited. The technology of mass fundraising tends to increase the power of state and national committees, especially the latter, so that increasingly the parties are centralized bureaucracies, less mediators *between* rulers and ruled than a *part* of the governmental tier.[40]

It makes matters worse that party contributors are likely to be activists and hence issue advocates or ideologues whose views are more extreme and more coherent than those of the rank and file. As a rule, such committed partisans care about electability as well as principle, but as Pomper remarked, they "like to believe . . . that the candidates closer to their favored program are also preferred by the voters."[41] Democrats ordinarily suffer most from this tipping of the intrapartisan balance: in the case of conservatives, ideology is tempered by their material interest in a Republican victory, but liberal activists—overwhelmingly middle class—have few *interested* reasons to hope for a Democratic triumph and are more likely to insist on purity.[42] Certainly, over the last quarter-century, the Democratic party has become more liberal in character and less working class.[43] Of course, Republicans have their own burgeoning problems, especially with the religious right, support that proved costly in 1992. Yet the fact that both parties risk drifting away from the center—and from the electorate—only underlines the weakening of the partisan link in the chain of democratic politics.[44]

The gathering urgencies of our public life point to the need to strengthen party organization, especially its base in the local places where citizens have a better chance to be known, have voices, and find a measure of dignity.[45] It would be worthwhile to challenge the Supreme Court's doctrine that campaign contributions are speech and hence are protected against effective regulation, even though that cause is probably a losing one. Even within the metes of *Buckley v. Valeo*, however, there is room to maneuver. It might be possible, for example, to limit or ban paid political advertising on television, redirecting expenditures into more traditional, local forms of campaigning. There are, moreover, ways to ease the burden of fundraising or to strengthen the role of party organizations in the nominating process by preprimary conventions, to say nothing of possible changes in primaries themselves.[46]

These possibilities, anything but a complete therapy for public life, would only be so many threads between the two tiers of our politics, but such ligatures are not to be despised. Human beings are political animals, and democratic politics has its own vitalities. Government and politicians are perennial targets of opportunity: they have shortcomings and to spare, but a great deal of the resentment that we express in politics derives from other sources of hurt, indignity, and frustration. It finds its way into public life precisely because, in politics much more than in economic and social life, we have some sort of voice, if only an inarticulate scream, and some quantum of representation. It is not much of an overstatement to say that Americans are inclined to hate politics because they need to love it, a proposition Tocqueville taught us long ago.[47] The first step toward that romance and the first imperative of public policy is to put citizens and their government on speaking terms.

The New Politics of Public Policy

MARC K. LANDY

MARTIN A. LEVIN

Gridlock is a myth. The detailed case studies of policy change contained in this volume demonstrate this.[1] Even in an era of divided government and institutional fragmentation and even with conservative chief executives occupying the White House, new and distinctly nonconservative policies have continued to be formulated in Washington. To claim that divided government and institutional fragmentation do not cause gridlock is not to denigrate their significance, however. The institutional conflict that they fuel has indeed had a devastating influence upon the polity, but it has not stemmed the tide of policy change.[2]

The inability of divided government and institutional fragmentation to prevent policy innovation is especially surprising when, as several of the cases in this book point out, the policies adopted were neither very popular nor unambiguously meritorious. It is therefore necessary to probe deeper to find the generator of such change. The brunt of the evidence contained in this book suggests that the root cause of much, if not most, of these innovations is neither institutional nor, narrowly speaking, political. It is intellectual. It involves the transformation of the very terms of policy discourse which has taken place over the last several decades, including, most importantly, a greatly expanded understanding of rights.

As previously conceived, rights were limited, for the most part, to participation in politics and freedom from various forms of government intrusion. The new view creates many new categories of rights—rights for the handicapped, the unborn, consumers, and even endangered species. These rights can only be secured through the active, programmatic involvement of government. Securing these new kinds of rights requires nothing less than the establishment of what amounts to a new constitutional order: a set of ideas and institutional arrangements that both supplements and supplants the order of 1789.

Unlike its predecessor, this new constitutional order was not established consciously and formally. Many of its most important elements are not incorporated into the Constitution itself but have been enshrined in legislative language, court dicta, and administrative routines. Because it is layered on top of a preexisting structure, its design is not composed of new institutions but of renovated existing ones. The preceding chapters have done much to delineate its various components and to show how they operate. In this conclusion we try to provide a composite sketch of this new order. But first it is necessary to substantiate our dismissal of gridlock as a description of the current policy process.

Gridlock

The gridlockeans err because their depiction of modern government is, in important ways, inaccurate. The major culprits that they think cause gridlock, divided government and institutional fragmentation, do not necessarily impede policy change.[3] They correctly identify government as being characterized by weak and fragmented governing institutions. But, instead of policy gridlock, the last decade has witnessed important innovative policies such as the Tax Reform Act of 1986, the Immigration Reform Laws of 1986 and 1990, the Clean Air Act of 1990, the Civil Rights for Disabled Americans Act, renewal of the Civil Rights Act, and the Superfund renewal of 1986. In the 1970s, during the Ford and Nixon presidencies, landmark legislation was passed and precedent-setting executive orders were issued in the areas of consumer protection, environmental protection, and transportation deregulation. The Carter presidency, representing the one brief window of undivided government during this entire epoch, was hardly more successful in enacting reforms than either its successors or predecessors.

Rather than creating stasis, institutional weakness and policy fragmentation have actually served to increase the competition for policy innovation and enhance the power of strategically placed policy entrepreneurs. The defenses against determined policy advocacy have broken down. The discipline that used to be provided by strong political parties and institutional checks and balances has weakened considerably.

DIVIDED GOVERNMENT: THE HYDRAULICS OF POLICY INNOVATION

Although the frustrations created by the Democrats' inability to conquer the White House and the Republicans failure to win control of

Congress no doubt heightened levels of partisan rancor poisoning the atmosphere of the Capitol, they did not bring about policy stasis. In fact, the heightened animosity and mistrust often fostered policy innovation. This unexpected dynamic is best exemplified by the Tax Reform Act of 1986, whose improbable success flew in the face of conventional political science wisdom.

The Tax Reform Act represented a massive change in the status quo, was not provoked by a widely perceived sense of crisis, did not stimulate a high level of public concern, and was subject to far more intense negative than positive lobbying pressure. It seemed to represent a classic example of a futile policy reform. Its benefits were dispersed (they would accrue to a large number of individual taxpayers and to the nation as a whole), and its costs were concentrated (they would accrue to a relatively small number of well-to-do, powerful, and highly organized individuals and groups who benefited from the existing loopholes). And yet, as chapter 5 shows, it passed because of a form of partisan competition that was actually enhanced and abetted by divided government.

Although both Republican and Democratic leaders knew that tax reform per se was not much on the minds of voters, they both sensed that it had real potential to become so. Neither side was willing to cede to the other a matter of such great potential concern to the broad middle class whom they knew to be beset by strong resentment against the tax code. At various crucial moments, when the reform effort seemed dead, key Republican and Democratic leaders revived it for fear of seeing their party take the blame for killing it. Although other factors thrust the issue onto the agenda, the politics of partisan blame avoidance led to its passage by a reluctant Congress and its endorsement by the White House.

A similar phenomenon accounted for the passage of the most expensive environmental reform of the 1980s, Superfund. Although it was formulated by Carter's EPA, it did not come up for a vote in Congress until after Carter's defeat. Yet the Republican leadership in the Senate chose to support it for fear of having the public view the Republicans as being insensitive to environmental health concerns.[4]

Partisanship is not static, and therefore the effect of divided government on a particular issue may change over time. As chapter 8 indicates, Reagan stymied Democratic efforts to revise the Clean Air Act during the 1980s, but both Nixon and Bush chose to support and, indeed, to claim credit for passing landmark clean air laws in 1970 and 1990. As both the tax reform and the two environmental examples suggest, divided government does not prevent innovation when partisan competitors feel that such action is the best means of courting public opinion.

FRAGMENTATION I — THE NEW CONGRESS AND POLICY VACUUM

Perhaps the clearest and most important example of institutional fragmentation in the last twenty years pertains to Congress.[5] Power within Congress has been dispersed, weakening the formal leadership. Committees have ceded power to a proliferating number of subcommittees, each with its own staff. At the same time, the autonomy of individual members has been encouraged by increases in their personal resources. But the right metaphor for understanding the influence of this fractionalization is not "logjam," but "vacuum," something that politics abhors. The effort to fill this vacuum has often proven quite productive of policy innovation.

As Paul Quirk points out in chapter 9, the diminished authority of congressional committee chairmen may hinder the passage of certain laws, but it also opens up the agenda and enables far more issues to receive congressional consideration. The net effect of more bills confronting a tougher screen may well be the passage of more laws.

Since congressional leaders are less capable of providing members with what Quirk terms *institutional cover* for voting against bills that are popular with constituents, members are increasingly disposed to buck the leadership and vote "aye." Because ordinary members feel increasingly on their own when it comes to reelection, they have a much greater need to develop their own "program material" with which to convince constituents that they are successful lawmakers. Thus, the very anarchic nature of the Congress vastly increases the pressure on representatives to find original and popular issues to champion and to press successfully for their passage.

The causal dynamic here is twofold. On the positive side, institutional fragmentation and atomization create new openings into which policy innovators can more easily enter. On the negative side, the lack of integrative institutions forces individual representatives to find ways to compensate. If members are no longer shielded by the leadership from organized interests and other outside pressures, they must find new means for protecting themselves and advancing their careers. These positive and negative pressures both work to increase the attractiveness of engaging in policy entrepreneurship and to decrease the political costs associated with it. They create the hydraulics whereby policy innovations are far more common than might have been anticipated.

FRAGMENTATION II — THE NEW FEDERALISM

The fragmentation of power between the states and the national government has also been assumed to be a source of policy gridlock. But, as Shep Melnick shows in chapter 2 regarding aid to the educationally handicapped, skilled policy advocates have been able to make use of this division of authority to accelerate policy change. In one state, a federal court suit spurred the governor to increase state spending for special education. In another, state court decisions led to the passage of a state law that became the model for the federal law. When states appealed to Congress for help, Congress used these requests as an opportunity to codify the rights of the handicapped children who were to receive the help. This, in turn, provided the courts with a further opportunity to insist on liberal interpretations of key phrases in the federal statute. As Melnick describes it, the results of this particular relationship between state and national courts and legislatures were that

> each institution made incremental changes that seemed small
> when viewed individually but that constituted major, rapid
> change when put together . . . This complex interaction of sepa-
> rated institutions allowed elected officials to take credit for help-
> ing the handicapped while avoiding blame for imposing costs.
> "Don't blame me, the courts made me do it." "Don't blame me,
> the feds require it." "Don't blame me, that is what the statute
> says." These were the constant refrains of policy makers who
> often understated the discretion available to them.[6]

Rather than continuing to serve as obstacles to federal policy change, the states now are just as likely to foster it. Rather than serving as a drag on such innovation, they can become part of a feedback process in which they create circumstances that seem to require federal action, which in turn "forces" them to upgrade and intensify their own efforts, and on and on.

Those who populate various government agencies at the national, state, and local levels are now less prone to view themselves as antagonists. Nor do they necessarily owe their primary allegiance to the particular city, state, or federal department that they are currently serving. Of far greater salience is the fact that they have so much in common: they have similar training, attend the same professional meetings, and can easily foresee the possibility that they will sooner or later serve at a level of government other than the one at which they now serve. The typical resume of today's successful public servant includes stints at both the state and federal level, not necessarily in that order. Most importantly, they very often share the same strong policy commitments. Therefore, it is only natural for them, regardless of whether they temporarily work at the state or federal level, to work in concert to achieve common goals.[7]

A New Constitutional Order

The arguments offered above are necessary but not sufficient for explaining the new politics of public policy. The dynamics of the parties, Congress, and federal-state relations are clearly permissive of policy innovation, but they do little to explain its shape and content. Not *every* policy proposal passes. What distinguishes those that do from those that do not? The exigencies of party competition increase the likelihood that popular ideas receive bipartisan support, but what makes a policy idea popular? Likewise, the fragmentation of Congress provides room for policy entrepreneurs to enter and maneuver, but why are some of their efforts successful and others not? Finally, as a result of the new dynamics of federalism that we describe, technocratic coalitions exist across the entire span of state and federal government, and yet not all of these coalitions have been equally successful in promoting their policy agendas.

What is so striking about the success of several of the reforms discussed in this volume is the lack of strong public endorsement of them. No public ground swell appeared to usher in aid to the handicapped or immigration reform, for example. Only in the environmental arena is there strong evidence of real public commitment to the principles that underlie stricter pollution regulation. This phenomenon supports Wilson C. McWilliams characterization of a "two-tiered politics" in which the mass electorate is "weakly articulated and greatly baffled" while "the world in and around the centers of government is dense with organized interests and policy advocates."[8]

Although each of these successful innovations is built upon a strong intellectual foundation forcefully framed by skilled policy entrepreneurs, the case for them is not necessarily logically or morally compelling, nor was it at the time they were passed. Eight years after enactment of the Tax Reform Act, its effects remain ambiguous.[9] In 1986 the moral climate of opinion favored ending loopholes and discouraging tax evasion by leveling the rates. But now many policy reformers, President Clinton included, are once again seeking to use tax incentives and progressive rates of taxation to pursue their versions of equity and social justice. When Superfund was reauthorized in 1986, it was subject to intense critical disapproval, which has continued ever since.[10] Likewise, critics claim that the costs imposed by the 1990 Clean Air Act will far exceed its benefits.[11]

If these policy innovations were not always popular and did not reflect an impartial consensus regarding their merits, then something else must act as a filter, blocking some types of policy initiatives while allowing others to shine brightly through. This filter is nothing other than the transformation of the terms of discourse in which policy discussion takes place. The crux of this transformation has been a vastly expanded understanding of what constitutes a person's rights. This transformation, aided and abetted by the partisan and institutional developments conventionally associated with "gridlock," has led to changes in the procedures and conduct of governing institutions that are so fundamental that they are best understood as making up a new constitutional order. Those policy realms most heavily influenced by these new terms of discourse have witnessed the greatest innovation. In those realms, the discipline imposed by the new constitutional order has thwarted conservative efforts to resist change despite the considerable success conservatives have achieved at the ballot box.

A constitutional order is a complex admixture of ideas and institutional arrangements. The order of 1789 sought to secure certain rights ("life, liberty, and the pursuit of happiness"). The Founders believed that those rights could best be upheld by a government whose powers and scope were severely limited, and they drafted an institutional design replete with checks and balances, separation of powers, and other barriers to positive action to serve as a means to that end. A more expansive view of rights must, perforce, alter those institutional arrangements. Its design is not geared to minimize government intrusion but rather to make sure that governmental authority is adequate for the broad set of ends it is now expected to attain.

Unlike the original constitutional order, this new regime was not established consciously and formally. No new constitutional convention was held. It was rather the result of an evolution of thinking about the purposes and principles of government, including the most basic understandings of liberty, equality, and justice. These new understandings became gradually embedded in statute and Supreme Court dicta. As James Q. Wilson remarks in chapter 10 (this volume), because they have been promulgated largely through courts and administrative agencies, they do not necessarily reflect the popular will. Indeed, their proponents have gone to great lengths to insulate many public policy fruits from popular judgment by etching them into stone via administrative regulation and court decree.

Because it is layered on top of a preexisting structure, the institutional design of this new order does not consist of new institutions, but rather the recontouring of existing ones. The three branches of government and the coexistence of the states and the federal government continue, but to vastly different effect. Thus, the Tenth Amendment of the Constitution has been consigned by the courts to virtual oblivion. It provides no serious impediment for the federal government to intrude upon what had previously been considered state prerogative.

The states still matter. They are an integral part of policy-generating technocratic coalitions. They have enhanced their role as "laboratories of democracy," creating policy experiments that point toward new possible avenues for national policy innovation. Likewise, the courts no longer provide much in the way of barriers to state action, but they have become extraordinarily important policy makers in their own right, as well as catalysts for state and national legislative action. The New Deal began the creation of the federal bureaucratic apparatus, and the courts and Congress have worked together to deprive its agents of much of their discretion to ensure that the administrative state adheres to the rights-oriented policies and principles contained in the statutes as interpreted by the courts.

The creation of this new order has antecedents in the Progressive Era. But as Sidney Milkis has shown, the new order was born during the New Deal and became fully mature during the 1960s and 1970s.[12] It was built on fertile soil. The old order was also based upon rights. The Declaration of Independence was framed in terms of the securing of rights. Its influence can be seen in the inclusion of a Bill of Rights in our founding document, and later in Lincoln's defense of the Union as a nation "conceived in liberty and dedicated to the proposition that all men are created equal." The Civil War, and Lincoln's rationale for it, constituted a second, rights-based founding of the republic. The constitutional underpinnings of this rededication of the political community are the Fourteenth and Fifteenth Amendments, which provide that the rights outlined in the Constitution would actually be protected by the federal government.

The New Deal expanded upon this revised understanding in two crucial ways. First, as outlined by FDR in his Commonwealth Club Address, it explicitly set out to create an economic constitution that would secure economic rights just as the political constitution secured political and civil rights. The content of these rights was not fully elaborated, but, at a minimum, they were considered to imply minimal levels of economic security, as provided for by old age pensions and unemployment compensation. Second, the National Labor Relations Act constitutionalized the relationship between unions and management, endowing workers with a right to form unions without fear of reprisal and compelling management to bargain with them in good faith.

The civil rights acts of the 1960s represent both a fulfillment of the Civil War "founding" and an extension of the New Deal principle of establishing rights in contexts heretofore viewed as lying outside the purview of government. Protecting the rights of racial minorities to vote, to assemble, and to enjoy a fair trial was simply making good on promises made a hundred years before. In banning discrimination in hiring and in the provision of certain forms of accommodations, how-ever, these laws were expanding upon the New Deal effort to endow people with publicly enforceable rights in arenas that had been previ-ously defined as private.

Building upon all of these precedents, the new constitutional order has come into full fruition as a result of the proliferation of rights claims since the mid-1960s. Shep Melnick dubs this phenomenon the *rights revolution*. "The rights revolution refers to the tendency to define near-ly every public issue in terms of legally protected rights of individu-als . . . the handicapped . . . workers . . . students, racial, linguistic, and religious minorities . . . women . . . consumers, the right of a hear-ing, the right to know—these have become the stock and trade of Amer-ican political discourse."[13]

A fuller enumeration of rights claims makes Melnick's point even more striking. Claims for the rights of aliens and the unborn extend the sphere of rights to encompass those not previously considered to be entitled to the full protection of American law and even to those not previously considered persons. The Endangered Species Act expands the universe of rights to the world of plants and animals.

This new order is not the product of a plot. It does not reflect a conscious effort by elites to undermine either the democratic process or the principle of limited government. Rather, it represents the inability of the dominant strata of opinion leaders to find an intellectually and morally defensible limit to rights expansion. If blacks, why not the handicapped? If the handicapped, why not aliens? If aliens, why not endangered species?

This expansion of right claims, which forms the core of the new constitutional order, is the spark that ignites the proliferation of policy. It provides policy innovators with a virtually unassailable argument. If one is entitled to something as a matter of *right*, then there is no fully defensible reason for being deprived of it. Therefore, if it is not obtain-able by other means, government should provide it. This does not mean that rights advocates win every battle. The unavailability of resources often forces them to beat strategic retreats. But the moral superiority of their position gives them the high ground from which to launch an endless series of assaults, leading to eventual victory.

The Making of a Constitutional Order

A full depiction of what brought the new constitutional order into being is beyond the scope of this chapter. In these few pages it is possible only to sketch the highlights. Essentially, the new constitutional order was forged by presidential rhetoric, supreme court dicta, statute, and the impact of collective action on the popular imagination.

PRESIDENTIAL RHETORIC

Beginning with FDR, the bully pulpit of the presidency has served to instill new conceptions of rights in the public mind. In his Commonwealth Club Address, FDR laid out a new understanding of rights in which economic rights were added to political ones.[14] He expanded upon his understanding of economic rights in his famous 1941 "Four Freedoms" address, in which he provided a rationale to the American public for coming to the aid of the foes of Nazism. In his State of the Union message of 1944, he gave his fullest elaboration of what he termed "an Economic Bill of Rights." It went beyond mere freedom from want to include the right to a "useful and remunerative job . . . a decent home . . . adequate medical care and the opportunity to achieve and enjoy good health . . . and the right to a good education."[15] Harry Truman showed his fidelity to FDR's "Second Bill of Rights" by quoting it verbatim in his "Fair Deal" speech of 6 September 1945.[16]

The fullest and broadest expansion of rights was enunciated by LBJ in his commencement address at Howard University in 1965. Not only did rights now encompass social and economic ends as well as political ones, but also inherent in the very idea of rights was that those rights be *actual* and not merely *potential.* Johnson proclaimed that "it is not enough to open the gates of opportunity. All our citizens must have the ability to walk through those gates . . . We seek not just equality as a right and a theory but equality as a fact and a result."[17]

Significantly, conservative presidents have not made a comparable effort to use rhetoric for the purpose of moderating and modulating these claims to rights. In fact, Reagan and Bush added new claims. Both spoke out forcefully in favor of the rights of the unborn, and Bush made a civil rights bill for the handicapped one of the chief domestic policy goals of his administration.

As Sidney Milkis has shown, the conservative response to these rights claims was insufficiently political and was therefore also only marginally effective.[18] Faced with a hostile Congress, Reagan did not dare to launch a full-fledged legislative assault upon this new constitutional order. Despite his reputation as a "great communicator," he made few attempts to use rhetoric to educate the public about the excesses of "the rights revolution." Instead, he relied primarily on administrative means to vitiate it. Such means could have only limited effect.

Whatever momentum these nonstatutory efforts might have had

was blocked by the interim congressional elections, which strengthened the Democrats and robbed Reagan of his ability to claim that his actions had public sanction. The net effect of these initiatives was to contribute further to the very government centralization he claimed to abhor. Given the moral and intellectual strength of the rights revolution, an effort to wage political warfare on the basis of principled support for limited government might well have failed, but the continued policy expansion during the Reagan-Bush years bears eloquent testimony to the failure of the alternative strategy of boring from within.

THE SUPREME COURT

As the final arbiter of the Constitution, the Supreme Court is clearly the single most effective instrument for redefining the constitutional order. In sphere after sphere of American life, it has been willing to interpret the Bill of Rights and other parts of the Constitution to grant rights to persons and others that the earlier understanding of the constitution denied. The Court has even been willing to create rights, the right to privacy being the most important example, that cannot plausibly be derived from any specific constitutional language but that somehow emanate from the spirit of the document when it is viewed in its entirety.

Although the president appoints Supreme Court justices, the postwar Republican dominance of the presidency has done little to staunch its rights-expanding tendencies. Several of the most important rights-oriented justices—Brennan, Warren, Blackmun, and Stevens—were appointed by Eisenhower and Nixon. Other Nixon, Reagan, and Bush appointees have joined in seminal rights-extending decisions. This would seem to indicate that the broad intellectual climate in which these judges operate—including the influence of their own clerks, who are more attuned to the current intellectual fashions as those are displayed in law journals, legal symposia, and so forth—exerts at least as much influence on their decision making as does their partisan allegiance.

STATUTE

The efforts of presidents and the court to build a new constitutional order based on an expanded conception of rights have been complemented and supplemented by acts of Congress. The broad enabling statutes that form the cornerstones of contemporary public policy cannot be understood simply in instrumental terms. They are also "mini" constitutions in that they contain the same elements and perform some of the same functions as does the "real" constitution: they establish broad ends, prescribe specific institutional arrangements, define powers, and delimit membership.[19] Many of the most important rights that the Court has "found" were first postulated in the preambles of seminal environmental, consumer protection, and civil rights statutes. For example, the Occupational Safety and Health Act, signed into law by President Nixon, does not simply set standards and rules for improving working conditions; it establishes a right to a safe and healthy workplace.

COLLECTIVE ACTION AND THE POPULAR IMAGINATION

The president and Congress are popularly elected, and even the members of the Supreme Court have been known to read the newspaper. Their efforts to build a new order could and would have been undone if they had proven unpopular. Instead, they seem to have found popular acceptance or at least acquiescence. The susceptibility of the public to rights expansion no doubt has many causes, but one of the very most important has to do with the specific political circumstances in which the crucial expansionary moves were made.

The extension of rights claims from the political to the economic realm took place during the Great Depression. This unprecedented economic cataclysm, which rendered most Americans economically insecure, if not actually devastated, did much to undermine public faith in limited government. After all, if the government could not preserve a modicum of freedom from want, what good was its ability to preserve political freedom? The first palpable extensions of rights went to segments of the public whose claims were particularly strong—retirees and workers seeking to bargain collectively. It was very hard to argue, particularly in the context of the Depression, that old people were *not* entitled to a pension and that workers were *not* entitled to a voice in decisions affecting their work lives.

In a similar vein, the extension of civil rights to black people was, initially at least, exceedingly popular. For anyone old enough to have seen it, the televised real-life drama of well-dressed, well-behaved young black men and women sitting down at Southern lunch counters and accepting brutal beatings without complaint or resistance certainly ranks as the bravest, noblest episode in modern American political history. Who could possibly favor denying a claim to rights under such circumstances?

The popularity of the labor movement of the 1930s and the civil rights movement of the late 1950s and early 1960s established a presumption in the public mind in favor of rights claims more generally. As long as claimants could cloak themselves in similar garb, judgments rendered by the popular media of opinion were likely to be in their favor. Thus, every subsequent effort to obtain rights—be it for the handicapped, women, trees, or the unborn—has self-consciously sought to mimic the tactics and the symbols pioneered by labor and perfected by the civil rights movement. Thus, gay rights groups demand that President Clinton ban discrimination against homosexuals in the military with "a stroke of the pen," as Truman did for blacks.

The fruits of these efforts are somewhat paradoxical. On the one hand, mimicry has resulted in grants of rights to women, the handicapped, aliens, and endangered species analogous to those previously accorded to workers and blacks. But the organizations representing these newer rights claimants, as well as the contemporary incarnations of the older ones, are treated by the public with skepticism verging on scorn. They have come to be identified by voters as *special interests*, a term previously reserved for lobbies that are obviously and openly narrowly self-interested.

The Politics of the New Constitutional Order

A constitutional order creates its own form of politics and policy. As Theodore Lowi has shown, the distributional policy and pluralist politics that dominated so much of our history were made possible by the checks and balances and separation of powers set forth in the Constitution, which made broader forms of political cohesion difficult if not impossible to secure.[20] As Sam Beer has argued, the new constitutional order of the New Deal made possible a more class-based politics exemplified by the New Deal Democratic Party.[21] However, this class orientation did not last. Rather, it marked a transition from pluralist politics to rights-based coalitions. The labor movement, the backbone of the New Deal Democratic Party, was unable to expand upon its successes in creating the Wagner Act and the Fair Labor Standards Act to devise a full-fledged European style welfare state. FDR fought successfully to prevent the labor movement from becoming the dominant force in the party, as its British and German counterparts were able to do. Instead, as rights-based policies came increasingly to the fore, labor lost its commanding position to other political coalitions who were better situated to exploit rights rhetoric for their political and policy purposes.

Robert Katzmann has shown how valuable rights rhetoric is in holding together reform coalitions, such as the American Coalition for Citizens with Disabilities (ACCD). It is questionable whether the ACCD could have been born without the rights premise. If government defined federal policy toward the disabled as a matter of claims involving the allocation of finite resources, then presumably each of the many groups within the ACCD would have competed with the others to secure funds for its own constituency. Because the government defined the issue in terms of rights, however, questions of cost became irrelevant; each group could champion the demands of others without financial sacrifice.[22]

A similar dynamic occurs in the environmental sphere. If the funds available for hazardous waste cleanups were finite, neighborhood groups and hazardous waste treatment companies would view themselves largely as competitors. If the pie is fixed in size, then the more the treatment companies are allowed to charge, the less actual cleanup will take place. But, because the cleanup of abandoned sites has been defined in terms of the rights of the victims, the treatment companies and the citizens' groups are able to form a successful coalition. Since the goal of any cleanup is defined as freedom from risk, there is, in principle, no limit to the amount of money to be spent on a given cleanup. Therefore, both the treatment companies and the citizens' groups want the law to require the highest conceivable level of cleanup. As Landy indicates in chapter 8 (this volume), in 1986 the national environmental groups and the association representing hazardous waste treatment companies united to amend the law governing abandoned waste sites, nicknamed Superfund, to require all sites to meet extraordinarily high air and water quality standards without the application of any test as to whether the health benefits of attaining such standards justified the cost.

Peter Schuck's depiction of the politics of immigration reform in chapter 3 (this volume) is also consistent with this analysis. Immigration policy is normally a zero-sum game. Increases in quotas for one nationality come at the cost of another in the past. But to the extent that the policy is now defined in terms of universally applicable rights, all potential beneficiaries have a basis upon which to coalesce politically. They can improve their circumstances by fighting for a principle that is equally helpful to their coalition partners. As Schuck demonstrates, such a political redefinition of the idea of international human rights actually occurred in the course of the battle for immigration reform. "In a world in which the number of refugees vastly exceeds the willingness of receiving nations to accept them, admission of one group on the basis of human rights principles can be viewed by others as little more than special interest group favoritism. The idea of universal humanitarian principles, although violated in many instances, helped to contain this favoritism and thus maintain the coalition."[23]

The constitutional order is influential in creating the political actors who then come to compose it. The very existence of the modern labor movement rests upon the constitutive policies of the New Deal—first section 7a of the NIRA and then the Wagner Act, which proclaimed labor's right to organize. Likewise, the emblematic political actor of the 1970s and 1980s, whom Milkis and Harris aptly dub "the Public Lobby," is itself largely the creation of the rights revolution. This lobby scarcely existed when the landmark environmental and consumer protection laws were passed. It owes its success to the political dynamics established by those laws.

Rights are created statutorily, but they are made meaningful only when they are successfully invoked. It is the special skill of the public lobby to be able to press for those rights in court and to work with its allies in Congress to amend legislation to permit the courts continually to expand the definition of those rights and to provide broader avenues for judicial intervention.

The Politics of Ideas and Expertise

The important policy reforms of the 1970s and 1980s were not based exclusively on rights claims. The two outstanding examples of non–rights-based innovations were the deregulation of transport and the Tax Reform Act of 1986.[24] They passed by virtue of the partisan competitive dynamic described earlier. Neither party in Congress wanted to be dubbed as pro-inflation or anti–middle class. But these policies could only be so clearly identified as anti-inflationary or pro–middle class because of the compelling nature of the ideas upon which they were based—efficiency, in the case of deregulation, and horizontal equity, in the case of tax reform. These ideas only became compelling because of the depth of the expert consensus that formed behind them. Congress and the public at large were barraged by expert testimony attesting to the role of competitive efficiency in reducing inflation and of horizontal equity in eliminating the unfairness of the tax code.

The industrial organization subdiscipline of the economics profession had grown united in support of deregulation. Its journals were littered with articles touting the efficiency gains to be reaped by removing the dead hand of regulation from transportation, banking, retail, and communications. Treasury Department specialists and their counterparts at the major Washington think tanks and congressional committees were similarly like-minded about the benefits of ending tax loopholes even at the price of diminished progressivity. In a former time, such consensus might not have proven so influential; in the wake of the great professionalization of reform that has occurred since World War II, however, politicians were loath to countervail such an impressive show of solidarity among those who were supposed to know.

Even so, this unity might have been insufficient to elicit action if it had not happened to coincide with the perceived political interests of key decision makers. Presidents Ford and Carter were desperate to find methods to combat inflation. Deregulation had the economists' stamp of approval as a certified inflation fighter, and therefore these two presidents were willing to endorse it despite the lack of public clamor for it and its other significant political liabilities. Although tax reform was not itself a popular issue, the expert consensus behind it left them highly vulnerable to charges that they were mere shills for the special interests if they failed to support it.

The existence of such consensus should not be taken to imply that the merits of these and other expert-endorsed reforms are unassailable. The achievement of consensus within the relevant reform professional community is not the same as a "scientific" consensus. It is less an intellectual than a political and cultural phenomenon. In any particular policy sphere, the array of intellectuals and analysts with a pipeline to the policy process may or may not be a microcosm of the broader scientific or social scientific community whose research and analysis is relevant to the policy issues at stake.

The tax policy debate was dominated by lawyers on the staffs of the congressional tax-writing committees, the Treasury Department, and leading Washington think tanks. Within those circles, a consensus had long existed about the need to remove the tax code's influence on economic decision making. However, in the wider circle of economists and policy analysts, there were many who would argue that tax incentives are crucial weapons in the arsenal of economic policy making. Eight years after the passage of the Tax Reform Act, its effects remain ambiguous. And, as critics predicted at the time, tremendous political pressure is building to repeal the compromise that lay behind the reform to either add steeper tax brackets or incorporate new loopholes.

The record of experts influencing policy is markedly uneven. In the environmental arena, academic experts have been much less influential. Among environmental economists there is a consensus about replacing "command and control" regulation with market incentives that is quite comparable to the expert consensus regarding deregulation that exists among industrial organization economists. And yet environmental economists have played only a marginal role in the formulation of environmental policy. Although they scored a major success in convincing Congress to adopt a tradeable permit system for controlling acid rain emissions, the vast bulk of pollution regulation continues to be done on a command and control basis.

Likewise, many environmental scientists are skeptical about whether global warming represents a serious environmental problem; nonetheless, the issue has achieved a significant place on the national policy agenda. A similar disparity existed regarding the health risks associated with hazardous waste. Public health experts are divided about whether such wastes pose a serious health threat and yet a whole edifice of laws and regulations based on those dire claims has been put in place.

Expertise has proven less powerful in the environmental realm because it has run afoul of the rights premise. Opponents of deregulation and tax reform were never able to make a credible case that the beneficiaries of regulation and of the existing tax code had a right to those benefits. Although unionized truck drivers clearly benefited from trucking regulation, the public did not take seriously the idea that the Teamsters were entitled to those advantages. Also, the Public Lobby weighed in on the side of deregulation. It claimed that the cause of consumer rights would benefit from ending transportation and communication oligopoly. By contrast, the public has a much stronger tendency to define environmental issues as matters of right and has been strongly encouraged to do so by the environmental wing of the Public Lobby. In that context, ideas about efficiency and probability, even when proffered by certified experts, have not proven so compelling.

In describing the improbable triumph of immigration reform (chapter 3, this volume) Peter Schuck demonstrates the advantages that a policy innovation derives when it is both based on a rights claim and has expert consensus in its favor. In addition to benefiting from the principle of universalistic human rights, the cause of immigration reform was aided by the formation of an expert consensus regarding its efficiency.

> Labor economists testified that the existing system . . . was highly inefficient . . . and that a restructured system expanding admissions of the "right" kind of immigrants could create immense social benefits while imposing few social costs. Although many business interests had long embraced these ideas, the general hostility to immigration evident at the beginning of the decade had pushed them to the margins of the debate. But the decade's free market, libertarian zeitgeist, nurtured by prominent academics, influential mass media, and conservative think tanks, succeeded in grounding and sharpening these notions. Influential conservatives like Alan Simpson and liberals like Bruce Morrison came to accept them and to incorporate them into their policy proposals.

The Dogs That Haven't Barked

Although it is true, as James Q. Wilson has argued, that the presupposition against federal government initiatives—the legitimacy barrier—that characterized the pre–New Deal polity has weakened considerably, it has not by any means disappeared. Much can be learned about the new politics of public policy by noticing what policy innovations did *not* transpire during the 1970s and 1980s—D.C. statehood, labor law reform, and family leave. In these cases, the sheer existence of divided government did matter. These are core partisan issues in which the vital interests of a very important constituent element of one or both of the two parties is at stake.

Despite the overall popularity of both gun control and family leave, Republican presidents felt called upon to demonstrate their loyalties to two Republican stalwarts, the gun lobby and the business community. This notion of core partisanship should not be viewed as entirely static. Presidents show some flexibility in what they deem to be a strictly partisan issue. For example, Reagan prevented reauthorization of the Clean Air Act for his entire term on the grounds that it was too costly to business. Bush, having run for office as "the environmental president," chose to support it. The end of divided government in 1992 brought with it enactment of both a family leave bill and a ban on assault weapons. The return of divided government in 1994 once again made these issues objects of partisan conflict.

Policy making has also been highly constrained by the budget deficit. With the exception of defense, no new laws that place major new burdens on the federal budget have been passed since the Great Society. The design of those major policy innovations that have taken place has been painstakingly crafted to minimize their budgetary effect. The tax reform was explicitly designed to be revenue neutral. Superfund is to be paid for by liable parties and by a special tax earmarked for that purpose. This need to avoid federal spending has created an enormous bias in the direction of regulatory legislation that deflects costs onto the private sector. The Clean Air Act and the law establishing civil rights for the handicapped both impose billions of dollars in costs on business and consumers, but their direct budgetary effect is minimal. Since the deficit continues to mushroom, policies requiring vast federal expenditure will continue to languish.

The "Old" Politics of Public Policy

The authors in this volume have emphasized what's new about our politics, but in the process they have also served to remind us about crucial aspects of what is old and enduring. As Kagan and Morone both emphasize, the burgeoning demand for new policy has not brought with it a concomitant support for and appreciation of government. Despite their insistence that it do more, Americans have in no way overcome their distaste for and fear of the state. Even as their expectations increase, they continue to place more and more barriers in the face of effective action. Thus, the rise of what Kagan terms *adversarial legalism*, an expanded reliance on the judicial process both to produce desirable results and to protect individual liberties. This is true gridlock, for it reveals both the inability of the courts to deliver such results themselves and their readiness to hamstring the ability of government agencies to deliver them. Not only does this implementational gridlock leave citizens dissatisfied, but also it reinforces their belief that government does not work and therefore makes them even less willing to provide government with the resources that would make more successful implementation possible.

As Kagan's example of the inability of government to complete the dredging of Oakland Harbor successfully shows, there are kinds of policy that are much less likely to be achieved now than in the past. It is hard to imagine the federal government initiating any project to compare with the Interstate Highway System, the Tennessee Valley Authority, or even the Postal Service. The Democrats campaigned in 1992 on a platform that included major infrastructural expansion. It remains to be seen whether the major roadblocks to the implementation of such a program—citizen suits, environmental impact statements, endangered species protections, and so forth—which the new politics of public policy have set in place can indeed be overcome.

Conclusion

The expansion of the concept of rights to apply to an ever more diverse array of issues and problems is the core of the new constitutional order that animates the new politics of public policy. From the standpoint of republican rule, this expansion has proven to be quite problematic.

The great virtue of rights is that they are nonnegotiable. Their value transcends calculation. They *are* subject to limitation. One cannot shout "fire" in a crowded theater. But limits apply only in the extreme. For the most part, they are exempt from a full and probing evaluation of their merits and their costs. It is literally unthinkable to attempt a serious consideration of the benefits of reinstituting slavery or eliminating trial by jury. Newer rights, like Social Security, have achieved almost as hallowed a status, as Ronald Reagan quickly discovered when he dared to question it. Also, since one has them "by right," rights need not be earned. The right to freedom of speech does not require one to speak wisely. Rights tell us what are owed, not what we owe. Therefore, the virtues to be obtained by establishing rights may well clash with other crucial virtues of republican rule—responsibility and deliberation. This is especially likely if the rights being established go beyond the political guarantees contained in the Bill of Rights to encompass economic and social goals that require programmatic government action.

To protect the public's capacity to discuss and weigh alternative courses of action and to promote civic obligation, entitlements should be established parsimoniously. Not every wrong should make a right. The great strength of the new constitutional order is its openness to claims of unfairness; its grave weakness is its equation of any legitimate grievances with violations of rights.

We have seen how rights-based policies served to create rights-based political coalitions which, in turn, worked to support and sustain such policies and the constitutional order on which they were based. To curb excessive rights claims requires new policies to support and sustain a more responsible and deliberative politics, a politics that clarifies choice.

Rights politics obscures choice. Because demands can be framed in noncompetitive terms, as open-ended entitlements, diverse claimants need not view one another as rivals. They have cause to cohere politically as champions of rights. This does not deprive legislators of the necessity of making choices. After all, using resources to fund new entitlements means that fewer resources will be available for some other purposes. But it does hinder their ability to make a deliberative choice. The logic of the rights claim deprives legislators of the opportunity to discuss and debate the wisdom of this demand for resources against the alternatives. If policies could be framed so as to turn rights claims back into ordinary claims, legislators could more easily recognize the finiteness of the choices they confront. A major obstacle hampering their capacity to judge the merits of different claims would be removed.

Health policy is illustrative. So long as health is viewed as an entitlement, the public need not consider how to choose among the demands of various health claimants and those claimants have an incentive to join together in a rights-based coalition geared toward increasing the size of health entitlements. But if a cap is placed on health care expenditures, such a coalition falls apart and pressure is created to force choices among rival claims.

A similar logic applies to the environment. The coalition described earlier between environmental groups and hazardous waste treatment companies would fall apart in the face of a budgetary cap on site cleanup. In such an atmosphere, environmental groups would be forced to shift from favoring the most expensive cleanups to devising a system for ensuring that the limited funds available were spent wisely.

Since rights are by definition universal, the bias of rights politics is expansionary, encompassing the broadest possible political territory. By contrast, the bias of responsibility-based politics is constrictive, toward the narrowest possible political space. It is much easier to make appeals for civic duty and public obligation at the level of the neighborhood or the community than it is at broader political levels where citizens are strangers. At the local level citizens can participate directly in these choices and therefore not feel that such burdens are being foisted upon them. They cannot fail to recognize that a relationship exists between the costs they will have to bear and the benefits bestowed by policy.

Seen in this light, such policy innovations as state and local revenue sharing and global budgeting are much more than administrative gimmicks. They have real constitutional significance in that they encourage certain forms of public participation, discourage others, and nurture the development of responsible civic attitudes. They are hardly panaceas, but it is the very resort to panaceas that is so much to blame for the current impoverishment of public discourse. Students of politics and policy can do much to enrich public debate by rekindling respect for the virtues of civic responsibility and deliberation and by suggesting practical means, however modest, for incorporating those virtues into the concrete objectives and design of public policy.

Notes

1. OF INTERESTS AND VALUES: THE NEW POLITICS AND THE NEW POLITICAL SCIENCE

1. Arthur Bentley, *The Process of Government* (Bloomington: University of Indiana Press, 1949); David Truman, *The Governmental Process* (New York: Knopf, 1951); Robert Dahl, *Polyarchy: Participation and Opposition* (New Haven: Yale University Press, 1971).

2. Ted Lowi, *The End of Liberalism*, 2d ed. (New York: Norton, 1979).

3. Herbert Simon, *Administrative Behavior* (New York: Macmillan, 1947).

4. Martin Shapiro, *Who Guards the Guardians?* (Athens: University of Georgia Press, 1988).

5. Aaron Wildavsky, "Choosing Preferences by Constructing Institutions: A Cultural Theory of Preference Formation," *American Political Science Review* 81 (1987): 3–22.

6. James Q. Wilson, *Bureaucracy* (New York: Basic Books, 1989).

2. SEPARATION OF POWERS AND THE STRATEGY OF RIGHTS: THE EXPANSION OF SPECIAL EDUCATION

This chapter is based on research undertaken by the author under the auspices of the Brookings Institution. A more extensive discussion of both special education and the broader themes of this chapter appears in R. Shep Melnick, *Between the Lines: Interpreting Welfare Rights* (Washington, D.C.: Brookings, 1994).

1. Judith Singer and John Butler, "The Education for All Handicapped Children Act: Schools as Agents for Social Reform," 57 *Harvard Education Review* 57 (1987): 125; Paul E. Peterson, "Background Paper," in *Making the Grade: Report of the Twentieth Century Fund Task Force on Federal Elementary and Secondary Education Policy* (New York: Twentieth Century Fund, 1983), 119–26; David Kirp, "Professionalization as a Policy Choice: British Special Education in Comparative Perspective," in Jay Chambers and William Hartman, eds., *Special Education Policies: Their History, Implementation, and Finance* (Philadelphia: Temple University Press,

1983), 74–112; Jack Tweedie, "The Politics of Legalization in Special Education Reform," in Chambers and Hartman, *Special Education Policies*, 48–73.

2. John Pittenger and Peter Kuriloff, "Educating the Handicapped: Reforming a Radical Law," *Public Interest* 66 (Winter 1982): 73. Also see Peterson, "Background Paper," 119.

3. *Pennsylvania Association for Retarded Children (PARC) v. Commonwealth of Pennsylvania*, 343 F. Supp 279 (E.D. Pa., 1972); *Mills v. Board of Education of the District of Columbia*, 348 F. Supp. 866 (D. D.C., 1972).

4. *San Antonio v. Rodriguez*, 411 U.S. 1 (1973).

5. David Neal and David Kirp, "The Allure of Legalization Reconsidered: The Case of Special Education," *Law and Contemporary Problems* 48 (1985): 68.

6. Quoted in Kirp, "Professionalization," 95.

7. Robert Stafford, "Education for the Handicapped: A Senator's Perspective," *Vermont Law Review* 3 (1978): 71, 72–73.

8. A number of works explore the history of these decisions: Leopold Lippman and I. Ignacy Goldberg, *Right to Education: Anatomy of the Pennsylvania Case and Its Implications for Exceptional Children* (New York: Teachers College Press, 1973); Frederick J. Weintraub, ed., *Public Policy and the Education of Exceptional Children* (Reston, Va.: Council for Exceptional Children, 1976); Erwin Levine and Elizabeth Wexler, *PL 94-142: An Act of Congress* (New York: Macmillan, 1981), chap. 2; David Kirp, William Buss, and Peter Kuriloff, "Legal Reform of Special Education: Empirical Studies and Procedural Proposals," *California Law Review* 62 (1974): 40.

9. Subcommittee on the Handicapped of the Senate Committee on Labor and Public Welfare, *Education for All Handicapped Children, 1975: Hearings*, 94th Cong., 1st sess., 1975, 312.

10. William Wilkin and David Porter, *State Aid for Special Education: Who Benefits?* (Washington, D.C.: Legislators' Education Action Program, National Conference of State Legislators, 1976), 1.

11. Quoted in Tweedie, "Politics of Legalization," 53.

12. *Mills* at 878.

13. *Brown v. Board of Education*, 347 U.S. 483 (1954).

14. *San Antonio School District v. Rodriguez*, 411 U.S. 1 at 20.

15. Thomas K. Gilhool, "Education: An Inalienable Right," in Weintraub, *Public Policy and Exceptional Children*, 18.

16. Kirp, Buss, and Kuriloff, "Legal Reform," 63.

17. "Education for the Handicapped Act Amendments of 1975," Senate Report 94-168, 94th Cong., 1st sess., 1975, 8.

18. The GAO and OCR studies are described in William Clune and Mark Van Pelt, "A Political Method of Evaluating the Education for All Handicapped Children Act of 1975 and the Several Gaps of Gap Analysis," *Law and Contemporary Problems* 48 (1985): 15–16.

19. See Susan Olson, *Clients and Lawyers: Securing the Rights of Disabled Persons* (Westport, Conn.: Greenwood, 1984), 42–56.

20. Robert Katzmann, *Institutional Disability: The Saga of Transportation Policy for the Disabled* (Washington, D.C.: Brookings, 1986), 111.

21. Gilhool, "Education: An Inalienable Right," 20.

22. Alan Abeson, "Litigation," in Weintraub, *Public Policy and Exceptional Children*, 240.

23. *Harrison v. Michigan*, 350 F. Supp. 846 (E.D. Mich., 1972); *Tidewater Society for Autistic Children v. Virginia*, #426-72-N (E.D. Va., 26 December 1972).

24. *San Antonio v. Rodriguez*, 411 U.S. 1 at 30, 33, and 42.

25. Tweedie, "Politics of Legalization," 54. Tweedie's findings are based on extensive interviews with participants.

26. Pittenger and Kuriloff, "Educating the Handicapped," 72; Richard Weatherley, *Reforming Special Education: Policy Implementation from State Level to Street Level* (Cambridge: MIT Press, 1981), 1.

27. "Additional Views" of Representatives Quie, Bell, Erlenborn, Buchanan, Pressler, and Goodling, in *Education for All Handicapped Children Act of 1975*, House Report 94-332, 94th Cong., 1st sess., 1975, 60.

28. Eugene Eidenberg and Roy Morey, *An Act of Congress: The Legislative Process and the Making of Education Policy* (New York: Norton, 1969).

29. Levine and Wexler, *PL 94-142*, 33.

30. Tweedie, "Politics of Legalization," 58.

31. *Congressional Record*, 20 May 1974, 93d Cong., 2d sess., 15269.

32. Ibid., 15272.

33. Neal and Kirp, "Allure of Legalization Reconsidered," 74; Clune and Van Pelt, "A Political Method," 13–14.

34. Gerald Ford, "Aid to Education of Handicapped Approved: President's Statement," quoted in *CQ Almanac* 31 (1975): 656.

35. Edward Koch, "The Mandate Millstone," *Public Interest* 61 (Fall 1980): 42.

36. *Battle v. Pennsylvania*, 629 F.2d 269 (3rd Cir., 1980) at 280.

37. *Alamo Heights Independent School District v. State Board of Education*, 790 F.2d 1153 (5th Cir., 1986) at 1158.

38. See, for example, *Georgia Association for Retarded Children v. McDaniel*, 716 F.2d 1565 (11th Cir., 1984); *Crawford v. Pittman*, 708 F.2d 1028 (5th Cir., 1983); and *Yaris v. Special School District*, 558 F. Supp. 545 (E.D. Mo., 1983).

39. See *Alamo Heights v. State Board* at 1158.

40. Judith Wegner, "Variations on a Theme," *Law and Contemporary Problems* 48 (1985): 200; Thomas Mooney and Lorraine Aronson, "Solomon Revisited: Separating Educational and Other than Educational Needs in Special Education Residential Placements," *Connecticut Law Review* 14 (1982): 531.

41. *North v. D.C. Board of Education*, 471 F. Supp. 136 (D.C., 1979) at 141. Also see *Kruelle v. New Castle County School District*, 642 F.2d 687 (1981).

42. *Abrahamson v. Hershman*, 701 F.2d 223 (1983) at 228.

43. *Parks v. Pavkovic*, 753 F.2d 1397 (7th Cir., 1985); *Christopher T. v. San Francisco Unified School District*, 553 F. Supp. 1107 (N.D. Calif., 1982).

44. James Stark, "Tragic Choices in Special Education: The Effects of Scarce Resources on the Implementation of PL 94-142," *Connecticut Law Review* 14 (1982): 477, 495–96.

45. *TG v. Board of Education*, 576 F. Supp. 420 (D. N.J., 1983); *Doe v. Anrig*, 651 F. Supp. 424 (D. Mass., 1987); *Papacoda v. Connecticut*, 528 F. Supp. 68 (D. Conn., 1981). But also see *Darlene L. v. Illinois State Board of Education*, 568 F. Supp. 1340 (N.D. Ill., 1983), and *McKenzie v. Jefferson*, 566 F. Supp. 404 (D. D.C. 1983).

46. *Dept. of Education v. Katherine D.*, 727 F.2d 809 (9th Cir., 1983).

47. *Tatro v. Texas*, 468 U.S. 883 (1984).

48. This was the theme of an influential law review article, "Enforcing the Right

to an 'Appropriate' Education: The Education for All Handicapped Children Act of 1975," *Harvard Law Review* 92 (1979): 1103. A number of judges cited this article, including the district court in *Rowley* (discussed below).

49. *Bales v. Clark,* 523 F. Supp. 1366 at 1370–71. Also see *Pinkerton v. Moye,* 509 F. Supp. 107 (1981).

50. For a detailed discussion of differences among the courts, see Wegner, "Variations on a Theme," 179, and Katherine Bartlett, "The Role of Cost in Educational Decisionmaking for the Handicapped Child," *Law and Contemporary Problems* 48 (1985): 7, 18.

51. *Henrick Hudson District Board of Education v. Rowley,* 458 U.S. 176 (1982).

52. *Henrick Hudson v. Rowley,* 483 F. Supp. 528 (S.D. N.Y., 1980) at 535.

53. *Henrick Hudson v. Rowley,* 458 U.S. 176 (1982) at 190, n.11, and 204, n.26.

54. *Henrick Hudson v. Rowley,* 458 U.S. 176 (1982) at 118–19, 206, 190, 204, 192, and 200 (emphasis added).

55. *Clearinghouse Review* (January 1984): 69–71. Examples of judges continuing to insist on an "independent" judicial assessment of IEPs include *Roncher v. Walter,* 700 F.2d 1058 (6th Cir., 1983); *Adams v. Hanson,* 632 F. Supp. 858 (1985); *Clevenger v. Oak Ridge School Board,* 744 F.2d 514 (6th Cir., 1984); and the cases discussed below.

56. *Doe v. Anrig,* 736 F.2d 773 at 806. One judge on the panel commented, "The thrust of this is hard to square with *Rowley*" (at 813).

57. *Springdale School District v. Grace,* 693 F.2d 41 (1982); *Abrahamson v. Hershman,* 701 F.2d 223 (1st Cir., 1983).

58. *David D. v. Dartmouth School Committee,* 775 F.2d 411 (1985) at 419.

59. The other cases are *Geis v. Board of Education,* 774 F.2d 575 (3rd Cir., 1985), and *Students of California School for the Blind v. Honig,* 736 F.2d 538 (9th Cir., 1984).

60. *Smith v. Robinson,* 468 U.S. 992 (1984). The quotations come from, respectively, Senator Weicker, Senator Kennedy, and Senator Kerry, *Congressional Record,* daily ed. (30 July 1985): S10397, S10399.

61. *Alyeska Pipeline Serv. Co. v. Wilderness Society,* 421 U.S. 240 (1975).

62. See, for example, Pittenger and Kuriloff, "Educating the Handicapped"; Neal and Kirp, "Allure of Legalization Reconsidered"; Kirp and Jensen, "What Does Due Process Do?"

63. Milton Budoff and Alan Orenstein, *Due Process in Special Education: On Going to a Hearing* (Ware Press, 1982), 119.

64. Morris Fiorina, *Congress: Keystone of the Washington Establishment,* 2d ed. (New Haven: Yale University Press, 1989), 46–47, 67.

3. THE POLITICS OF RAPID LEGAL CHANGE: IMMIGRATION POLICY IN THE 1980s

Peter H. Schuck is the Simeon E. Baldwin Professor of Law at Yale Law School. This chapter was commissioned by the Gordon Public Policy Center at Brandeis University, and it benefited from a faculty workshop there. Muzzafer Chishti, Richard Day, John Ellwood, Lawrence Fuchs, Carl Hampe, Stephen Legomsky, Bonnie Maguire, Bruce Morrison, Rogers Smith (who deserves special thanks), and Jerry Tinker graciously commented on earlier drafts. Margo Schlanger, Yale Law School class of 1993, provided fine research assistance. An earlier draft was the subject of a panel discussion at the annual research conference of the Association for Public Policy Analysis and Management in October 1991. A longer, more heavily footnoted version of this chapter was published in *Studies in American Political Development* 6 (Spring 1992): 37.

1. For an illuminating discussion on this point, see Rogers M. Smith, "If Politics Matters: Implications for a 'New Institutionalism,'" *Studies in American Political Development* 6 (Spring 1992): 1.

2. On the concept of normal politics, see Bruce A. Ackerman, "The Storrs Lectures: Discovering the Constitution," *Yale Law Journal* 93 (1984): 1013.

3. In this chapter I use the conventional "diversity" label to describe a set of provisions—enacted in IRCA, extended in 1988, and further extended and refined in the 1990 act—that give favored treatment to immigrants from countries that were "underrepresented" or "disadvantaged" in the post-1965 immigrant flows. As discussed below, these labels can be somewhat misleading.

4. Not counting the almost 900,000 amnestied aliens who adjusted to legal status in 1990 and swelled the number of legal admissions for that year, the United States admitted a total of 529,120 aliens: 231,680 nonquota immigrants (i.e., immediate relatives, special immigrants, etc.); 214,550 people under the family preferences; 53,729 under the occupational preferences; 20,371 under the program for aliens from countries "adversely affected" by the 1965 act; and 8,790 under the so-called diversity program. During fiscal 1993 the total admissions were 904,292, including 147,012 for employment-based immigrants, 33,468 for diversity, 226,776 for family-sponsored immigrants, 255,059 for immediate relatives, 127,343 for refugee and asylee adjustments, and the remainder for miscellaneous categories. These figures do not include refugees and asylees who were admitted but not yet adjusted to the status of permanent resident during these years. In 1993, 132,000 refugees and asylees were admitted but not yet adjusted. Telephone conference with Eloise Thornton, Statistics Division, INS, 1 August 1994.

5. Peter A. Hall, ed., *The Political Power of Economic Ideas: Keynesianism across Nations* (Princeton: Princeton University Press, 1989).

6. Olmstead v. U.S., 277 U.S. 438, 435 (1928) (dissenting opinion).

7. In summarizing the role of ideas on immigration politics, I have used the word *elite* advisedly. Most Americans revere the nation's immigrant past and admire immigrants whom they know, but they do not favor an expansionist immigration policy. This was true before the 1980s, and it is almost certainly true today. Policy activists, with high educational and professional status, are different. Elite public opinion in the 1980s, as articulated by liberal and conservative editorialists alike, strongly endorsed pro-immigration reforms, and these views exerted considerable influence in Congress and in the upper reaches of the executive branch.

8. Shortly after this chapter was completed, several events involving immigrants made the headlines. Terrorist attacks against the World Trade Center and other sites were allegedly planned and executed by aliens, some of whom were admitted to the United States through State Department and INS incompetence. Chinese immigrants were smuggled into the United States on derelict vessels after having suffered appalling mistreatment. Along with illegal migration, these events aroused much indignation and handwringing. In California and other states, proposals to crack down on illegal aliens made headway. As of early August 1994, however, Congress had not yet moved to amend in any fundamental way the expansionist policies institutionalized in the 1990 act. Instead, it was focusing on proposals to expedite the processing of asylum claims by undocumented aliens, proposals Congress had con-

sidered and rejected for more than a decade. Even if enacted, these measures will hardly affect the higher legal immigration levels of recent years. Should this restrained public response to restrictionist pressures and anti-immigrant rhetoric continue, it will provide perhaps the most striking evidence that the expansionist consensus described in this chapter has firm political roots.

4. ADVERSARIAL LEGALISM AND AMERICAN GOVERNMENT

This chapter is a substantially revised version of "Adversarial Legalism and American Government," *Journal of Policy Analysis and Management* 10 (1991): 369–405. Support for the research and writing was provided by the Center for Advanced Study in the Behavioral Sciences, Stanford, California, and the College of Law, Ohio State University.

1. Derek Bok, "A Flawed System of Law Practice and Training," *Harvard Magazine* (May/June 1983): 38–45, 70, but see Robert A. Kagan and Robert Rosen, "On the Social Significance of Large Law Firm Practice," *Stanford Law Review* 37 (1985): 399–443, and Ronald Gilson, "Value Creation by Business Lawyers: Legal Skills and Asset Pricing," *Yale Law Journal* 94 (1984): 239–313.

2. Lawrence Susskind and Gerard McMahon, "The Theory and Practice of Negotiated Rulemaking," *Yale Journal on Regulation* 3 (1985): 134; Gary Bryner, *Bureaucratic Discretion: Law and Policy in Federal Regulatory Agencies* (New York: Pergamon Press, 1987), 117.

3. Thomas B. Metzloff, "Researching Litigation: The Medical Malpractice Example," *Law and Contemporary Problems* 51 (1988): 199–242; Richard Miller and Austin Sarat, "Grievances, Claims and Disputes: Assessing the Adversary Culture," *Law and Society Review* 15 (1981): 525; David Caplovitz, *Consumers in Trouble: A Study of Debtors in Default* (New York: Free Press, 1974).

4. Marc Galanter, "Reading the Landscape of Disputes: What We Know and Don't Know (and Think We Know) about Our Allegedly Contentious and Litigious Society," *UCLA Law Review* 31 (1983): 4; Molly Selvin and P. A. Ebener, *Managing the Unmanageable: A History of Civil Delay in the Los Angeles Superior Court* (Santa Monica: Institute for Civil Justice, 1984); Wayne McIntosh, "150 Years of Litigation and Dispute Settlement: A Court Tale," *Law and Society Review* 15 (1980–81): 823; Robert A. Kagan, "The Routinization of Debt Collection: An Essay on Social Change and Conflict in the Courts," *Law and Society Review* 18 (1984): 323; David S. Clark, "Civil Litigation Trends in Europe and Latin America since 1945: The Advantage of Intracountry Comparisons," *Law and Society Review* 24 (1990): 549–69; Heleen F. P. Ietswaart, "The International Comparison of Court Caseloads: The Experience of the European Working Group," *Law and Society Review* 24 (1990): 571–93.

5. David Engel, "The Oven Bird's Song: Insiders, Outsiders, and Personal Injuries in an American Community," *Law and Society Review* 18 (1984): 551.

6. Peter Edelman, "Japanese Product Standards as Non-tariff Trade Barriers: When Regulatory Policy Becomes a Trade Issue," *Standard Journal of International Law* 24 (1988): 292; David Vogel, "Consumer Protection and Protectionism in Japan," *Journal of Japanese Studies* 18 (1992): 119–54.

7. Among the most perceptive cross-national comparisons are Joseph L. Badaracco, *Loading the Dice: A Five Country Study of Vinyl Chloride Regulation* (Boston: Harvard Business School Press, 1985); Derek Bok, "Reflections on the Distinctive Character of American Labor Laws," *Harvard Law Review* 84 (1971): 1394–1463 (on

the selection of labor union representatives); John Braithwaite, *To Punish or Persuade: Enforcement of Coal Mine Safety* (Albany: SUNY Press, 1985); Ronald Brickman, Sheila Jasanoff, and Thomas Ilgen, *Controlling Chemicals: The Politics of Regulation in Europe and the United States* (Ithaca, N.Y.: Cornell University Press, 1985) (on the regulation of carcinogens); Patricia Day and Rudolf Klein, "The Regulation of Nursing Homes: A Comparative Perspective," *Milbank Quarterly* 65 (1987): 303–47; Mary Ann Glendon, *Abortion and Divorce in Western Law* (Cambridge: Harvard University Press, 1987) (on abortion, divorce, and child support); Steven Kelman, *Regulating America, Regulating Sweden: A Comparative Study of Occupational Safety and Health Policy* (Cambridge: MIT Press, 1981); David L. Kirp, "Professionalization as a Policy Choice: British Special Education in Comparative Perspective," *World Politics* 34 (1982): 137 (on education for handicapped children); John Langbein, "The German Advantage in Civil Procedure," *University of Chicago Law Review* 52 (1985): 823–66 (on civil litigation methods); Gary Schwartz, "Product Liability and Medical Malpractice in Comparative Context," in P. Huber and R. Litan, eds., *The Liability Maze* (Washington, D.C.: Brookings, 1991); David Vogel, *National Styles of Regulation: Environmental Policy in Great Britain and the United States* (Ithaca, N.Y.: Cornell University Press, 1986).

8. Jerry L. Mashaw, *Bureaucratic Justice: Managing Social Security Disability Claims* (New Haven: Yale University Press, 1983).

9. Badaracco, *Loading the Dice.*

10. John Langbein, "The German Advantage in Civil Procedure," *University of Chicago Law Review* 52 (1985): 823–66.

11. Compare John Thibaut and Laurens Walker, "A Theory of Procedure," *California Law Review* 66 (1978): 541–66.

12. P. S. Atiyah and Robert S. Summers, *Form and Substance in Anglo-American Law: A Comparative Study of Legal Reasoning, Legal Theory, and Legal Institutions* (Oxford: Clarendon Press, 1987).

13. See, for example, Martin Levin, "Urban Politics and Judicial Behavior," *Journal of Legal Studies* 1 (1972): 193–221; C. K. Rowland and Robert A. Carp, "The Relative Effects of Maturation, Period, and Appointing President on District Judges' Policy Choice: A Cohort Analysis," *Political Behavior* 5 (1983): 109–34; John Gottschall, "Reagan's Appointments to the U.S. Courts of Appeals," *Judicature* (June/July 1986): 49–54.

14. Bert Niemeijer, "Urban Land-Use and Building Control in The Netherlands: Flexible Decisions in a Rigid System," *Law and Policy* 11 (1989): 121–52; Frank K. Upham, *Law and Social Change in Postwar Japan* (Cambridge: Harvard University Press, 1987).

15. Robert A. Kagan, "What Makes Uncle Sammy Sue?" *Law and Society Review* 21 (1988): 717.

16. Richard H. Sander, "Elevating the Debate on Lawyers and Economic Growth," *Law and Social Inquiry* 17 (1992): 665; Richard H. Sander and E. Douglas Williams, "Why Are There So Many Lawyers? Perspectives on a Turbulent Market," *Law and Social Inquiry* 14 (1989): 434–35.

17. James S. Kakalik et al., *Costs of Asbestos Litigation* (Santa Monica: Institute for Civil Justice, 1983); James S. Kakalik and Nicholas M. Pace, *Costs and Compensation Paid in Tort Litigation* (Santa Monica: Institute for Civil Justice, 1986); Task Force on Medical Liability and Malpractice, *Report* (Washington, D.C.: Department

of Health and Human Services, 1987), 16; Institute for Civil Justice, *Annual Report, 1989–1990* (Santa Monica: Institute for Civil Justice, 1990), 49–54.

18. Two law professors, fresh from a major American Law Institute study of the tort system, offered this summary: "Tort law is a highly unsatisfactory system of compensation. Random victims are protected at giant overhead costs. Large sums go to lawyers rather than to compensating victims or funding additional accident reduction." Kenneth S. Abraham and Lance Liebman, "Private Insurance, Social Insurance, and Tort Reform: Toward a New Vision of Compensation for Illness and Injury," *Columbia Law Review* 93 (1993): 108.

Even in workers' compensation systems, designed to replace expensive tort litigation, lawyers' fees (for both sides) and other contestation costs have been estimated to be 30 percent of each dollar paid in claims—Task Force on Medical Liability and Malpractice, *Report* (Washington, D.C.: Department of Health and Human Services, 1987), 16; Sara R. Pease, *Performance Indicators for Permanent Disability: Low Back Injuries in Texas* (Workers Compensation Research Institute, 1988)—and in more serious permanent partial disability cases, "friction" costs in several states are two-thirds the average award—CWCI, *Litigation Incidence* (San Francisco: California Workers Compensation Institute, 1991).

19. Peter Menell, "The Limitations of Legal Institutions for Addressing Environmental Risks," *Journal of Economic Perspectives* 5 (1991): 108.

20. Stephen D. Sugarman, "The California Vehicle Injury Plan (VIP): Better Compensation, Fairer Funding, and Greater Safety," Working Paper 21 (Berkeley: Earl Warren Legal Institute, University of California, 1993), 3–4.

21. Dow Chemical Co. has stated that its 1986 legal and liability insurance expenditures in the United States were five times its overseas costs for a comparable volume of business—Franklin Nutter and Keith Bateman, *The U.S. Tort System in the Era of the Global Economy* (Schaumburg, Ill.: Alliance of American Insurers, 1989), 20.

In 1986, Canadian physicians paid medical malpractice protection fees ranging from $288 to $3,500 a year, depending on their specialties. In the same year, the St. Paul Insurance Co., a leading American malpractice insurer, said that its typical annual premiums ranged from $1,365 for an Arkansas general practitioner to $106,000 for a Miami neurosurgeon—Peggy Berkowitz, "In Canada, Different Legal and Popular Views Prevail," *Wall Street Journal*, 4 April 1986, 21.

The average American physician's malpractice premium in 1986 was eleven times the average Canadian premium—Donald Dewees, Michael Trebilcock, and Peter Coyte, "The Medical Malpractice Crisis: A Comparative Empirical Perspective," *Law and Contemporary Problems* 54 (1991): 221.

22. Allen Myerson, "Soaring Liability Payments Burden New York's Budget," *New York Times*, 29 June 1992, A15; Peter W. Huber, *Liability: The Legal Revolution and Its Consequences* (New York: Basic Books, 1988), 3–4.

23. Franklin Zimring and Gordon Hawkins, *Capital Punishment and the American Agenda* (Cambridge: Cambridge University Press, 1986); Keith Hawkins, *Environment and Enforcement: Regulation and the Social Definition of Pollution* (Oxford: Oxford University Press, 1984); Kelman, *Regulating America, Regulating Sweden.*

24. Task Force on Medical Liability, *Report.*

25. Kenneth Prager, "Clozoril: Torts' Dangerous Side Effects," *Wall Street Journal*, 6 December 1990, A18.

26. Jane Cooper Alexander, "Do the Merits Really Matter? A Study of Settlements in Securities Class Actions," *Stanford Law Review* 43 (1991): 497−598: Margaret S. Race, "Critique of Present Wetlands Mitigation Policies in the United States Based on Analysis of Past Restoration Projects in San Francisco Bay," *Environmental Management* 9 (1988): 71−82; L. Mastroianni et al., eds., *Developing New Contraceptives: Obstacles and Opportunities* (Washington, D.C.: National Academy Press, 1990); George L. Priest, "Can Absolute Manufacturer Liability Be Defended?" *Yale Journal of Regulation* 9 (1992): 237−62.

27. Albert N. Alschuler, "The Vanishing Civil Jury," *University of Chicago Legal Forum* (1990): 5−6.

28. James Blumstein, Randall Bovberg, and Frank Sloan, "Beyond Tort Reform: Developing Better Tools for Assessing Damages for Personal Injury," *Yale Journal on Regulation* 8 (1990): 174; Audrey Chin and M. Peterson, *Deep Pockets, Empty Pockets: Who Wins in Cook County Jury Trials?* (Santa Monica: Institute for Civil Justice, 1985); Peter W. Huber, "Junk Science and the Jury," *University of Chicago Legal Forum* (1990): 273.

29. Gerald Williams, *Legal Negotiation and Settlement* (1983), 6; Douglas Rosenthal, *Lawyer and Client: Who's in Charge?* (New York: Russell Sage Foundation, 1974), 202−7; Michael J. Saks, "Do We Really Know Anything about the Behavior of the Tort Litigation System? And Why Not?" *Pennsylvania Law Review* 140 (1992): 1215, 1223; Marc Galanter, "The Quality of Settlements," *Journal of Dispute Resolution* (1988): 55.

30. Stephen D. Sugarman, "Doing Away with Tort Law," *California Law Review* 73 (1985): 592−95; Marc Galanter, "The Civil Jury as Regulator of the Litigation Process," *University of Chicago Legal Forum* (1990): 220−21.

31. David Brereton and Jonathan D. Casper, "Does It Pay to Plead Guilty? Differential Sentencing and the Functioning of Criminal Courts," *Law and Society Review* 16 (1981): 45−70; Thomas M. Uhlman and Darlene Walker, " 'He Takes Some of My Time, I Take Some of His': An Analysis of Sentencing Patterns in Jury Cases," *Law and Society Review* 14 (1979): 323.

32. Kagan, "Routinization of Debt Collection," 338, 348−49; Stewart Macaulay, "Lawyers and Consumer Protection Laws," *Law and Society Review* 14 (1979): 115.

33. R. Shep Melnick, *Regulation and the Courts: The Case of the Clean Air Act* (Washington, D.C.: Brookings, 1983); Jeremy Rabkin, *Judicial Compulsions: How Public Law Distorts Public Policy* (New York: Basic Books, 1989).

34. John Mendeloff, *The Dilemma of Rulemaking for Toxic Substances* (Cambridge: MIT Press, 1987); John Dwyer, "The Pathology of Symbolic Legislation," *Ecology Law Quarterly* 17 (1990): 233−316; Jerry L. Mashaw and Daniel Harfst, "Regulation and Legal Culture: The Case of Motor Vehicle Safety," *Yale Journal on Regulation* 4 (1987): 257−316.

35. Robert Ellickson, "The Homelessness Muddle," *Public Interest* 99 (1990): 56.

36. Thomas W. Church and Robert Nakamura, *Cleaning Up the Mess: Implementation Strategies in Superfund* (Washington, D.C.: Brookings, 1993).

37. Eugene Bardach and Robert A. Kagan, *Going by the Book: The Problem of Regulatory Unreasonableness*, a Twentieth Century Fund study (Philadelphia: Tem-

ple University Press, 1982); John T. Scholz, "Cooperation, Deferrence and the Ecology of Regulatory Enforcement," *Law and Society Review* 18 (1984): 601–46.

38. National Academy of Science, *Decisionmaking at the U.S. Environmental Protection Agency* (Washington, D.C.: National Academy Press, 1977), 79–81.

39. Steven Kelman, "Adversary and Cooperationist Institutions for Conflict Resolution in Public Policymaking," *Journal of Policy Analysis and Management* 11 (1992): 186.

40. David Bayley, *Forces of Order: Police Behavior in Japan and the United States* (Berkeley: University of California Press, 1976), 150.

41. Vogel, *National Styles of Regulation*, 254, 259.

42. National Research Council, *Dredging Coastal Ports* (Washington, D.C.: National Academy Press, 1986).

43. Joanie Mackowski, "Port, Fishermen, Shipping Lines, Environmentalists Join Oakland Mud Battle," *Pacific Shipper*, 23 May 1988, 26–27.

44. The Corps of Engineers may be right in asserting that disposal at Alcatraz has no significant adverse environmental effects; see U.S. Army Corps of Engineers, *Appendix D, Finding of No Significant Impact and Environmental Assessment, Oakland Inner Harbor 38-Foot Separable Element of the Oakland Harbor Navigation Improvement Project* (San Francisco: U.S. Army Corps of Engineers, 1992). But that conclusion is passionately disputed by knowledgeable (if perhaps biased) environmental advocates and bay fishermen. It is clear that the bay is an important ecological area, severely stressed in many ways. Environmentally harmful scenarios sketched out for the bay are much more detailed and plausible than are any spelled out for deep water areas off the continental shelf.

45. Robert Bowman, "Federal Officials Downplay Government's Role in Dredging, Port Projects," *Pacific Shipper*, 19 March 1990, 7–8.

46. *Pacific Shipper*, "Exxon Tanker Runs Aground in Long Beach Harbor," 16 April 1990, 6–8.

47. National Research Council, *Dredging Coastal Ports*, 3, 77.

48. Scott McCreary, "Resolving Science-intensive Public Policy Disputes: Lessons from the New York Bight Initiative," Ph.D. diss., MIT, 1989, 43.

49. Charles Strum, "U.S. Grants Permit for Dredging of Newark Bay Berths," *New York Times*, 27 May 1993, B7; *New York Times*, "Suit to Stop Dumping of Sediment Filed," *New York Times*, 2 June 1993, A5; Charles Strum, "Judge Allows Dredging to Continue," *New York Times*, 8 June 1993, B5.

50. National Research Council, *Dredging Coastal Ports*, 89–90; Ann E. Wessel and Marc J. Hershman, "Mitigation: Compensating the Environment for Unavoidable Harm," in Marc J. Hershman, ed., *Urban Port and Harbor Management* (New York: Taylor and Francis, 1988); Joanie Mackowski, "Strict Environmental Regulation Expands Duties, Stresses Budgets at Pacific Coast Port Facilities," *Pacific Shipper*, 12 September 1988, 22.

51. Michael O'Hare and Lawrence Bacow, *Facility Siting and Public Opposition* (New York: Van Nostrand, 1983); Bernard J. Frieden, "The New Regulation Comes to Suburbia," *Public Interest* 55 (1979): 15–27.

52. Richard J. Pierce, Jr., "Two Problems in Administrative Law: Political Polarity on the District of Columbia Circuit Court and Judicial Deterrence of Agency Rulemaking," *Duke Law Journal* 1988: 300–28; R. Shep Melnick, "Administrative Law and Bureaucratic Reality," *Administrative Law Review* 44 (1992): 247.

53. Richard B. Stewart, "Madison's Nightmare," *University of Chicago Law Review* 57 (1990): 347. Reflecting on his experience as Assistant Attorney General for Environment and Natural Resources, Richard Stewart, in a passage that seems to reinforce the exemplary character of the Oakland harbor story (pp. 346–47), wrote that

> a combination of bureaucratic hearings and review by unelected judges is an unlikely process for selecting and implementing measures in the general interest. Courts and agencies are buried in lengthy adversary hearings that often take many years to resolve . . . Interest groups can circumvent state and local political processes by bringing federal court actions . . . No one bears clear responsibility for decisions. The already severe fragmentation of central authority is exacerbated by treating each agency decision as an isolated event to be judicially reviewed on the basis of its separate evidentiary record.

54. Kenneth Hanf and Cor Smits, "Maintenance Dredging in the Port of Rotterdam: Trading Off Environmental Quality and Economic Development" (Paper presented at the annual meeting of the Law and Society Association, Amsterdam, 26–29 June 1991); Robert A. Kagan, "The Dredging Dilemma: Economic Development and Environmental Protection in Oakland Harbor," *Coastal Management* 19 (1991): 313–41.

55. Bruce A. Ackerman and William T. Hassler, *Clean Coal/Dirty Air* (New Haven: Yale University Press, 1981).

56. Peter H. Schuck, *Suing Government: Citizen Remedies for Official Wrongs* (New Haven: Yale University Press, 1983).

57. Marc Galanter, "Law Abounding: Legalisation around the North Atlantic," *Modern Law Review* 55 (1992): 10; Marc Galanter, "The Life and Times of the Big Six; or, the Federal Courts since the Good Old Days," *Wisconsin Law Review* (1988): 921–54; William Nelson, "Contract Litigation and the Elite Bar in New York City, 1960–1980," *Emory Law Review* 39 (1990): 413–62.

58. Sander and Williams, "Why So Many Lawyers?" 434–35; Joseph Sanders and Craig Joyce, " 'Off to the Races': The 1980s Tort Crisis and the Law Reform Process," *Houston Law Review* 27 (1990): 216.

59. Robert A. Kagan, "Constitutional Litigation in the United States," in R. Rogowski and T. Gawron, eds., *Constitutional Courts in Comparison* (Gummersbach, West Germany: Theodor Huess Academie, 1987).

60. Lawrence M. Friedman, *Total Justice* (New York: Russell Sage Foundation, 1985).

61. Peter A. Kohler and Hans F. Zacher, *The Evolution of Social Insurance, 1881–1981: Studies of Germany, France, Great Britain, Austria and Switzerland* (New York: St. Martin's Press, 1982); Sheila B. Kamerman and Alfred J. Kahn, "What Europe Does for Single-Parent Families," *Public Interest* 93 (1988): 70–86.

62. Niemeijer, "Urban Land-Use in the Netherlands;" Vogel, *National Styles of Regulation.*

63. Aaron Wildavsky, "A World of Difference—the Public Philosophies and Political Behaviors of Rival American Cultures," in Anthony King, ed., *The New American Political System*, 2d ed. (Washington, D.C.: AEI Press, 1990).

64. Aaron Wildavsky, "Robert Bork and the Crime of Inequality," *Public Interest* 98 (1990): 98–117.

65. Samuel Huntington, *American Politics: The Promise of Disharmony* (Cambridge, Mass.: Belknap Press, 1981).

66. See James Q. Wilson, *The Politics of Regulation* (New York: Basic Books, 1980).

67. Bardach and Kagan, *Going by the Book*, chap. 2; Robert Litan and William Nordhaus, *Reforming Federal Regulation* (Washington, D.C.: Brookings, 1983), 44.

68. Martin Shapiro, *Who Guards the Guardians? Judicial Control of Administration* (Athens: University of Georgia Press, 1988).

69. George L. Priest, "The Invention of Enterprise Liability: A Critical History of the Intellectual Foundations of Modern Tort Law," *Journal of Legal Studies* 14 (1985): 461–527; Edmund Ursin, "Judicial Creativity and Tort Law," *George Washington Law Review* 49 (1981): 229; Schuck, *Suing Government.*

70. W. Robert Curtis, "The Deinstitutionalization Story," *Public Interest* (Fall 1986): 34; David J. Rothman and Sheila M. Rothman, *The Willowbrook Wars* (New York: Harper and Row, 1984).

71. Mirjan Damaska, *The Faces of Justice and State Authority: A Comparative Approach to the Legal Process* (New Haven: Yale University Press, 1986).

72. Ibid., 13.

73. Contrary to popular belief, motions to suppress illegally obtained evidence rarely enable the criminal suspect to walk out of the courtroom a free person; see Thomas Y. Davies, "A Hard Look at What We Know (and Still Need to Learn) about the 'Costs' of the Exclusionary Rule," *American Bar Foundation Research Journal* 1983: 611. But pretrial hearings on such motions occur, according to some studies, in almost one in every ten criminal prosecutions—Peter F. Nardulli, "The Societal Cost of the Exclusionary Rule: An Empirical Assessment," *American Bar Foundation Research Journal* 1983 (1983): 594—and in almost 40 percent of prosecutions that rely on evidence obtained via search warrant (Davies, "A Hard Look," 664). For an insightful account of the legal uncertainty and limits of adversarial legalism as a mode of regulating the police, see Craig Bradley, *The Failure of the Criminal Procedure Revolution* (Philadelphia: University of Pennsylvania Press, 1993).

74. Michael McCann, *Taking Reform Seriously: Perspectives on Public Interest Liberalism* (Ithaca, N.Y.: Cornell University Press, 1986).

75. Roger Davidson, "Subcommittee Government: New Channels for Policy Making," in Thomas Mann and Norman Ornstein, eds., *The New Congress* (Washington: American Enterprise Institute, 1981).

76. Huntington, *American Politics*; Nelson Polsby, *The Consequences of Party Reform* (New York: Oxford University Press, 1983); Austin Ranney, "The President and His Party," in Anthony King, ed., *Both Ends of the Avenue: The Presidency, the Executive Branch and Congress in the 1980s* (Washington, D.C.: American Enterprise Institute, 1983).

77. Michael Greve, "Environmentalism and Bounty Hunting," *Public Interest* 97 (1989): 15–29.

78. Terry M. Moe, "The Politics of the Bureaucratic State," in J. Chubb and P. Peterson, eds., *Can the Government Govern?* (Washington, D.C.: Brookings, 1989).

79. Marc Landy, Marc Roberts, and Stephen Thomas, *The Environmental Protection Agency: Asking the Wrong Questions* (1990); Robert B. Reich, "Public Administration and Public Deliberation," *Yale Law Journal* 94 (1985): 1622.

80. Marc Landy and Mary Hague, "The Coalition for Waste: Private Interests and

the Superfund," in M. Greve and F. Smith, eds., *Environmental Politics: Public Costs, Private Rewards* (New York: Greenwood, 1992).

81. Edward L. Rubin, "Legislative Methodology: Some Lessons from the Truth-in-Lending Act," *Georgetown Law Review* 80 (1991): 233.

82. Melnick, *Regulation and the Courts;* John T. Scholz and Feng Heng Wei, "Regulatory Enforcement in a Federalist System," *American Political Science Review* 80 (1986): 1249.

83. Rabkin, *Judicial Compulsions;* Mashaw, *Bureaucratic Justice.*

84. For example, despite badgering by congressional oversight committees and advocacy group lawsuits, the EPA has managed to meet only about 14 percent of the scores of statutory deadlines for regulatory action that Congress has built into pollution control statutes—Environmental Law Institute, *Statutory Deadlines in Environmental Legislation* (Washington, D.C.: ELI, 1985), 12. Rather than increase agency capacity to meet them, however, Congress responded during the 1980s by enacting new and more specific deadlines, thereby inviting new lawsuits each time a financially crimped and demoralized EPA misses a statutory deadline again; see R. Shep Melnick, "Pollution Deadlines and the Coalition for Failure," in M. Greve and F. Smith, eds., *Environmental Politics: Public Costs, Private Rewards* (New York: Greenwood, 1992), 89–102.

85. Stephen Smith, *Call to Order: Floor Politics in the House and Senate* (Washington: Brookings, 1989); Peter H. Schuck, "Legal Complexity: Some Causes, Consequences, and Cures," *Duke Law Journal* 42 (1992): 27–29. For an illuminating comparison of American and British statutory drafting, see Atiyah and Summers, *Form and Substance in Law,* 298–335.

86. Shapiro, *Who Guards the Guardians?* 172.

87. Francis Blake, "The Politics of the Environment: Does Washington Know Best?" *American Enterprise* (March/April 1990): 6–7; Hilary Stout, "Codified Confusion: Tax Law Is Growing Ever More Complex, Outcry Ever Louder," *Wall Street Journal,* 12 April 1990, 1, 8.

88. For example, the federal Superfund law imposes strict, retroactive, and joint and several liability on all firms that have ever used a disposal site but does not say what level of "cleanliness" must be achieved (and hence how much money must be spent) in cleaning up the site—which, of course, leads to endless litigation; see Church and Nakamura, *Cleaning Up the Mess.*

89. Atiyah and Summers, *Form and Substance in Law,* 37–40, 305–8.

90. Pierce, "Two Problems in Administrative Law"; Gottschall, "Reagan's Appointments."

91. Marc Galanter and Joel Rogers, "The Transformation of American Business Disputing? Some Preliminary Observations" (Working Paper DPRP 10-3, Institute for Legal Studies, University of Wisconsin, Madison, 1991); Nelson, "Contract Litigation and the Elite Bar."

92. Mark J. Roe, "A Political Theory of American Corporate Finance," *Columbia Law Review* 91 (1991): 10–67.

93. Robert B. Reich, "Bailout: A Comparative Study in Law and Industrial Structure," *Yale Journal on Regulation* 2 (1985): 163–224; Lester Thurow, "Communitarian vs. Individualistic Capitalism," *Responsive Community* 2 (Fall 1992): 24–30.

94. See James B. Stewart, *The Partners: Inside America's Most Powerful Law Firms* (New York: Simon and Schuster, 1983).

95. Alexander, "Do the Merits Matter?"; Roberta Romano, "The Shareholder Suit: Litigation without Foundation?" *Journal of Law, Economics, and Organization* 7 (1991): 55.

96. Ronald Gilson, "How Many Lawyers Does It Take To Change an Economy?" *Law and Social Inquiry* 17 (1993): 639.

97. J. Rogers Hollingworth, Jerald Hage, and Robert Hanneman, *State Intervention in Medical Care: Consequences for Britain, France, Sweden, and the United States* (Ithaca, N.Y.: Cornell University Press, 1990).

98. In Japan, motor vehicle liability insurance companies are privately owned but apparently less competitive; they operate more like public utilities. Claims are processed by a single, independent organization, which in turn apportions losses and profits among the member companies. Rates are controlled by the government, and the government reinsures 60 percent of all coverage—Takao Tanase, "The Management of Disputes: Automobile Accident Compensation in Japan," *Law and Society Review* 24 (1990): 651–87. The consequence is a far less adversarial relationship between motorists and liability insurance companies. "An insurance company is, in the eyes of the injured party, not so much an adversary as an agent." Tanase, "The Management of Disputes," 668.

99. Robert J. Flanagan, *Labor Relations and the Litigation Explosion* (Washington, D.C.: Brookings, 1987).

100. Joel Rogers, "Divide and Conquer: Further 'Reflections on the Distinctive Character of American Labor Laws,'" *Wisconsin Law Review* 1990: 1–147; Robert A. Kagan, "How Much Does Law Matter? Labor Law, Competition, and Waterfront Labor Relations in Rotterdam and U.S. Ports," *Law and Society Review* 24 (1990): 35–69.

101. Flanagan, *Labor Relations and Litigation Explosion*; James Dertouzos, Elaine Holland, and Patricia Ebener, *The Legal and Economic Consequences of Wrongful Termination* (Santa Monica: Institute for Civil Justice, 1992).

102. Reich, "Bailout"; Shapiro, *Who Guards the Guardians?*; Peter H. Schuck, "Litigation, Bargaining and Regulation," *Regulation* 3 (1979): 26; Susskind and McMahon, "Theory and Practice of Rulemaking."

103. Joel F. Handler, "Dependent People, the State, and the Modern/Postmodern Search for the Dialogic Community," *UCLA Law Review* 35 (1988): 999–1113.

104. Mashaw, *Bureaucratic Justice*.

105. Badaracco, *Loading the Dice*.

106. See Abraham and Liebman, "Private Insurance, Social Insurance"; Jeffrey O'Connell, "Expanding No-Fault beyond Auto Insurance: Some Proposals," *Virginia Law Review* 59 (1973): 749; Stephen D. Sugarman, *Doing Away with Personal Injury Law: New Compensation Mechanisms for Victims, Consumers, and Business* (New York: Quorum Books, 1989); Sugarman, "California Vehicle Injury Plan (VIP)"; Paul C. Weiler, *Medical Malpractice on Trial* (Cambridge: Harvard University Press, 1991).

107. Robert A. Kagan, "Do Lawyers Cause Adversarial Legalism? A Preliminary Inquiry," *Law and Social Inquiry* 19 (1994): 1–62, esp. 56–58.

5. POLICY MODELS AND POLITICAL CHANGE: INSIGHTS FROM THE PASSAGE OF
TAX REFORM

1. James MacGregor Burns, *The Deadlock of Democracy* (Englewood Cliffs, N.J.: Prentice-Hall, 1963).

2. See especially Lloyd N. Cutler, "To Form a Government," *Foreign Affairs* 59 (Fall 1980): 126–43, James L. Sundquist, *Constitutional Reform and Effective Government* (Washington, D.C.: Brookings, 1986), and Michael Mezey, *Congress, the President, and Public Policy* (Boulder, Colo.: Westview, 1989).

3. Compare Stanley S. Surrey, *Pathways to Tax Reform* (Cambridge: Harvard University Press, 1973), Stanley S. Surrey and Paul R. McDaniel, *Tax Expenditures* (Cambridge: Harvard University Press, 1985), and Joseph A. Pechman, *Federal Tax Policy*, 4th ed. (Washington: Brookings, 1983).

4. John F. Witte, *The Politics and Development of the Federal Income Tax* (Madison: University of Wisconsin Press, 1985), 380.

5. David G. Davies, *United States Taxes and Tax Policy* (New York: Cambridge University Press, 1986), 287.

6. Earl Latham, "The Group Basis of Politics," *American Political Science Review* 46 (June 1952): 390.

7. Compare Witte, *Politics and Development.*

8. The classic statement is Stanley S. Surrey, "The Congress and the Tax Lobbyist: How Special Tax Provisions Get Enacted," *Harvard Law Review* 70 (May 1957): 1145–82.

9. Davies, *Taxes and Tax Policy*, 285.

10. Quoted in *Tax Notes*, 31 December 1985, 1. On contributions to committee members see "Pac-ing the Deck," *Common Cause News*, 13 June 1985, 1; "Gimme a Break," *Common Cause News*, 11 February 1986, and *Financing the Finance Committee* (Washington, D.C.: Common Cause, March 1986).

11. Interview with Rep. Thomas Downey, 3 April 1987. Subsequent quotations that lack specific attribution were obtained from some seventy interviews conducted as part of a broader research project from which this chapter is drawn. See Timothy J. Conlan, Margaret T. Wrightson, and David R. Beam, *Taxing Choices: The Politics of Tax Reform* (Washington: CQ Press, 1990).

12. Examples include home mortgage deductions, defended by the realtors and home builders, and most fringe benefits, a great concern to unions and insurance companies.

13. Treasury I was released to the public in November 1984, Treasury II the next May.

14. Arthur Anderson and Co., *Tax Reform 1986: Analysis and Planning* (Arthur Anderson, 1986), 3–4.

15. For a discussion, see James L. Sundquist, "Needed: A Political Theory for the New Era of Coalition Government in the United States," *Political Science Quarterly* 103 (Winter 1988–89): 624–25.

16. Susan B. Hansen, *The Politics of Taxation: Revenue without Representation* (New York: Praeger, 1983), 62.

17. Sundquist, *Constitutional Reform*, 75–76.

18. Jim Jones, quoted in "Taxes behind Closed Doors," *Frontline* 411 (Boston: WGBH TV Transcripts, 1986), 3.

19. Tom Downey, quoted in "Taxes behind Closed Doors," 22; On the importance of such future-oriented strategic calculations generally in congressional behavior, see Gary C. Jacobson and Samuel Kernell, *Strategy and Choice in Congressional Elections* (New Haven: Yale University Press, 1981). The growing importance of blame avoidance in congressional behavior is discussed in R. Kent Weaver, *Automatic Government: The Politics of Indexation* (Washington, D.C.: Brookings, 1988).

20. One poll conducted during the month of TRA's passage found only 19 percent of interviewees favorable, with a nearly equal 16 percent opposed. Another poll the next April showed only marginal improvements in the sense of "tax fairness." See Barry Sussman, *What Americans Really Think and Why Our Politicians Pay No Attention* (New York: Pantheon Books, 1988), 153–54.

21. James Q. Wilson, ed., *The Politics of Regulation* (New York: Basic Books, 1980), 370.

22. What is here described as the "new" reform politics was actually quite influential during the Progressive Era. On the role of experts and muckraking journalists in securing the passage of early food and drug legislation, see Mark V. Nadel, *The Politics of Consumer Protection* (Indianapolis: Bobbs-Merrill, 1964), 383–84.

23. Wilson, *The Politics of Regulation*, 372.

24. Deborah A. Stone, *Policy Paradox and Political Reason* (Glenview, Ill.: Scott-Foresman, 1988), 25. See also John W. Kingdon, *Agendas, Alternatives, and Public Policies* (Boston: Little, Brown, 1984), 131–32.

25. Daniel P. Moynihan, "The Professionalization of Reform," *Public Interest* 1 (Fall 1965): 6–16.

26. Samuel H. Beer, "Federalism, Nationalism, and Democracy in America," *American Political Science Review* 72 (March 1978): 17.

27. The origins of the concept may be traced to the work of Henry C. Simons and Robert M. Haig. See Simons' *Personal Income Taxation: The Definition of Income as a Problem of Fiscal Policy* (Chicago: University of Chicago Press, 1938), and Robert M. Haig, ed., *The Federal Income Tax* (New York: Columbia University Press, 1921).

28. See Joseph A. Pechman, "Erosion of the Individual Income Tax," *National Tax Journal* 10 (March 1957). Summaries of key reform proposals appeared in Joseph A. Pechman, ed., *A Citizen's Guide to the New Tax Reforms: Fair Tax, Simple Tax, Flat Tax* (Totawa, N.J.: Rowman and Allanheld, 1985).

29. Former Assistant Treasury Secretary John E. Chapoton observed that "[The White House] wanted to be able to say, 'Me No Alamo, I don't know what Treasury is doing,' so as not to get it mixed up in the presidential race."

30. Donald T. Regan, *For the Record: From Wall Street to Washington* (New York: Harcourt, Brace, Jovanovich, 1988): 206.

31. Many of the same features had also appeared in the earlier Bradley-Gephardt bill, which helped to ensure bipartisan support for the Treasury proposal.

32. Interview with Rob Leonard.

33. Interview with Congressman Robert Matsui.

34. Steven Kelman, "Why Public Ideas Matter," in Robert B. Reich, ed., *The Power of Public Ideas* (Cambridge, Mass.: Ballinger, 1988), 31.

35. Compare Charles D. Elder and Roger W. Cobb, *The Political Uses of Symbols* (New York: Longman, 1983).

36. Congressman Dan Rostenkowski, quoted in Strahan, "Committee Politics and Tax Reform," 25–26.

37. Mark Moore, "What Sort of Ideas Become Public Ideas?" in Reich, *The Power of Public Ideas*, 79.

38. Compare "Corporate Taxes in the Reagan Years," Citizens for Tax Justice, October 1984. See the discussion in Joseph J. Minarik, *Making Tax Choices* (Washington, D.C.: Urban Institute, 1985), 7.

39. See Kingdon, *Agendas, Alternatives, and Public Policies*, for extensive discussions of policy entrepreneurship.

40. Wilson, *The Politics of Regulation*, 371.

41. Nelson W. Polsby, *Political Innovation in America: The Politics of Policy Initiation* (New Haven: Yale University Press, 1984): 171–72.

42. Compare E. E. Schattschneider, *The Semi-Sovereign People: A Realist's View of Democracy in America* (New York: Holt, Rinehart, and Winston, 1960).

43. Nadel, *Politics of Consumer Protection*, 192.

44. S. Robert Lichter, Stanley Rothman, and Linda S. Lichter, *The Media Elite: America's New Power Brokers* (Bethesda, Md.: Adler and Adler, 1986), 57.

45. Ibid., 130.

46. A content analysis of indexes under the headings *tax policy* and *tax reform* indicates that the *Washington Post* placed tax reform on its front page twelve times in 1984, fifty-four times in 1985, and forty-six times in 1986. Similarly, the *New York Times* ran fifteen such front page stories in 1984, fifty-three in 1985, and forty-six in 1986.

47. Martha Derthick and Paul J. Quirk, *The Politics of Deregulation* (Washington, D.C.: Brookings, 1985), 103.

48. Ibid., 241.

49. Compare Anthony King, "The American Polity in the Late 1970s: Building Coalitions in the Sand," in Anthony King, ed., *The New American Political System* (Washington, D.C.: American Enterprise Institute, 1978), 393.

50. Hedrick Smith, *The Power Game: How Washington Works* (New York: Random House, 1988), 14–15.

6. THE POLITICS OF THE ENTITLEMENT PROCESS

1. Martha Derthick, *Policymaking for Social Security* (Washington, D.C.: Brookings, 1979), 290.

2. Senate Committee on the Budget, Task Force on Entitlements, Uncontrollables, and Indexing, *Hearings on the Administration's FY1984 Medicare and Medicaid Budget Proposals*, 98th Cong., 1st sess., February 1983, 2.

3. Ibid., 35.

4. Allen Schick, "Controlling the 'Uncontrollable': Budgeting for Health Care in an Age of Mega-Deficits" (Paper presented at the AEI New Fellows Conference, Washington, D.C., 1 November 1985), 1–2.

5. See Aaron Wildavsky, "Doing Better and Feeling Worse: The Political Pathology of Health Policy," *Daedalus* 95, no. 1 (1976): 105–23.

6. See Margaret Greenfield, *Medicare and Medicaid: The 1965 and 1967 Social Security Amendments* (Westport, Conn.: Greenwood, 1968).

7. Randall R. Bovbjerg and John Holahan, *Medicaid in the Reagan Era: Federal*

Policy and State Choices (Washington, D.C.: Urban Institute, 1982), 8.

8. Ibid.

9. Congressional Budget Office, "Reducing the Federal Budget: Strategies and Examples, Fiscal Years 1982–1986," 118, quoted in *Report to the Congress by the Comptroller General of the United States: What Can Be Done to Check the Growth of Federal Entitlement and Indexed Spending* (Washington, D.C.: Government Printing Office), 36.

10. Schick, "Controlling the 'Uncontrollable,'" 27–28.

11. Budget of the United States Government, FY 1983 (Appendix), Executive Office of the President: Office of Management and Budget, I-1014-15.

12. Bernard Popick, "The Social Security Disability Program: III. The Black Lung Benefits: An Administrative Case Study," *Journal of Occupational Medicine* 13, no. 7 (July 1971): 337.

13. L. E. Kerr, "Black Lung," *Journal of Public Health Policy* 1, no. 1 (March 1980): 57.

14. Alan Derickson, "The Origins of the Black Lung Insurgency," *Journal of Public Health Policy* 4, no. 1 (March 1983): 32–33.

15. Richard Corrigan, "Miners Rally To Block Black Lung Benefit Cuts," *National Journal* 5 (28 March 1981): 101–14; *Congressional Quarterly Almanac* 46 (1981): 115.

16. Kerr, "Black Lung," 59.

17. "Plan To Wipe Out Deficit in Lung Trust Fund Is Approved by Congress," *Congressional Quarterly* (26 December 1981): 2569.

18. R. A. Rettig, "The Policy Debate on Patient Care Financing for Victims of End-Stage Renal Disease," *Law and Contemporary Problems* 40, no. 4 (Autumn 1976): 217.

19. R. A. Rettig, "End Stage Renal Disease and the 'Cost' of Medical Technology," in *Medical Technology: The Culprit behind Health Care Costs?* (Washington, D.C.: Department of Health and Human Services, 1979), 103.

20. Rettig, "Policy Debate on Financing," 203–4.

21. Ibid., 216.

22. Ibid., 219.

23. Schick, "Controlling the 'Uncontrollable,'" 1.

24. J. K. Iglehart, "Funding the End-Stage Renal Disease Program," *New England Journal of Medicine* 306, no. 8 (25 February 1982): 492.

25. Rettig, "Policy Debate on Financing," 220.

26. R. A. Rettig, "The Politics of Health Cost Containment: ESRD," *Bulletin of New York Academy of Medicine* 56, no. 1 (January/February 1980): 131, 133.

27. D. Greenberg, "Renal Politics," *New England Journal of Medicine* 298, no. 25 (22 June 1978): 1428.

28. I. F. Denkovich, "Kidney Dialysis Payment May Be Test of Reagan's Commitment to Competition," *National Journal* 5 (5 December 1981): 2162.

29. R. J. Pristave and J. B. Riley, "HCFA Publishes Final ESRD Prospective Reimbursement and Regulations," *Dialysis and Transplantation* 12, no. 6 (June 1983): 452.

30. Allen Schick, "Budgetary Adaptations to Resource Scarcity," in Charles H. Levine and Irene Rubin, eds., *Fiscal Stress and Public Policy* (Beverly Hills: Sage Publications, 1980).

31. "1967 Law Is Giving States Windfall in Federal Funds," *New York Times*, 7

August 1972, 1; "How the Government 'Bought' Mississippi," *Washington Post*, 8 June 1972, 1.

32. Joel Havemann, "Revenue Sharing Plan Likely to Be Extended, Changed," *National Journal Reports* 6 (20 July 1974): 1074; John F. Tomer, "Revenue Sharing and the Intrastate Fiscal Mismatch," *Public Finance Quarterly* 5 (October 1977): 446.

33. Quoted in Wildavsky, *The New Politics of the Budgetary Process*, 345.

34. Joel Havemann, " 'Most Powerful Lobby' Faces First Test—Revenue Sharing," *National Journal Reports* 7 (27 December 1975): 1718–20.

35. Joel Havemann, "Ford to Recommend Few Changes in Revenue Sharing," *National Journal Reports* 7 (18 January 1975): 92.

36. Jerry Hagstron and Neal R. Pierce, "The Cities, Not the States, May Bear the Brunt of Revenue Sharing Cutbacks," *National Journal Reports* 12 (19 April 1980): 636–39; Joel Havemann, "It Will Be 'No-Holds Barred' When House Takes Up Revenue Sharing," *National Journal Reports* 8 (5 June 1976): 783.

37. Sargent Shriver, interview by Jeanette Valentine, in Edward Zigler and Jeanette Valentine, *Project Head Start: A Legacy of the War on Poverty* (New York: Free Press, 1979), 52, 56.

38. Daniel P. Moynihan, *The Politics of Guaranteed Income* (New York: Random House, 1973), 42, 197.

39. Bureau of the Census, "Economic Characteristics of Households in the United States: Second Quarter 1984," in *Current Population Reports*, ser. P-70, no. 4 (Washington, D.C.: Government Printing Office, 1985); Reuben Snipper, "Interactions among Programs Providing Benefits to Individuals: Secondary Effects of the Budget," Congressional Budget Office Report, May 1982, xii.

40. House Committee on Ways and Means, *Background Material and Data on Major Programs within the Jurisdiction of Committee on Ways and Means*, 97th Cong., 2d sess., 18 February 1982, 309.

41. Kathryn Waters Gest, "Major Food Stamp Overhaul Near Approval," *Congressional Quarterly Weekly Report* 34 (6 August 1977), 1642–47; "The Food Stamp Controversy," *Congressional Digest* 60 (January 1981): 42–47.

42. Congressional Budget Office, "Major Legislative Changes in Human Resources Programs since January 1981," August 1983, 41.

43. Senate Committee on Agriculture, Nutrition and Forestry, *Child Nutrition Programs: Description, History, Issues and Options*, 98th Cong., 1st sess., January 1983, 60–72.

44. Jonathan Rauch, "Women and Children's Food Program Is 'Off Limits' to Reagan Budget Cutbacks," *National Journal* 8 (17 November 1984): 2197.

45. Congressional Budget Office, "Major Legislative Changes," vii–viii.

46. Senate Subcommittee on Nutrition of the Committee on Agriculture, Nutrition, and Forestry, *Hearing*, 23 February 1982.

7. ELUSIVE COMMUNITY: DEMOCRACY, DELIBERATION, AND THE RECONSTRUCTION OF HEALTH POLICY

1. James Q. Wilson, "New Politics, New Elites, Old Publics," chap. 10, this volume.

2. See James A. Morone, "American Political Culture and the Search for Lessons from Abroad," *Journal of Health Politics, Policy and Law* 15, no. 1 (1990): 129–43.

3. The notion of an American democratic faith is developed at length in James

Morone, *The Democratic Wish: Popular Participation and the Limits of American Government* (New York: Basic Books, 1990). Portions of this chapter are drawn from chap. 7 of that book.

4. See the powerful critique of the American Medical Association by the editors of the *Yale Law Journal*, "The American Medical Association: Power, Purpose and Politics in Organized Medicine," *Yale Law Journal* 63 (May 1954): 933–1022, esp. 950–53, quoted at 953. On the more general issue of professional dominance over entry requirements, see George Stigler, "The Theory of Economic Regulation," *Bell Journal of Economics*, 2, no. 1 (Spring 1971): 3–21.

5. For the classic analysis of both Medicare and American interest group politics, see T. R. Marmor, *The Politics of Medicare* (London: Routledge Kegan Paul, 1970), 111–12. Contrast the British case described by Harry Eckstein, *Interest Group Politics* (Stanford: Stanford University Press, 1960).

6. Paul Starr, *Transformation of American Medicine* (New York: Basic Books, 1982), 253; Odin Anderson, "The Legislative History of Medicare," in Eugene Feingold, ed., *Medicare: Policy and Politics* (San Francisco: Chandler Publishing, 1966), 90; Max Skidmore, *Medicare and the American Rhetoric of Reconciliation* (University: University of Alabama Press, 1970), 105.

7. The tone of the debate is captured by Marmor, *The Politics of Medicare*; Richard Harris, *Sacred Trust* (New York: New American Library, 1966); Skidmore, *Medicare and Rhetoric of Reconciliation*; and Arthur M. Schlessinger, Jr., *A Thousand Days* (New York: Houghton Mifflin, 1965), chap. 25.

8. Skidmore, *Medicare and Rhetoric of Reconciliation*, 138.

9. Senate Committee on Finance, *The Social Security Act*, (Washington, D.C.: Government Printing Office, 1976), 399, Title xviii, sections 1801, 1802, 1803.

10. See Frank Thompson, *Health Care and the Bureaucracy* (Cambridge: MIT Press, 1981), chap. 5; Judith Feder, *Medicare: The Politics of Federal Hospital Insurance* (Lexington, Mass.: D.C. Heath, 1977).

11. Ben Wattenberg, *Statistical History of the United States* (New York: Basic Books, 1976), 74; see the revised numbers in U.S. Bureau of the Census, *Statistical Abstract of the United States, 1986*, 106th ed. (Washington, D.C., Government Printing Office, 1985), 102–3.

12. Starr, *Transformation of American Medicine*, 381.

13. Percentage of gross national product computed from Wattenberg, *Statistical History of the United States*, 74; federal spending taken from Drew Altman, Richard Greene, and Harvey Sapolsky, *Health Planning and Regulation* (Washington, D.C.: AUPHA Press, 1981), 5.

14. See Paul Starr's penetrating "The Politics of Therapeutic Nihilism," *Hastings Center Reports* (October 1986): 24–30. Perhaps the harshest critic of the profession was Ivan Illich, *Medical Nemesis: The Expropriation of Health* (New York: Pantheon, 1976). See also Rick Carlson, *The End of Medicine* (New York: John Wiley, 1975). For more mainstream worrying about the state of medicine, see John Knowles, *Doing Better and Feeling Worse* (New York: Norton, 1977).

15. Basil Mott, "The New Health Planning System," in Arthur Levin, ed., *Health Services: The Local Perspective* (New York: Academy of Political Science, 1977), 238–41; J. H. Parkum and V. C. Parkum, *Voluntary Participation in Health Planning* (Harrisburg: Bureau of Comprehensive Health Planning, Pennsylvania Department

of Health, 1957); Altman, Greene, and Sapolsky, *Health Planning and Regulation*, 21–22.

16. Starr, *Transformation of American Medicine*, 400–401.

17. Public Law 93-641 was passed by Congress in December 1974 and signed by President Ford in January 1975. Dominick is quoted in *Congressional Record*, 19 December 1974. For a vague discussion of the vague congressional intent, see *The Report by the Committee on Interstate Commerce and Foreign Commerce on the National Health Policy, Planning and Resources Development Act of 1974*, report 93-1382 (Washington, D.C.: Government Printing Office, 26 November 1974).

18. The different mandates can be found in the following sections of the act: Preface (Purpose #1), 1513(a)(2), 1513(a)(5), 1502(a)(9), 1502(a)(2), and 1502(a)(10).

19. PL 93-641, 1512(b)(3)(c)(i). For an analysis of the implicit theories of representations, see James Morone and T. R. Marmor, "Representing Consumer Interests: The Case of National Health Planning," *Ethics* 91 (April 1981): 431–50.

20. G. Gregory Raab, "National/State/Local Relationships in Health Planning: Interest Group Reaction and Lobbying," in *Health Planning in the United States* (Washington, D.C.: National Academy Press, 1981), 2:120.

21. Daniel P. Moynihan, *Maximum Feasible Misunderstanding* (New York: Free Press, 1969), xx.

22. I include my own judgment in this litany as a gesture of conciliation to a group of scholars I admire enormously (despite their appearance here as something of straw men). The quotes are taken, respectively, from T. R. Marmor and James A. Morone, "Representing Consumer Interests: Imbalanced Markets, Health Planning and the HSAs," *Milbank Memorial Fund Quarterly: Health and Society* 58, no. 1 (1980): 161; Lawrence D. Brown, "Some Structural Issues in the Health Planning Program," in *Health Planning in the United States*, 2:1; Harvey Sapolsky, "Bottoms Up Is Upside Down," in *Health Planning in the United States*, 143; Thompson, *Health Care and the Bureaucracy*, 48, 50.

23. On regulatory capture generally, see Barry Mitnick's literature review and taxonomy, *The Political Economy of Regulation* (New York: Columbia University Press, 1980). On the HSA case, see Lawrence Brown, who termed the effort *self-regulating localism*—"Political Conditions of Regulatory Effectiveness: The Case of PSROs and HSAs," *Bulletin of the New York Academy of Medicine* 58, no. 1 (1982): 78.

24. See Bruce Vladeck, "Interest Group Representation and the HSAs: Health Planning and Political Theory," *American Journal of Public Health* 67 (January 1977): 23–29. This is still one of the best articles written on the agencies—despite predictions that were wrong.

25. Brown, "Some Structural Issues," 24.

26. See James A. Morone, "The Real World of Representation," in *Health Planning in the United States*, 273.

27. Guy Peters, *American Public Policy* (Chatham, N.J.: Chatham House, 1986), 185.

28. There are two alternate explanations for why the agencies pursued cost control. First, many providers pursued certificate-of-need regulation to gain competitive advantage over rival providers. Second, the staff members balanced the providers and dominated the agency with their rationalizing vision. The former did occur in some

health care markets, but even in the many places where providers put up a united, staunchly antiregulatory front, the agencies pursued the cost-cutting mission. As for staff, they too abandoned their own agendas—rational planning, community organizing—to pursue cost cutting through certificate-of-need regulation. The pressures of organizational maintenance tended to work on all members of the agencies—consumers, providers, and staff. For a fuller account, see James Morone, *The Democratic Wish* (Basic Books, 1990), 292, 314–16.

29. Gay Sands Miller, "Agencies Act to Lower Health Bills by Saying No to Bigger Hospitals: Citizen Planners Turn Down Expansions, Push Clinics, Promote Shared Services," *Wall Street Journal*, 5 May 1977; Altman, Greene, and Sapolsky, *Health Planning and Regulation;* Codman Research Group, "The Impact of Health Planning and Regulation on the Patterns of Hospital Utilization in New England," executive summary, DHEW contract 291-76-0003, September 1977. On national effects of certificate of need, see Andrew B. Dunham, "Health and Politics: The Impact on Certificate of Need Regulation," Ph.D. diss., University of Chicago, 1981. See also Morone, *The Democratic Wish*, 286–327.

30. For the long-term political implications of these developments, see James A. Morone and Andrew B. Dunham, "Slouching to National Health Insurance: The New Health Care Politics," *Yale Journal of Regulation* 2, no. 2 (1985): 263–91. For a longer account of the development of the new payment mechanism, see Dunham and Morone, *The Politics of Innovation: Hospital Regulation in New Jersey* (Princeton, N.J.: Health Research and Education Trust, 1982).

31. Judith Kosterlitz, "Cookbook Medicine," *National Journal* (9 March 1991): 574.

32. Ibid., 575; Brian Cox, "Illinois Blues Begin Physician Evaluation Program," *National Underwriter*, 20 January 1992, 13; Spencer Rich, "Medicare: Can the Doctors Be Trusted?" *Washington Post*, 18 February 1991. For discussion, see James A. Morone, "The Bureaucracy Empowered," in James Marone and Gary Belkin, *National Health Care Reform* (Durham, N.C.: Duke University Press, 1994), 148–64.

8. THE NEW POLITICS OF ENVIRONMENTAL POLICY

1. Ronald Inglehart, *Culture Shift in Advanced Society* (Princeton: Princeton University Press, 1990), 5.

2. These words were uttered at the Windstar Foundation Conference in 1989 and were reported in *Earth Ethics*, Summer 1990, 13. Following up on that idea, the Windstar Federation mounted a campaign for a constitutional amendment to ensure "the right of every American to a clean and healthy environment." Eight earlier attempts to pass such an amendment had been made between 1968 and 1972. "All eight died in committee, and passage of such specific remedial legislation as the Clean Air Act and the Safe Drinking Water Act reduced the immediate pressure for such a constitutional amendment." *Earth Ethics*, Summer 1990, 13.

See also the following statement of three commissioners of the National Commission on Air Quality: Richard Ayres, staff attorney for the Natural Resources Defense Council; John Sheehan, United States Steel Workers; and Anne Marie Crocetti. Although they dissented from much of the report issued by the commission, they used the following language to praise its decision to recommend retention of the national air quality standards of the Clean Air Act: "Through these standards, Congress recognized Americans' *basic right to air that is fit to breathe*" (emphasis added).

The thirteen-member National Commission on Air Quality was created by Congress in 1977 under the Clean Air Amendments of 1977 to make an independent analysis of air pollution control and alternative strategies for achieving the goals of the act. This quotation is from its report, *To Breathe Clean Air* (Washington, D.C.: Government Printing Office, 1981), 5–31.

3. For an excellent depiction of this evolution, see R. Shep Melnick, "The Courts, Congress, and Programmatic Rights," in Richard A. Harris and Sidney M. Milkis, eds., *Remaking American Politics* (Boulder, Colo.: Westview, 1989), 188–212.

4. See Louis Cassarett and John Doull, eds., *Toxicology: The Basic Science of Poison,* 1st ed. (New York: Macmillan, 1975), chap. 2.

5. For an account of Muskie's political career, see Theodore Lippman, Jr., and Donald C. Hansen, *Muskie* (New York: Norton, 1971).

6. Charles O. Jones, *Clean Air: The Policies and Politics of Pollution Control* (Pittsburgh: University of Pittsburgh Press, 1975), 202.

7. John C. Esposito et al., *Vanishing Air* (New York: Pantheon, 1970), 306–10.

8. For an account of the competition between Nixon and Muskie over clean air policy, see Marc Landy, Marc Roberts, and Stephen Thomas, *The Environmental Protection Agency: Asking the Wrong Questions* (New York: Oxford University Press, 1990), 28–30.

9. R. Shep Melnick, *Regulation and the Courts* (Washington, D.C.: Brookings, 1983), 239.

10. Esposito, *Vanishing Air,* viii.

11. Ibid., 9.

12. Senate Debate on S. 4358, September 21, 1970, in Senate Committee on Public Works, *A Legislative History of the Clean Air Act of 1970,* 93d Cong., 2d sess., 1974, 220, 227.

13. Melnick, *Regulation and the Courts,* 188.

14. U.S. Congress, House Subcommittee on Conservation and Natural Resources, Committee on Government Operations, Hearings, 1970, *The Environmental Decade: Action Proposals for the 1970s,* 91st Cong., 2d sess., February 2–6, March 13, April 3. Cited in Richard Harris and Sidney Milkis, *The Politics of Regulatory Change* (New York: Oxford University Press, 1989), 236–37 (emphasis added).

15. On the intellectual climate of that period, see especially E. J. Dionne, *Why Americans Hate Politics* (New York: Simon and Schuster, 1991), 31–54.

16. On the formulation of Superfund, see Landy, Roberts, and Thomas, *Environmental Protection Agency,* 133–71. On Superfund more generally see also Thomas W. Church and Robert Nakamura, *Cleaning Up the Mess: Implementation Strategies in Superfund* (Washington, D.C.: Brookings, 1993); Marc Landy and Mary Hague, "The Coalition for Waste: Private Interests and Superfund," in Michael S. Greve and Fred Smith, Jr., *Environmental Politics: Public Costs, Private Rewards* (New York: Praeger, 1992), 67–88; and Daniel Mazmanian and David Morell, *Beyond Superfailure: America's Toxics Policy for the 1990s* (Boulder, Colo.: Westview, 1992).

17. Landy, Roberts, and Thomas, *Environmental Protection Agency,* 141–42.

18. Office of Policy Analysis, USEPA, *Unfinished Business: A Comparative Assessment of Environmental Problems* (February 1987), I-28–I-34.

19. Landy and Hague, "Coalition for Waste," 68–71.

20. Peter Huber, *Liability: The Legal Revolution and Its Consequences* (New York: Basic Books, 1988), 65–82.

21. John Lyons, "Deep Pockets and CERCLA," *Stanford Environmental Law Journal* 6 (1986–87): 271.

22. For fuller accounts of this process, see Alfred A. Marcus, *Promise and Performance* (Westport, Conn.: Greenwood, 1980), and John C. Whitaker, *Striking a Balance: Environment and Natural Resources in the Nixon-Ford Years* (Washington, D.C.: American Enterprise Institute, 1976).

23. For a broad assessment of the EPA, see the symposium "Assessing the Environmental Protection Agency after Twenty Years: Law, Politics and Economics," ed. Christopher H. Schroeder and Richard J. Lazarus, *Law and Contemporary Problems* 54 (Autumn 1991).

24. Landy, Roberts, and Thomas, *Environmental Protection Agency*, 39–440.

25. Ibid., 40–42.

26. Melnick, *Regulation and the Courts*, 99.

27. For a full account of the NSPS controversy, see Bruce A. Ackerman and William T. Hassler, *Clean Coal Dirty Air: or How the Clean Air Act Became a Multibillion Dollar Bail-Out for High-Sulfur Coal Producers and What Should Be Done about It* (New Haven: Yale University Press, 1981).

28. Melnick, *Regulation and the Courts*, 99.

29. Ackerman and Hassler, *Clean Coal*, 79–103.

30. R. Shep Melnick, "Pollution Deadlines and the Coalition for Failure," in Greve and Smith, *Environmental Politics*, 89–104.

31. On Congress and environmental policy, see Michael Kraft, "Environmental Gridlock: Searching for Consensus in Congress," in Michael Kraft and Norman Vig, eds., *Environmental Policy in the 1990s*, 2d ed. (Washington, D.C.: CQ Press, 1994), 97–120. On the role of Congress in the formulation of the Clean Air Act, see Richard E. Cohen, *Washington at Work: Backrooms and Clean Air* (New York: Macmillan, 1992).

32. Cohen, *Washington at Work*, 2–30.

33. Julie Kosterliz, "Watch Out for Waxman," *National Journal* (11 March 1989): 577–81.

34. Michael E. Kraft, "Environmental Gridlock: Searching for Consensus in Congress," in Norman J. Vig and Michael E. Kraft, *Environmental Policy in the 1990s* (Washington, D.C.: CQ Press, 1990), 103–24.

35. "Bush Vows to Fight Pollution," *Washington Post*, 1 September 1988, A-1.

36. A detailed summary of the act appears in *1990 CQ Almanac*, 248–74. For a broad discussion of the act, see Gary C. Bryner, *Blue Skies, Green Politics* (Washington, D.C.: CQ Press, 1993).

37. Henry Waxman, "An Overview of the Clean Air Act Amendments of 1990," *Environmental Law* 21 (1991): 1743–44.

38. Waxman, "An Overview," 1742.

39. "Clean Air Act Rewritten, Tightened," *1990 CQ Almanac*, 248–49.

40. U.S. Congress, House Committee on Energy and Commerce, *Clean Air Act Amendments of 1990* (H.R. 3030), 101st Cong., 2d sess., 17 May 1990, rept. 101-490, pt 1, 322.

41. *1990 CQ Almanac*, 275.

42. Bryner, *Blue Skies*, 130.

43. Ibid., 95–96; Cohen, *Washington at Work*, 55–60.

44. Jan Paul Acton and Lloyd S. Dixon, *Superfund and Transaction Costs: The*

Experience of Insurers and Very Large Firms (Santa Monica, Calif.: Rand Institute for Civil Justice, 1992).

45. Landy and Hague, "Coalition for Waste," 73–75.

46. Ibid., 75.

47. Ibid., 78–81.

48. The phrase is Bruce Yandle's. See Bruce Yandle, "Bootleggers and Baptists: The Education of a Regulatory Economist," *Regulation* 7 (May/June 1983): 12–16.

49. Holly Idelson, "The Cost of Cleaning Up," *CQ Weekly Report* (25 April 1992): 1069.

50. National Commission on Air Quality, *To Breathe Clean Air,* 5–36.

51. Melnick, "Pollution Deadlines," 98.

52. On the role of economists in the transportation deregulation debate and of Kahn in particular, see Martha Derthick and Paul Quirk, *The Politics of Deregulation* (Washington, D.C.: Brookings, 1985).

53. For a broader discussion of EPA officials as civic educators, see Landy, Roberts, and Thomas, *Environmental Protection Agency,* 7–8, 79–82, 279–82, 290–97.

54. As coined by Herbert Kaufman, *neutral competence* means "to do the work of government expertly, and to do it according to explicit, objective standards rather than to personal or party or other obligations and loyalties." Kaufman, "Conflicts in Doctrines of Public Administration," *American Political Science Review* 50, no. 4 (December 1956): 1060.

55. I am indebted to Charles Rubin for helping me with this formulation.

9. POLICY MAKING IN THE CONTEMPORARY CONGRESS: THREE DIMENSIONS OF PERFORMANCE

1. James L. Sundquist, *The Decline and Resurgency of Congress* (Washington, D.C.: Brookings, 1981).

2. Research on the effects of reform looks mainly at matters like the number of floor amendments or the number of pages of legislation. For examples of such research, see Leroy Rieselbach, ed., *Legislative Reform: The Policy Impact* (Lexington, Mass.: Lexington Books, 1978).

3. Both cases are discussed for different purposes in Martha Derthick and Paul J. Quirk, *The Politics of Deregulation* (Washington, D.C.: Brookings, 1985).

4. For a general treatment, see Leroy Rieselbach, *The Politics of Congressional Reform* (Washington, D.C.: CQ Press, 1986).

5. John Ellwood, "The Great Exception: The Congressional Budget Process in an Age of Decentralization," in Lawrence C. Dodd and Bruce I. Oppenheimer, eds., *Congress Reconsidered,* 3d ed. (Washington, D.C.: CQ Press, 1985), 315–42.

6. Roger A. Davidson, ed., *The Postreform Congress* (New York: St. Martin's Press, 1991); Steven S. Smith, *Call to Order: Floor Politics in the House and the Senate* (Washington, D.C.: Brookings, 1989); Stanley Bach and Steven S. Smith, *Managing Uncertainty in the House of Representatives* (Washington, D.C.: Brookings, 1988).

7. For a more detailed discussion of these issues, with emphasis on developments in the postreform Congress, see Paul J. Quirk, "Structures and Performance: An Evaluation," in Davidson, *The Postreform Congress,* 303–24. Jane Mansbridge, *Beyond Adversary Democracy* (Chicago: University of Chicago Press, 1983), made a somewhat similar appeal to the hypothetical deliberations of an idealized direct democracy as benchmark for evaluating political institutions. Under some theoreti-

cal assumptions, such as those of majority-rule voting models in social-choice theory, this criterion would be strictly undefined and therefore useless because of intransitivities in majority preferences. However, this conception of an ideal direct democracy is roughly analogous to a cooperative, n-person, nonzero-sum game. One can think of the policy choices that would result from such a democracy in much the same way as game theorists think of the solution concepts for such games. See Peter Ordeshook, *Game Theory and Political Theory: An Introduction* (New York: Cambridge University Press, 1986).

8. Morris P. Fiorina, "The Decline of Collective Responsibility in American Politics," *Daedalus* 109, no. 3 (1979): 25-45; Kenneth A. Shepsle, "Representation and Governance: The Great Legislative Trade-off," *Political Science Quarterly* 103 (1988): 461-84.

9. Derthick and Quirk, *The Politics of Deregulation*; R. Douglas Arnold, *The Logic of Congressional Action* (New Haven: Yale University Press, 1991).

10. Roger Davidson, "Subcommittee Government: New Channels for Policy Making," in Thomas E. Mann and Norman J. Ornstein, eds., *The New Congress* (Washington, D.C.: American Enterprise Institute, 1981), 99-133.

11. Smith, *Call to Order*.

12. The principal works are Arthur Maass, *Congress and the Common Good* (New York: Basic Books, 1983); Joseph M. Bessette, "Is Congress a Deliberative Body?" in Dennis Hale, ed., *The United States Congress* (Chestnut Hill, Mass.: Boston College, 1982); William Muir, *Legislature* (Berkeley: University of California Press, 1986); and Jane J. Mansbridge, "Motivating Deliberation in Congress," in Sarah Baumgartner Thurow, ed., Constitutionalism in America, vol. 2 (New York: University Press of America, 1988).

13. I leave aside for now ambiguities about the amount of investment in information gathering and the potential indeterminacy of decisions due to majority-rule disequilibrium.

14. Compare the excellent discussions of these conditions in Muir, *Legislature*, and Mansbridge, *Motivating Deliberation in Congress*. Such discussion assumes an American-style, independent legislature.

15. Keith Krehbiel, *Information and Legislative Organization* (Ann Arbor: University of Michigan Press, 1991).

16. Paul J. Quirk, "The Cooperative Resolution of Policy Conflict," *American Political Science Review* 83 (1989): 905-21.

17. This tendency may, however, cause difficulty for administrators, who are subjected to ever-increasing and often inconsistent legislative constraints. See Martha Derthick, *Agency under Stress* (Washington, D.C.: Brookings, 1990), and James Q. Wilson, *Bureaucracy: What Government Agencies Do and Why They Do It* (New York: Basic Books, 1989).

18. Bach and Smith, *Managing Uncertainty in the House*.

19. For a study that refutes claims of the immobilism of recent American politics with reference to social regulation, see Richard A. Harris and Sidney M. Milkis, *The Politics of Regulatory Change: A Tale of Two Agencies* (New York: Oxford University Press, 1989).

20. My discussion of trucking deregulation follows Derthick and Quirk, *The Politics of Deregulation*, and Dorothy Robyn, *Braking the Special Interests: Truck-*

ing Deregulation and the Politics of Policy Reform (Chicago: University of Chicago Press, 1986).

21. Clifford Winston, "Economic Deregulation: Days of Reckoning for Microeconomists," *Journal of Economic Literature* (September 1993): 1263–89.

22. Gordon Tullock, "Achieving Deregulation—a Public-Choice Perspective," *Regulation: AEI Journal on Government and Society* 2 (1987): 50–54; Robyn, *Braking the Special Interests.* In the next session, however, Congress enacted a form of tax relief to offset the losses suffered by trucking companies whose operating certificates had become worthless in an environment of virtually free competitive entry. Presumably, the industry would have done still better if it had offered in timely fashion to accept such a program in trade for its support of deregulation.

23. My account of this case is derived from Pietro Nivola, *The Politics of Energy Conservation* (Washington, D.C.: Brookings, 1986).

24. Nivola, *The Politics of Energy Conservation.*

25. Gary M. Mucciaroni, *Reversal of Fortune: Public Policy and Private Interest* (Washington, D.C.: Brookings, forthcoming).

26. See also Paul J. Quirk and Bruce Nesmith, "Explaining Deadlock: Domestic Policymaking in the Bush Presidency," in Lawrence C. Dodd and Calvin Jillson, eds., *New Perspectives on American Politics* (Washington, D.C.: CQ Press, 1994), 191–211, and Anthony King and Giles Austin, "Good Government and the Politics of High Exposure," in Colin Campbell and Bart A. Rockman, eds., *The Bush Presidency: First Appraisals* (Chatham, N.J.: Chatham House, 1991), 249–86.

10. NEW POLITICS, NEW ELITES, OLD PUBLICS

1. William M. Lunch, *The Nationalization of American Politics* (Berkeley: University of California Press, 1987), 130.

2. Morton Keller, *Affairs of State* (Cambridge: Harvard University Press, 1977).

3. James Buchanan, "The Moral Dimensions of Debt Financing," *Economic Inquiry* 23 (1985): 1–6.

4. *Federalist* No. 10

5. Benjamin Ginsberg and Martin Shefter, *Politics by Other Means* (New York: Basic Books, 1990).

6. James Macgregor Burns, *The Deadlock of Democracy* (Englewood Cliffs, N.J.: Prentice-Hall, 1963).

7. Hedrick Smith, *The Power Game* (New York: Random House, 1988).

8. Ronald Dworkin, *Taking Rights Seriously* (Cambridge: Harvard University Press, 1977).

9. Cf. Lloyd N. Cutler, "To Form a Government," *Foreign Affairs* (Fall 1980): 126–43.

11. TWO-TIER POLITICS AND THE PROBLEM OF PUBLIC POLICY

1. Dan Walters, *The New California: Facing the Twenty-first Century* (Sacramento: California Journal, 1986).

2. Charles Murray, "The Shape of Things to Come," *National Review,* 8 July 1991, 29–30; Robert Reich, "The Secession of the Successful," *New York Times Magazine,* 20 January 1991, 17ff.

3. In California, state law requires the Secretary of State to prepare a booklet for

voters containing arguments for and against each initiative proposition. Under the dutiful supervision of March Fong Eu, the current incumbent, that volume has often resembled a telephone directory. By contrast, the media campaigns waged over such initiative propositions are ordinarily no more than meretricious sloganeering.

4. John Kenneth Galbraith, "Coolidge, Carter, Bush, Reagan," *New York Times,* 12 December 1988, A16.

5. Letter of Cato to the *New York Journal,* undated, in Herbert J. Storing, ed., *The Complete Anti-Federalist* (Chicago: University of Chicago Press, 1981), 2:111.

6. Machiavelli, *Discourses,* book III, chap. 21.

7. Richard Zeiger, "Few Citizens Make Decisions for Everyone," *California Journal* (November 1990): 527, 529.

8. Leslie Gelb, "Throw the Bums Out," *New York Times,* 23 October 1991, A23. In 1992, Bush and Clinton supporters faulted Congress as an institution but had some confidence in their own representatives; Perot's followers disdained both by a significant majority—Dan Balz and E. J. Dionne, Jr., "In a Quirky Year, Perot Could Be a Loose Cannon," *Washington Post National Weekly,* 4–10 May 1992, 8.

9. David Rosenbaum, "The Paralysis of No-Pain Politics," *New York Times,* 19 April 1992, E1.

10. James Q. Wilson, "The Newer Deal," *New Republic,* 2 July 1990, 34; Daniel Yankelovitch, *Coming to Public Judgment* (Syracuse: Syracuse University Press, 1991).

11. Marc K. Landy et al., *The Environmental Protection Agency: Asking the Wrong Questions* (New York: Oxford University Press, 1990).

12. Michael Paul Rogin, "JFK: The Movie," *American Historical Review* 97 (1992): 502, 505; Sidney Blumenthal, "He's a New Age Demagogue," *New York Times,* 5 April 1992, E17.

13. Benjamin Ginsberg and Martin Shefter, *Politics by Other Means* (New York: Basic Books, 1990). The media are the obvious example, but Perot's movement, though it expressed itself in electoral politics, is a variation on the same theme— Gerald M. Pomper et al., *The Election of 1992* (Chatham: Chatham House, 1993), 197–201.

14. Gerald M. Pomper et al., *The Election of 1988* (Chatham: Chatham House, 1989), 194–195.

15. Pomper et al., *The Election of 1992,* 192–193.

16. Garry Wills, "Ross Perot and the Immaculate Election," *Washington Post National Weekly,* 1–7 June 1992, 23; Michael Schrage, "Perot: A Man of Revolution, Not Evolution," *Washington Post,* 1 May 1992, B3; Steven Greenhouse, "Hardly Laissez-Faire," *New York Times,* 27 June 1992, 19. The term *tamed prince,* of course, is taken from Harvey C. Mansfield, Jr., *Taming the Prince: The Ambivalence of Modern Executive Power* (New York: Free Press, 1989).

17. In this and what follows, I have drawn on my "The Anti-Federalists, Representation and Party," *Northwestern University Law Review* 84 (1989): 12–38.

18. In fact, Madison observed, American institutions are unique in being wholly representative, characterized by the "total exclusion of the people in their collective capacity" from any role in government. *The Federalist* #63.

19. *The Federalist* #10, 53, 56, 57; David Epstein, *The Political Theory of the Federalist* (Chicago: University of Chicago Press, 1984).

20. Essays of Brutus in the *New York Journal,* 18 October and 29 November 1787, in Storing, *Complete Anti-Federalist,* 2:369–371, 384–385.

21. Letter of Cato in the *New York Journal,* undated, in Storing, *Complete Anti-Federalist,* 2:111.

22. Harvey C. Mansfield, Jr., *America's Constitutional Soul* (Baltimore: Johns Hopkins University Press, 1991), 170.

23. Despite media ballyhoo about self-reformation, this did not improve in 1992—*New York Times,* 11 July 1992, L7. See also Todd Gitlin, "On Being Sound-Bitten," *Boston Review* (December 1991), 17.

24. Dorothy B. James, "Television and the Syntax of Presidential Leadership," *Presidential Studies Quarterly* 18 (1988): 737–39; Gerald Marzorati, "From Tocqueville to Perotville," *New York Times,* 28 June 1992, E17.

25. John Tierney, "Now, Journalists Renege on Election Promises," *New York Times,* 31 January 1992, A12.

26. Ellen Hume is cited by Richard Berke, "Campaign '92," *New York Times,* 26 June 1992, A13; see also Roger Masters, Sigfried Frey, and Gary Bente, "Dominance and Attention: Images of Leaders in German, French and American TV News," *Polity* 23 (1991): 393.

27. Walter Goodman, "Why Clinton Can't Go on TV and Fix Everything," *New York Times,* 30 May 1993, H27.

28. Letter from the Federal Farmer to the Republican, 31 December 1787, in Storing, *Complete Anti-Federalist,* 2:268–69.

29. Letter of Cato to the *New York Journal,* undated, in Storing, *Complete Anti-Federalist,* 2:112.

30. The original terms of the proposed first amendment, never ratified by the states, provided that there should be "not less than one Representative for every fifty thousand persons." A last minute change revised "less" to "more." *Annals of Congress* 1 (1789): 913.

31. Essay of Brutus in the *New York Journal,* 18 October 1787, in Storing, *Complete Anti-Federalist,* 2:370–71.

32. Essay of Brutus in the *New York Journal,* 15 November 1787, in Storing, *Complete Anti-Federalist,* 2:380.

33. Speech of Patrick Henry to the Virginia Ratifying Convention, 12 June 1788, in Storing, *Complete Anti-Federalist,* 5:243–244.

34. Speech of Melancton Smith to the Convention of the State of New York, 21 June 1788, in Storing, *Complete Anti-Federalist,* 6:157–59.

35. Letter from the Federal Farmer to the Republican, 31 December 1787, in Storing, *Complete Anti-Federalist,* 2:269, 290–92; essay of Brutus in the *New York Journal,* 10 April 1788, in Storing, *Complete Anti-Federalist,* 2:444–45; speech of Melancton Smith to the Convention of the State of New York, 25 June 1788, in Storing, *Complete Anti-Federalist,* 6:164–65.

36. Walter Dean Burnham, *Critical Elections and the Mainsprings of American Politics* (New York: Norton, 1970), 133.

37. Woodrow Wilson, *Constitutional Government in the United States* (New York: Columbia University Press, 1908), 218.

38. Gerald M. Pomper, *Passions and Interests: Political Party Concepts of American Democracy* (Lawrence: University Press of Kansas, 1992), 118–121, 129.

39. Laura L. Vertz, John P. Fendress, and James L. Gibson, "Nationalization of the Electorate in the United States," *American Political Science Review* 81 (1987): 961-66.

40. This is the sound, critical basis of Theodore Lowi's flawed prescription for a third party—"The Party Crasher," *New York Times Magazine*, 23 August 1992, 28ff. On the general points, see Leon Epstein, *Political Parties in the American Mold* (Madison: University of Wisconsin Press, 1986), esp. 205-25, 272-309.

41. Pomper, *Passions and Interests*, 64; see also 53-67 passim.

42. Ibid., 67

43. Thomas Byrne Edsall, *The New Politics of Inequality* (New York: Norton, 1984). Even in 1992, with a candidate eager to move the party to the center, Democrats denied Robert Casey, Pennsylvania's antiabortion governor, the right to address the party's convention.

44. E. J. Dionne, Jr., *Why Americans Hate Politics* (New York: Simon and Schuster, 1991).

45. "It is through such a system," Samuel Huntington observed, "rather than broad appeals to public opinion, that Presidents achieve the policy results they desire." *American Politics: The Promise of Disharmony* (Cambridge: Harvard University Press, 1981), 219.

46. For some proposals, see Pomper, *Passions and Interests*, 146-49.

47. Alexis de Tocqueville, *Democracy in America* (Garden City: Doubleday, 1969), 243.

12. THE NEW POLITICS OF PUBLIC POLICY

1. *Gridlock* has become a commonplace of political analysis among political scientists, journalists, and practitioners. The *Washington Post* compiled a record of President Clinton's use of the term in his public utterances. Between January and July 1993, he used the term ninety-six times. Some examples: "Hallelujah! The gridlock was broken yesterday, and the United States Congress passed the Motor-Voter Bill." "Tonight the House said 'No' to gridlock." (After passage of the House Budget Plan)

The most important journalistic account of gridlock is in Hedrick Smith's *The Power Game: How Washington Works* (New York: Random House, 1988).

In political science see (for example) Randall Ripley, who has this to say about the results of divided government: "In general, not much legislation is produced . . . particularly on domestic matters. What domestic legislation does pass is likely to be bland and inconsequential." *Congress, Process and Policy* (New York: Norton, 1983), 355. Or "At such times (of divided government) the normal tendency of the U.S. system towards deadlock becomes irresistible." James Sundquist, "The Crisis of Competence in Our National Government," *Political Science Quarterly* (1980): 192.

We are not the first to criticize this view. See especially David Mayhew, *Divided We Govern: Party Control, Lawmaking and Investigations, 1946-1990* (New Haven: Yale University Press, 1991), and Morris Fiorina, *Divided Government* (New York: Macmillan, 1992), 86-112.

2. For an account of the debilitating effects of gridlock, see Benjamin Ginsberg and Martin Shefter, *Politics by Other Means: The Declining Importance of Elections in America* (New York: Basic Books, 1990), esp. 131-61.

3. For example, "voters added the most fractious division of all: the gridlock of divided government . . . The partisan division of government is a crucible for stalemate . . . Our national political irresolution derives from the ambivalence of voters on many central issues and from the lack of an overarching political force to organize and manage government." Smith, *The Power Game*, 652.

4. Marc Landy, Marc Roberts, and Stephen Thomas, *The Environmental Protection Agency: Asking the Wrong Questions* (New York: Oxford University Press, 1990), 160.

5. See Paul Quirk's chap. 9 in this volume. See also Thomas Mann and Norman Ornstein, eds., *The New Congress* (Washington, D.C.: American Enterprise Institute, 1981).

6. R. Shep Melnick, chap. 2 in this volume.

7. "Between different levels of government, common disciplines and subdisciplines promote cooperation within vertical hierarchies. These bureaucratic elements in turn establish cordial relations with specialized elements and with groups of consumers who benefit from their services." Samuel H. Beer, "A New Public Philosophy," in Anthony King, ed., *The New American Political System*, 1st ed. (Washington, D.C.: American Enterprise Institute, 1978), 22.

8. Wilson C. McWilliams, chap. 11 in this volume.

9. For evaluations of the effects of the 1986 Tax Reform Act on various aspects of economic performance, see Joel Slemrod, ed., *Do Taxes Matter? The Impact of the Tax Reform Act of 1986* (Cambridge: MIT Press, 1990); for its influence on income distribution, see Edward M. Gramlich, Richard Kasten, and Frank Sammartino, "Growing Inequality in the 1980s: The Role of Federal Taxes and Cash Transfers," in Sheldon Danziger and Peter Gottschalk, eds., *Uneven Tides: Rising Inequality in America* (New York: Russell Sage Foundation, 1993), 223–50, and B. B. Kern, "The Tax Reform Act of 1986 and the Progressivity of the Individual Income Tax," *Public Finance Quarterly* 18, no. 3 (1990): 259–72.

10. For a compendium of such criticism, see Keith Schneider, "New View Calls Environmental Policy Misguided," *New York Times*, 21 March 1993, 1. Also Marc Landy and Mary Hague, "The Coalition for Waste: Private Interests and Superfund," in Michael Greve and Fred Smith, Jr., eds., *Environmental Politics: Public Costs, Private Rewards* (New York: Praeger, 1992), 67–88.

11. Paul R. Portney, "Economics and the Clean Air Act," *Journal of Economic Perspectives* 4 (Fall 1990): 173–81.

12. Sidney M. Milkis, *The President and the Parties: The Transformation of the American Party System since the New Deal* (New York: Oxford University Press, 1993). This book brilliantly depicts the rise of "programmatic liberalism" from the New Deal to the present.

13. R. Shep Melnick, "The Courts, Congress, and Programmatic Rights," in Richard A. Harris and Sidney M. Milkis, eds., *Remaking American Politics* (Boulder, Colo.: Westview, 1989), 188.

14. Franklin Delano Roosevelt, "New Conditions Impose New Requirements upon Government and Those Who Conduct Government," Campaign Address on Progressive Government at the Commonwealth Club, San Francisco, Calif., 23 September 1932, in *Franklin Delano Roosevelt: Public Papers and Addresses*, ed. Samuel Rosenman (New York: Random House, 1938), 1:742–56.

15. Franklin Delano Roosevelt, "Unless There Is Security Here at Home, There

Cannot Be Lasting Peace in the World," Message to the Congress on the State of the Union, 11 January 1944.

16. *Public Papers of the Presidents: Harry S. Truman* (Washington, D.C.: Government Printing Office, 6 September 1945), 1:263–308.

17. Lyndon B. Johnson, Commencement Address at Howard University, 1965.

18. Milkis, *President and Parties*, 261–84.

19. Marc Landy, "Public Policy and Citizenship," in Helen Ingram and Steven Rathgeb Smith, eds., *Public Policy for Democracy* (Washington, D.C., 1993), 19–44.

20. Theodore J. Lowi, *The End of Liberalism: Ideology, Policy and the Crisis of Public Authority* (New York: Norton, 1969).

21. Beer, "New Public Philosophy," 9.

22. Robert Katzmann, *Institutional Disability: The Saga of Transportation Policy for the Disabled* (Washington, D.C.: Brookings, 1986), 111.

23. Peter Schuck, chap. 3 in this volume.

24. On transportation deregulation see Martha Derthick and Paul Quirk, *The Politics of Deregulation* (Washington, D.C.: Brookings, 1985).

List of Contributors

DAVID R. BEAM is associate professor of political science and director of the Master of Public Administration program at the Illinois Institute of Technology. A former senior analyst with the U.S. Advisory Commission on Intergovernmental Relations, his published works examine contemporary American federalism and his current writings address the political challenges facing public policy analysts and ethical issues in privatization.

TIMOTHY J. CONLAN is associate professor of government and politics at George Mason University, where he directs the university's Federalism and Public Policy Research Center. Previously he served as assistant staff director of the Senate Subcommittee on Intergovernmental Relations and as a Senior Analyst with the Advisory Commission on Intergovernmental Relations. Conlan is the author of *Federal Regulation of State and Local Governments: The Mixed Record of the 1980's; Taxing Choices: The Politics of Tax Reform;* and *New Federalism: Intergovernmental Reform from Nixon to Reagan.*

ROBERT A. KAGAN is professor of political science and law at the University of California, Berkeley, and director of the university's Center for the Study of Law and Society. His writings include *Regulatory Justice; Going by the Book: The Problem of Regulatory Unreasonableness* (with Eugene Bardach); and articles on legal history, law enforcement, comparative legal systems, the legal profession, and regulatory processes. His current research concerns American "adversarial legalism" as a distinctive style of policy implementation and dispute resolution.

MARC K. LANDY is professor of political science at Boston College and a senior fellow at the Gordon Public Policy Center. He is an author (with

Marc Roberts and Stephen Thomas) of *The Environmental Protection Agency from Nixon to Clinton: Asking the Wrong Questions*. His recent essay "Citizenship and Public Policy" appears in Helen Ingram and Steven Rathgeb Smith, eds., *Public Policy for Democracy* (1993).

MARTIN A. LEVIN is professor of political science at Brandeis University and founding director of its Gordon Public Policy Center. He is the author of *The Political Hand: Policy Implementation and Youth Employment Programs* (1985), *Urban Politics and the Criminal Courts* (1977) and coauthor of *Making Government Work* (1994). In 1991, Levin was elected president of the Association of Public Policy Analysis and Management (APPAM), the leading national association of academic and government policy analysts and managers.

WILSON CAREY MCWILLIAMS is professor of political science at Rutgers University. He is the author of *The Idea of Fraternity in American Politics* and of numerous essays about American political thought and American politics. He is a frequent contributor to *Commonweal*.

R. SHEP MELNICK is professor and chair in the Politics Department of Brandeis University. He is the author of *Between the Lines: Interpreting Welfare Rights* (1994) and *Regulation and the Courts: The Case of the Clean Air Act* (1983). He is co-chair of the Harvard Program on Constitutional Government and has been on the staff of the Brookings Institution.

JAMES A. MORONE is professor of political science at Brown University. His *The Democratic Wish: Popular Participation and the Limits of the American Government* won the American Political Science Association's Gladys M. Kammerer Award. Professor Morone's latest book is *The Politics of Health Care Reform* (1994).

PAUL J. QUIRK is a professor in the Department of Political Science and the Institute of Government and Public Affairs at the University of Illinois at Urbana-Champaign. He is the author of *Industry Influence in Federal Regulatory Agencies* (1981) and is coauthor of *The Politics of Deregulation* (1985), which won the Louis Brownlow Award of the National Academy of Public Administration. He has also published numerous articles and essays on the presidency, Congress, and regulatory politics. His current research is on legislative-executive relations and the performance of government.

PETER H. SCHUCK is Simeon E. Baldwin Professor of Law at Yale and author of *Suing Government: Citizen Remedies for Official Wrongs* (1983); *Citizenship without Consent: Illegal Aliens in the American Policy* (1985); and *Agent Orange on Trial: Mass Toxic Disasters in the*

Courts (1987). He has also been principal deputy assistant secretary for planning and evaluation in the U.S. Department of Health, Education, and Welfare (1977–79); director of the Washington Office of Consumers Union (1972–77); and consultant to the Center for Study of Responsive Law (1971–72).

MARTIN SHAPIRO is Coffroth Professor of Law at Berkeley's Boalt Hall School of Law. He is one of the founders of Berkeley's program on Juris-prudence and Social Policy. Professor Shapiro's books include *Who Guards the Guardians: Judicial Control of Administration* (1988); *Courts: A Comparative and Political Analysis* (1981); and *Law and Politics in the Supreme Court.*

The late AARON WILDAVSKY was the Class of 1940 Professor of Political Science at the University of California, Berkeley. He had been the founding dean of the Graduate School of Public Policy, and, earlier, chairman of the Political Science Department. He was past president of the American Political Science Association, as well as the recipient of the association's James Madison Award for a Career of Distinguished Scholarship. He was author and co-author of more than thirty books, including *The Politics of the Budgetary Process, Risk and Culture, Implementation,* and *Speaking Truth to Power.*

Since 1985 JAMES Q. WILSON has been the James Collins Professor of Management at the University of California, Los Angeles. Before that for twenty-six years he was the Shattuck Professor of Government at Harvard University. He is the author or coauthor of thirteen books, including *The Moral Sense; American Government; Bureaucracy; Thinking about Crime; Varieties of Police Behavior; Political Organizations;* and *Crime and Human Nature* (with Richard J. Herrnstein). He was chairman of the White House Task Force on Crime in 1966 and chairman of the National Advisory Commission on Drug Abuse Prevention in 1972 and 1973. He is currently chairman of the Board of Academic Advisers of the American Enterprise Institute.

MARGARET WRIGHTSON is assistant director in the Budget Issues group at U.S. Government Accounting Office (GAO). She also teaches policy analysis as an adjunct professor at Georgetown University. She is an author of *Taxing Choices: The Politics of Tax Reform* and *Managing Regulatory Reform: The Reagan Strategy and Its Impact.*

Index

LIBRARY OF CONGRESS CATALOGING-IN-PUBLICATION DATA

The New politics of public policy / edited by Marc K. Landy, Martin A. Levin.
    p.   cm.
    Includes bibliographical references and index.
    ISBN 0-8018-4877-6 (alk. paper). — ISBN 0-8018-4878-4 (pbk. : alk. paper)
    1. United States—Economic policy—1981–1993—Decision
making. 2. United States—Politics and government—1981–1989—
Decision making. 3. United States—Politics and government—1989–
1993—Decision making. I. Landy, Marc Karnis. II. Levin, Martin A.
HC106.8.N496 1995
338.973—dc20   94-24379